SISTERS OF THE SOUL
A Devotional Exploring Women In God's Word

Messages of Love, From Father God
To His Beloved Daughters
A 365-Day Women's Study Devotional

By Wanda F. Hicks
Author, Teacher, and Beloved Daughter

Copyright © 2023 Wanda F. Hicks
For permissions to use this book, contact Wanda F. Hicks at wandahicks2008@yahoo.com

All rights reserved. No portion of this book may be reproduced, distributed, or transmitted in any form or by any means without the prior written permission of the author, except as permitted by US Copyright law.

Printed in the United States of America.
ISBN No. 978-1-7349595-3-6 (eBook)
ISBN No. 978-1-7349595-1-2 (PB)

Published By: Lystra Wilson - LystraInspires.com
Cover Design: Badrudeen Mikaheel - freelancerguru222@gmail.com

---

Listed alphabetically below are the Bible translations used for Scripture quotations referenced throughout **Sisters of the Soul**:

AMP–The Amplified Bible. Copyright © 1954, 1958, 1962, 1964, 1965, 1987 by The Lockman Foundation. Used by permission. All rights reserved.

ASV–The American Standard Version. Public domain.

BSB–The Bereans Study Bible

ESV–The Holy Bible, English Standard Version. Copyright © 2001 by Crossway Bibles, a division of Good News Publishers. Used by permission. All rights reserved.

GNT–Good News Translation Bible. Copyright © 1992 by American Bible Society.

GWT–God's Word Translation Bible. Copyright © 1995 by God's Word to the Nations. Used by permission of Baker Publishing Group.

HCSB–The Holman Christian Standard Bible®. Copyright © 1999, 2000, 2002, 2003 by Holman Bible Publishers. Used by permission.

ICB–The International Children's Bible (ICB). The Holy Bible, International Children's Bible® Copyright © 1986, 1988, 1999, 2015 by Tommy Nelson™, a division of Thomas Nelson. Thomas Nelson is a registered trademark of Harper Collins Christian Publishing, Inc. All rights reserved.

KJV–The King James Version (KJV). Public domain.

MSG–The Message–NavPress Copyright © 1993, 2002, 2018 by Eugene H. Peterson

NCV–The New Century Version®. Copyright © 2005 by Thomas Nelson. Used by permission. All rights reserved.

NHE–New Heart English Bible. Copyright ©2022 New Heart English Bible, Public Domain. Edited by Wayne A. Mitchell. Public Domain 2008-2022.

NIV–The New International Version®. Copyright ©1973, 1978, 1984, by International Bible Society. Used by permission of Zondervan. All rights reserved.

NKJV–New King James Version ® (NKJV®). Copyright © 1982 by Thomas Nelson, Inc. Used by permission. All rights reserved.

NLT–The New Living Translation. Derived from the Living Bible. Copyright 1996, 2004, 2007, 2013, 2015. Used by permission of Tyndale House Publishers, Inc. All rights reserved.

NASB®–The New American Standard Bible®. Copyright © 1960, 1962, 1963, 1968, 1971, 1972, 1973, 1975, 1977, 1995 by The Lockman Foundation. Used by permission.

PHILLIPS–J.B. Phillips New Testament (PHILLIPS). The New Testament in Modern English by J.B. Phillips copyright © 1960, 1972 J. B. Phillips. Administered by The Archbishops' Council of the Church of England. Used by permission.

Dedications

Above all, I want to thank my LORD and Savior Jesus Christ for His inspiration and the completion of this devotional book.

To my husband and co-writer, Pastor Willie Hicks of Harvest Care Christian Fellowship: I could not have completed this book without your love and patience.

To my daughter Leigh and son Ethan: Thank you for your untiring love and support of your mother throughout this endeavor.

A very special thanks to Lystra Wilson and Carla Springs for all of the support you provided towards the editing and publishing of this devotional.

To our Women's Bible Study Group: A special thanks to all of you for all of your support.

Finally, to my friend, Debbie Kenne, "my Jonathan." The fruition of this devotional comes from your first having given me the idea — I am forever grateful to you!

Endorsement

It is a privilege and pleasure to endorse this beautifully written women's study devotional, **Sisters of the Soul, Messages of Love, From Father God To His Beloved Daughters,** on behalf of my sister in the Lord, Wanda F. Hicks.

The spiritual jewels contained throughout the devotionals are priceless! It is inspirational and thought provoking! I recommend having a notebook or tablet ready to further develop what the Holy Spirit deposits into your heart and mind for the next 365 days! You will discover you're on a journey with twelve actual women of the Bible, their families, and their real-life circumstances.

If you think you have learned all there is to know about the women in the Bible, I humbly suggest you think again! As Christians, we know the Bible is our primary source of reference; and our author, Wanda Hicks, knows that too! She does just that as she delves into the lives of these twelve women. She has filled each devotional with God's Word, personal insight, and practical applications we can all benefit from today.

You know, I think we sometimes take lightly the testimonies of individuals—everyone has a story! When shared, especially in the context of ministry, the Lord will use those stories to help bring healing to others. Throughout each devotion and prayer, I came to appreciate how Wanda transparently poured out her heart and soul through parts of her own personal testimonies. She writes as though she is physically beside not only the twelve women she's written about, but also with her readers; observing and addressing various issues they may undergo. Most importantly, she concludes each devotion with inclusive thoughts and prayers to the Lord on behalf of us all (including herself).

Sisters of the Soul is not just written about these twelve women from the Bible; it is not just a short devotional where you read a scripture, have an inspirational thought, pray, and go about your day. Hopefully, you will still do those things, but don't be surprised if you find yourself digging even deeper into thought, entering into the presence of our Lord, and it resulting in an even more, closer relationship with Him. I know it did for me! This is the point where I found our Father God, relaying personal messages of love to His daughters—you and me!

Have you ever come across one of those stories in the Bible where you seemed to wander and wonder? I mean, times where you literally found yourself in the story itself? For example, what about voluntarily sharing your husband with another woman, such as Sarah did with Hagar? If you were Rachel, would you have let your sister deceitfully marry your man just because of cultural tradition or because your dad said so? Would you have tried to warn your fiancé? What would you have done if you were in Hannah's shoes when it came to her husband's other wife, menacing Peninnah? Would you have taken all that ridicule off of her? Warning: As you read through each devotion, remember, you are in the 21st century, not thousands of years ago. This will help you say to yourself, "Oh, that was then so, let me calm down!" So many, many questions and "what if's," right? Well… **Sisters of the Soul** gets into some of those issues and won't leave you hanging. It will provide you with insight and responses from our Lord's perspective.

We know and believe there is only one true source of God's Word—the Bible. From it, many devotionals, commentaries, and other resource tools have been written and developed. We are thankful for this because it has helped many of us to understand God's Word, His ways, His will, and His purpose more clearly for our lives.

Sisters of the Soul is one of those resources which digs deeper into the souls of the twelve individual women Wanda Hicks has selected to write about. Not only does she provide Scriptural references, but as a woman, she goes straight to the point of what may not be clearly seen in Scripture—the mind, heart, and soul of a woman. In other words, she addresses things about these women we've all wondered about, but could not tap into directly; and she does it without leaving the principles of God's Word.

I love the concentration of one woman per month. It gives us a more in-depth look into their daily lives and/or the situations they faced. It causes us to reflect and see how the women of that time period were not much different from us today. Sure, our cultures are different; but when it comes down to the soul of the matter, we're all women and can relate to how they must have felt. We can read between the lines, without ignoring the Word of God which surrounds it.

Whether you are considering accepting Jesus Christ as your Lord and Savior, new in your relationship with Him and studying His Word, or perhaps a veteran, you will thoroughly enjoy and benefit spiritually and emotionally by reading **Sisters of the Soul**! I know I did, and I pray you will too!

Carla A. Springs
Endearment Ministries

Devotional Features

Devotional Content: A month-by-month list of all devotional topics written for each day of the year. Contents reveal the name of the biblical daughter featured for the specified month.

Devotional Title: Name of devotional reading for the day.

Scripture: Scripture text (with referenced translation) related to the day's reading topic.

Devotional Reading: Tied to the day's Scripture reading, the daily devotional messages communicate the remarkable love and attentiveness God gives to all His daughters. The Author touches on those deeper subjects, not commonly seen or talked about, but often thought of. Through the auspices of the Holy Spirit, the messages will provide the reader with thought-provoking insight into God's love, promises, plans, and purpose for His beloved daughters.

The Woman and Us: Connecting Scripture, the devotional message, and the featured biblical woman, the author briefly transparently explores what the message is saying to us today.

God Speaks: Using Scripture and paraphrase, the author provides insight into what she feels God is saying as it relates to the devotional topic.

Wanda's Prayer: An inclusive, brief prayer by the author, in response to the day's devotion.

Contents

INTRODUCTION	**SISTERS OF THE SOUL!**	1
JANUARY		2
INTRODUCTION	**THE STORY OF EVE**	3
January 1	THE "HANDS-ON" GOD	5
January 2	BREATH OF GOD	6
January 3	BUILDING EVE'S HOUSE	7
January 4	REAL MEN WORK	8
January 5	FREEDOM	9
January 6	ALONE	10
January 7	THE COMPANION	11
January 8	SLEEP, REST	12
January 9	RIB AND BONE	13
January 10	BONE DEEP	14
January 11	ONE PLUS ONE EQUALS—ONE	15
January 12	NAKED TRUTH	16
January 13	CAREFUL LITTLE EARS	17
January 14	CAREFUL LITTLE MOUTH	18
January 15	SIN'S SOUFFLé (Part One)	19
January 16	SIN'S SOUFFLé (Part Two)	20
January 17	EYE PROBLEMS	21
January 18	THE FALLOUT	22
January 19	HIDING FROM LOVE?	23
January 20	WHERE ARE YOU?	24
January 21	AFRAID	25
January 22	GOOD LISTENER	26
January 23	YOU'RE NAKED?	27
January 24	BLAME GAME (Part 1)	28
January 25	BLAME GAME (Part 2)	29
January 26	CURSED CORRECTED	30
January 27	SIN'S SORROW	31
January 28	YOUR AUTHORITY—YOUR RESPONSIBILITY	32
January 29	MOTHER OF THE LIVING	33
January 30	NEW CLOTHES	34
January 31	GOT TO GO	35
FEBRUARY		36
INTRODUCTION	**SARAH (MOTHER OF THE JEWS)**	37
February 1	HOW ROYAL	39
February 2	BEAUTIFUL AND BARREN	40
February 3	CHANGE IN SCENERY	41
February 4	NEW WORLD	42
February 5	RIDE OR DIE CHICK	43
February 6	FAITH FAMINE	44
February 7	EGYPT'S PRICE	45
February 8	HELEN WHO?	46

February 9	PROSTITUTE'S PRICE	47
February 10	"SINNER'S" SERMON	48
February 11	WEIGHT OF WAITING	49
February 12	BAD IDEA	50
February 13	"UH-OH"	51
February 14	CONTENTIOUS	52
February 15	IT'S WORSE	53
February 16	HAGAR'S SON	54
February 17	NAME CHANGE	55
February 18	GETTING STARTED	56
February 19	"NO!"	57
February 20	REPEAT	58
February 21	LAUGHING	59
February 22	LITTLE LIAR	60
February 23	HAND'S OFF	61
February 24	SET TIME	62
February 25	REALLY LAUGH	63
February 26	MOCKING	64
February 27	GOT TO GO!	65
February 28	SUM OF LIFE	66

MARCH   67

INTRODUCTION	**HAGAR (FROM BONDAGE TO FREEDOM)**	**69**
March 1	HOW DID I GET HERE?	71
March 2	"FLIGHT"	72
March 3	SLAVE NO MORE!	73
March 4	HAGAR, THE MAID	74
March 5	FOUND YOU	75
March 6	GO BACK	76
March 7	GREAT GOD!	77
March 8	HEARD YOU	78
March 9	CAKE TOPPER	79
March 10	SEES ME	80
March 11	LIVING ONE	81
March 12	YOUR SON	82
March 13	WHICH ONE	83
March 14	DISTRESSED	84
March 15	FORGOTTEN PROMISES	85
March 16	WANDERING	86
March 17	DESPONDED	87
March 18	ONE PRAYS	88
March 19	GET GOING	89
March 20	EYE OPENING	90
March 21	PAPA GOD	91
March 22	FOREVER	92
March 23	FULFILLED	93
March 24	HAGAR'S LEGACY (Part 1)	94
March 25	HAGAR'S LEGACY (Part 2)	95
March 26	HAGAR'S LEGACY (Part 3)	96

March 27		GREATEST DAD	97
March 28		TRUE HUSBANDMAN	98
March 29		ROCK TOWER	99
March 30		CHRIST'S FREEDOM	100
March 31		CHRIST THE GREAT EMANCIPATOR	101

APRIL — 102

INTRODUCTION		**REBEKAH**	**103**
April 1		WRONG PLACE	105
April 2		THE FATHER'S WISDOM	106
April 3		WILLING HEART	107
April 4		A GOD THING	108
April 5		WHAT'S IN YOUR WALLET!	109
April 6		SEEK GOD FIRST	110
April 7		A REQUEST	111
April 8		INSTANT ANSWER	112
April 9		WEIGHT IN GOLD	113
April 10		WHO YO' PEOPLE?	114
April 11		PRAISE TIME!	115
April 12		MI CASA, SU CASA	116
April 13		TESTIMONY	117
April 14		CHOOSE	118
April 15		"YES" HAS PRIVILEGES	119
April 16		BLESSINGS	120
April 17		SURRENDERED BRIDE!	121
April 18		THE HUSBAND	122
April 19		WHO'S THAT MAN?	123
April 20		I DO…MY WIFE	124
April 21		DAD'S SINS REVISTED	125
April 22		BABY CARRIAGE?	126
April 23		PROBLEM?	127
April 24		STOLEN BLESSING?	128
April 25		THE FRUITS OF FEAR	129
April 26		WICKED PLAN	130
April 27		NO STOPPING NOW	131
April 28		THE STRESS	132
April 29		THE EXCUSE	133
April 30		"WEEPING"	134

MAY — 135

INTRODUCTION		**LEAH**	**137**
May 1		OLDER WEAKLING	139
May 2		DADDY'S HELP	140
May 3		DECEIVED	141
May 4		GOD SAW—GOD ACTED	142
May 5		SONS CAN'T BUY LOVE (Part 1)	143
May 6		SONS CAN'T BUY LOVE (Part 2)	144
May 7		SON'S CAN'T BUY LOVE (Part 3)	145

May 8	JUST PRAISE	146
May 9	DONE! NOW REST	147
May 10	THE BABY WAR	148
May 11	GOOD FORTUNE?	149
May 12	HAPPY?	150
May 13	DESPERATE	151
May 14	TWISTED FACTS	152
May 15	AIN'T TOO PROUD TO BEG	153
May 16	I HEAR YOU	154
May 17	GOD'S WAGES?	155
May 18	MORE LOVE	156
May 19	FATHER GOD	157
May 20	PEACE PLEASE	158
May 21	APPLE'S EYE	159
May 22	JUST A NAME?	160
May 23	WIFE NO. 2	161
May 24	UNITY AND PEACE	162
May 25	THE JOURNEY	163
May 26	NO god HERE	164
May 27	I'M GLAD I KNOW WHO MY REAL HUSBAND IS	165
May 28	A DAUGHTER'S HURT—MOM'S PAIN	166
May 29	LESS + GOD = ABUNDANCE	167
May 30	LEAH GETS HER DUE	168
May 31	GOD'S EPITAPH	169

JUNE   170

INTRODUCTION	**RACHEL**	**171**
June 1	JUST ONE LOOK!	173
June 2	A SHEEP THING	174
June 3	LOVE MOVES—LARGE STONES	175
June 4	YEP, SHE'S THE ONE	176
June 5	WE ARE FAMILY	177
June 6	THE BRASS TACKS	178
June 7	NO-BRAINER	179
June 8	CLEAR CHOICE	180
June 9	JUST DO IT	181
June 10	MY WIFE, PLEASE	182
June 11	GREAT DECEPTION	183
June 12	TRICKS CAN'T KILL LOVE	184
June 13	I WILL DO IT AGAIN	185
June 14	AHHH…FOR THIS I WORKED	186
June 15	EVERYONE MUST BE LOVED—RIGHT	187
June 16	WHEN HUMAN LOVE IS NOT ENOUGH	188
June 17	WOMAN, I CAN'T HELP YOU	189
June 18	NO… LORD, I WON'T PRAY—I GOT THIS	190
June 19	THIS WAS A "HUMAN THANG"	191
June 20	THIS IS PERSONAL	192
June 21	WELL, IT WAS A COMPLETE KNOCK OUT	193
June 22	GOD MAKES A POINT	194

June 23	GOD'S TIMING IS NEVER LATE—TO GOD	195
June 24	IN A LEAGUE ALL BY HIMSELF	196
June 25	IT IS TIME FOR A TRUCE	197
June 26	THE THRILL IS GONE	198
June 27	POOR THING, NOW YOU'VE GOT TO HIDE god	199
June 28	OK, THE GODS HAVE GOT TO GO!	200
June 29	A TRAGIC ENDING TO A WONDERFUL LIFE	201
June 30	A TESTAMENT TO A GREAT LADY	202

JULY — 203

INTRODUCTION	**HANNAH**	**205**
July 1	NOW THAT'S A NAME	207
July 2	A GOOD REASON FOR A BAD DECISION	208
July 3	PLAYING FAVORITES	209
July 4	WHAT'S IN A NAME	210
July 5	THE HOLIDAY BLUES	211
July 6	KIND BUT CLUELESS	212
July 7	HERE IS THE PLACE—NOW IS THE TIME	213
July 8	TAKE THIS BURDEN AND KEEP IT	214
July 9	JUDGING A BOOK BY ITS COVER	215
July 10	SINCE YOU DIDN'T ASK, I'LL TELL YOU	216
July 11	BABY IS ON THE WAY	217
July 12	PRAISE ON CREDIT	218
July 13	TIMING	219
July 14	LORD, I SAID IT AND I MEANT IT	220
July 15	A PROMISE MADE IS A PROMISE KEPT	221
July 16	NOW LET'S BREAK OUT IN PRAISE	222
July 17	IN A CATEGORY OF HIS OWN	223
July 18	BONDAGE AND FREEDOM	224
July 19	I'VE GOT THE POWER	225
July 20	GOD FLIPS THE SWITCH	226
July 21	CAN'T STOP PRAISING HIS NAME	227
July 22	GOD CALLS THE SHOTS	228
July 23	LOVE LIFTED ME	229
July 24	I STAND ON A SOLID ROCK	230
July 25	A CONTINUED REMINDER	231
July 26	POWERLESSNESS	232
July 27	DON'T EVEN THINK ABOUT IT	233
July 28	A SPECIAL GIFT FOR HIS "HIGHLY FAVORED ONE"	234
July 29	THAT'S MY BABY	235
July 30	YOUR KIDS WILL BLESS YOU	236
July 31	A MEGA DOSE OF GRACE	237
Bonus	HANNAH'S TESTIMONY	238

AUGUST — 239

INTRODUCTION	**ELIZABETH**	**241**
August 1	ANCESTRY	243
August 2	ELIZABETH—THE NAME	244

August 3	A SOLD-OUT LIFE	245
August 4	A GODLY LIFE, BUT NOT PAIN FREE	246
August 5	I'M WAITING TO BLESS YOU	247
August 6	I HEARD YOUR PRAYERS—I ANSWERED	248
August 7	I'M GIVING A SON TO ENJOY	249
August 8	REJOICE WITH ME	250
August 9	MORE ABOUT YOUR BOY	251
August 10	HOLINESS IN, HOLINESS OUT	252
August 11	HOLY POWER PURIFIES COMPLETELY	253
August 12	YOUR GREATEST GIFT TO HUMANITY	254
August 13	THE DUMBEST QUESTION	255
August 14	HE WAS RIGHTEOUS, BUT NOT SINLESS	256
August 15	YOU MAY FORGET, BUT I DON'T	257
August 16	MOVE AND LET ME PRAISE HIM	258
August 17	BLESSED TO BE A BLESSING	259
August 18	I'VE GOT TO SEE THIS FOR MYSELF	260
August 19	JUMPING FOR JOY!	261
August 20	THE INFECTIOUS SPIRIT	262
August 21	THE COMFORTER	263
August 22	THE CONFIRMER	264
August 23	A PLACE OF HONOR	265
August 24	GIRL, I GOTTA TELL IT!	266
August 25	YOU'RE MY HERO	267
August 26	I WILL SING OVER YOU NOW	268
August 27	DON'T JUST COME FOR A VISIT—STAY!	269
August 28	LOVE'S PERFECT TIMING	270
August 29	GOD'S GOODNESS ON DISPLAY	271
August 30	I'M DOING WHAT GOD SAID!	272
August 31	HONEY, I GOT THIS	273

SEPTEMBER — 274

INTRODUCTION	**MARTHA**	275
September 1	HELLO, I'M MARTHA	277
September 2	I DON'T HAVE TIME TO SIT	278
September 3	DRIVEN TO DISTRACTION	279
September 4	DRIVEN FROM DISTRACTION TO THE FEET OF JESUS	280
September 5	OK LORD, I'VE GOT SOMETHING TO SAY	281
September 6	MARTHA'S MAD MELTDOWN	282
September 7	IT'S ALRIGHT BABY	283
September 8	TOO STRESSED TO FEEL BLESSED	284
September 9	KEEP THE MAIN THING THE MAIN THING	285
September 10	MARTHA, THERE'S A BETTER WAY	286
September 11	YOU CAN REFUSE YOUR MEAL BUT I'M NOT TAKING HERS	287
September 12	STANDING STILL	288
September 13	IT'S ALL YOURS AND YOU CAN HAVE IT	289
September 14	IN ALL YOUR GETTING, GET GOD'S PERSPECTIVE	290
September 15	MARTHA, DON'T FORGET WHAT YA' KNOW	291
September 16	IN THE COMPANY OF FRIENDS	292
September 17	JESUS, AREN'T YOU JUST A LITTLE LATE?	293

September 18	A CHANGE OF HEART	294
September 19	THANKS FOR ANSWERING MY PRAYER LORD, BUT THAT'S OK	295
September 20	MIND EXPANSION (Part 1)	296
September 21	MIND EXPANSION (Part 2)	297
September 22	MIND EXPANSION (Part 3)	298
September 23	THE BALL IS IN YOUR COURT—SISTER	299
September 24	THE GIGANTIC LIE: GOD DOESN'T HURT WHEN YOU HURT	300
September 25	JUST TAKE A STEP MARTHA	301
September 26	LORD, I OBJECT	302
September 27	OK MS. MARTHA, LET ME TELL YOU ONE MO' GIN!	303
September 28	THE POWER OF SURRENDER	304
September 29	WE'RE IN THIS THING TOGETHER	305
September 30	IN PERFECT ORDER	306

OCTOBER — 307

INTRODUCTION	**MARY**	**309**
October 1	MARY, IT'S A PRIORITY THANG	311
October 2	THIS IS THE PLACE FOR ME	312
October 3	DON'T BE HATIN'	313
October 4	JESUS TO THE RESCUE	314
October 5	I'VE GOT TO HAVE IT	315
October 6	LORD, NOW WHAT?	316
October 7	MY CHILD, I HEARD YOU—DO YOU HEAR ME?	317
October 8	I GOT YOUR WORD, BUT MY PROBLEM AIN'T FIXED	318
October 9	I'VE GOT THE HOOK UP	319
October 10	WILL THE REAL MARY… SIT DOWN?	320
October 11	TIME TO BLOW THIS POPSICLE STAND	321
October 12	THEY'RE WATCHING ME	322
October 13	THIS IS A GOOD TIME FOR WORSHIP	323
October 14	A DOUBLE TAKE AT THE VERSE	324
October 15	I FEEL THE PAIN OF SIN—AND IT ANGERS ME	325
October 16	TAKE ME TO YOUR PLACE OF SORROW	326
October 17	WHY ARE YOU CRYING MY LORD?	327
October 18	LOOK AND SEE—MY GOD DOES CARE	328
October 19	THE CRITIC—THERE'S ONE IN EVERY CROWD	329
October 20	YOUR FEELINGS MOVE ME	331
October 21	TAKE A RETAKE, NOW WHAT DO YOU SEE?	332
October 22	MARY, I'VE GOT YOUR HEART—NOW TRUST MY WORD	333
October 23	CATCH AN EAR FULL MARY	334
October 24	LOVE RESTORES LIFE	335
October 25	WHAT'S IN YOUR DOGGY BAG?	336
October 26	BEING IN HIS PRESENCE MOVES ME	337
October 27	THE EMPTY JAR	338
October 28	WHAT'S THAT I SMELL?	339
October 29	THE HIT DOG ALWAYS HOLLERS	340
October 30	THE LORD TO THE RESCUE—AGAIN	341
October 31	MARY'S EPITAPH	342

NOVEMBER — 343

INTRODUCTION	**THE SAMARITAN WOMAN**	345
November 1	GOD'S GOT HER ON HIS MIND	347
November 2	ALL IN THE FAMILY	348
November 3	HONEY, I'M HERE	349
November 4	WHAT A LINE	350
November 5	IT'S JUST ME AND YOU	351
November 6	YOU TALKIN' TO ME!	352
November 7	WOMAN CHILL! I'VE GOT WHAT YOU NEED	353
November 8	SHOW ME THE BUCKET	354
November 9	THE CHALLENGE	355
November 10	WRONG WATER—WRONG WELL	356
November 11	RIGHT WELL—SATISFYING WATER	357
November 12	OK, I BITE—I'LL TAKE IT	358
November 13	BEFORE I POUR IN THE NEW, LET ME FLUSH OUT THE OLD	359
November 14	OUCH! YOU TOUCHED A NERVE	360
November 15	I'LL CUT IT ALL OUT	361
November 16	I CAN'T CONNECT THE DOTS	362
November 17	I CHASE RABBITS	363
November 18	YOU'RE IN THE WRONG PLACE	364
November 19	THE DIVIDING LINE	365
November 20	LET'S BE CRYSTAL CLEAR	366
November 21	I'LL TELL YOU WHY	367
November 22	I'M PEEKING THROUGH THE KEYHOLE	368
November 23	SHE HIT THE MOTHER LODE	369
November 24	LISTEN, DID YOU HEAR THE PIN DROP?	370
November 25	I GOTTA' NEW RUN NOW!	371
November 26	JUST KNOWING JESUS	372
November 27	I'M COMING, WAIT ON ME	373
November 28	A MESSAGE FROM THE MASTER'S HEART	374
November 29	A BUMPER CROP	375
November 30	WE NEED MORE WATER	376
Bonus	A TESTAMENT OF HER TESTIMONY	378

DECEMBER — 379

INTRODUCTION	**MARY, THE MOTHER OF JESUS**	381
December 1	A PROMISE KEPT	383
December 2	THE ULTIMATE PRIVILEGE	384
December 3	I'M HAPPY—YOU'RE… TROUBLED	385
December 4	GUESS WHO'S COMING TO YOUR WOMB?	386
December 5	NOW, ABOUT THE BABY!	387
December 6	QUESTIONS—QUESTIONS	388
December 7	LITTLE GIRL, THE ANSWER IS SIMPLE	389
December 8	HOLD ON TO THIS LITTLE NUGGET	390
December 9	FATHER, I'M YOURS!	391
December 10	CAN I GET A WITNESS PLEASE?	392
December 11	"DON'T LOOK FOR WHAT YOU ALREADY HAVE"	393
December 12	LET THE BLESSINGS FLOW	394

December 13	IT WAS NEVER ABOUT ME	395
December 14	A CARING GOD FATHER	396
December 15	THE PRAISES KEEP COMING	397
December 16	THE LONG ARM OF OUR GOD	398
December 17	THE GOODNESS OF GOD ON DISPLAY	399
December 18	CAN'T STAY ON THE MOUNTAINTOP FOREVER	400
December 19	MY DARK LONELY VALLEYS	401
December 20	MARY, I'LL TALK TO HIM	402
December 21	GOD'S MAN DOES WHAT GOD TELLS HIM	403
December 22	WE'LL HONEYMOON IN—BETHLEHEM?	404
December 23	UNWELCOME RECEPTION	405
December 24	HEAVENLY CONFIRMATION	406
December 25	DO YOU WANT ANOTHER SIGN?	407
December 26	I HAVE ANOTHER WITNESS	408
December 27	HE'S ONLY ON LOAN TO YOU	409
December 28	HAVE YOU MET MY BOY—HE'S GOD!	410
December 29	THE PIERCING OF THE SOUL (Part 1)	411
December 30	THE PIERCING OF THE SOUL (Part 2)	412
December 31	A SON'S PROVISION	413
Bonus	IT'S ALL RIGHT NOW	414

Introduction

SISTERS OF THE SOUL!

Sisters of the Soul is a 365-day women's study devotional book, specifically dedicated to twelve women in the Bible—seven from the Old Testament and five from the New Testament.

Each month will feature one of the twelve women. As the Word of God reveals them to us, we will not only explore and carefully examine their lives, but perhaps we will discover areas in our own lives we closely identify with. We will touch on some of those subjects rarely talked about, but often thought of.

These devotionals came out of my personal time of study, daily reflections, and questions I have had with the Lord. It resulted in my wanting to share them with you too! I figured if they blessed me, they may bless you as well! I hope you too, will gain a fresh perspective into how God loves, cares for, relates to, interacts with, intervenes on behalf of, provides, protects, and treasures all of His daughters—from the Creation of his first daughter Eve to all of you today!

All the glory goes to God alone. As I praise Him for what He has revealed to me, I hope that for all women who read the devotionals, He will reveal His love to you personally, as seen in His dealings with His daughters, found throughout Scripture.

My sister in Christ Jesus, as you continue in your own personal study of God's love letter to us—the Bible, may **Sisters of the Soul** enhance and deepen your knowledge and understanding of His Word concerning you as His beloved daughter. May it cause you to have a deeper, more passionate relationship and bond with the LORD OF LOVE—drawing you even closer to Him than ever before!

Finally, each day as you conclude your devotional reading throughout **Sisters of the Soul**, I pray it will leave you feeling motivated, strengthened, confident, fulfilled, and most of all, loved by God—our precious Heavenly Father.

Your Sister of the Soul,
Wanda F. Hicks

Notes

January

INTRODUCTION

THE STORY OF EVE

Eve, the first lady of Creation, was formed as a companion and helper to Adam. Eve's life is mostly found in the first few chapters of Genesis.

As the first woman of Creation, God formed her into a perfectly sinless environment. Her untried innocence would be the catalyst Satan would use for earth's downfall.

Throughout this first month of January, we will see how God displays His tenderness to Eve, as He attends to her needs. He does this by giving her His loving provisions and a grand purpose for her life. Later He gives her His covering for sin, and eventual pardon through His death on the Cross.

Come, let us journey back in time and see the beauty and wonder of the Heavenly Father's love, as shown to daughter Eve. In glancing at her life, we will see how God's love is so magnificently shown in our own lives.

Notes

January 1

THE "HANDS-ON" GOD

"AND THE LORD GOD FORMED MAN OF THE DUST OF THE GROUND, AND BREATHED INTO HIS NOSTRILS THE BREATH OF LIFE; AND MAN BECAME A LIVING BEING." (GENESIS 2:7 NKJV)

The beginning of Eve's world, her life, begins with her husband—Adam. Our LORD wanted a "hands on" relationship with His human Creation. He proved this to us when He formed Eve's husband-to-be from the dust of the ground. A glance at Genesis, chapter one reveals how God spoke everything into perfect order. An example of this is when God said, "Let there be light, and there was light." (Genesis 1:2) By the end of the first chapter of Genesis, God in the person of Jesus Christ spoke an entire world into place. The powerful Words of our LORD and Creator form an entire universe by a mere utterance. He simply speaks and in an instant, Creation obeys (John 1:1 and Hebrews 1:1). Jesus could have directly spoken the man into place, but instead, He scoops up dust and gives it the privilege of being personally shaped into "The image and likeness of the Creator God …" (Genesis 1:26) Our loving Father holds and handles His newly created son, as any loving parent would. Eve's husband-to-be would be a man of God's hands on Creation. Our LORD is intimately connected with this man. I believe our Lord forms Adam with Eve in mind!

EVE AND US: What is the lesson here? I see three: (1) I think our LORD wants the same "hands on" relationship with us, the daughters of Eve, as He had with Adam and Eve. (2) God's design for His "hands on" woman is to have a "hands on" man. (3) That godman will have a deep abiding and intimate relationship with his Maker and Lord, as well as his wife-to-be (Eve). God's markings will be clearly seen in his life. Father God wants to give to all His daughters, the same as He gave to His first daughter, Eve.

GOD SPEAKS: "Then he put his hands on her, and immediately she straightened up and praised God." (Luke 13:13 NIV) What is your sickness? Do you need a touch from the Lord Jesus about issues in your life? What are they? Bring them to Him now! Do not delay—He is waiting.

WANDA'S PRAYER: "Lord, we leave it all to You—take over!"

January 2

BREATH OF GOD

"AND THE LORD GOD ... BREATHED INTO HIS NOSTRILS THE BREATH OF LIFE; AND MAN BECAME A LIVING BEING." (GENESIS 2:7 NKJV)

Notice what a beautiful thing our loving LORD does for Eve, His daughter-to-be. After forming her husband-to-be (Adam) from delicate dust, God then breathes His own breath into this fragile substance. It is God's breath which gives the man life. The result of our LORD touching, forming, and breathing the breath of life into dust is a creature made in the image of the Most High God. It is not hard to form "mud pies" from wet dirt; but dust forms nothing in human hands except a round—sort of fur ball. However, dust in the hands of the Omnipotent, All-Powerful God, becomes a creature, a man, capable of ruling this planet. That dust, called Adam, filled with the "breath of God," is now the son of his Father—God. He is totally filled with his "Dad's" Spirit—God's very own breath. He is God's boy through and through. In glancing at Adam, we see the heart of our Heavenly Father. The outcome is a priceless Creation, a man fit for Eve. Father God would give this precious gift to His first daughter of Creation.

EVE AND US: Eve's husband was made from a very fragile substance. I heard someone once say that the minerals which make up a human being were only worth two dollars. Only our Heavenly Father can breathe into two dollars' worth of scrap metals and turn it into a priceless commodity which would rule the planet. (Genesis 1:26) God wants to fill us with His breath, the Holy Spirit, as He did for Eve's husband. The Creator God wants to take our bruised and battered lives and make them priceless commodities as well.

GOD SPEAKS: "Then he breathed on them and said, 'receive the Holy Spirit.'" (John 20:22 NLT) Allow the Breath of God to make you into God's priceless Creation.

WANDA'S PRAYER: Father God, breathe Your perfect breath of life into us.

January 3

BUILDING EVE'S HOUSE

"NOW THE LORD GOD HAD PLANTED A GARDEN IN THE EAST, IN EDEN; AND THERE HE PUT THE MAN HE HAD FORMED." (GENESIS 2:8 NIV)

Look at how our LORD does things. The Father works with perfect order; after all, He is the Master builder. Before building and uniting the first family of Creation, our LORD would build other things first. Father God knew He would build into Eve, two great needs which would have to be met first. Those needs were security and stability. So how does our LORD meet the yet to be created, Eve's needs? Through Adam, of course! For security, God supplies His first man, the perfect home—the Garden of Eden. This garden home is filled with matchless beauty and splendor. Picture the rolling hillsides and clear crystal waters, which are teamed with exotic creatures of every sort. Into this picture-perfect paradise, our LORD placed His son, Adam. This paradise home, which was to be the couple's first forever home, met Eve's need for stability. Though Eve has not yet been created, the perfect Dad (God) is already meeting her needs perfectly.

EVE AND US: As Christians, we have the same Builder as Eve; we do not have to envy her perfect world at all. Instead, let us take note of how Father God, in great anticipation, meets her needs before He creates her. The Builder of Eve's home is quite capable of building our homes as well.

GOD SPEAKS: "Unless the Lord builds the house, they labor in vain who build it. … it is vain for you to rise up early, to sit up late, to eat the bread of sorrows; for so he gives his beloved sleep." (Psalm 127:1-2 NKJV) Allow Me (God) to build your house from start to finish, just as I did Eve's. Simply give Me your all—trust and rest in My perfect architectural skills.

WANDA'S PRAYER: Lord, be at home in our hearts and lives; and fashion us after Your will.

January 4

REAL MEN WORK

"THE LORD GOD TOOK THE MAN AND PUT HIM IN THE GARDEN OF EDEN TO WORK IT AND TAKE CARE OF IT." (GENESIS 2:15 NIV)

See the great "work" our God has put into the design of our planet. The first two chapters of Genesis give us lengthy descriptions of Adam's new home. The Father (God) went through a great deal of work building this home for the first couple. This place had "everything" imaginable. "The LORD made all kinds of trees to grow out of the ground—trees which were pleasing to the eye and good for food." (Genesis 2:9) Our "Heavenly Dad" thought of everything. The garden came with the first natural sprinkler system— "Dew from the ground watering the earth." (Genesis 2:6) After giving Adam his dream home, our "Dad" gave His baby boy a job (work) to do. This work (which was not difficult work) gave him a sense of purpose, and it would meet another of Eve's basic needs—provision. Adam's work was to be the "husbandman" or garden caretaker to the Eden Gardens. If Adam could properly care and tend to lowly shrubs and animals, he would certainly care nicely for Eve. We can also see that Eve's husband is a totally God-led man. The Father puts him in the garden with duties and he stays in the garden doing the work he was told to do. Adam, aware that he is forever in the presence of God, carries out his assigned work flawlessly.

EVE AND US: Again, our LORD shows His care for the yet created Eve, through the traits He gives Adam. The idea of working provides purpose and structure. She also needed someone which not only had God's purpose of protector and provider, but someone who would follow God's leading. We see in Adam that he was a chip off the old "Rock" (Christ Jesus, our LORD God). God's provision of Eve shows us He will also provide for us as well.

GOD SPEAKS: "But Jesus said to them, 'my Father never stops working. And so I work too.'" (John 5:17 ICB) "In all the work you are doing, work the best you can. Work as if you were working for the Lord, not men." (Colossians 3:23 ICB) Our LORD would say, "I am your perfect example … I work, and you work too."

WANDA'S PRAYER: "Father, work out those character traits You want to work in us."

January 5

FREEDOM

"AND THE LORD GOD COMMANDED THE MAN, 'YOU ARE FREE TO EAT FROM ANY TREE IN THE GARDEN; BUT YOU MUST NOT EAT FROM THE TREE OF THE KNOWLEDGE OF GOOD AND EVIL, FOR WHEN YOU EAT FROM IT YOU WILL CERTAINLY DIE.'" (GENESIS 2:16-17 NIV)

Adam and the (to be created) Eve are given a lot of freedom. They are "FREE" to eat from "ANY TREE IN THE GARDEN." There would have been miles and miles of delectable, edible foliage. To maintain order and to build faithfulness and commitment into Adam's character (a necessary quality valued by "womankind"), God gave him one simple command. Take note from the above verses that freedom is not just an opportunity, it is a command! Our LORD is saying, "be free" but do not be unrestrained. Freedom without limits is chaos. Obedience on Adam's part shows the greatest demonstration of love. The Father God does not leave His son to wonder "why," nor to "guess at," the outcome of disobedience. The Father informs Adam of the deadly results before He even created Eve. (Genesis 2:17) Adam would demonstrate his love to his Father and LORD by obeying His word. The burden of keeping the home and family intact is given to him. As long as he leads and cares for his family, the way his Father directs, then all would remain in perfect bliss. The job of family "guardian," is a wonderful gift our LORD was giving to His first daughter of Creation.

EVE AND US: God has given Eve's future husband all any man could ever ask for, or dream of. With the perfection and beauty man is given, he is also given real freedom. True freedom is the freedom to obey a perfect and Holy God, and thus remain in perfect fellowship with Him. This was God's way of providing for Eve. Our LORD was giving her a man who loved Him and kept His word. God's provision for Eve shows His love and care for me too! I believe this is God's desire for all women everywhere.

GOD SPEAKS: "It was for freedom that Christ sets us free; therefore keep standing firm and do not be subject again to a yoke of slavery." (Galatians 5:1 NASB) I came to give you true freedom.

WANDA'S PRAYER: Lord, give us the freedom to say "yes" to Your perfect will for our lives.

January 6

ALONE

"AND THE LORD GOD SAID, 'IT IS NOT GOOD THAT THE MAN SHOULD BE ALONE; I WILL MAKE HIM AN HELP MEET FOR HIM.'" (GENESIS 2:18 KJV)

During the first week of Creation, our Lord made everything good. The sights and sounds of a perfect paradise were evident at every turn. Every fluffy cloud, every singing bird of the air, and fish of the sea had the words from God "I love you" stamped on them. The Father beheld the clear skies, the rolling hillsides—perfumed with a thousand fragrances that scented the air from His floral Creation. Then turning to look at the crystal-clear waters, bursting full of sea creatures, God's view was one of breath-taking beauty. He said of His Creation, "This is good!" All was good; all was perfect, except one thing. "It was not good that the man should be alone." (Genesis 2:18) Loneliness to GOD is not good. The God who dwells in tri-unity knew this even before the man discovered it. The man needed suitable companionship. Our Father knew all too well that just any companion would not do. The answer to Adam's dilemma was the woman, Eve. She was that suitable helper to Adam.

EVE AND US: I think the lesson to us is that loneliness is never good. Our LORD knew this from the beginning. He provided a solution to the problem then and now. He wants us to allow Him to provide suitable help and companionship for us; but it starts with Him.

GOD SPEAKS: "My soul waits in silence for God alone; From Him comes my salvation. He alone is my rock and my salvation, My stronghold; I will not be greatly shaken." (Psalm 62:1-2 NASB). "and you are complete in Him, who is the head of all principality and power." (Colossians 2:10 NKJV) There is a substantial difference between being single and being alone. I am forever and always with you. The Lord says, "I would never leave or forsake you," and I meant every word. Therefore, you are never alone. Eve and every one of her daughters, including you, were made for My incredibly special purpose—to be My special blessings. Let your fullness be in Me alone. The status of being single or married should not alter the plans I have for you, child of Mine. You are my "Bride" and joy. Your earthly marital status does not change this fact. You are my jewel, so shine and sparkle for Me. You are to be My light and joy. Now you go girl, and glorify Me in all you do.

WANDA'S PRAYER: Wow, LORD, you sure know how to make a girl feel special. Father, fill us with Your glory. Make us into that priceless jewel!

January 7

THE COMPANION

"OUT OF THE GROUND THE LORD GOD FORMED EVERY BEAST OF THE FIELD AND EVERY BIRD OF THE AIR, AND BROUGHT THEM TO ADAM TO SEE WHAT HE WOULD CALL THEM. AND WHATEVER ADAM CALLED EACH LIVING CREATURE, THAT WAS ITS NAME. SO ADAM GAVE NAMES TO ALL CATTLE, TO THE BIRDS OF THE AIR, AND TO EVERY BEAST OF THE FIELD. BUT FOR ADAM THERE WAS NOT FOUND A HELPER COMPARABLE TO HIM." (GENESIS 2:19-20 NKJV)

Isn't it interesting what God does with His son here? The previous verse tells us our Lord knew the man needed companionship. But reading this text, we might wonder, "Did God forget or get off track with His normal order of Creation?" No! Looking carefully at this Scripture, gives us a glimpse of the Father's perfect will. Our Lord sees Adam's physical need for companionship. He will meet Adam's need in His perfect time. But Adam must learn that nothing supersedes commitment to his Father and carrying out His Father's will. Our Loving LORD must be priority one for Adam! So, the Father gives him the task of naming every creature on the planet. Wow! What's fascinating is that he names them in less than a day. Remember Adam, Eve, and the land creatures are all created on day six of the Creation week. (Genesis 1:26) Adam obeys the Father, and names all the creatures; then realizes he is alone. There is no comparable helper for him. Now that Adam and God are aware of the problem, Father God goes to work on the solution—the Creation of Eve. To Eve, God gives a man with an eternal focus. Adam's desire is to carry out his Father's will above his own.

EVE AND US: See how the perfect Dad thinks, and how He works out His flawless plan on behalf of Eve. Notice the man was not idly waiting for companionship. Instead, he is about his Dad's business. This seems to be a universal concept for me to adapt. Trust my loving LORD fully and carry out the work I am assigned to do.

GOD SPEAKS:
"But seek ye first the kingdom of God, and his righteousness; and all these things shall be added unto you." (Matthew 6:33 KJV) "I am a companion of all them that fear thee, and of them that keep thy precepts. (Psalm 119:63 KJV) Put God's kingdom and His way of doing things first, and your needs will be met as well. Make Him your focus—He will provide all your needs.

WANDA'S PRAYER: Lord, change our focus from selfish needs to seeking You first in all areas of our lives.

January 8

SLEEP, REST

"AND THE LORD GOD CAUSED A DEEP SLEEP TO FALL ON ADAM, AND HE SLEPT; AND HE TOOK ONE OF HIS RIBS, AND CLOSED UP THE FLESH IN ITS PLACE." (GENESIS 2:21 NKJV)

Our Lord is the Master surgeon. He proves it here. With equipment-free anesthesia, He causes the man to fall into a deep sleep—a deep rest. On the sleeping, resting Adam, the Father does His flawless work with no artificial life support. But why put the man to sleep? God could have done the work with an awake and watching Adam. There are great lessons for us here. (1) The Lord does not need Adam's help in doing what is best for him. He already knows what to do and will do it perfectly. (2) An awake Adam might offer well intended, but misguided input. After all, his only models for mates were the animals. He had never seen another human, much less a female creature. (3) I think the greatest lesson to be seen is that of resting, in the complete and perfect work of the LORD. As Adam lay in a restful sleep, our Lord sustained His man and performed flawless surgery on him. God's mind is far superior to ours. Unlike us flawed humans, He does not need life support machinery, chemical anesthesia, or even a scalpel for His surgical procedure. This perfect "doing" by God, absent of man's input, builds confidence and trust into the heart of the future Mrs. Adam (Eve). This part of the story tells her she can rest in the finished work of her Lord.

EVE AND US: Lord, it is so good to know that even as we rest in sleep; You are at work on our behalf. We can clearly see how You supplied Eve's need before she was even created. You never sleep or slumber; but You do rest when Your perfect work is done. (Genesis 2:2) Eve shows us how our perfect Lord does everything perfectly.

GOD SPEAKS: "Come to me, all you who are weary and burdened, and I will give you rest." (Matthew 11:28 NIV) "I go to bed and sleep in peace. Lord, only you keep me safe." (Psalm 4:8 ICB) Our LORD wants us to REST IN HIM. He does His work perfectly.

WANDA'S PRAYER: Lord, teach us to rest in You now; and not at some time in the distant future.

January 9

RIB AND BONE

"THEN THE RIB WHICH THE LORD GOD HAD TAKEN FROM MAN HE MADE INTO A WOMAN, AND HE BROUGHT HER TO THE MAN." (GENESIS 2:22 NKJV)

Here is another display of our Lord's awesome power. With the skill of a Master surgeon, the Father removes a rib (a bone) from the man. From that rib, He completely "builds or forms (fashions)" it into a woman. There is no limit to our Dad's abilities. He just speaks, and it comes. He forms dust into a man, who then rules a planet. Now, He takes a bone from the man and creates his mate. The bone from Adam's chest would forever have his heart. Our Lord is not only Creator, but designer as well. A point worth mentioning is how Father God sets humans apart from animals, birds, and sea creatures. He called, and these creatures came forth. (Genesis 1:20-21) However, in the case of human beings, our LORD gently touches and handles His man and woman. The woman's beginning came from the man. She is of him, and his offspring will forever be of her. Imagine the tender care displayed by the Father in forming Eve. God hand-crafted each curve of her shapely body—lips, eyes, face, hands, etc. She is a sculpted masterpiece from head to foot with Adam in mind. No other life on this planet can make this boast. The man and woman—comparable companions would be linked together forever. This link is not just a physical attachment, but our LORD provided an emotional attachment to the heart as well. At his side, Adam would blossom to heights unimagined. Eve was truly Adam's comparable helper, support, and friend.

EVE AND US: Eve's life started with a single bone. It is amazing what our LORD can do with so little. Our little truly becomes much in His hands.

GOD SPEAKS: "… Can these bones live? …Surely I will cause breath to enter into you, and you shall live…then you shall know that I am the Lord." (Ezekiel 37:3-6 NKJV) You serve the God that can give life to any bone!

WANDA'S PRAYER: LORD, breathe on our dry, brittle bones; and give them and our hearts new life!

January 10

BONE DEEP

"AND ADAM SAID: 'THIS IS NOW BONE OF MY BONES AND FLESH OF MY FLESH; SHE SHALL BE CALLED WOMAN, BECAUSE SHE WAS TAKEN OUT OF MAN.'"
(GENESIS 2:23 NKJV)

Adam was taken aback by what he saw in the woman! He had been looking at animals and birds all day. The man could not have imagined what an indescribable beauty his Father would provide for him. Our Father must have informed the man she was a part of him—taken from his bones. Adam, in utter excitement and joy, exclaimed, "Bone of my bone and flesh of my flesh!" So ecstatic is Adam about what his Father has done for him, he continues to say, "She shall be called woman, because she was taken from the man." In looking at Eve, Adam knew this was his suitable helper and companion for life. She was like him, yet so amazingly different. Eve added spice to his life. Here was someone to whom he could express his deepest feelings. He could and would love her until his dying breath. In creating Eve this way, our LORD makes another statement. The man and woman are forever intertwined. She originally came from him, and ever after, mankind would come from her. This was a forever connection.

EVE AND US: Even though Eve was the only person on the planet for Adam, she was all he needed. How could she not be? She was perfect, and who can improve on perfection? Our LORD does things right the first time—He does not need to do retakes.

GOD SPEAKS: "… Suddenly a rattling; and the bones came together, bone to bone … the flesh came upon them, and the skin covered them over, …thus says the Lord God: Come from the four winds, O breath, and breathe … I will put my Spirit in you, and you shall live …" (Ezekiel 37:7-14 NKJV) Do you see how enormously powerful your God is?

WANDA'S PRAYER: Lord, we praise You! You can speak to dry dead bones and make them live! There is NOTHING TO HARD FOR YOU.

January 11

ONE PLUS ONE EQUALS—ONE

"THEREFORE SHALL A MAN LEAVE HIS FATHER AND HIS MOTHER, AND SHALL CLEAVE UNTO HIS WIFE: AND THEY SHALL BE ONE FLESH." (GENESIS 2:24 KJV)

The words, "… the two shall be one flesh" are very powerful, as they flow from the mouth of our Eternal God. The two, in a marriage, equals one. Marriage, in God's eyes, calls for a man and woman to leave their parents and cleave (cement) to each other as husband and wife. The two must be one flesh. Our LORD started with one flesh, the man. From a piece of that man, God formed his mate. In marriage, the two would once again become one. In marriage, singleness is the goal. GOD adds one plus one and gets one! She is in him, and he is in her, with Christ at its center—this is God's goal for marriage. A Godly marriage represents God. "For our LORD is one." A godly marriage also reflects Heaven. In eternity, GOD is one, but HE exists in three persons: FATHER, SON, and HOLY SPIRIT. A marriage is like a finely woven fabric, intricately put together.

EVE AND US: LORD, divorce rips the finely woven fibers of the fabric in two, and both pieces are destroyed. Many of us have gone down this terrible path; we have felt the ripping of the fibers. We know You heal the tears; however, some scars remain. At times, we can feel like a torn cloth with jagged edges.

GOD SPEAKS: "And the two shall become one flesh;' so then they are no longer two, but one flesh." (Mark 10:8 NKJV) I am in the business of making people whole and pure. In Jesus Christ, is the fullness of GOD in bodily form. (Colossians 2:9) Let Me live in your heart. I, your Father, and LORD, will complete you. Whether married or single, know that I am your Husband, and you are My bride. Believe it and move forward. As Eve joined human to human, be now joined as it was meant to be; humanity indwelt by Divinity.

WANDA'S PRAYER: LORD, as the songwriter says, "Let Your love consume, fill me with Your glory." We empty ourselves before You; pour into us as much of You as we can hold.

January 12

NAKED TRUTH

"NOW THE MAN AND HIS WIFE WERE BOTH NAKED, BUT THEY FELT NO SHAME." (GENESIS 2:25 NLT)

I picture Adam and Eve in their paradise home, strolling through the foliage as naked as can be. The fig leaves are still on the tree. The only covering this couple has is that they are clothed in the silk linen of God's perfect love and righteousness. This perfect LOVE not only casts out fear, but it does away with shame and guilt as well. The life which the first couple lived before God is pure and "guilt free." The couple is one with their LORD, and one with each other. This oneness with God is good and sin free. God's goodness is seen in the display of complete nudity and a total emptying of themselves. They have no inhibitions to each other, or to their LORD. Everything for this perfect couple was open and naked before each other, and before their LORD. Think of it, they did not have to play emotional or physical hide and seek. This is the way Father God meant things to be. Truly, this is "the marriage bed undefiled." (Hebrews 13:4)

EVE AND US: Eve's world is so different from ours. After all, she lived in paradise. In her world, there was no sin. Question: "Can we have that kind of emotional nakedness in our world?" The answer is a resounding "yes!" Our Lord desires to give us openness and freedom in the marriage He designs. The LORD Jesus was the center of Adam and Eve's world. Problems will arise, but quickly bring everything to Him. Give God total control. Allow Him to reign over your marriage and life. When we go astray like run-away sheep, God's correction rod brings us back into the fold.

GOD SPEAKS: "Above all, clothe yourselves with love, which binds us all together in perfect harmony." (Colossians 3:14 NLT) My child, "you are complete in Me." Remember again the Creation story. Do not forget it was I, your LORD, who completed the first man and his wife. I did it then and I can still do it now in you if you would only allow me to. My question to you is, "Do you want to be made whole?" Be complete in Christ and be made whole.

WANDA'S PRAYER: Father God, Your Word says, "… But all things are naked and open to the eyes of HIM to whom we must give account." (Hebrews 4:13b NKJV) Lord, let there be no distance between us. May we be naked before You always.

January 13

CAREFUL LITTLE EARS

"NOW THE SERPENT WAS MORE CUNNING THAN ANY BEAST OF THE FIELD WHICH THE LORD GOD HAD MADE. AND HE SAID TO THE WOMAN, 'HAS GOD INDEED SAID, YOU SHALL NOT EAT OF EVERY TREE OF THE GARDEN?'" (GENESIS 3:1 NKJV)

We are not told why Eve was singled out to assist the man in the downfall of humanity. However, one thing is clear—the fact that the serpent spoke to her meant she was close enough to hear him. So, the question I ask is, why was Eve close enough to the serpent to hear his lying words? Somehow, Eve had gotten herself in "earshot" of Satan to hear his deceptive words. So, what grand scheme did the "hater" of God and man (Satan) use to cause the fall of Creation? He dropped a few seeds of doubt into the innocent soil of Eve's heart. "Eve," the serpents says; "Are you sure you heard God right? Did God really say what you thought He said?" With these words, "did God really say," the serpent starts to play mind games with innocent Eve. In one quick blow, Satan gets her to doubt the perfect truth of God, His love, and devotion to her. His success and our failure usually come when we place ourselves in earshot of him.

EVE AND US: Thousands of years later, we still fall prey to Satan's same trick. Our fall comes in when we allow him to get close enough to whisper evil, "sweet nothings" in our ear. When we obey his words, we too, like Humpty Dumpty, have our great fall. Help Lord!

GOD SPEAKS: "Give ear and hear my voice, listen and hear my speech." (Isaiah 28:23 NKJV) Listen to My words, with a heart to obey them.

WANDA'S PRAYER: LORD, keep us in earshot of You and Your words always. Give us strong legs to run from Satan and sin. Help us hear You, with a heart to obey. Teach us not to question, but to comply with Your Word.

January 14

CAREFUL LITTLE MOUTH

"AND THE WOMAN SAID TO THE SERPENT, 'WE MAY EAT THE FRUIT OF THE TREES OF THE GARDEN; BUT OF THE FRUIT OF THE TREE WHICH IS IN THE MIDST OF THE GARDEN, GOD HAS SAID, YOU SHALL NOT EAT IT, NOR SHALL YOU TOUCH IT, LEST YOU DIE.'" (GENESIS 3:2-3 NKJV)

Eve's lingering at the "Tree of sin" placed her in a no-win situation. No matter what she would answer, Satan would have a better response. Remember, the serpent is "cunning and crafty." In cases like this, the best defense would have been to "RUN" into the arms of her loving LORD or to her husband. It was God's command, so maybe she should have referred Satan to God, the Creator and Maker of the command, in the first place. But I have a question. Why didn't the man speak up? The Bible says he was "with her" (Genesis 3:6). Why didn't he come to the defense of his wife? Where were those protector skills when Eve needed them most? But Eve, what could she have said to Satan? Her only defense against the attacks of her enemy is the Word of God. Eve, girl, just stick to and say what you know. All she knew was "don't eat from the tree." So, Eve, do not eat, do not talk, just walk… away… from the tree. There is no shame in running away from the big bad Satan—Sista' girl. After all, as my rhyme goes, "He who turns and runs away, can let the LORD fight your battles another day." Or she could have taken a page out of Adam's book and said nothing at all.

EVE AND US: We cannot beat up on Eve too much because we are guilty of the same things. We speak when we should be quiet. Battles we should allow our LORD to fight, we try fighting ourselves, only to receive a good beat down from the devil. Again, Lord, show us Your way of escape.

GOD SPEAKS: "that you may with one mind and one mouth glorify the God and Father of our Lord Jesus Christ." (Romans 15:6 NKJV) "But you, O man of God, flee these things and pursue righteousness, godliness, faith, love, patience, gentleness." (1 Timothy 6:11 NKJV) Are you facing the real possibility of crashing and burning in sin? Praise God and run to His exit door—Flee the temptation! After fleeing, RUN to your LORD. "Pursue righteousness, godliness, faith, love …" These are all attributes which describe ME, the God of Heaven. Come to Me and I will protect you.

WANDA'S PRAYER: "Let the words of my mouth and the meditation of my heart Be acceptable in Your sight, O LORD, my strength and my Redeemer." (Psalm 19:14 NKJV)

January 15

SIN'S SOUFFLÉ (PART ONE)

"THEN THE SERPENT SAID TO THE WOMAN, 'YOU WILL NOT SURELY DIE.'" (GENESIS 3:4 NKJV)

Satan, the serpent, shows his craft in full array. First, that cunning snake starts his recipe with a large cup of doubt. "Did God really say what you thought He said?" (Genesis 3:1) He carefully stirs Eve's doubtful thoughts, allowing them to simmer slowly in her mind. He knows the aroma created with his words is now gradually reaching their boiling point of discontent, and will soon spill over into open rebellion. While on slow cook, the master chef of sin throws in one of his main ingredients—one pound of a "big lie." He says to Eve, "You will not surely die." Satan looks Eve directly in the face, with batting eyes and with a sweet soft voice says, "Girl, you're not 'gonna die—you're 'gonna be 'god." (Writer's paraphrase) Now he has Eve on his hook.

EVE AND US: We can relate to Eve because we have all been there. Soft lights or no lights, the right music and lots of sweet-sounding words all added up to my fall. Like Eve, the match was lit, and I too was burning. Now, because of my sin, I am separated from the true love, Jesus Christ. I am left bruised, battered, alone, and wondering how do I get back home. Lord, speak to my heart and give me Your answers.

GOD SPEAKS: "The thief's purpose is to steal and kill and destroy. My purpose is to give them a rich and satisfying life." (John 10:10 NLT) As you consider the temptation to sin, consider My words, "… My purpose is to give you a rich and satisfying life." Satan's words always bring death of some kind—God's words bring life! Do not trust your feelings—stick to My words, "They are truth and life."

WANDA'S PRAYER: "Just as I am without one plea, but that thy (Jesus') blood was shed for me. And that You bid me to come to thee, Oh Lamb of God, I come, I come." (Hymn: "Just As I Am")

January 16

SIN'S SOUFFLÉ (PART TWO)

"FOR GOD KNOWS THAT IN THE DAY YOU EAT OF IT YOUR EYES WILL BE OPENED, AND YOU WILL BE LIKE GOD, KNOWING GOOD AND EVIL." (GENESIS 3:5 NKJV)

To complete his soufflé, Satan throws in four pounds of top choice "ego batter" into the mix. Here he says to Eve, "Your 'LORD of Love' is only lying to you. You will not die, as God says. Eve, He is actually holding back something very special from you. God is scared you will take over His job—that you will be 'god.' He is cheating you out of this glorious new lifestyle. I, at great peril and sacrifice to myself, will help you get what is yours." Satan continues, "Eve, do not stop at just being part of Creation. Oh no! I have secret information—you, my dear woman, can be god!" (Writer's paraphrase) These words were the last and perfect ingredients needed to finish the devil's soufflé. Satan had mixed his lies, mingled with a hit of truth in just the right portions. He was right about the good and evil part. Eve had always known "good." She was a flawless woman living in paradise. In choosing to listen to Satan, she would know the endless pit of evil. With crafty, cunning words, he stirred his sin mixture well. He placed it gently in the oven of her preheated mind. Now the devil had only to just allow the soufflé of sin to bake in Eve's mind—and bake it did.

EVE AND US: Looking at Eve's story, Lord, it is very scary to know Satan is waiting to pounce on us with destruction. Lord, give us words of comfort to conquer these fears which may otherwise consume our hearts.

GOD SPEAKS: "Thou shalt have no other gods before me." (Exodus 20:3 KJV) Don't even worship the "god of self." Tell the enemy of God to, "… Get thee behind me, Satan: for it is written, Thou shalt worship the Lord thy God, and him only shalt thou serve." (Luke 4:8 KJV) No matter what you go through, take hold of My perfect love, and let Me cast out all your doubts and fears. Now give Me praise.

WANDA'S PRAYER: You alone are God and besides You there is no other God! We will bless the LORD with our whole heart.

January 17

EYE PROBLEMS

"SO WHEN THE WOMAN SAW THAT THE TREE WAS GOOD FOR FOOD, THAT IT WAS PLEASANT TO THE EYES, AND A TREE DESIRABLE TO MAKE ONE WISE, SHE TOOK OF ITS FRUIT AND ATE. SHE ALSO GAVE TO HER HUSBAND WITH HER, AND HE ATE." (GENESIS 3:6 NKJV)

As we shall see, Eve has eye problems. Satan, having prepared his appetizing meal of sin, sits back, and waited for Eve to take a little nibble. Having heard the "god" of evil's words and digested them well, her mind is now clouded. Eve's lingering too long at the "sin tree" has fogged her view of right and wrong. The start of her eye problems is that she now sees what was once "forbidden," as gourmet food. Since "the tree was pleasant to look at," Eve casts off her fear of the forbidden tree. She now embraces it like a long-lost love. Its fruit could make her wiser than the God of Heaven, she thought. She now sees this fruit, not her LORD, as the answer to all her needs. She believed in this new thing to make her happy, so she left her loving Father for it. Finally, she took the bait, ate, and digested it well. How awful! Not only does she engage in the devilish deed, but she takes her husband with her. My advice to Eve: "Girl, enjoy the sweetness of the fruit in your mouth, for when that fruit hits your belly, it is going to sour in your stomach."

EVE AND US: Eve's "eye problems" would be instrumental in assisting in the fall of Creation. She influenced her husband to do evil, and not good. Her actions speak to us; how often we can be used as influences for evil, and not for good? Notice, too, how sin loves company.

GOD SPEAKS: "The eye is the light for the body. If your eyes are good, then your whole body will be full of light. But if your eyes are evil, then your whole body will be full of darkness …" (Matthew 6:22-23 ICB) Eve had "Eyeitis". This malady causes total self-absorption. Concerned only about her own needs, she turns from God's truth to Satan's lies. She had My perfect and complete truth! Yet, that was not enough, so she began focusing on the lie. "Eyeitis" is terminal to not only the first couple, but to all their offspring as well—thanks Eve!

WANDA'S PRAYER: Father, You are the only cure for "Eyeitis." Immunize us from self-absorption. Teach us to keep our eyes on You only.

January 18

THE FALLOUT

"THEN THE EYES OF BOTH OF THEM WERE OPENED, AND THEY KNEW THAT THEY WERE NAKED; AND THEY SEWED FIG LEAVES TOGETHER AND MADE THEMSELVES COVERINGS." (GENESIS 3:7 NKJV)

Like the explosion of a thousand atomic bombs, the fallout from Adam and Eve's sin would alter the existence of life on planet Earth forever. Adam joined his wife in eating from the tree of sin. Fallout No. 1: "both of their eyes were opened…" But just what were their eyes open to? Answer: Nakedness without God! Fallout No. 2: Disobedience to God's expressed command caused the removal of the Spirit which God had breathed into them at Creation. The result was Fallout No. 3: They could see sin's results, from God's view. They saw that sin brought an ugly and shameful nakedness. Immediately, in a vain and desperate attempt to cover the guilty act, "they sewed fig leaves together and made themselves coverings." Compare this nakedness with the one in Genesis 2:25. The nakedness with God is a holy and peaceful beauty. It was "nakedness" lived with God, in His will. This "new" nakedness is shameless and guilt laden. In an attempt to hide and cover the sin problem, they grab fig leaves. Fallout No. 4: In only moments, they have gone from perfect bliss to the depths of sin. Satan was right on this point— "they now knew evil," and evil was very ugly. Stripped of the warmth of God's Spirit which held them close in His loving arms, they must now face evil, and its consequences. In their confused state, they must have wondered, "Where are the promised diadems and regal robes to show they were now 'gods'?" This 'being god,' was a big lie! This shameful nakedness needed a covering.

EVE AND US: Eve's fallout was terrible; what must she have been thinking at this moment? Satan's promised lies were like puffs of smoke—they had just vanished! What lies has Satan sold to you? Mine are too many to count. In the end, like Eve, I too was left trying to cover my guilt and shame.

GOD SPEAKS: "David said to Gad, 'I am in deep distress. Let us fall into the hands of the LORD, for his mercy is great; but do not let me fall into human hands.'" (2 Samuel 24:14 NIV) Entering into sin and its consequences always cause deep distress. But the God of Heaven is merciful.

WANDA'S PRAYER: Thank You, Father, for the wonderful love and mercy You are ever ready to give to us. What a great God we serve!

January 19

HIDING FROM LOVE?

"AND THEY HEARD THE SOUND OF THE LORD GOD WALKING IN THE GARDEN IN THE COOL OF THE DAY, AND ADAM AND HIS WIFE HID THEMSELVES FROM THE PRESENCE OF THE LORD GOD AMONG THE TREES OF THE GARDEN."
(GENESIS 3:8 NKJV)

This scene would be comical if it were not so sad. The time to run and hide was when the serpent first spoke to Eve! But sin can twist the mind and warp the perception; so much to where both Eve and her husband saw **"good" as "evil" and "evil" as "good."** In this text, after His day was done, we see a picture of a loving Father—the Creator of the Universe, who could not wait to come, and spend precious time with His kids, after a long, hard, day of work. The text gives us the picture of "Daddy" God, having daily face-to-face time with His kids (Adam and Eve). But this day differs from other days. Instead of running to their Father God as before, they run from Him in stark fear. They run and hide from the LORD of LOVE! The spirit of sin has replaced God's Holy Spirit. Sin had them believing that their loving Lord was going to hurt them for their evil act. I once heard a preacher say, "Sin is a mental disease." Here I can see he was right! Adam and Eve are confused and scared, so they run from the God of love like frightened rats. How sad is that? Can you see God's perfect heart breaking in two?

EVE AND US: Eve and her husband did not know what to do or where to go. The loud voice of Satan now screams to them to just run and hide—get away and fast! How many times have we been in Eve's situation? In our failings and sins, we too run like a wild rat. We, too, are in the vise grip of fear.

GOD SPEAKS: Again, I refer you to David—listen and hear My voice. "Where can I go from Your Spirit? Or where can I flee from Your presence? If I ascend into heaven, You are there; If I make my bed in hell, behold, You are there ..." (Psalm 139:7-12 NKJV) Read the entire chapter sometime—it will blow you away. You will discover I do not want to harm you—just LOVE you back to Myself.

WANDA'S PRAYER: Lord, what more can we say, but thank You for your awesome love. Father, never leave us.

January 20

WHERE ARE YOU?

"THEN THE LORD GOD CALLED TO ADAM AND SAID TO HIM, 'WHERE ARE YOU?'" (GENESIS 3:9 NKJV)

Words really cannot do justice to the act of love displayed in this verse. My Lord comes from His Heaven to get His wayward kids who have sinned. He was very well aware of what they had done. The spotless God makes the first move towards reconciliation. See Him reaching out to Adam, in an attempt to bridge the gap Adam's sin had caused. The Heavenly Dad knows His sin-scared kids will not come to Him, so He goes to them. He seeks them out. He tenderly and softly calls to His man, "… where are you?" In other words, "Adam, My son, do you know where your disobedience has taken you?" (Writer's paraphrase) Father God knows Adam's feelings and thoughts. He would woo His family back to Himself. If they are lost, it will not be due to God's hand. This is a beautiful display of love by our Father. Note, though, they both sinned; however, our LORD goes to the one who was left in charge—Adam.

EVE AND US: Do we realize how far sin can take us from our loving LORD? The delusion of sin says, "You have sinned, and God is angry. He is going to punish you harshly, so RUN, RUN!" Or sin says, "Go fix the problem, then come back." You will never return because you cannot fix the problem.

GOD SPEAKS: "… I will never leave or forsake you." (Hebrews 13:5 NKJV) "O Death, where is your sting? O Hades, (Grave) where is your victory?" "But thanks be to God, who gives us the victory through our Lord Jesus Christ." (1 Corinthians 15:55, 57 NKJV) You do not ever have to worry; I am not going anywhere. You might try to run and hide, but I will come for you and save you.

WANDA'S PRAYER: What comforting words these are. Lord, we will rest in You and in Your words.

January 21

AFRAID

"SO HE SAID, 'I HEARD YOUR VOICE IN THE GARDEN, AND I WAS AFRAID BECAUSE I WAS NAKED; AND I HID MYSELF.'" (GENESIS 3:10 NKJV)

Adam, as spokesman and head of this planet, speaks up. He tells the Father he was afraid because of his nakedness. Adam says, "I heard you call me, but I'm naked and exposed—I was scared of You God." (Writer's paraphrase) In Adam's speech, he admits fear and shame. Sin caused both things. The Father breathed into Adam's nostrils, His own breath. Thus, the "rightness" (or righteousness) that Adam and Eve possessed was from God alone. Though Adam and Eve were naked prior to sinning, that nakedness caused no shame because they were in a right and Holy relationship before their LORD. Adam's act of disobedience has broken this wonderful relationship with their loving LORD. They are now stripped of God's righteousness and left cold, scared, and naked. The nakedness of sin brings fear. Fear brings flight from God, who alone can save them. They are blind to truth and can only see the pain of evil. Sin is now out of Pandora's Box. Once the lid was lifted, the contents of evil spilled out and contaminated our world.

EVE AND US: Poor Eve, what she must think about all this? She may have thought: "It wasn't supposed to be this way; I feel ashamed and scared." Like Eve, we have all broken God's laws (sinned). We can relate to her feelings of fear and shame because of our actions. What is the answer, LORD?

GOD SPEAKS: "Fear not; you will no longer live in shame. don't be afraid; there is no more disgrace for you …" (Isaiah 54:4 NLT) You no longer have to live in shame or fear. My perfect love has cast them both out.

WANDA'S PRAYER: We thank You, Father, for looking beyond our faults and loving us in the midst of our deepest needs. Help us always to live in this remarkable love.

January 22

GOOD LISTENER

"SO HE SAID, 'I HEARD YOUR VOICE IN THE GARDEN, AND I WAS AFRAID BECAUSE I WAS NAKED; AND I HID MYSELF.'" (GENESIS 3:10 NKJV)

Picture the scene—it is the cool of the day. This is the time when Father God lovingly meets with His new family. However, this day is different—it is the day after the sin. Adam and Eve are dressed in drying fig leaves and cowering like frightened rats. They are hiding behind one of the trees in the Garden of Eden; in a futile attempt to escape the eye of the All-Seeing God. The compassionate Father (aware of their location), calls out to His confused, trembling son, "Where are you?" This incident is heart breaking to our LORD. It was crushing for the perfect Father of love, to hear the words, "I'm scared of You, because I have sinned." The Father, like the wonderful Dad He is, just listened and loved his wayward son. Notice in this scene, there are no lightning flashes or clashing thunder; just a quiet listen by our LORD to His boy.

EVE AND US: Despite her fears, the love of Father God must have struck Eve. There was no scolding or finger pointing. Our LORD just listened to Adam's explanation. She no doubt experienced his same fears, as well as thought, "I gave him the fruit of sin; which caused all the mess." Looking back over our lives, we, like Eve, can see our many mess ups. These "mess ups" separate us from our LORD.

GOD SPEAKS: "… for the lord has heard (listened) of your misery." (Genesis 16:11 NIV) Father God hears us also; do not run away from His loving arms.

WANDA'S PRAYER: Father, never let go of us. Always keep us in Your loving arms.

January 23

YOU'RE NAKED?

"AND HE SAID, 'WHO TOLD YOU THAT YOU WERE NAKED? HAVE YOU EATEN FROM THE TREE OF WHICH I COMMANDED YOU THAT YOU SHOUD NOT EAT?'"
(GENESIS 3:11 NKJV)

One attribute of our All-Powerful God is that He is All-knowing! Here is a great demonstration of this. The LORD knew Adam's dilemma, and the heart of His wayward son. God asks Adam a simple question; "You say that you are naked. So, tell Me, this 'new nakedness' you are talking about, who told you about it? Have you disobeyed Me and eaten from the forbidden tree?" (Writer's paraphrase) The Father's heart toward His erring son is one of tender compassion. The All-Knowing God could have said, "You messed up, Adam, and that's why you are naked!" But those words could never come from a Father, whose heart is LOVE personified. Our God, the Daddy of our universe, is waiting for Adam and Eve's confession, so that He can pounce forgiveness, cleansing, and restoration upon his kids. The symptom is the nakedness. The problem is disobedience. So, to God's question, "Have you eaten from the forbidden tree?" Adam's answer should have been, "Yes, Father God, I messed up; I disobeyed You—please forgive me. Please make things all right between You and me." Those words to our LORD would have thrilled His heart.

EVE AND US: I imagine as Eve stood beside her husband, she, too, felt the chilly breeze from the nakedness which sin had brought on. She must have also thought soon she, too, must answer for the deeds she had done. In looking at this story, we can ask ourselves, "What sins and misdeeds have we done to strain our relationship with our loving Dad?"

GOD SPEAKS: "… wretched, miserable, poor, blind, and naked. I counsel you to buy from Me gold refined in the fire, that you may be… clothed, that the shame of your nakedness may not be revealed; and anoint your eyes with eye salve, that you may see. As many as I love, I rebuke and chasten. Therefore be zealous and repent." (Revelation 3:17b-19 NKJV) To mankind, healing is free for the asking; but it cost the Son of God His life. Come, get cleansing and restoration. I am here waiting for you.

WANDA'S PRAYER: Lord, we are totally messed up! Clean us completely. Empty us of self, and fill our hearts with You.

January 24

BLAME GAME (PART 1)

"THEN THE MAN SAID, 'THE WOMAN YOU GAVE TO BE WITH ME, SHE GAVE ME OF THE TREE, AND I ATE.'" (GENESIS 3:12 NKJV)

Adam has just confessed his nakedness and fears to God. However, Adam's confession only deals with the fruit of his problem. The LORD wants to get to the root, which is disobedience. This is the cause of the nakedness, which brought the fear and shame. The Father is ever ready to forgive and draw him back into fellowship. To begin the fix, the LORD asks Adam a simple question with an easy answer. "Who told you that you were naked or without a covering? Did you eat from the forbidden tree?" In other words, just confess the wrong and ask for forgiveness. But no! Adam would not confess. Instead, he goes on the "blame game tour." He blames the woman, Eve, and he blames God. "LORD," he says, "The problem as I see it, is this woman, that YOU … gave me. Yeah, I ate but that (woman and You), were the cause of the problem." (Writer's paraphrase) The sting of sin had now infected him like a deadly virus. It (sin) comes in, attacks his mind, and has taken over. The result is humanity's destruction. Before sin, words like fear, hiding, and now blaming were not a part of the innocent pair's vocabulary. Now, only moments after the fall of man, those words ooze out so effortlessly from Adam's lips.

EVE AND US: These words must have pierced Eve's soul. The love of her life has just reduced her to "the woman You gave me." At this point, Eve must have felt very alone. I remember once many years ago, after having been intimate with a certain man, everything was later exposed. I, too, heard those stinging words spoken of me, and I felt as naked as Eve. The words cut like a knife, leaving me aching for months. Reader, have you had a similar experience?

GOD SPEAKS: "Nevertheless we, according to His promise, look for new heavens and a new earth in which righteousness dwells. Therefore, beloved, looking forward to these things, be diligent to be found by Him in peace, without spot and blameless;" (2 Peter 3:13-14 NKJV) This world is now stained by sin. With God's Spirit in you, your job is to live like you are preparing for the new world to come.

WANDA'S PRAYER: Father God, continue to fill us with your Spirit, so we can give You glory.

January 25

BLAME GAME (PART 2)

"AND THE LORD GOD SAID TO THE WOMAN, 'WHAT IS THIS YOU HAVE DONE?' THE WOMAN SAID, 'THE SERPENT DECEIVED ME, AND I ATE.'" (GENESIS 3:13 NKJV)

Eve goes on the "blame game tour" with her husband, Adam. She blames the serpent's deception for her downfall. In her case, however, she is somewhat correct. "But I fear, lest somehow, as the serpent deceived Eve by his craftiness, so your minds may be corrupted from the simplicity that is in Christ." (2 Corinthians 11:3 NKJV) Yes, Eve had been deceived, but no one forced her to linger near the tempting serpent. No one pried her mouth open and shoved the forbidden fruit down her throat. The Father's words were so simple and so plain… "do not eat from the forbidden tree." Standing naked before her loving Dad in drying fig leaves, cowering in fear, she must have wondered, "How did I get in this mess?" I cannot end this dialogue without pointing out how loving and gracious the Father is in this situation. Notice He does not accuse. The text could have read, "Eve, you wicked woman, just look at what you've done!" But the words our LORD spoke to Eve caused her to think about her actions. "The LORD God said to the woman, what is this you have done?" (Genesis 3:13 NKJV). Or "Eve, are you aware of what you have done?" (Writer's paraphrase) God was very aware of what happened—He saw it all. Yet, He allows the erring Eve to explain her side of things, thus allowing her to reflect upon her actions. The correct answer should have been, "LORD, I really messed up; please forgive me." However, Eve's answer is, "It's not my fault; that snake did it to me—I'm a victim."

EVE AND US: How often do we, like Eve, fail to come clean for our actions? Instead, we play the blame game and make ourselves the victim. Our Lord gives us the chance to simply confess the sin; yet we choose to do just like Eve did and play the lame blame game. Without true confession to our LORD, victims will never have victory.

GOD SPEAKS: "If we confess our sins, He is faithful and just to forgive us our sins and to cleanse us from all unrighteousness." (1 John 1:9 NKJV) If you would just lay all the dirty laundry of your sins at My feet, you will see that I (your LORD), am so very trustworthy. I will not only cleanse you from that one sin, but I will also clean up all the "evil" ways which remain in your heart.

WANDA'S PRAYER: "Jesus keep me near the cross…" Father, keep us in Your Word, and ever close to You.

January 26

CURSED CORRECTED

"SO THE LORD GOD SAID TO THE SERPENT: 'BECAUSE YOU HAVE DONE THIS, YOU ARE CURSED MORE THAN ALL CATTLE, AND MORE THAN EVERY BEAST OF THE FIELD; ON YOUR BELLY YOU SHALL GO, AND YOU SHALL EAT DUST ALL THE DAYS OF YOUR LIFE. AND I WILL PUT ENMITY BETWEEN YOU AND THE WOMAN, AND BETWEEN YOUR SEED AND HER SEED; HE SHALL BRUISE YOUR HEAD, AND YOU SHALL BRUISE HIS HEEL.'" (GENESIS 3:14-15 NKJV)

There are some fascinating morsels that come from this conversation above. First, the Father never asks the serpent to explain his side of things. I think it is because He knew everything from his mouth would be a lie. Next, the Father informs the serpent and the couple that everything on the planet is now cursed, with the serpent being the most cursed. The serpent now becomes a creature that will forever crawl on its belly and eat the dust of the ground. Finally, the Lord corrects the problem where it began—with the woman. She was the catalyst which caused the sin. Thus, it would be the seed of the woman who would crush the serpent's head. The name of the seed is Jesus Christ. He would come through the woman, by way of the Holy Spirit. This brought Eve much comfort and gave her something to look forward to. She knew she had played a big part in the mess up. Now her Dad was giving her a kind of big hand in cleaning up. Little did she know, she would not be around for it.

EVE AND US: As children of our LORD, we can see where He has cleaned up the many messes made in our lives. As we glance back over our life highways, we can see all our mistakes; and the rotten consequences which closely followed. We can only go forward by looking at Jesus. He cleans up the city dumps of our lives. In its place, He has built something new and clean, where the trash used to be.

GOD SPEAKS: "…Though your sins are like scarlet, They shall be as white as snow; Though they are red like crimson, They shall be as wool. If you are willing and obedient, You shall eat the good of the land; (Isaiah 1:18-19 NKJV) Come, let Me give you a nice clean bath.

WANDA'S PRAYER: LORD, we are ready for our baths now.

January 27

SIN'S SORROW

"TO THE WOMAN HE SAID: 'I WLL GREATLY MULTIPLY YOUR SORROW AND YOUR CONCEPTION; IN PAIN YOU SHALL BRING FORTH CHILDREN; YOUR DESIRE SHALL BE FOR YOUR HUSBAND, AND HE SHALL RULE OVER YOU.'" (GENESIS 3:16 NKJV)

I love how the Lord fixes things. He dealt with the serpent and now He deals with the second link in the broken chain—Eve. God tells her the consequences of her actions (sin always has consequences), will not bring the heavenly bliss as she was told. She will instead have pain and sorrow in conception, and in having children. Centuries later, we as women are still finding the pain and sorrow in child conception and childbirth to be very, very, true. Even if you had anesthesia to numb the pain before delivery, you will still feel it after the medication wears off. Next, our Father addresses a problem that has come about as the result of sin—the struggle to control. He tells her that her desire will be to control her husband; but he would control her. We daughters of Eve have witnessed this negative control on both sides down through the centuries.

EVE AND US: Thousands of years later, the age-old problem of sin still exists. Much pain and sorrow still surround conception and childbirth to this day. The sorrows of women are varied and many. How often do we read of everything from human trafficking of young girls, increase in teen pregnancies, fetal and maternal mortalities? All these pains and sorrows can be traced back to the first disobedient act in Creation.

GOD SPEAKS: "Surely He has borne our griefs and carried our sorrows…" (Isaiah 53:4 NKJV) I AM the bearer of all your pain and sorrows. Give them to me.

WANDA'S PRAYER: Father, thank You for loving us enough to take our burdens.

January 28

YOUR AUTHORITY—YOUR RESPONSIBILITY

"THEN TO ADAM HE SAID, 'BECAUSE YOU HAVE HEEDED THE VOICE OF YOUR WIFE, AND HAVE EATEN FROM THE TREE OF WHICH I COMMANDED YOU, SAYING, 'YOU SHALL NOT EAT OF IT': CURSED IS THE GROUND FOR YOUR SAKE; IN TOIL YOU SHALL EAT OF IT ALL THE DAYS OF YOUR LIFE. BOTH THORNS AND THISTLES IT SHALL BRING FORTH FOR YOU, AND YOU SHALL EAT THE HERB OF THE FIELD. IN THE SWEAT OF YOUR FACE YOU SHALL EAT BREAD TILL YOU RETURN TO THE GROUND, FOR OUT OF IT YOU WERE TAKEN; FOR DUST YOU ARE, AND TO DUST YOU SHALL RETURN.'" (GENESIS 3:17-19 NKJV)

As Eve listened to the pronouncements of judgment given to her husband by our Lord, the words, "Because you have heeded the voice of your wife, and have eaten from the tree of which I commanded you, saying, 'you shall not eat of it'" … She could not help but to think, this man listened to me over God, and now look at the mess it has caused. This would be the beginning of her "if only's." "If only," I hadn't talked to the snake; "If only" I had run from the scene, before eating the forbidden fruit or giving him the fruit to eat. But the Father is merciful. He does not blame Eve for Adam's responsibility. Instead, He says, "Adam, you listened, and you ate from the tree I told you not to eat from. Now your entire world has changed because of your one sin." (Writer's paraphrase) Eve influenced Adam away from God's original design, and now the result was the destruction of both of their worlds. He would know sweat and toil until death. We can clearly see that sin is never a private matter. Her one transgression affected the entire planet for thousands of centuries to come.

EVE AND US: The lessons are crystal clear. (1) The men in our lives must hear from Father God and follow His leadings. If he hears from and obeys the Father, he will not go wrong. (2) We, too, must not influence the men in our lives for evil, but for good. We must always remember, if we influence him negatively, it may destroy both of our worlds.

GOD SPEAKS: "But I want you to know that the head of every man is Christ, the head of woman is man, and the head of Christ is God." (1 Corinthians 11:3 NKJV) Spend your time learning and operating in your place, and allow Me to put everyone else in theirs. I am so much better at directing things than you are. My order is perfect, and I make no mistakes. You are to pray for the "wrongs" you see, and allow Me to speak My perfect will and plan. Remember, "The law of the LORD is perfect, converting the soul; The testimony of the LORD is sure, making wise the simple;" (Psalm 19:7 NKJV)

WANDA'S PRAYER: Father, help us trust you. Help us pray to You for the men in our lives; that You will give them Your perfect direction. Thank you Father.

January 29

MOTHER OF THE LIVING

"AND ADAM CALLED HIS WIFE'S NAME EVE, BECAUSE SHE WAS THE MOTHER OF ALL LIVING." (GENESIS 3:20 NKJV)

I love happy endings, don't you? Here is an example of one. It comes just before the man and his wife are forced to leave the Garden of Eden, and before she gives birth to her first child. Adam turns to his wife with love and gives her the name Eve. The name means "life" in Hebrew, or "to bear, to conceive seed." Adam no longer saw his wife as "that woman" who caused him to sin. In the midst of all that sorrow and pain, he was given a great revelation. He remembered what the Lord had said of Eve—that she would bear the Seed, which would crush the serpent. This revelation comforted him and drew him closer to his wife. The LORD had provided a "fix" for this grand mess up, and He would use his wife Eve as part of the solution. Our LORD would truly use Eve to be the mother of the living. Every child would come from her and "woman kind." A woman would bring the God man into the world. After leaving Eden, the fruit of that intimacy would produce children and a deeper closeness. This closeness would see them through their trials—in a world racked by sin.

EVE AND US: Father, what a lovely picture! You brought beauty and love out of all this mess. Remind us again how you can do it in our lives.

GOD SPEAKS: "To console those who mourn…, To give them beauty for ashes, The oil of joy for mourning, The garment of praise for the spirit of heaviness; That they may be called trees of righteousness, The planting of the LORD, that He (I) may be glorified." (Isaiah 61:3 NKJV) I created you for My praise, and when you give your life to Me, I still can, and will, make it a thing of beauty.

WANDA'S PRAYER: Lord and Father, take our lives and use them for Your glory. Always keep us close—so very close to you.

January 30

NEW CLOTHES

"UNTO ADAM ALSO AND TO HIS WIFE DID THE LORD GOD MAKE COATS OF SKINS, AND CLOTHED THEM." (GENESIS 3:21 KJV)

What a very pitiful site we are witnessing in the Garden of Paradise. The once holy couple, now spoiled by sin, stands before the Lord of the Heavens, draped in drying fig leaves, in a feeble attempt to cover sin's nakedness. The Father is so very loving and gracious. He knows that human covering for sin will never do. Our feeble attempt to mask our sin is but drying fig leaves; it hides nothing and will soon fall off. Notice the clothing our LORD provides His fallen pair. "The Lord made them coats of skin and clothed them." Adam and Eve's self-made clothing was never good enough. You might ask, "why?" Considering how fig leaves dry out in four to five days; their clothing would not last. However, the clothing our Lord made for them from skins was much more durable. And most of all, the clothing the Lord gave them came with an especially important lesson. The lesson is that someone would have to die for the man and the woman to live. You cannot get "skins" from a live animal. The slaughter of this innocent animal was a lesson to the couple that the Son of God would give His own life as payment for our sins. What a terrible lesson to learn.

EVE AND US: As Eve watched the killing of this innocent animal, I am certain she realized the high cost of sin. "This animal died to clothe me, so I might live." That animal pointed to the Lamb of God, which would take away the sin of the world for all time. (John 1:36)

GOD SPEAKS: "I will greatly rejoice in the LORD, My soul shall be joyful in my God; For He has clothed me with the garments of salvation, He has covered me with the robe of righteousness, ..." (Isaiah 61:10 NKJV) Our God is so worthy of praise.

WANDA'S PRAYER: Father, thank you for Your love, Your goodness, and Your mercy for us. Live in us now, and help us to always appreciate this love.

January 31

GOT TO GO

"SO THE LORD GOD BANISHED THEM FROM THE GARDEN OF EDEN, AND HE SENT ADAM OUT TO CULTIVATE THE GROUND FROM WHICH HE HAD BEEN MADE." (GENESIS 3:23 NLT)

For the first family of Creation, this was the ultimate price for their sin. The couple was forced out of their paradise home. Was the Holy God unfair? NO!!! Had the couple continued living in their paradise home after their sin, they would have had the opportunity to eat from the "Tree of Life." Thus, the couple would live forever in their sinful state. Imagine living in a world of forever sin—now that would be evil! They would produce children who would be perpetual sinners as well. The end result would have been an entire planet of everlasting sinners! In His grace, God only gave us a season (a long season) of sin. Imagine, however, never ending crime, injustice, and inhumanity to man. This is what would have happened if the fallen couple had access to the tree of eternal life. To prevent this mother of evils, our LORD had a plan to destroy sin, its cause, and to give us paradise once again. Now this is something worth shouting praise to our LORD about! I am sure Eve, forced from her paradise home, and left to face sin's cold consequences, could see nothing to shout about.

EVE AND US: At times, sin seems to be the debt we keep paying for. Reader, can you think of past sins in your life, which seem to haunt you to this day? I can.

GOD SPEAKS: "And I will put enmity between thee and the woman, and between thy seed and her seed; it shall bruise thy head, and thou shalt bruise his heel." (Genesis 3:15 KJV) I paid the price for you because I love you. You can bury—lay those sins to bed.

WANDA'S PRAYER: Thank You Father, for paying the cost of our sins. Thank You for providing a way back to the tree of life, but as a blood-bought saint.

Notes

February

INTRODUCTION

SARAH (MOTHER OF THE JEWS)

Our second woman of study is (Sarai) or Sarah, as her name would later be called. As Eve is the "Mother of the Living," so Sarah is the "Mother of the Jews."

Our LORD would use this elderly woman and her elderly husband to produce the Jewish nation; out of which He would bring His Messiah, the Savior of the world.

In walking through the pages of her life as presented to us in God's Holy Word, we will glean many beautiful and valuable lessons of life. The book of Hebrews refers to Sarah as a woman of faith. She was that, and so much more.

So, take this journey with me as we travel back in time to the life of God's first woman of faith.

Notes

February 1

HOW ROYAL

"THEN ABRAM AND NAHOR TOOK WIVES: THE NAME OF ABRAM'S WIFE WAS SARAI … " (GENESIS 11:29 NKJV)

Our first introduction to Sarai is an interesting one. She bursts on the scene in the lineage of Abram, son of Terah. Abram wanted a wife, so he took Sarai. Her name means "my princess" according to the Blue Letter Bible (BLB). The word princess means to be of royal blood. Scripture does not tell us that Sarai was a descendent of an earthly monarch, but in Abram's eyes, she must have been like royalty because he loved her and saw her as his "princess." We are told in Scripture that Sarai was strikingly beautiful. This may have been why she was known as "princess." Other scholars render Sarai's name to mean "contentious and argumentative" (BLB). As we look at this "princess" of Abram's, we shall see that side as well.

SARAI AND US: It must be nice to be characterized as royalty, or someone's princess, as Sarai was. Us "plain Jane's" of the world, may want to envy her a little, Father. Lord, help us "plain Jane's" to deal with our jealous tendencies. Show us we are special.

GOD SPEAKS: "But you are a chosen generation, a royal priesthood, a holy nation, His own special people, that you may proclaim the praises of Him who called you out of darkness into His marvelous light;" (1 Peter 2:9 NKJV) You have no reason to "hate" on Sarai. As a saved and sanctified child of the King of Heaven, you have royal, heavenly blood coursing through your veins.

WANDA'S PRAYER: Lord, thanks for the wonderful reminder.

February 2

BEAUTIFUL AND BARREN

"BUT SARAI WAS BARREN; SHE HAD NO CHILD." (GENESIS 11:30 NKJV)

The beautiful Sarai was blessed with many things: good looks, an adoring husband, and a close-knit, caring family. But with all her blessings, there would be one thing in life which would give her much pain— "Sarai was barren; she had no child." Those seven little words cut like daggers through her heart and soul. For all that she could give her husband, she could not give him what he would crave—an heir to carry on his lineage. Childlessness was a shameful thing—then and now. Right off the bat, women are asked, "Are you married—do you have any children?" All the women around Sarai were having children, while her womb lay empty. Genesis 22:20-23 tells us Sarai's sister-in-law Milcah had eight sons. Her brother-in-law even had sons with his concubine. The ache in her heart must have been great. Yep! Sarai, like the rest of us on the planet of sinners, have missing pieces. None of us are perfect. That missing piece hung heavy on her heart and weighed on her soul.

SARAI AND US: Like Sarai, we all have missing pieces and barren areas of our lives. I saw my barren areas as a failed first marriage, and having to raise my kids as a single mom. Reader, what are the barren areas of your life which hang heavy on your heart and soul? Sarai, you, and I need to refocus. Let us focus on and count our blessings, not our barren areas.

GOD SPEAKS: "Sing, O barren, You who have not borne! Break forth into singing, and cry aloud, …Do not fear, for you will not be ashamed; Neither be disgraced, for you will not be put to shame; ..." (Isaiah 54:1-4 NKJV) Are you empty and unfulfilled? My life-giving Spirit can fill that hollow space. I AM that missing piece of your life's puzzle; I am what you need. You may say, "I love the Lord, and I still feel empty." In this instance, remember, you still need filling and refilling. So, seek Me, drink of me, and consume Me—hourly, daily if need be, until you are filled. Allow Me to occupy every inch of you completely. Trust Me and know that "I will withhold no good thing from you." "Seek first, My kingdom and My righteousness…" (Matthew 6:33), and I will birth in you a new, pure, and right desire. Then I will satisfy the desires of your heart. Trust Me to add the things you really need; and believe that I have your absolute best in mind.

WANDA'S PRAYER: Father God, You have blessed and completed us with many things in this world. But mostly, You have completed us with You—thank You Lord. Personally, I want to give You "crazy praise" right now! You have been so very good to me. Help us all to refocus and continue to focus only on You—not on the barren areas of our lives.

February 3

CHANGE IN SCENERY

"AND TERAH TOOK HIS SON ABRAM AND HIS GRANDSON LOT, THE SON OF HARAN, AND HIS DAUGHTHER-IN-LAW SARAI, HIS SON ABRAM'S WIFE, AND THEY WENT OUT WITH THEM FROM UR OF THE CHALDEANS TO GO THE LAND OF CANAAN; AND THEY CAME TO HARAN AND DWELT THERE." (GENESIS 11:31 NKJV)

Sarai has moved from Ur of Chaldeans to Haran, at the command of her father-in-law Terah. What caused this over 600-mile move? Abram, the husband, was told by the God of Heaven to leave his homeland, its people, and to follow Him to a place of His choosing. (Acts 7:2-4) However, in this strongly patriarchal society, the oldest male and father are considered as "king". Terah, Abram's father, decides to leave town with his son. This change in scenery must have been a welcomed one for Sarai. Though I am sure she missed her loved ones, she was a new person and in a new place. In this place, there would be little reminders of her childlessness—after all, she did not know anyone, and no one knew her. She could hide in anonymity. But heartaches and disappointments of the soul always seem to find their way into her emotional "suitcases," thus, carrying them with her. Though Sarai left the familiar reminders of her "barrenness," she carried the emptiness of her childlessness with her, and unpacked its heartache wherever she went.

SARAI AND US: All of us, if we are not careful, carry around emotional baggage. We, like Sarai, carry these unwelcome but familiar emotional companions wherever we go. These "trinkets" of hurt and pain are our constant companions. For years, my "emotional baggage" was my singleness. Since I did not fully give it to the Lord, I carried it with me wherever I went.

GOD SPEAKS: "For He satisfies the longing soul, And fills the hungry soul with goodness." (Psalm 107:9 NKJV) Bring all of your "emotional suitcases" to Me, and leave them there. Allow Me to satisfy you with Myself. I alone can "satisfy the longing soul and fill the hungry soul with goodness.

WANDA'S PRAYER: LORD, give us that satisfaction now, and feed our hungry souls.

February 4

NEW WORLD

"NOW THE LORD HAD SAID TO ABRAM: 'GET OUT OF YOUR COUNTRY, ... TO A LAND THAT I WILL SHOW YOU. I WILL MAKE YOU A GREAT NATION; I WILL BLESS YOU AND MAKE YOUR NAME GREAT; AND YOU SHALL BE A BLESSING. AND IN YOU ALL THE FAMILIES OF THE EARTH WILL BE BLESSED.' ... AND ABRAM WAS SEVENTY-FIVE YEARS OLD WHEN HE DEPARTED FROM HARAN."
(GENESIS 12:1-4 NKJV)

Just when it seemed Sarai's life was settling down in a new place, she experienced another tragedy—Terah, her father-in-law, dies. Abram's earthly father is gone, and the LORD God steps right in his place. The LORD now assumes His rightful role as Abram and Sarai's mentor and Dad. He calls to His son and talks with him. To this old man (Abram 75) and his barren wife (Sarai 65), God makes a wonderful promise; "Get up, leave your home, get away from your father's house, and go where I will show you. If you do that, Abram, I will make a great nation out of you. I will bless you beyond your wildest dreams. I will make you and your barren wife, a great nation." (Genesis 12:1-3) (Writer's paraphrase). "… Abraham believed God, and it was accounted to him for righteousness." (Romans 4:3 NKJV) Sarai had a man who not only loved her, but also heard God's voice and would follow his LORD'S orders—Abram "departed from Haran." Sarai is off to a new world. She must have quietly rejoiced in her heart to her LORD, knowing that He had not forgotten her long-awaited, unanswered prayers.

SARAI AND US: Sarai's blessings are two-fold. First, Sarai has a man after God's heart; one who hears His voice and obeys it. Second, through Abram, she was assured God heard her prayers and would answer the deep passion of her heart. It is so good to be reminded that God hears and will answer the cries of our heart. Reader, tell Him your heart cries.

GOD SPEAKS: "Likewise the Spirit also helps in our weaknesses. …, but the Spirit Himself makes intercession for us with groanings which cannot be uttered. Now He who searches the hearts knows what the mind of the Spirit is, because He makes intercession for the saints according to the will of God." (Romans 8:26-27 NKJV) I (God) love you so much and I have anticipated your every need. I am so intimately involved in your life that My Spirit will pray for My perfect will to be accomplished in your life. I ask you, how loving is that?

WANDA'S PRAYER: Father, thank You for this deep abiding love You have for us.

February 5

RIDE OR DIE CHICK

"THEN ABRAM TOOK SARAI HIS WIFE AND LOT HIS BROTHER'S SON, AND ALL THEIR POSSESIONS THAT THEY HAD GATHERED, AND THE PEOPLE WHOM THEY HAD ACQUIRED IN HARAN, AND THEY DEPARTED TO GO TO THE LAND OF CANAAN. SO THEY CAME TO THE LAND OF CANAAN."
(GENESIS 12:5 NKJV)

I am fascinated by the fact that Abram, an old man, just picks up and moves at God's bidding. It is clear from this text the LORD had truly blessed this couple with great possessions and servants. I marvel at Sarai's faith. She has not received a direct word from God; and at 65 she is no spring chicken. Yet this "ride or die chick" just goes with her husband to this strange land. There is no scriptural record of her complaining or questioning his decision at this point. Though Sarai has not had her own personal relationship with the God of Heaven, she knows Him well through His interactions with her husband. The beauty of Sarai's character is she acts on what she knows. She knows her husband is truly committed to the unseen God. She knows her husband loves her and is truly committed to their marriage. Through her many years of barrenness, Abram never sought the comfort of another woman's arms. Abram was a one-woman man. She caught his eyes years before and still held his heart forever. The fact she was childless did not daunt his love for her, nor his commitment to her. She took great confidence in that thought. This "ride or die chick" would follow her man to the ends of the earth. Though she had not met this loving LORD for herself, she knew Him well through her husband.

SARAI AND US: Sarai shows us what true marital commitment looks like. Ladies, this is the kind of man you want in your life; a man who will show you Jesus. Through slips and falls, your man still has his eyes on Jesus.

GOD SPEAKS: "Then Jesus said to his disciples, 'If anyone desires to come after Me, let him deny himself, and take up his cross, and follow me.'" (Matthew 16:24 NKJV) Are you a disciple of your LORD'S? Then deny yourself and follow Me.

WANDA'S PRAYER: Father, help us die to self. Empty us of ourselves and totally fill us with You.

February 6

FAITH FAMINE

"NOW THERE WAS A FAMINE IN THE LAND, AND ABRAM WENT DOWN TO EGYPT TO DWELL THERE, FOR THE FAMINE WAS SEVERE IN THE LAND." (GENESIS 12:10 NKJV)

In Genesis 12:6-9, we see a beautiful passage. Abram arrives safely from Haran to Canaan. Our LORD greets him on his arrival by appearing to him. The Father gives him a word of prophecy: "To your offspring I will give this land." Abram is so thrilled about this promise that "He builds an altar to the LORD…" Abram surveys the "promised land" the LORD gives him. He then builds another altar in a place call Bethel (House of God). At Bethel, he worships the LORD. The LORD dwelt with Abram and Sarai in this place. If Sarai had not seen this invisible God before, she sees Him now. She sees His power of deliverance from the town of Haran to Canaan land, and she sees how much He means to her husband. So, what happens between the faith of Genesis 12:7-8, and the fear of Genesis 12:10? Why was this man of God leaving the House of God? The answer was simple: "There was a famine in the land and the famine was severe." He may have tried for a time to weather it out, but the famine was too severe. The land is very parched and dry. Since there was no water, perhaps people and livestock were dying. And so Abram develops a famine of faith. The drought struck fear in his heart. Fear turns Abram from trusting the God of Heaven to trusting the god of self-reliance. As Abram is going through his "faith famine," we read nowhere in the text that Abram calls on his Lord, as he had done earlier. To Abram, the answer was clear—go down to Egypt with wife and family. Meanwhile, Sarai is quietly taking it all in.

SARAI AND US: Though their faith was new to the elderly couple, Sarai saw her husband commune with his LORD. She may have been unaware that she, too, could talk with God. We, however, have no such excuse. We can go boldly before the "throne of grace and receive help and mercy." (Hebrews 4:16) Yet we let our "faith famines" drive us to our "Egypt's" (the world) for help. Reader, what drives you to your "Egypt's"?

GOD SPEAKS: "The LORD knows the days of the upright, And their inheritance shall be forever. They shall not be ashamed in the evil time, And in the days of famine they shall be satisfied." (Psalm 37:18-19 NKJV) "For I will pour water on him who is thirsty, And floods on the dry ground; …" (Isaiah 44:3 NKJV) Bring your "faith famines" to Me and watch how I will satisfy you. I will flood your dry ground with My Living water.

WANDA'S PRAYER: Thank You, Father, for always reminding us of how dependable You are; especially when our world is always changing.

February 7

EGYPT'S PRICE

"AS HE WAS ABOUT TO ENTER EGYPT, HE SAID TO HIS WIFE SARAI, 'I KNOW WHAT A BEAUTIFUL WOMAN YOU ARE. WHEN THE EGYPTIANS SEE YOU, THEY WILL SAY, 'THIS IS HIS WIFE.' THEN THEY WILL KILL ME BUT WILL LET YOU LIVE. SAY YOU ARE MY SISTER, SO THAT I WILL BE TREATED WELL FOR YOUR SAKE AND MY LIFE WILL BE SPARED BECAUSE OF YOU.'" (GENESIS 12:11-13 NIV)

Say it is not so Abram! Has it come to this—the prostitution of your wife, to save your own skin? Going down to Egypt (turning from God and to the world) always leads to compromise and degradation, as in this sad case. Abram is asking his beautiful "princess" to lie for him and to be taken as Pharaoh's mistress. In essence, "good old father of the faithful" was about to pimp his wife so that, "I (Abram) will be treated well for your sake and my life would be spared." Abram had not only abandoned the Lord, but his wife as well. The price of living in Egypt was very high. I once heard that "Sin takes you farther than you wish to go, and keeps you longer than you ever thought. In the end, sin will cost you more than you ever dreamed." This is so true in this case. As if Abram's crimes were not bad enough, Sarai's response was mind blowing. She silently consents to her husband's degrading plan. She submitted to his headship as husband. At this point, without saying it, she calls him lord. She completely trusted her husband's judgment in this matter. Wow!

SARAI AND US: Would you do "a Sarai" to save your man? Before you and I answer a loud "NO," we need to remember all the compromises and concessions we have made to hold on to a man. I was once involved with a man who never acknowledged me in public, "so that it would be well for his sake." For months, I carried on with this act. All the while, I felt horrible on the inside. I had sold myself to my Egypt, and I was the slave.

GOD SPEAKS: "Therefore, I urge you, brothers and sisters, in view of God's mercy, to offer your bodies as a living sacrifice, holy and pleasing to God—this is your true and proper worship. Do not conform to the pattern of this world, but be transformed by the renewing of your mind. Then you will be able to test and approve what God's will is—his good, pleasing and perfect will." (Romans 12:1-2 NIV) Oh, I (your LORD) wish you would be a slave to My perfect will for your life. I have such wonderful plans for you.

WANDA'S PRAYER: It is true Lord; we have trusted in our own plans most of our lives. Today, again, we want to present our bodies as a living sacrifice for You.

February 8

HELEN WHO?

"WHEN ABRAM CAME TO EGYPT, THE EGPYTIANS SAW THAT SARAI WAS A VERY BEAUTIFUL WOMAN. AND WHEN PHARAOH'S OFFICALS SAW HER, THEY PRAISED HER TO PHARAOH, AND SHE WAS TAKEN INTO THE PALACE." (GENESIS 12:14-15 NIV)

It is said of Helen of Troy, "She had the face that launched a thousand ships." They could well say this of Sarai, that her beauty moved the country of Egypt. From the moment Sarai entered Egypt, she was the talk of an entire nation. At 65, her beauty was so striking that she was ushered almost immediately into the palace of Pharaoh. Sarai's inner beauty, not her outer, is what fascinates me. She is not occupied or consumed with her looks at all. Her actions display a woman in love with her husband. She is intent on submitting to his authority. Abram has a jewel of a wife. We see Sarai doing what he has instructed, even to her own peril. This is a great act of faith on Sarai's part. She did not know what would happen to her in Pharaoh's court, yet she believed her actions were for the best, and she carried out her job to the fullest. Sarai's only hope was in her husband's unseen God.

SARAI AND US: At first glance, we may think, "She's not too bright, and she is too trusting in her self-serving husband, who sold her out to save his own skin." One might admire the fact that she followed her heart and her "lord's" plan. How often do we follow our heart and not God's Word for many decisions of life? LORD, we need Help!

GOD SPEAKS: "The heart is deceitful above all things and beyond cure. Who can understand it? "I the LORD search the heart and examine the mind, to reward each person according to their conduct, according to what their deeds deserve." (Jeremiah 17:9-10 NIV)

WANDA'S PRAYER: Lord, give us a heart after Yours'!

February 9

PROSTITUTE'S PRICE

"HE (PHARAOH) TREATED ABRAM WELL FOR HER SAKE, AND ABRAM ACQUIRED SHEEP AND CATTLE, MALE AND FEMALE DONKEYS, MALE AND FEMALE SERVANTS, AND CAMELS. BUT THE LORD INFLICTED SERIOUS DISEASES ON PHARAOH AND HIS HOUSEHOLD BECAUSE OF ABRAM'S WIFE SARAI." (GENESIS 12:16-17 NIV)

Here we see Abram profiting at Sarai's expense; lying, calling her his sister. This is the prostitute's price for all the "stuff" Pharaoh gives him. Truthfully speaking, Sarai is his half-sister, but he was married to her, thus overriding the "half-sister thing." They lived as husband and wife—not brother and sister. What must Sarai be thinking at this point? "Is this how the story is supposed to go?" (Writer's paraphrase) This scene shows the difference between the flesh-filled husband (Abram) and the Spirit-filled Husband (Father God). The flesh-filled husband worries primarily about himself and his needs. A Spirit-filled husband cares for His wife and family. Circumstances limit the flesh-filled husband. The Spirit-filled husband operates in divine, unlimited circumstances. His reliance is on God's power. Sarai's Maker—God, shows what a true husband does. Despite Abram's temporary insanity, God's mind was on His daughter. She had followed her husband and spared his life. Father (God) would wonderfully honor that. The deliverance was miraculous. "… The Lord inflicted serious diseases on Pharaoh and his household because of Abram's wife Sarai." (Genesis 12:17 NIV). Father God is never stumped on how to deliver His daughters from trouble. Pharaoh would not have this woman tonight, or any other night! The Father has a perfect plan, and Abram's foolishness, nor Pharaoh's folly, could stop it. God delivers His daughter out of trouble. Sarai is not forgotten or forsaken. Pharaoh's household afflictions were proof of that.

SARAI AND US: We are not much different from Sarai; let us go back down memory lane. How many times have we "gone along, to get along," in a toxic situation? How many scary situations have we begged the LORD to deliver us out of? Our LORD was faithful to deliver us.

GOD SPEAKS: "For I am the LORD your God, the Holy One of Israel, your Savior; I give Egypt for your ransom, … in your stead. Since you are precious and honored in my sight, and because I love you, I will give people in exchange for you, nations in exchange for your life. Do not be afraid, for I am with you; … (Isaiah 43:3-5 NIV) No price is too high to save what is Mine, and you are Mine!

WANDA'S PRAYER: Thank you, Father, for letting us know how much you love us.

February 10

"SINNER'S" SERMON

"SO PHARAOH SUMMONED ABRAM. 'WHAT HAVE YOU DONE TO ME?' HE SAID. 'WHY DIDN'T YOU TELL ME SHE WAS YOUR WIFE? WHY DID YOU SAY, 'SHE IS MY SISTER,' SO THAT I TOOK HER TO BE MY WIFE? NOW THEN, HERE IS YOUR WIFE. TAKE HER AND GO!' THEN PHARAOH GAVE ORDERS ABOUT ABRAM TO HIS MEN, AND THEY SENT HIM ON HIS WAY, WITH HIS WIFE AND EVERYTHING HE HAD."
(GENESIS 12:18-20 NIV)

Realizing that God plagued his house for having the married Sarai, Pharaoh calls Abram on the carpet for his deceptive sins. Here is the sinner giving the saint a sermon on morality; how very sad when this happens. Sarai's chastisement is indirect, since the two of them were one in this devilish deed, though Pharaoh knew she was following the instructions of her husband. Despite Abram's slap on the hand, Father God spares their lives, and He blesses them! "So, Abram went up from Egypt to the Negev, with his wife and everything he had, and Lot went with him." (Genesis 13:1) Abram kept all of his ill-gotten gain. This act of disobedience would later haunt them. Sarai could breathe an enormous sigh of relief. She was rescued just in the nick of time. She has now witnessed first-hand how the invisible God of Heaven makes Himself very visible in time of need. So, in quiet thankfulness, she returns to Abram's side. Upon returning to the land of promise, Abram rededicates his heart to the Lord. (Genesis 13:3-4) Abram led his house back to God. Repentance from sin and a cleansing of the heart is just what the family needed after this journey into sin.

SARAI AND US: Can you remember living in your spiritual "Egypt?" How was your relationship with the LORD? What was the distance like? What is it like now, to be in right relationship with Him? If you are not right with Him, get right NOW—DO NOT WAIT!

GOD SPEAKS: "At one time we too were foolish, disobedient, deceived and enslaved by all kinds of passions and pleasures. We lived in malice and envy, being hated and hating one another. But when the kindness and love of God our Savior appeared, he saved us, not because of righteous things we had done, but because of his mercy. He saved us through the washing of rebirth and renewal by the Holy Spirit, whom he poured out on us generously through Jesus Christ our Savior," (Titus 3:3-6 NIV) I, your LORD, did all this, just for you!

WANDA'S PRAYER: Thank you, loving Father, for loving and saving us.

February 11

WEIGHT OF WAITING

"NOW SARAI ABRAM'S WIFE BARE HIM NO CHLDREN…" (GENESIS 16:1 KJV)

Sarai and Abram were back in the home of promise, the land of Canaan. The first thing Abram does is to call on the name of the Lord. (Genesis 13:4) Time continues ebbing, as Sarai and Abram remain childless. Abram's nephew Lot moves away. Time is slowly drifting away, and God speaks words of comfort and assurance to Abram. Our LORD is saying to His son and daughter, "Just hold on a little while longer." (Writer's paraphrase) (Genesis 13:14-18) With years slowly passing by it would seem Sarai's biological clock has died and gone to "clock heaven," as she awaits the fulfillment of God's promise. Life goes on as Abram meets King Melchizedek, ruler of Salem, and High Priest, to the everlasting LORD; and receives his blessing. Sarai's waiting continues. Perhaps she does not know that she, too, can go directly to the Father. The God who saved her from Pharaoh's bed is just waiting for her to come to Him. So, she waits on the Lord for that expected son from the fruit of her womb. A decade of silence from the God of Heaven has passed since she had left her childhood home of Ur. The Father had promised her husband a son. So, the aging couple sits in hollow silence, waiting for the fulfillment of God's Word. In this awful silence, she wears her barrenness like an albatross around her neck. Waiting on the Lord is a heavy weight—seeming too much for her to carry.

SARAI AND US: Oh, how we can all relate to Sarai. Who has not waited for that __ (write in your prayer request) to happen? We, like Sarai, must just "bear" our weight of waiting. Father God, give us Your pleasant words of comfort to our dry, parched souls.

GOD SPEAKS: "Truly my soul waiteth upon God: from him cometh my salvation." (Psalm 62:1 KJV) So drop those weights at MY feet—the feet of your Lord, and get yourself some much-needed rest.

WANDA'S PRAYER: Oh Lord, we give You the pain and heartache we feel. Thank You for letting us know You are already at work on the problem. We know it will all be worked out in Your perfect timing. We will drop not only this problem, but all of our cares at Your feet. Hallelujah!

February 12

BAD IDEA

"AND SARAI SAID UNTO ABRAM, 'BEHOLD NOW, THE LORD HATH RESTRAINED ME FROM BEARING: I PRAY THEE, GO IN UNTO MY MAID; IT MAY BE THAT I MAY OBTAIN CHILDREN BY HER.' AND ABRAM HARKENED TO THE VOICE OF SARAI." (GENESIS 16:2 KJV)

Sarai had waited long enough, she thought. She would take off her "weight of waiting." I can hear her rationale as she plots, "Where are You God, and why are You taking so long…? I am an old, menopausal, barren woman. It is obvious I will never have children, but maybe my husband Abram can. Perhaps there is another way." (Writer's paraphrase) The weight of waiting drove her to this "bad idea." "Abram, take my handmaid and have our child through her. Surely this is God's will. Abram, you will have your heir, and I will have my long-lost child. It can work husband; I know it can—it just feels right." (Writer's paraphrase) MISTAKE! MISTAKE! MISTAKE! This plan is doomed to disaster from the start—a catastrophe waiting to happen. Shouldn't you run this crazy plan by God first? If Sarai had only allowed her frustrations to drive her to the feet of her Lord, it would have all worked out. Her loving Father knew what she was going through; He was willing and waiting to hear her heart's cry. Time and time again, Abram had already communed with his Dad, in disappointment and despair. Each time he received comfort, as he continued to wait for the promise. (Genesis 13:14-18) In Genesis 15, the Lord comes to Abram, and they discuss the matter of the promised heir. He receives the Father's assurance then; "he (Abram) believed in the LORD, and He accounted it to him for righteousness." (Genesis 15:6). After this encounter with God, Abram worshipped his Lord. So why couldn't he have taken five minutes to run this plan by God? Perhaps in his heart Abram knew he was in the wrong, but had grown weary of the waiting.

SARAI AND US: We, too, grow tired of waiting. There have been many times in life where we have had to just wait—on relationships, kids, and finances. We, too, need to allow our frustrations to drive us to the feet of our LORD.

GOD SPEAKS: Like Sarai, your problem is that you let go of My hand all too quickly in times of trials. "Trust in the Lord with all your heart, (Especially in times of severe trial and doubt) And lean not on your own understanding; In all your ways acknowledge Him (me), And He (I) shall direct (make straight) your paths." (Proverbs 3:5-6 NKJV)

WANDA'S PRAYER: Father, teach us to practice this verse in all of our dealings. Thanks!

February 13

"UH-OH"

"SO HE (ABRAM) WENT IN TO HAGAR, AND SHE CONCIEVED. AND WHEN SHE SAW THAT SHE HAD CONCEIVED, HER MISTRESS BECAME DESPISED IN HER EYES." (GENESIS 16:4 NKJV)

Genesis 16:3 says Sarai gives her maid to her husband Abram to be his wife, after Abram had dwelt ten years in the land of Canaan. Sarai gives her husband to another woman! It does not take a rocket scientist to see that sounds like a terrible idea. Did she really think the "slave girl" turned wife would just go back to being a slave again? I do not think so! The slave girl (Hagar) knew she was carrying in her womb, the promised heir to Abram's dynasty. As far as Hagar was concerned, she is now the rightful wife. In her mind, the old girl (Sarai) needs to just step aside. Hagar saw herself as "Queen of this kingdom"—thank you very much! This happens when we try to solve spiritual problems in the flesh. In carrying out this disastrous scheme, Abram and Sarai were saying to the Lord, "You were taking too long, so we're just helping You out." They forgot, however, that it was God's promise—not theirs! Wasn't it the Father who spoke to Abram while he was still in the Ur of Chaldeans saying, "And I will make of your descendants as the dust of the earth…" (Genesis 13:16 NKJV) Again, the Lord said to Abram, "… Look now toward heaven, and count the stars if you are able to number them." And He said to him, "So shall your descendants be." (Genesis 15:5 NKJV) Since it was the Creator's monumental promise to Abram, it was up to Creator God alone, to fulfill His promise. Their only job was to wait on the fulfillment of the promise. And when they had questions or complaints about His timing or His process during the waiting period, they needed only to go to their Dad; the Lord, and Maker of the Universe, for answers. He was just an "altar" call away.

SARAI AND US: All of us can relate to Sarai. How often have we tried to "help the Lord" out by putting our evil, and many times ungodly, plans in place? Only to have our "Hagar situations" blow up in our face, time and time again.

GOD SPEAKS: Decide which of us is God and Lord of your life. If you are god, okay, then I will step aside. But do not blame Me (God), when things go wrong. The other and best option is to "Be still, and know that I am God; (over your entire life—every nook and cranny) I will be exalted among the nations, I will be exalted in the earth! The Lord of Hosts is with us; The God of Jacob is our refuge. Selah" (Psalm 46:10-11 NKJV)

WANDA'S PRAYER: Lord, sometimes we really understand and get this; then, sometimes it seems like a foreign concept to us. Please keep us close to You. It is only by having Your Spirit to fill us daily (sometimes hourly), that we can live the life You have destined for us.

February 14

CONTENTIOUS

"THEN SARAI SAID TO ABRAM, 'MY WRONG BE UPON YOU! I GAVE MY MAID INTO YOUR EMBRACE; AND WHEN SHE SAW THAT SHE HAD CONCEIVED, I BECAME DESPISED IN HER EYES. THE LORD JUDGE BETWEEN YOU AND ME.'"
(GENESIS 16:5 NKJV)

Another meaning for Sarai is contentious. Here she contends with her husband and God, by blaming them for her sins (that sounds familiar). She says to her husband, "Abram, I did wrong; I gave my maid to you. She got pregnant and now she hates me. It is your fault for my wrong. Yeah, I know I played god because I could not wait for the true God to do His job. I messed up; but it is your fault, husband." (Writer's paraphrase) She ends by contending with God as she brings Him into the mess, "Oh and by the way, may God now judge between you and me." (Writer's paraphrase) This all started from a prior act of faithlessness. Abram went to Egypt instead of God for famine relief. (Genesis 12:11-15) Hagar the handmaid, was part of the buyout Abram received for selling Sarai to Pharaoh. This young handmaid, used and abused by the two of them, now used her pregnancy as a bargaining chip. Hagar may have been a slave, but she was no one's fool. Abram knew this was wrong. In the previous chapter, the Lord had just affirmed His promise of the heir coming through his loins. (Genesis 15) Had he not seen with his own eyes how his loving Father had protected his wife from the Pharaoh's arms? Why did he not just tell his wife, "Honey, I know this sounds like a good idea, but this is not God's plan. God told me He will bless us with a child—doing this crazy scheme will end up in disaster. So darling, this plan is a "no go," okay?" The "Genesis" of the war between the Arabs and Jews started here, and would cost billions of lives. Sin is never a private matter, or an isolated incident. No, sin is the hurt that keeps on hurting.

SARAI AND US: Sarai shows us, as Jesus says, "It's the little foxes that spoil the vine." (Song of Solomon 2:15) My "little sins" of entering an "unequally yoked marriage caused my two wonderful children to grow up in a fatherless home. The painful effects on my kids are evident to this day!

GOD SPEAKS: "Thus says God the LORD, Who created the heavens and stretched them out, Who spread forth the earth and that which comes from it, Who gives breath to the people on it, And spirit to those who walk on it: I, the LORD, have called You in righteousness, And will hold Your hand; I will keep You..." (Isaiah 42:5-6 NKJV) Believe that I am God! I saw the mess before you got into it; now believe in My Mighty hands to get you out.

WANDA'S PRAYER: Lord, always keep us in the hollow of Your hands.

February 15

IT'S WORSE

"SO ABRAM SAID TO SARAI, 'INDEED YOUR MAID IS IN YOUR HAND; DO TO HER AS YOU PLEASE.' AND WHEN SARAI DEALT HARSHLY WITH HER, (HAGAR) SHE FLED FROM HER PRESENCE." (GENESIS 16:6 NKJV)

What a sad shame, shown in the picture painted in the above Scripture. Instead of someone getting on their knees and repenting, the situation is allowed to carry on and grow from bad to worse. Abram realizes his part in the mess; but having received what he feels is his promised heir, wants no part in the disciplinary process of his chaotic household. His cowardice leaves that duty to his wife. Sarai, already out of order from the start of this complete debacle, is primed to make the whole matter much worse. And that is exactly what she does. Sarai treats Hagar harshly. Hagar runs, taking with her (in the womb) Abram's heir. Is this a mess or what? I do not blame Hagar for running for her life. The shame is that we have both the patriarch (the father of the faithful) and the matriarch of the Jewish nation, acting like scoundrels. With witnesses like these, who would listen to, much less believe in, the God of Heaven?

SARAI AND US: Looking at Sarai's life at this point should cause us to reflect on the times when we have not acted Christ-like to those around us. I am especially embarrassed when my poor behavior has been around those I have tried witnessing to about Jesus, aren't you?

GOD SPEAKS: Cleaning up messes is one of my specialties. Give Me your mess and, "Praise the LORD! For it is good to sing praises to our God; For it is pleasant, and praise is beautiful. He heals the brokenhearted And binds up their wounds. He counts the number of the stars; He calls them all by name. Great is our Lord, and mighty in power; His understanding is infinite." (Psalm 147:1,3-5 NKJV)

WANDA'S PRAYER: Father and Lord, we do praise You. It was You who brought us through those incredibly sad times in our lives. Thank You Father, for the ongoing love and grace you provide for our families.

February 16

HAGAR'S SON

"ABRAM WAS EIGHT-SIX YEARS OLD WHEN HAGAR BORE ISHMAEL TO ABRAM." (GENESIS 16:16 NKJV)

Well, this ends the cliff hanger; we see Hagar went back to Sarai and Abram's home. (Genesis 16:7-14) Hagar gave birth to Abram's son, naming him Ishmael. Sarai's vendetta is put on hold. From the silence, I assume Sarai just dealt with the situation as best she could. After all, what else could she have done? Notice there is no celebration for this boy—isn't he the heir of Abram? There is just a footnote in Scripture; only a mention that Hagar had Abram's son, and then a sigh. Sin is funny that way. Satan offered Abram and Sarai great and glorious alternatives to their loving Father's design for their lives. If that sounds familiar, see Eve's story. He paints such beautiful masterpieces on the canvases of their minds. "Catch the vision, people, and see what I see," the devil whispers to Sarai and Abram. They, too, believed the lies and plunged headlong into disobedience. When it is all over, all they can do is to look back and see all the damaged lives which were affected and destroyed; scattered about, like litter on an abandoned highway. When all is said and done, Sarai and Abram realize they have only themselves to thank for all the mess they have made.

SARAI AND US: This part of the lesson speaks volumes about things we all can relate to. How many "city dumps" (figuratively speaking) have we created with our poor choices? Like Sarai, all we can do now is sigh, and say "oh well." Father, we need many words of comfort.

GOD SPEAKS: "For God so loved the world that he gave his one and only Son, that whoever believes in him shall not perish but have eternal life. For God did not send his Son into the world to condemn the world, but to save the world through him. Whoever believes in him is not condemned, but whoever does not believe stands condemned already because they have not believed in the name of God's one and only Son." (John 3:16-18 NIV) "If we confess our sins, he is faithful and just and will forgive us our sins and purify us from all unrighteousness." (1 JOHN 1:9 NIV) My heart is never to condemn you; I came only to save and replace your life with Mine. Stop looking back. I do not remember your sins, so why should you? I placed your sins in the depths of the sea.

WANDA'S PRAYER: Thank You so much, Father! Our hearts are overflowing with thanksgiving and praise.

February 17

NAME CHANGE

"THEN GOD SAID TO ABRAHAM, 'AS FOR SARAI YOUR WIFE, YOU SHALL NOT CALL HER NAME SARAI, BUT SARAH SHALL BE HER NAME.'" (GENESIS 17:15 NKJV)

In my opinion, Genesis 17 is one of the most beautiful chapters in all of Scripture. After coming through the tragic events of Genesis 16, Genesis 17 paints such a wonderful picture of rescue, grace, mercy, and forgiveness. For thirteen long years, the prodigal couple had been at a distance from their loving Lord. Life in the prodigal kingdom was dry and empty; aimlessly wandering on a journey leading nowhere. They were far from God's design and purpose for their lives. Jesus would be their road map home. "When Abram was ninety-nine years old, the LORD APPEARED TO ABRAM AND SAID TO HIM, 'I AM ALMIGHTY GOD; walk before ME and be blameless.'" (Genesis 17:1 NKJV) The Father comes to his boy and says, "son, you have been gone long enough. My door is open wide; come back home to Me. I will take away the blame." (Writer's paraphrase) Our Heavenly Father is so loving, so very good, and so full of compassion. He does not scold His wayward son. He just shows up and begins things right where they should be—a Father and son in harmony. Abram's response is also very touching. Like a man dying of thirst, "he falls on his face and God talked with him…" (Genesis 17:3) It is as if he was saying, "Thank You, LORD, for bringing me back home." After reaffirming the relationship with His son, He reminds Abram the original plans have not changed, despite some minor detours (i.e., Hagar and Ishmael). Then the Lord of love does an unbelievably beautiful thing; He made all things new concerning Abram and Sarai. The Father gave them new names! "No longer shall your name be called Abram, but your name shall be Abraham; for I have made you a father of many nations… As for Sarai, your wife, you shall not call her Sarai, but Sarah shall be her name." (Genesis 17:5, 15 NKJV). The Father says to them, "you are blameless," because of My righteousness. To prove it, I am changing what has hung over you all your lives—your names: Abram (exalted father), who was without children for over 80 years, your name is now father of multitudes. And Sarai (the contentious one), you are now Sarah, the noble lady." (Writer's paraphrase) God did not see them as they were, but as the exalted positions He called them to be.

SARAH AND US: What are some names you have been called, or names you have called yourself? It really does not matter, because our LORD has a new name for you.

GOD SPEAKS: "… I will give him a white stone, and on the stone a new name written which no one knows except him who receives it." (Revelation 2:17 NKJV)

WANDA'S PRAYER: Change our names, LORD!

February 18

GETTING STARTED

"AND I WILL BLESS HER (SARAH) AND ALSO GIVE YOU A SON BY HER; THEN I WILL BLESS HER, AND SHE SHALL BE A MOTHER OF NATIONS; KINGS OF PEOPLES SHALL BE FROM HER." (GENESIS 17:16 NKJV)

This is the first time Sarah was named in Scripture as heir to the promise. While it was always assumed she would be the mother of the promised child, because of the great mess up of Genesis 16, further clarification was needed. In making this promise to Sarah, Father God was also affirming His original design of marriage—between one man and one woman. The Lord's perspective on things is so much simpler, as well as much better than ours. The Lord refers to Sarah as Abraham's only wife. (Genesis 17:15) Sarah had given Hagar to Abraham as a wife, to conceive children. (Genesis 16:3) With the birth of Hagar's son, things had become complicated. But Dad (Father God) put things back in their proper order. The Father knew the "Hagar plan" was not of His creation, and thus it was not a union He would recognize. Now, having placed things back in the God-set order, the Father moved forward with His original plans without missing a beat. "And I will bless her (Sarah) and also give you a son by her; then I will bless her, and she shall be a mother of nations; kings of people shall be from her." (Genesis 17:16 NKJV) In essence, the Lord was saying: I knew his wife was old, when I made the promise to Abram back in Ur. This miraculous event would be for My glory.

SARAH AND US: In looking at this event (two very old people having a child) everyone who will read this story down through the ages will know that NOTHING is too hard for the Almighty God.

GOD SPEAKS: "Listen to Me, O house of Jacob, And all the remnant of the house of Israel, Who have been upheld by Me from birth, Who have been carried from the womb: Even to your old age, I am He, And even to gray hairs I will carry you! I have made, and I will bear; Even I will carry, and will deliver you." (Isaiah 46:3-4 NKJV) You can put your name in the middle of that promise. I will never leave or ever forsake you, my precious child.

WANDA'S PRAYER: Father God, thank you for Your love and mercy. Thank You also for Your reminder that nothing is too hard for You. We are loved by the Lord of Love.

February 19

"NO!"

"THEN GOD SAID: 'NO, SARAH YOUR WIFE SHALL BEAR YOU A SON, AND YOU SHALL CALL HIS NAME ISAAC; I WILL ESTABLISH MY COVENANT WITH HIM FOR AN EVERLASTING COVENANT, AND WITH HIS DESCENDANTS AFTER HIM.'"
(GENESIS 17:19 NKJV)

In this dialogue, Dad (God) is speaking to Abraham regarding Sarah giving birth to the promised heir. Abraham wrestled with two issues here: (1) His faith is being stretched to believe the Lord would cause a 100-year-old man, and a 90-year-old woman, to bear children. (2) The rejection of Ishmael as heir to the divine promise. Why would the Lord do things the hard way? Wouldn't it be easier to just accept the child already here as the heir? To answer this question, we will start with the fact that Ishmael's conception was through a human, willful disobedience to God's design. Our LORD made a promise, knowing Sarah's post-menopausal womb, could only bear a child through His (God's) divine intervention. This would be a God act! This story is a lesson in how we are saved into God's Kingdom. We are not saved by our acts, but by believing in His death on the cross for our sins. Just as Ishmael, a work of the flesh is unacceptable, so our "goodness" will never be enough to earn Heaven. We offend our Holy LORD when we offer our human token, to satisfy His divine promise. Abraham and Sarah were to totally depend on their Father to fulfill the promise. Just as it was impossible for Sarah's post-menopausal womb to produce a child, so it is just as impossible for us to be saved into God's Kingdom by our own works.

SARAH AND US: When this story is shared with others (either spoken or by reading), it will tell of how the All-Powerful God works on behalf of individuals. Down throughout all history, it has, and continues to, build faith in millions. God's people—past, present, and future could say, since the Lord worked so powerfully on Abraham and Sarah's behalf, He can, and will do the same for us.

GOD SPEAKS: "Now to him (that HIM is THE LORD) who is able to do exceedingly abundantly above all that we ask or think, according to the power that works in us." (Ephesians 3:20 NKJV) Faith for you, is holding in your hands, "things hoped for," according to My will, the evidence (the proof) of things not seen. (Hebrews 11:1) (Writer's paraphrase)

WANDA'S PRAYER: Father, these words are so easy to hear, but extremely difficult to live out. Help us to believe and walk in faith, as we say, "Lord, I believe."

February 20

REPEAT

"BUT MY COVENANT I WILL ESTABLISH WITH ISAAC, WHOM SARAH SHALL BEAR TO YOU BY THIS SET TIME NEXT YEAR." (GENESIS 17:21 NIV)

I am struck by several things in this verse. The first is that this verse is a repeat of verse nineteen. Next, how the LORD names this child. Father God is really "hammering home" the point that this 90-year-old woman and her 100-year-old husband, are YES, REALLY GOING TO HAVE A SON! God is giving sad Sarah not just something to make her smile, but to cause her to break out into hysterical LAUGHTER! But our LORD goes further. You will notice in Genesis 16 how the Lord did a similar thing for Hagar. He told Hagar in Genesis 16, and Sarah in Genesis 17, they would both have boys. He gave both boys their names. We can see our LORD does not play favorites. For most of Sarah's life, she may have been sad and miserable because of her barrenness, but our LORD will give her "Laughter (Isaac) at a set time next year." In Genesis 17:16, we see Sarah will have a son and that she will be the mother of many nations. In fact, Kings of nations will be among her descendants. Unlike Hagar, her son will not just have earthly kings in his lineage. Sarah's son will be in the lineage to be the KING OF KINGS AND LORD OF LORDS - JESUS CHRIST.

SARAH AND US: Sarah's life shows us we can know with absolute certainty that the God in whom we trust can do all things. We can know our loving Father always keeps His promises. How many times has the LORD had to repeat Himself to you? Are you slow of heart to believe, like me?

GOD SPEAKS: "Rejoice in the Lord always. Again I will say, rejoice!" (Philippians 4:4 NKJV) In other words, repeat—do this verse OVER AND OVER AGAIN! REJOICE! REJOICE!

WANDA'S PRAYER: LORD, help us rejoice and praise You always.

February 21

LAUGHING

"THEREFORE SARAH LAUGHED WITHIN HERSELF, SAYING 'AFTER I HAVE GROWN OLD, SHALL I HAVE PLEASURE, MY LORD BEING OLD ALSO?'" (GENESIS 18:12 NKJV)

God's care and concern for His own is so evident in how the Father relates to Abraham and Sarah. After the Lord re-establishes the broken relationship of Genesis 16, it seems He visits them constantly. Here in Genesis 18, our Dad comes again for a visit with His kids. This time, however, He does not just speak; He shows up in human form, with two others with Him. Abraham recognizes His Dad and prepares a meal. The Father affirms to his son again (Genesis 18:10) that Sarah will have the son of promise. In looking at this story, I can see just how very personal the Father of the Heavens is to His children. The verse says, "Now Abraham and Sarah were old, well advanced in age; and Sarah had passed the age of childbearing." (Genesis 18:11) In fact, Sarah was approaching ninety, and Abraham, one hundred years old. Sarah had long past menopause. She had waited years and years for a promise left unfulfilled. Now in her heart of hearts she felt, "It's too late, why bother—I'm too old for this." So, when she overheard the Lord talking with her husband about her having a child, she sneered, "After I have grown old, shall I have pleasure, my lord being old also." (Genesis 18:12) Sarah's laugh was not one of joy, but I believe, of anger and obvious disbelief. "Why would God wait until nothing can be done on my part to help me have this child? Now, after all these years of going through reproach, pain, and heartache, now You will give me a child?" Sarah was absolutely correct. The supernatural works of God are so far above and beyond anything we could ever think of or hope to accomplish. If we would just grasp this single truth, then we would stop worrying and just wait in joyful expectancy for the fulfillment of His promises in our lives.

SARAH AND US: Like Sarah, we can think back on wasted years, wasted time, and wasted energy in being angry at God for our failed hopes and dreams. Father, speak to our hearts.

GOD SPEAKS: "For I know the thoughts that I think toward you, says the LORD, thoughts of peace and not of evil, to give you a future and a hope." (Jeremiah 29:11 NKJV) If you can only allow these words to settle in your spirit. "Then you will call upon Me and go and pray to Me, and I will listen to you. And you will seek Me and find Me, when you search for Me with all your heart." (Jeremiah 29:12-13 NKJV) Nothing is EVER wasted with the LORD. There is always a lesson. Look for it.

WANDA'S PRAYER: Father God, help us trust You; Help us bring You our all.

February 22

LITTLE LIAR

"IS ANYTHING TOO HARD FOR THE LORD? AT THE APPOINTED TIME I WILL RETURN TO YOU, ACCORDING TO THE TIME OF LIFE, AND SARAH SHALL HAVE A SON. BUT SARAH DENIED IT, SAYING, 'I DID NOT LAUGH,' FOR SHE WAS AFRAID. AND HE (GOD) SAID, 'NO, BUT YOU DID LAUGH!'" (GENESIS 18:14-15 NKJV)

This verse is very rich with insight on how the loving, faithful Father deals with His faithless kids, of which I am one. Notice how our Lord does not mind repeating Himself. He says to Abraham and Sarah (who is in the tent eavesdropping on her husband's conversation with the LORD), "I'll see you on the due date of little Laughter's (Isaac's) birth." Upon hearing this, Sarah lets out a sneering, contemptuous laughter of unbelief. The Father calls her out on this sneering response. In fear, she flat out lies and denied she laughed. She tells the All-Knowing God; He did not hear what He knew He heard. But God shows His Omniscience (He knows all) to Sarah; "Stop lying—you and I both know you laughed." (Writer's paraphrase)

SARAH AND US: Our LORD shows us it is ok to be honest with Him. Confession is for us, not Him. Confession cleanses our souls and removes the barrier which our sins erect. The end result is a deeper and more fulfilling relationship with our LORD.

GOD SPEAKS: "Cast all your anxiety on him because he cares for you." (1 Peter 5:7 NIV) You do not have to be anxious with your Lord; or lie about your feelings. Just place them at My feet.

WANDA'S PRAYER: Father, help us to always be real with You. We never want to be at a distance with You.

February 23

HAND'S OFF

"AND ABRAHAM JOURNEYED FROM THERE TO THE SOUTH, AND DWELT BETWEEN KADESH AND SHUR, AND STAYED IN GERAR. NOW ABRAHAM SAID OF SARAH HIS WIFE, 'SHE IS MY SISTER.' AND ABIMELECH KING OF GERAR SENT AND TOOK SARAH. BUT GOD CAME TO ABIMELECH IN A DREAM BY NIGHT, AND SAID TO HIM, 'INDEED YOU ARE A DEAD MAN BECAUSE OF THE WOMAN WHOM YOU HAVE TAKEN, FOR SHE IS A MAN'S WIFE.'" (GENESIS 20:1-3 NKJV)

Our Lord, the Savior, is beautiful and loving. He is indeed my Knight in shining Armor. I love watching love stories on TV or the movies. But no Hollywood script can compare to what the Loving Lord does for us in real life. After the promise of Isaac's birth is given in Genesis 17 and 18, one would think that Abraham (the father of the faithful), could trust his Heavenly Dad in all things. I guess not though, because he starts up with his old trick of lies, which is what got him into all the mess of his past sins in the first place. I can appreciate Abraham's weak faith because my faith is weak, also. Anyway, the Nomadic Abraham journeys up and down through the land of promise, until he comes to Gerar. Fear paralyzes the old patriarch, and he reverts to his old ways of self-survival and completely forgets the All-Powerful God. Sad to say, this is a role Sarah is all too comfortable with, and she plays along with her man. If I were God, I would say, "I have had enough of you two; I am going to find someone else to give My promises to." But no! To the loving Father and Lord, a promise made is a promise kept. My Lord will be faithful even when His kids are faithless. The Lord Himself comes down to a heathen king and puts the fear of God in him. The Father tells Abimelech, "you're a dead man, because she is another man's wife." (Genesis 20:3). Abimelech, who had not become intimate with Sarah, pleads for his life to the Lord. God hears and responds to him. (Genesis 20:4-7) God's response—his life will be spared. (Genesis 20:7-11) Once again, Sarah has a firsthand account of God's deliverance made on her behalf.

SARAH AND US: Are you not so very glad that our salvation does not depend on our ability to do right, but on the Heavenly Father's power to deliver us from our sins?

GOD SPEAKS: "…Then the LORD said in His heart, "I will never again curse the ground for man's sake, although the imagination of man's heart is evil from his youth; …" (Genesis 8:21 NKJV) "Behold, I was brought forth in iniquity, (evil tendencies) and in sin did my mother conceive me." (Psalm 51:5 NKJV) I know what you will do, as well as what you have already done. Despite what I know about you (which is everything), My love for you is the same. Now rest in this, and in Me.

WANDA'S PRAYER: Wow! We just want to say thank You again, Father, for Your wonderful love.

February 24

SET TIME

"AND THE LORD VISITED SARAH AS HE HAD SAID, AND THE LORD DID FOR SARAH AS HE HAD SPOKEN. FOR SARAH CONCIEVED AND BORE ABRAHAM A SON IN HIS OLD AGE, AT THE SET TIME OF WHICH GOD HAD SPOKEN TO HIM." (GENESIS 21:1-2 NKJV)

This is certainly true in Sarah's case—God came, "… At the set time of which God had spoken to him (Abraham)." (Genesis 21:2 NKJV) "Is anything too hard for the LORD? At the appointed time I will return to you, according to the time of life, and Sarah shall have a son." (Genesis 18:14 NKJV) Until now our LORD had not given a set time. He had given a set promise, but not a set time. The Father always keeps His appointments—how refreshing to remember during those long wait times. I cannot wait to get to Heaven to ask Sarah about her pregnancy and the labor process. Those nine months could not have been easy for a ninety-year-old woman. It was not easy for me, and I was twenty-nine when I had my last child. The joy, however, in finally giving birth to the long-awaited child must have been worth every bout of nausea and labor pains. It is such a wonderful thing when the LORD so wonderfully answers our prayers, beyond what we could have ever imagined.

SARAH AND US: My testimony about the ON-TIME GOD! Many moons ago, I was a struggling, single mom in nursing school, and needed money for school. All other sources failed, so I prayed to the Lord. He almost drowned me with MORE MONEY THAN I NEEDED. Now, what is your story? How did the LORD supply your needs?

GOD SPEAKS: "Then the LORD appointed a set time, saying, 'Tomorrow the LORD will do this thing in the land.'" (Exodus 9:5 NKJV); "Taste and see that the LORD is good. Oh, the joys of those who take refuge in him! Even strong young lions sometimes go hungry, but those who trust in the LORD will lack no good thing." (Psalm 34:8,10 NLT) I am very good and very capable of satisfying your every need.

WANDA'S PRAYER: If only we would remember these words when we are in the middle of our struggles. Hide Your words in our hearts, Lord, so that we do not sin against You.

February 25

REALLY LAUGH

"NOW ABRAHAM WAS 100 YEARS OLD WHEN HIS SON ISAAC WAS BORN TO HIM. AND SARAH SAID, 'GOD HAS MADE ME LAUGH, AND ALL WHO HEAR WILL LAUGH WITH ME.'" (GENESIS 21:5-6 NKJV)

Can you hear Sarah's outrageous joy leap from this verse? For so long, I imagine her family and friends had been laughing at her and her husband. Can you hear the snickers? They were old when the promise first came; Abram was seventy-five and Sarai was sixty-five when the Lord spoke to him. Many well-meaning friends or relatives must have said, "Let me get this straight… Abraham, you are nearly one hundred and Sarah is pushing ninety; and you are telling me that God told you the two of you are going to have a kid? Give it up, you two; you are too old for this pleasure." As we read the verse, we can hear the pent-up frustration, as it now gushes out of Sarah's soul. She also said, "who would have said to Abraham that Sarah would nurse children? For I have borne a son for him in his old age." (Genesis 21:7) This barren woman was singing for joy, and she would not be silent. Sarah reminds all the doubters and may have said, "See, the Lord did just what He said he would do! My God has taken away my mountain of reproach and pain, heaped upon me for all these years." The long night of silent weeping over her childlessness, and her vain attempts at fixing her problem, was over. The Lord had brought her joy this beautiful morning. For this joy, she would laugh and laugh and laugh. Every time she looked at and held Laughter (Isaac) in her arms, she would no longer remember the pain, but the everlasting joy.

SARAH AND US: Thousands of years later, we read this story and can still laugh with our sister Sarah; as we celebrate her wonderful joy at having given birth to the promised son. We can thank our Heavenly Father that through the line of Abraham, He gave us Jesus as the payment for our sins.

GOD SPEAKS: "…For the LORD has heard the voice of my weeping." (Psalm 6:8 NKJV) "… His favor is for life; Weeping may endure for a night, But joy comes in the morning. (Psalm 30:5 NKJV) "… To comfort all who mourn, … To give them beauty for ashes, The oil of joy for mourning, The garment of praise for the spirit of heaviness; That they may be called trees of righteousness, …" (Isaiah 61:2-3 NKJV)

WANDA'S PRAYER: We will "Sing Hallelujah to my Lord!" He is so very worthy of all our praise and adoration. We cannot thank Him enough for His goodness and mercy shown to us.

February 26

MOCKING

"SO THE CHILD GREW AND WAS WEANED. AND ABRAHAM MADE A GREAT FEAST ON THE SAME DAY THAT ISAAC WAS WEANED. AND SARAH SAW THE SON OF HAGAR THE EGYPTIAN, WHOM SHE HAD BORNE TO ABRAHAM, SCOFFING."
(GENESIS 21:8-9 NKJV)

It is funny how the spiteful tendencies of our flesh are never far from us. At just the right time, it comes back to bite us where it really hurts; such is the case here. Abraham and Sarah are in grand celebration over the weaning of their son Isaac from breast feeding. As you may recall, there was no party given for Ishmael's birth. (Genesis 16:15-16) Hagar's child was just here—that is all! No doubt, the boy Ishmael must have realized that his position as Abraham's favorite son was now over. Here is the child of promise—this is the true heir! So possibly out of Ishmael's own hurt, resentment, or jealousy, came the serpent's bite of mocking Isaac. This would be a tragedy except with our Lord, nothing is wasted. The Father uses this story to illustrate a beautiful point of freedom and slavery. According to Galatians 4, this whole scenario of Isaac and Ishmael represents two covenants (agreements) on how we reach God. Ishmael, born to the slave woman, represents the bondage of trying to keep the Law given on Mount Sinai. Isaac represents the promise of Salvation given through Jesus Christ. It is important to understand we can never be saved in God's Kingdom by keeping the Law. This is because we were born sinners; and thus, we sin. Sinners cannot inherit the Kingdom of God.

SARAH AND US: I am so grateful for this story appearing in Scripture, and for its interpretation given by Paul, in Galatians 4. It lets us know it is not about the rules, but about the relationship we have in Jesus Christ. The Law (given on Mount Sinai), point out our flaws and shows us how far we are from reaching the standard of perfection. The relationship with Christ (His Spirit living in us), gives us power to live a life as He lived, and to obey His will.

GOD SPEAKS: "IF YOU ABIDE IN ME, AND MY WORDS ABIDE IN YOU, YOU WILL ASK WHAT YOU DESIRE, AND IT SHALL BE DONE FOR YOU." (JOHN 15:7 NKJV) So then, how do we reach God? How do we take away the stain of our sin? Answer: Only through the Child of Promise—Jesus Christ, who died for our sins. We live by His Spirit living inside of us. It is His Spirit, which empowers us to live as He directs.

WANDA'S PRAYER: Father, help us obey You—to do those things and live in Your Spirit.

February 27

GOT TO GO!

"THEREFORE SHE SAID TO ABRAHAM, 'CAST OUT THIS BONDWOMAN AND HER SON; FOR THE SON OF THIS BONDWOMAN SHALL NOT BE HEIR WITH MY SON, NAMELY WITH ISAAC.'" (GENESIS 21:10 NKJV)

When I first read this, I thought, "Oh, here Sarah goes again." She is about to make another bad decision. She is the one who put this bondwoman in this predicament, with her grand idea of getting a son for herself and Abraham. (Genesis 16) Now, over a little ill treatment of her 'precious' son, she will cause Hagar and her son to be homeless. How cruel can she be? But I must keep in mind, the All-Seeing and All-Knowing God knows what is going on and will take care of all parties involved in this mess. As hard as this is for Abraham, Hagar, and Ishmael, it must be done. The Lord provides for Ishmael and his mother. (Genesis 21:12-21) The Father uses this illustration of Hagar/Ishmael versus Sarah/Isaac to bring home a crucial point. Abraham had two sons; one by a bondwoman (Hagar), and one by a freedwoman (Sarah). This sad story is used as an illustration to us. The point is this: we are saved by grace, through faith alone. It is God's gift to us through Jesus Christ, our Savior. We are not saved from sin by keeping rules. Saved people with Jesus Christ living in them will follow God's commands. The Law cannot save us. The job of the law is to point out sin. (It is a mirror). The law shows us we are predetermined sinners (born in sin). We come into the world breaking God's laws, and we are doomed to judgment from birth. Thus, salvation from sin comes when we are born again. There is nothing the flesh can do to save. Salvation, like Sarah's pregnancy and her giving birth to Isaac, is a supernatural event.

SARAH AND US: So, what is the conclusion of this matter? Answer: Like Sarah, we must cast out the bondage for freedom. "Knowing that a man is not justified by the works of the law but by faith in Jesus Christ… for by the works of the law no flesh shall be justified." (Galatians 2:16 NKJV)

GOD SPEAKS: "This only I want to learn from you: Did you receive the Spirit by the works of the law, or by the hearing of faith? Are you so foolish? Having begun in the Spirit, are you now being made perfect by the flesh?" (Galatians 3:2-3 NKJV) It is by the Spirit of God through the blood of Jesus Christ. This is the Spiritual rebirth. There is nothing the flesh can do to save. "Now to Abraham and his Seed were the promises made. He does not say, 'And to seeds,' as of many, but as of one, 'and to your Seed,' who is Christ.'" (Galatians 3:16 NKJV)

WANDA'S PRAYER: Lord, live in our hearts and keep us in Your perfect way.

February 28

SUM OF LIFE

"BY FAITH SARAH HERSELF ALSO RECEIVED STRENGTH TO CONCEIVE SEED, AND SHE BORE A CHILD WHEN SHE WAS PAST THE AGE, BECAUSE SHE JUDGED HIM FAITHFUL WHO HAD PROMISED." (HEBREWS 11:11 NKJV)

What is the sum of a life? When we pass into eternity, what will be said of us by those we leave behind? Sarah shows us that God's opinion of us is the only one that really matters. In looking back through the book of Genesis for the short over-view of Sarah's life, we can see her many flaws and failings. But when Father God sums up her life, He sees a daughter of faith. "By FAITH Sarah herself also received strength to conceive seed, and she bore a child when she was past age, because she judged HIM FAITHFUL WHO HAD PROMISED." (Hebrews 11:11 NKJV) In the end, Sarah passed the only test which really mattered. She counted our Father God faithful, to do what He said He would do. And Sarah said, "God has made me laugh, and all who hear will laugh with me." She also said, "who would have said to Abraham that Sarah would nurse children? For I have borne him a son in his old age." (Genesis 21:6-7) Sarah lived one-hundred and twenty-seven years, and she died. At the time of her death, Isaac was thirty-seven years old, and her husband was one-hundred and thirty-seven years old. I guess it did not matter what had transpired before Laughter (Isaac) came; for the last thirty-seven years before her death, the Father blessed her with laughter and much joy.

SARAH AND US: Sarah relied on God's strength to conceive and carry her through the pregnancy. God faithfully did what He said He would do. We can rely on the same strength Sarah did.

GOD SPEAKS: "Make a joyful shout to God, all the earth! Sing out the honor of His name; Make His praise glorious. (Psalm 66:1-2 NKJV) Though you may have no voice for singing, I will make beautiful music come from your life.

WANDA'S PRAYER: Father God, here is our life! Take it and use it as You see fit. In hurtful times and during those times when we do not understand, help us trust You anyway.

Notes

Notes

March

INTRODUCTION

HAGAR (FROM BONDAGE TO FREEDOM)

Hagar was a slave girl given to Abram (Abraham) in Egypt when he left Canaan during the famine. He told the people of Egypt that Sarai (Sarah) was his sister. (She was his half-sister, but they lived as husband and wife.) They gave Abram many gifts in exchange for giving his wife to Pharaoh; one of those gifts was Hagar, the slave.

Sarah would use Hagar to help Abraham and Sarah start a family, since Sarah was barren. As we journey through her life, we shall see how our LORD turns tragedy into triumph.

The LORD can do the same in our lives as He did for Hagar. Her life, however, is also used to illustrate higher truth. This higher truth is real freedom, which is never achieved through human efforts. Real freedom is only found in Jesus Christ. Every day of our lives, He stands before us and offers us freedom in Him. Do we accept it willingly, or do we feel we must do something to earn this freedom—to show our worthiness? WRONG THOUGHTS! The person who the Son of GOD sets free, they are free indeed. (John 8:36)

Abraham had two sons (Ishmael and Isaac); one by a slave (Hagar) and one by a free woman (Sarah). Hagar, the slave woman's son, came first. He was of human invention—a thing of the flesh. Hagar's son represents what we do when we try to earn GOD'S favor. We "work" out of our Salvation; not for it.

Like Ishmael, (Hagar's son of human effort) who was put out into the wilderness, our work for salvation must be put out of GOD'S sight. To the Father they are like filthy, dirty rags and are of no use to Him. On the other hand, when we surrender our poor miserable selves to our Heavenly Dad for His use, wonderful things happen! Unattainable feats are done!

Christ is working in us, His righteous acts. Although we are very sinful, He works through us, and this is what gets the job done; thus, His receiving all the Glory. Join me on this wonderful journey through the life of Hagar.

Notes

March 1

HOW DID I GET HERE?

"THEN PHARAOH GAVE ABRAM MANY GIFTS BECAUSE OF HER—SHEEP, GOATS, CATTLE, MALE AND FEMALE DONKEYS, MALE AND FEMALE SERVANTS, AND CAMELS." (GENESIS 12:16 NLT)

We find the background for this story in Genesis 12. The Lord had commanded Abram to leave his homeland to go to a place where He (the Lord) would direct him. In return for Abram's obedience, the Father would make him a great nation. Abram obeyed God's command and moved to the land of Canaan. After being there for a time, a famine came upon the land. Abram got scared, and without consulting the Lord, he went south to Egypt seeking relief. On the way to Egypt, he freaked out. In fear of being killed because of his wife's beauty, Abram asked her to tell a lie. "Say that you are my sister instead of my wife," he asks her. She agrees and is taken to become one of Pharaoh's wives. In return, Abram received a handsome payoff which is listed in the above verse (Genesis 12:16). Hagar is one of the female servants given in the payment package. Uprooted from her homeland and sold as a slave, Hagar could not have imagined what a pivotal role she would play not only in the life of the father of the Jewish nation, but in the world as well. Our loving Lord would use the yet unnamed slave to teach His lesson of love and care to single moms down through the annals of time. Hagar, a slave, was bartered out like an old rag to Abram. But in God's eyes, she was a person of beauty.

HAGAR AND US: The story of Hagar's captivity and pain teaches us several valuable lessons. Our world is flawed by sin. We are all held captive; either physically, spiritually, or both. Our Lord loves us so much and wants to draw us out of bondage, and to Himself. Like Hagar, despite our station in life, we too are so loved by our LORD.

GOD SPEAKS: "So I will restore to you the years that the swarming locust has eaten, The crawling locust, The consuming locust, And the chewing locust, My great army which I sent among you." (Joel 2:25 NKJV) You do not have a situation that I, the LORD, cannot take you through, or bring you out of.

WANDA'S PRAYER: Father, help us to always remember there is no problem in our lives, bigger than You. Teach us to go to You first and always, for answers and comfort.

March 2

"FLIGHT"

"NOW SARAI, ABRAM'S WIFE, HAD BORNE HIM NO CHILDREN. AND SHE HAD AN EGYPTIAN MAIDSERVANT WHOSE NAME WAS HAGAR." (GENESIS 16:1 NKJV)

Hagar's name means "flight." Sarai would use "flight" to try and escape the many years of her painful barrenness. If anyone had reason to want to escape their current situation, it was Sarai. She had spent ten long years in the land of promise, waiting on the "promised son." As time passed, her hopes of having a child waned. How could she escape her childless state and remove this reproach which haunted her day and night? Sarai's thoughts may have gone something like this: "God is moving so slow! His plan is not working, so I will go to Plan B. I have a young slave girl. She can have a child for me. People do it all the time. Lord knows I am too old to have kids. If she sleeps with my husband, the child will be his, and I will take over as mother." In Sarai's mind, this was the perfect plan. She pictured herself holding "her" baby, birthed by Hagar. Hagar, a large piece of this misguided puzzle, is not given much of an option. She is simply told she would be the second wife to Abram; taken and forced to bear a child. This terribly violates her rights; but as a slave, she had no rights. So, "Abram goes into Hagar, and she conceived." (Genesis 16:1-4)

HAGAR AND US: Our LORD created us as free moral agents with the ability to choose. Choices denied blatantly violate our basic human rights, it is abuse. In Hagar's case, it is also an act of violence. These acts of violence can leave deep painful scars; physically and emotionally. Our LORD never approves of, or sanctions abuse.

GOD SPEAKS: "But He was wounded for our transgressions, He was bruised for our iniquities; The chastisement for our peace was upon Him, And by His stripes we are healed." (Isaiah 53:5 NKJV) You have wounds? Do you have bruises? I know exactly what that feels like. I was also bruised and beaten for something I had no part in. Like Hagar, I did not say a word. The enormous difference is that My stripes, My wounds, and My pain bring you healing. I am the balm in Gilead for the healing of your wounds. So, bring Me all that pain, sorrow and hurt and I will take it all away. It will take time; but stay in Me, and I will heal your wounded soul. That is a promise!

WANDA'S PRAYER: Lord, thank You for dealing with our hurts and pains which we have laid at Your feet over the many years.

March 3

SLAVE NO MORE!

"SO HE WENT IN TO HAGAR, AND SHE CONCEIVED. AND WHEN SHE SAW THAT SHE HAD CONCEIVED, HER MISTRESS BECAME DESPISED IN HER EYES."
(GENESIS 16:4 NKJV)

It did not take Hagar long to figure out she had the "goods," and Sarai did not. She was the one carrying the heir in her womb, and not the old Sarai. After all, "Sarai, Abram's wife, took Hagar her maid, the Egyptian, and GAVE HER TO HER HUSBAND ABRAM TO BE HIS WIFE..." (Genesis 16:3) Now Hagar was coming into the fullness of her role as Abram's wife. In her mind, she (Hagar) was a slave no more. Hagar's thought in her mind was that Abram did not need two wives, thus Sarai had to go. In Hagar's thinking, Sarai could not have kids, so what good was she? Hagar began to despise her mistress. Translation: Hagar hated this old bag and wanted her out of the way. A tragic lesson from this is that people are not toys we can manipulate at will. The real problem is that Abram lacked an heir, and he lacked faith. God was the solution to his problem, not Hagar. It was the LORD that gave Abram the promise of having a child at seventy-five years of age. And therefore, it was the LORD'S responsibility to produce a child through this old couple. The wait became too long for Sarai; so instead of going to the LORD of the promise, she attempted a self-fix; not a God solution. Her solution was doomed to fail. Hagar, on the other hand, represents the natural woman who has no knowledge of God. Thus, her thoughts and actions are normal for a person who does not know God.

HAGAR AND US: While we can understand the old couple's dilemma, we can relate to Hagar as well. Remember, she was placed in an oppressive situation. Now she sees her chance to get the upper hand, and she takes advantage. She is a woman of the flesh, and she acts out the part.

GOD SPEAKS: "The LORD knows the thoughts of man, (a person) That they are futile. Blessed is the man (person) whom You instruct, O LORD, And teach out of Your law, That You may give him rest from the days of adversity,..." (Psalm 94:11-13 NKJV) (BECAUSE) "There is a way that seems right to a man, (or woman) But its end is the way of death." (Proverbs 14:12 NKJV) Acting in the flesh does no one, any good. The answer is to allow your LORD to fill you with His Holy Spirit in order to fix the problem.

WANDA'S PRAYER: Okay LORD, have Your own way in our lives!

March 4

HAGAR, THE MAID

"SO ABRAM SAID TO SARAI, 'INDEED YOUR MAID IS IN YOUR HAND; DO TO HER AS YOU PLEASE.' AND WHEN SARAI DEALT HARSHLY WITH HER (HAGAR), SHE FLED FROM HER PRESENCE."
(GENESIS 16:6 NKJV)

Sarai was old; but she was not stupid. She would not put up with the disdain of Hagar the slave towards her. She goes to Abram to discuss the matter. He takes a hands-off approach. "She's your maid honey, so, you handle it dear." (Genesis 16:5) (Writer's paraphrase) And handle it, Sarai did! She treats Hagar so harshly that Hagar runs away. We are not told what type of abuse Sarai dished out to Hagar, but whatever it was, it was so bad that Hagar ran from the house. "She fled from her presence!" This is what happens when everyone is operating in their flesh—you have a big mess! What we can learn from this text is that when we try to solve our problems without the Master problem solver, we too, will end up in a big mess such as this one. The Father waits, however, because He knows none of the parties involved. Though they desperately need Him, they cannot receive Him yet. The result is everything and everyone is out of order.

HAGAR AND US: Two wrongs can never make a right. Slavery and forced procreation is WRONG. Hagar's efforts to payback the old couple WAS WRONG ALSO. She is out of place. She should be taking a "servant's" position, and not one of superiority. In an effort to "get even," how often have we done the same thing?

GOD SPEAKS: "Seek the LORD while He may be found, Call upon Him while He is near. Let the wicked forsake his way, And the unrighteous man his thoughts; Let him return to the LORD, And He will have mercy on him; And to our God, For He will abundantly pardon. For My thoughts are not your thoughts, Nor are your ways My ways, says the LORD." (Isaiah 55:6-8 NKJV) There are two issues of conflict going on here between Hagar and Sarai. Hagar represents the wicked person who does not know God. Her mindset is, "Get all you can, and can all you get." Sarai represents the carnal Christian; she knows God, but is doing evil. They both must come to the LORD. The wicked (Hagar) must forsake her way and find God's way. The unrighteous (Sarai) must put away her unrighteous thoughts (which have now turned into evil actions and harsh treatment of Hagar). But that is not enough. Next, the wicked and the unrighteous must COME TO THE LORD. He will pardon and straighten out (fix) the problem. He alone has the solution.

WANDA'S PRAYER: Father, help us to humble ourselves in Your sight; I know You will then lift us up.

FOUND YOU

"NOW THE ANGEL OF THE LORD FOUND HER BY A SPRING OF WATER IN THE WILDERNESS, BY THE SPRING ON THE WAY TO SHUR. AND HE SAID, 'HAGAR, SARAI'S MAID, WHERE HAVE YOU COME FROM, AND WHERE ARE YOUR GOING?' SHE SAID, 'I AM FLEEING FROM THE PRESENCE OF MY MISTRESS SARAI.'"
(GENESIS 16:7-8 NKJV)

This verse shows us a perfect picture of Jesus Christ. Hagar represents one who does not know God. Yet, "The angel of the Lord" goes after her and finds her. "But God demonstrates His own love towards us, in that while we were still sinners, Christ died for us." (Romans 5:8 NKJV) Neither Abram nor Sarai goes after Hagar, but God does—how very touching this is. It speaks volumes about the Heavenly Father's heart. "For God so loved the world that He gave His only begotten Son, that whoever believes in Him should not perish but have everlasting life." (John 3:16 NKJV) The Lord of love not only chases her down, but He talks with her, and He listens to her. The Father knew exactly where Hagar was, and about the circumstances which brought her to this place. He asks her these questions so she can pour out her heart to Him. These verses point out how the Lord can meet our specific needs. Hagar needed the Wonderful Counselor, as well as the Mighty God; and the Forever Father was only too happy to help meet her needs. Hagar had a face-to-face encounter with God. He shows up not as a mean, harsh God, but as the Loving Lord and Savior. She was pregnant and alone in that wilderness. But she was not really alone, and she was not forsaken. Her Heavenly Father was right there to set things straight.

HAGAR AND US: Like Hagar, have there been times in your life when situations have become so bad that you just ran away? I have felt this way many times. But like Hagar, I am so glad God tackled me with His arms of love and did not let me go.

GOD SPEAKS: "For (I) God did not send His (My) Son into the world to condemn the world, but that the world through Him might be saved." (John 3:17 NKJV) My mission is to bring salvation and restoration. "for the Son of Man has come to seek and to save that which was lost." (Luke 19:10 NKJV) I also came to straighten out the saved ones as well. Let the love of God hold you like a vice grip as you deal with life.

WANDA'S PRAYER: Father, hold us closer and closer to Your heart.

March 6

GO BACK

"THE ANGEL OF THE LORD SAID TO HER, 'RETURN TO YOUR MISTRESS, AND SUBMIT YOURSELF UNDER HER HAND.'" (GENESIS 16: 9 NKJV)

The text listed above is interesting. Hagar is told to go back home and submit to her mistress. In the previous text, the Father reminds her she is the "maid of Sarai" (Genesis 16:8). Hagar agrees Sarai is her mistress, but to be told to go back to abuse seems hardly fair, especially for a God of Love. In this study, I realize the Lord God knows all. He knows He is not sending her back into an abusive situation. Sarai will abuse Hagar no more (Read the rest of Genesis 16). Having met her Heavenly Father, Hagar now knows He loves her and will protect her. She knows she can go to Him in time of need. Most importantly, "Dad" is dealing with Hagar and her sin. He will deal with Sarai later. Hagar was out of order when she stopped submitting to her mistress. Despite what she may have thought, Sarai was the mistress and Hagar was the servant—nothing more and nothing less. The Father wanted Hagar to perform her duties, and not question the duties of others. Hagar had met her Lord; He had revealed Himself to her. Now He would set her priorities in perfect order. The LORD just wanted Hagar to trust in His love for her. The proof of Hagar's trust would be seen in her obedience to her LORD.

HAGAR AND US: The lesson for Hagar seems to be, "two wrongs don't make a right." NONE OF US ARE GIVEN A LICENSE to abuse or commit any wrong when we have been hurt. "… Vengeance is Mine, I will repay, says the LORD!" (Romans 12:19 NKJV)

GOD SPEAKS: "Furthermore, we have had human fathers who corrected us, and we paid them respect. Shall we not much more readily be in subjection to the Father of spirits and live?" (Hebrews 12:9 NKJV) To be in subjection to Me, your Lord, is life. Got the Son of God? Then you have life! Everything apart from Me, is death.

WANDA'S PRAYER: In the book of Deuteronomy, You said You that set before us life and death and that You want us to choose life. Father, teach us to choose You; thereby always choosing life.

GREAT GOD!

"THEN THE ANGEL OF THE LORD SAID TO HER (HAGAR), 'I WILL MULTIPLY YOUR DESCENDANTS EXCEEDINGLY, SO THAT THEY SHALL NOT BE COUNTED FOR MULTITUDE.'" (GENESIS 16:10 NKJV)

Our Heavenly Father is no respecter of persons. He loves us all the same and gives good gifts to us all. At first glance, the promise given to Hagar looks a lot like the one the Father God made to Abram (See Genesis 13:16). The LORD says to Hagar, "I will multiply (your) descendants exceedingly, so that they shall not be counted for multitude." Our Lord is going to give Hagar a very large family. Hagar is the first liberated woman in Scripture; she is head of this house. Hagar's children are called Hagar's children and are not included as the heirs of the promise of Abraham and Sarah. Hagar's son, Ishmael, whose father is Abram, would not be in the lineage of the promised SEED, meaning CHRIST—THE SAVIOR OF THE WORLD. God's design was for Abram and his wife Sarai to accomplish this purpose. The "fathering" of Ishmael by Abram was never our Lord's design. Abram's only job was to just believe that his Lord would do what He had promised. The Lord loves to bless, and the Father wants to bless Hagar. He is telling her, "Yes, you have run away from home, and you are out here in this wilderness. I see you, Hagar! I see and have seen your life's circumstances; they have not escaped My All-Seeing eyes. Your problems have not gone unnoticed by your loving Lord. I send you back not to be abused, but as My witness. Just like Abram, I am going to bless you also. Hagar, I want you to believe that I am your Father as well."

HAGAR AND US: As with Hagar, we are not despised; but so well loved by the LORD. He is just waiting to take care of us. He wants to speak to our circumstances. As He so lovingly assured Hagar, our LORD wants to assure us too, of His tender love and care for us.

GOD SPEAKS: "See, I have inscribed you on the palms of My hands; Your walls are continually before Me." (Isaiah 49:16 NKJV) Your name is written on My nail-scarred hands. Those prison walls which confine you and shut Me out are ever before Me. I know all of your hurts and pains. Let Me tear down the walls and take away the pain. I can give you a love which you have never known; and a peace for which you have so longed.

WANDA'S PRAYER: Lord, we are ready! Take all of our hurts and our pain and replace them with Your love and peace.

March 8

HEARD YOU

"AND THE ANGEL OF THE LORD SAID TO HER: 'BEHOLD, YOU ARE WITH CHILD, AND YOU SHALL BEAR A SON. YOU SHALL CALL HIS NAME ISHMAEL, BECAUSE THE LORD HAS HEARD YOUR AFFLICTION.'" (GENESIS 16:11 NKJV)

This is another one of those beautiful gems from the life of Hagar, which speaks to my heart. The Father continues speaking to her. He tells her intimate and personal things about her life. It seems as if the Heavenly Father is putting His huge arms of love around Hagar and saying, "Hush now and do not cry; I know all about it. I saw the whole ugly mess. This baby you are having is a boy and I know how this pregnancy came about. I want you to call him Ishmael because I HEARD YOUR AFFLICTION. I AM THE GOD WHO HEARS. Honey, I hear, and I feel, what you are going through. I know all about your life. Despite your abuse, I am going to bless you. I am going to multiply your descendants, make them a nation, and bless them. From now on, when you look at your child, remember that you were never alone. I, your Lord, saw, heard, and fixed your circumstances." (Writer's paraphrase)

HAGAR AND US: Like Hagar, we can know comfort and peace right now, despite our past or even present misery. Allow God to deal with your every hurt and pain.

GOD SPEAKS: "Do not fear, for you will not be ashamed; Neither be disgraced, for you will not be put to shame; For you will forget the shame of your youth, And will not remember the reproach of your widowhood anymore. For your Maker is your husband, The LORD of hosts is His name; And your Redeemer is the Holy One of Israel; He is called the God of the whole earth." (Isaiah 54:4-5 NKJV) I know you and all of your circumstances by name. You are Mine; I will never let you go.

WANDA'S PRAYER: Thank you, Father, for dealing with every hurt and pain.

March 9

CAKE TOPPER

"HE SHALL BE A WILD MAN; HIS HAND SHALL BE AGAINST EVERY MAN, AND EVERY MAN'S HAND SHALL BE AGAINST HIM. AND HE SHALL DWELL IN THE PRESENCE OF ALL HIS BRETHREN."
(GENESIS 16:12 NKJV)

What I love about the LORD is how He gives us blessings beyond anything we could ever imagine. Here is a splendid example of this. The Eternal Father gives Hagar a glimpse into the future. The Father displays His Omnipresence by telling her some very personal and intimate details of her son's adult life. She is told these things while she is still pregnant with the child. Our Lord displays her child's life before her in panoramic view. Every detail of her life and her child's life is fully known by Him alone. Father God can do this because He has already seen it, and He is allowing it for His own glory. He sees her son grown up and the problems he will have. "Dad" (our LORD) assures her He will take care of her son. This gives Hagar (and us) great comfort because our "Dad" does not just see us, He knows us completely. It is one thing to build your faith in the kept promises of God, or even to have faith in the God who supplies the present, but to know for a certainty that the God of the Heavens has already taken care of your future? Now, this is the God in whom we can truly rest! The GOD who is All-Seeing, All-Knowing, All-Powerful—He is the God which we can trust not only with our yesterday's, but for our tomorrows as well.

HAGAR AND US: Like Hagar, our LORD comes to us in every station of life. He says, "Give Me this challenge, difficulty, or hardship—I will work it out." Whether we are married or single, the Lord is our Great Husband. The LORD Jesus wants to care for us, in and through all our walks of life.

GOD SPEAKS: "The LORD will keep you from all harm-he will watch over your life; the LORD will watch over your coming and going both now and forevermore." (Psalm 121:7-8 NIV) Even in your sad times, I am with you; I cry when you cry, and laugh when you laugh. I will never leave or forsake you.

WANDA'S PRAYER: Father, there are times when we feel very insecure. Thank you for your constant reassurance.

March 10

SEES ME

"THEN SHE CALLED THE NAME OF THE LORD WHO SPOKE TO HER, YOU-ARE-THE-GOD-WHO-SEES; FOR SHE SAID, 'HAVE I ALSO HERE SEEN HIM WHO SEES ME?'" (GENESIS 16:13 NKJV)

Hagar had listened to all the Lord had to say to her and it must have left her breathless! Finally, after taking in all the magnificent words the Father had spoken to her, she spoke. I imagine her thoughts were, "God, I know You are real. You are not the gods of my childhood—the ones I learned about in Egypt. You are a living-breathing God!" The God of Heaven had come down to dwell in her presence, and she lived to tell about it. She had done something few humans had ever done. She had an encounter with the LORD. That would have left me breathless, too. God had given Hagar a privilege that not even Sarai was given. The Lord gave information to Hagar directly. Sarai received her information second-hand from her husband. The Father and God of the universe had become her husband, and what a Great Provider He was. He had reached into the inner recesses of her heart and touched her deepest needs. To meet those needs, He offered Himself to her in a very personal way. The Father told and showed her He was all she would ever need.

HAGAR AND US: Though we have never seen God face-to-face as Hagar did, we do have the Spirit of God living in our hearts; and we have His written Word. I am sure we could all give testimonials of how He has made Himself real to us. I know I could write books on how the LORD has made Himself so very real to me.

GOD SPEAKS: "For in Him (Jesus) dwells all the fullness of the Godhead bodily; and you are complete in Him, who is the head of all principality and power." (Colossians 2:9-10 NKJV) I (GOD) complete you, because I am complete. Bring Me your joys and sorrows—your hopes and disappointments. Allow Me to reach inside of you and take away your hurt—I will replace it with My everlasting joy.

WANDA'S PRAYER: I am feeling really good now! Thank You, Father, for being all we will ever need.

March 11

LIVING ONE

"THEREFORE THE WELL WAS CALLED BEER-LAHAI-ROI; OBSERVE, IT IS BETWEEN KADESH AND BERED." (GENESIS 16:14 NKJV)

The words Beer-Lahai Roi, means "well of the Living one who sees me." (Nelson's Bible Dictionary) It is a well in the wilderness between Kadesh Barnea and Bered, which is in southern Israel. This is the area where Hagar would eventually make her home. This wilderness was a dry, parched desert land with few sources of water. Life in such an area can be very difficult to live in. This so aptly represented Hagar's life. As an Egyptian slave, she was given away, stripped from her family, taken many miles from her home, and forced to surrogate a child. What a desolate life. Hagar was truly in her wilderness in every way. In the middle of her wilderness, the LORD provides Himself as the Living water to quench her insatiable thirst. Hagar drinks from the well that never runs dry. Bursting with the satisfaction of having been filled to overflowing, she names this place and calls it, "The Well of the Living One who sees me." The Living One had given her Living water. She is the first woman mentioned in Scripture to drink from the "Well of life," but would not be the last. Her testimony would not only be a source of spiritual strength to her, but to others as well, like Isaac. (see Genesis 24:62 and Genesis 25:11).

HAGAR AND US: Reader, the Lord is the Living One who sees you as well. Have you seen Him? He wants to fill you with His Spirit.

GOD SPEAKS: "(When he said "living water," he was speaking of the Spirit, who would be given to everyone believing in him…" (John 7:39 NLT) This water is for you!

WANDA'S PRAYER: LORD, fill us up with Your Living water.

March 12

YOUR SON

**"SO HAGAR BORE ABRAM A SON; AND ABRAM NAMED HIS SON, WHOM HAGAR BORE, ISHMAEL."
(GENESIS 16:15 NKJV)**

The first-born son of Abram was here. He was not the son of promise, but of human effort. Sarai went through a great deal of effort to create this son; yet Ishmael's birth was not a time of joy and celebration. The fruits of sin are never as joyous as its promises claim. In looking at the above verse, it seems the boy was nearly forgotten. Despite the obvious despair found in the text, it offers much hope. The verse tells me several things: First, Hagar obeyed the voice of her LORD and returned back. The LORD had given Hagar a heart of surrender. Having submitted all things to her loving LORD, she could submit to those He had placed in authority over her. Hagar could obey in peace, with full assurance that the God of Heaven (and not Abram or Sarai) was in charge of her life. She had been given assurance in the wilderness, that the everlasting Father loved her with an everlasting love. Finally, the text tells me that Abram listened to Hagar's story of her encounter with the LORD, and believed her. He named the child Ishmael; which is the name God told Hagar to give her unborn child. This was Hagar's witness to the old patriarch and his wife. The Father had taken care of Hagar's situation with Sarai too; we read of no more rough treatment from Sarai at this point.

HAGAR AND US: Like Hagar, we can know that if no one else loves us, the LORD OF LOVE supremely loves us. We see His great love for us in His care.

GOD SPEAKS: "For God so loved the world that He gave His only begotten Son, that whoever believes in Him should not perish but have everlasting life." (John 3:16 NKJV) I will never leave or let you go from My sight. Just as I was with Moses and Hagar, I am with you always. Comfort yourself in these words.

WANDA'S PRAYER: Father, thank you for always reassuring us of Your tender love for us. Lord, keep us in the middle of those giant arms of love.

March 13

WHICH ONE

"BUT SARAH SAW THAT THE SON WHOM HAGAR THE EGYPTIAN HAD BORNE TO ABRAHAM WAS MOCKING, AND SHE SAID TO ABRAHAM, 'GET RID OF THAT SLAVE WOMAN AND HER SON, FOR THAT WOMAN'S SON WILL NEVER SHARE IN THE INHERITANCE WITH MY SON ISAAC.'" (GENESIS 21:9-10 NIV)

The background of this text is that the LORD has just blessed Sarah with a son, Isaac. The boy, Isaac, has just been weaned from breast feeding. (Genesis 21:8) A great feast (a giant party) was taking place to celebrate this event. At the party, it seems that Sarah saw Ishmael "mocking" or making fun of the situation or her son. The text says, "Ishmael was mocking." The word for mocking (scoffing) used here means to laugh outright (in merriment or scorn)—to make sport or to mock. Sarah saw Ishmael's actions as a put down of her and her son, and she wanted him out. Just how he was mocking or what he was saying, we are not told. We can assume Ishmael is acting out his anger of being "dethroned as heir to Abraham's kingdom." This was the beginning of the fulfillment of the prophecy, the LORD had spoken over Ishmael before his birth in Genesis 16:12, "… his hand will be against every man, and every man's hand will be against him…" Sarah's harsh attitude and hand was definitely against him. Perhaps she was releasing 13 years of stored-up anger since Ishmael's birth to Hagar. The scripture in Genesis 21:9 does not give us Hagar's thoughts at this moment, but no doubt she must have been quite upset. Thirteen years ago, she had left because of Sarah's harsh treatment of her. Now, 13 years later, she and her child were both receiving the wrath of this angry woman. She would be thrust out into the cold. She would learn that her security did not lie in Abraham.

HAGAR AND US: Like Hagar, we too must learn that our security does not lie in the hands of man, but in the hands of the Eternal God of Heaven.

GOD SPEAKS: "Humble yourselves, therefore, under God's mighty hand, that he may lift you up in due time." (1 Peter 5:6 NIV) It is I the LORD, and not man, who is your true help.

WANDA'S PRAYER: LORD, thank you for being our strong tower and hiding place.

March 14

DISTRESSED

"THE MATTER DISTRESSED ABRAHAM GREATLY BECAUSE IT CONCERNED HIS SON. BUT GOD SAID TO HIM, 'DO NOT BE SO DISTRESSED ABOUT THE BOY AND YOUR SLAVE WOMAN. LISTEN TO WHATEVER SARAH TELLS YOU, BECAUSE IT IS THROUGH ISAAC THAT YOUR OFFSPRING WILL BE RECKONED.'"
(GENESIS 21:11-12 NIV)

We find the background of the above text in Genesis 21:9. They had given a great feast in little Isaac's honor. Sarah sees Ishmael, Hagar's son, scoffing (mocking) at everything going on. Sarah saw Ishmael's actions as a putdown of her and her son, and she wanted him out. In the above text, we see Abraham had grown attached to his son Ishmael, and his mother. "The matter (of putting Hagar and Ishmael out) distressed him greatly…" He did not want them to leave, and probably would not let them go. The LORD had to step in and tell Abraham to send Hagar and Ishmael away. When the LORD speaks, and we listen, it is always a good thing! With all other voices hushed, the man of GOD must hear and receive the final word from GOD. It was ok to hear his wife's opinion, but he must get HIS INSTRUCTIONS FROM THE LORD. And the LORD said, "It's time for Hagar to go!" But why would the LORD tell Hagar to go back to the patriarch's home and then, after only thirteen years later, tell her to leave? Answer: Divine appointment and not human planning. To everything, God has a season. This story would be a lesson for centuries to come. First of all, thirteen years earlier, Hagar decided to leave because of adverse circumstances. In her wilderness experience, she met the LORD. The Father displayed His love for her and assured her He alone was her provider (Genesis 16:7-16). Hagar would have to rely on God's promises alone. It would teach her (and us) the surety of His words. Finally, this story would represent a lesson to us all. We must die to self and totally surrender our lives over to the LORD.

HAGAR AND US: How often are we distressed when man lets us down? We need not look to the hands of man; instead, always look to the hands of God for our deliverance!

GOD SPEAKS: "… My heart within me is distressed … Cause me to hear Your lovingkindness in the morning, For in You do I trust; …" (Psalm 143:4,8 NKJV) Bring Me all of your distresses.

WANDA'S PRAYER: LORD, teach us to rely on You alone. Teach us to go to You first for all things.

March 15

FORGOTTEN PROMISES

"YET I WILL ALSO MAKE A NATION OF THE SON OF THE BONDWOMAN, BECAUSE HE IS YOUR SEED." (GENESIS 21:13 NKJV)

I (like Hagar), often forget the goodness of our LORD; taking for granted that He speaks no idle words. In Genesis 21:13, the Father reminds us of this in His dealings with Hagar and Ishmael. Amidst the tragedy of a family about to be ripped to shreds, the LORD reminds Abraham and (indirectly Hagar) of His love and care for them. He tells Abraham, I will take care of Ishmael because he is "your seed." Therefore, "I WILL ALSO MAKE A NATION OF THE SON OF THE BONDWOMAN …" Hagar was given a similar promise while she was still pregnant before her son's birth. (Genesis 16:10) The Father of all Creation steps in as father to Ishmael. The LORD asks Abraham to step back as father; Ishmael will not be abandoned. Super Dad will be his father and He will take care of him. Hagar can take great comfort in these words. The Father had spoken these same words to her thirteen years earlier in the wilderness near Shur. (Genesis 16:10) All Hagar needed to do was to hold on to the words of the LORD. Her test and trials were coming; but our LORD had given Hagar His guarantee of victory—He would bring her through. Now in her time of deepest need, Hagar needed to take hold of God's promises, with the force of a vise grip, and not let go.

HAGAR AND US: Like Hagar, our LORD has given us His Word; that Word is the Bible. Have you read His promises for you lately?

GOD SPEAKS. "We are hard pressed on every side, but not crushed; perplexed, but not in despair; persecuted, but not abandoned; struck down, but not destroyed. We always carry around in our body the death of Jesus, so that the life of Jesus may also be revealed in our body." (2 Corinthians 4:8-10 NIV) Go back and read Genesis, Chapters 1-2. In reading those verses, you will note that I spoke Creation into place, made man from dust, and woman from a single bone. I AM the LORD Almighty; your little problems are nothing to Me. Just dump all of them on Me, and watch how I work!

WANDA'S PRAYER: LORD, thanks for always reminding us of Your love and care for us. We love You Father.

March 16

WANDERING

"EARLY THE NEXT MORNING ABRAHAM TOOK SOME FOOD AND A SKIN OF WATER AND GAVE THEM TO HAGAR. HE SET THEM ON HER SHOULDERS AND THEN SENT HER OFF WITH THE BOY. SHE WENT ON HER WAY AND WANDERED IN THE DESERT OF BEERSHEBA." (GENESIS 21:14 NIV)

The scene given to us here is a very sad one. God has instructed Abraham to send Hagar and his son Ishmael away. Abraham is heartbroken. Hagar and her son are in deep despair. I imagine there was much wailing and tear shedding by all three. Hagar leaves Abraham and goes to the Wilderness of Beersheba, and wanders as if she is in a blinding fog in the dead of night. She is confused, frightened, and wandering. Why? Thirteen years prior, she had run from Sarah's wrath and ended up in a desert southeast of where she was now. In that desolate desert, she was all alone, pregnant, and "The LORD found HER …" (Genesis 16:7) In that desert near a spring, the LORD listened to her. He spoke so tenderly to her, His words of comfort. She named that place, "the Well of the Living One who sees me." (Genesis 16:12) The same Living God who saw her and attended to her needs thirteen years earlier, sees her now and is still quite capable of meeting her needs. Now thirteen years later, she is at Beersheba, or "The Well of Oaths." How fitting it is that she now finds herself at "The Well of Oaths," with the Oath's Giver; the God of Heaven. Thirteen years earlier, He had given Hagar His oath of safety and protection; therefore, she did not need to worry because His provisions were sure. She does not need to wander in a fog. He was as close as the mention of His Name.

HAGAR AND US: Like Hagar, at times we too wonder aimlessly in the fog over our circumstances; but we do not have to. His love for us is genuine and His promises are sure. He says that He is always with us, even to the end of the age.

GOD SPEAKS: "For all the promises of God in Him are Yes, and in Him Amen, to the glory of God through us." (2 Corinthians 1:20 NKJV)

WANDA'S PRAYER: Father, what can we say but "thank you!" Help us to stay with you in the good times, and to cling to you in the bad.

March 17

DESPONDED

"AND THE WATER IN THE SKIN WAS USED UP, AND SHE PLACED THE BOY UNDER ONE OF THE SHRUBS. THEN SHE WENT AND SAT DOWN ACROSS FROM HIM AT A DISTANCE OF ABOUT A BOWSHOT; FOR SHE SAID TO HERSELF, 'LET ME NOT SEE THE DEATH OF THE BOY.' SO SHE SAT OPPOSITE HIM, AND LIFTED HER VOICE AND WEPT." (GENESIS 21:15-16 NKJV)

Hagar reminds me of the boy who was an heir to untold wealth, but would not access it. She is in a needless, desponded state. Do not get me wrong; it is ok to cry and weep over our sad circumstances, but Hagar (and us), can do more than just weep and cry; we could use keys of deliverance. Those keys of deliverance are called: "Remember and Request." "Remember" when you were in a similar place, and "the Living One who sees" was there with you. He brought you peace and great comfort. The next key of deliverance is to "Request." Request the help of the All-Powerful "Living One." The Lord had placed Hagar there; His provisions were already in place for her well-being. Hagar was preparing for death, when in fact, the Living One was there. She forgot this fact and is now suffering. Life and help were just a prayer away, but Hagar's desponded state only prepared her for death.

HAGAR AND US: Oh, how many times we too prepare for death when life is just a prayer away!

GOD SPEAKS: "Call to Me, and I will answer you, and show you great and mighty things, which you do not know." (Jeremiah 33:3 NKJV) I love you with a forever love. As my daughter, I can assure you that I will always be with you, and I will take care of you. One day you will be with Me forever!

WANDA'S PRAYER: Father, those words are so comforting to hear and feel. Thank you for Your love and care for us, in the good and bad.

March 18

ONE PRAYS

"AND GOD HEARD THE VOICE OF THE LAD. THEN THE ANGEL OF GOD CALLED TO HAGAR OUT OF HEAVEN, AND SAID TO HER, 'WHAT AILS YOU, HAGAR? FEAR NOT, FOR GOD HAS HEARD THE VOICE OF THE LAD WHERE HE IS.'" (GENESIS 21:17 NKJV)

In this story, mothers (especially single ones), can take much comfort. The previous two verses of this chapter tell us the water had run out for Hagar and Ishmael. She places her thirteen-year-old son under a shrub, awaits death, and laments this imminent event. (Genesis 21:15-16) The lad is very weak, frail, and at the point of death; so, he cries out to the LORD. How do I know this? Jeremiah 33:3 NKJV says, "Call to Me, and I will answer you, and show you great and mighty things, which you do not know." Finally, the text says, "And GOD HEARD the voice of the lad... fear not, for GOD HAS HEARD THE VOICE OF THE LAD..." (Genesis 21:17). See how very close Father God is to us? He is as close as the mention of His Name. The Father had given Hagar so many precious and wonderful promises (see Genesis 16:10-12). He would not forsake her now. He was just waiting for someone to cry out to Him for help (not cry out to their problems). Apparently, Ishmael did just that.

HAGAR AND US: Isn't it sad when your child reminds you to pray? Hagar knew the LORD, but she forgot about Him. Now at the point of death, it is her child, not her, who calls out for help, to the Source of life.

GOD SPEAKS: "God is our refuge and strength, a very present help in trouble." (Psalm 46:1 NKJV) Take comfort in these words. You are mine, and I always take care of those who belong to me.

WANDA'S PRAYER: "Therefore we will not fear, Even though the earth be removed, and though the mountains be carried into the midst of the sea; Though its waters roar and be troubled, Though the mountains shake with its swelling. *Selah* There is a river whose streams shall make glad the city of GOD, The holy place of the tabernacle of the Most High. God is in the midst of her, she shall not be moved; GOD shall help her, just at the break of dawn. The LORD of host is with us (me); the GOD of Jacob is our (my) refuge. *Selah* Be still, and know that I am GOD..." (Psalm 46:2-5, 7,10 NKJV) Father, this is our prayer and praise to you; THANK YOU!

March 19

GET GOING

"ARISE, LIFT UP THE LAD AND HOLD HIM WITH YOUR HAND, FOR I WILL MAKE HIM A GREAT NATION." (GENESIS 21:18 NKJV)

When we last left our story, Hagar's son (Ishmael) was crying out to God for help. God wonderfully shows up and responds to the boy and his mother. He tells her to go to the lad (her son). She had distanced herself from him while awaiting his supposed death. There will be no death today, the LORD says, "… I WILL MAKE HIM A GREAT NATION." (Genesis 21:18) I love it when Father God, like the perfect Dad He is, just "shows up and shows out"! What a great and wonderful LORD we serve! God tells Hagar to go hold and comfort her child because deliverance is here! Again, Hagar is asked to step out in faith—into the loving arms of her Father and Savior. She can give comfort because the LORD has comforted her. He speaks to her as He had done thirteen years prior. This story gives hope; not only to her, but to all of us. It says the Comforter will never leave or forsake us. His presence in that wilderness to Hagar is the same presence we can feel and know today, thousands of years later.

HAGAR AND US: Like Hagar, it is so nice to know that when we do not know what to do, our LORD and Savior does, and He does it so very well. Many times, during a single day, I am assured of this fact.

GOD SPEAKS: "The Lord of host is with us; the God is Jacob is our refuge." (Psalm 46:7 NKJV) Remember, I am always with you.

WANDA'S PRAYER: Yes LORD, thank You for NEVER leaving me.

March 20

EYE OPENING

"THEN GOD OPENED HER EYES, AND SHE SAW A WELL OF WATER. AND SHE WENT AND FILLED THE SKIN WITH WATER, AND GAVE THE LAD A DRINK."
(GENESIS 21:19 NKJV)

In continuing our story, we see in Genesis 21:14, Hagar is wandering around in the Wilderness of Beersheba, after being put out by Abraham. The name of this place is called "Well of Oaths." "Well of Oaths" means, "there are wells of water in this place." She was in a similar place thirteen years earlier (Genesis 16:14). It was here where she had met the LORD and He spoke with her. He gave her many great and precious promises. Now thirteen years later, Hagar is having a "déjà vu moment," and does not even realize it. The Father had to open her eyes. The wells were there, but she could not see it, because tears of despair blinded her eyes from having been tossed aside like an old rag. All Hagar sees is imminent death. However, the Father of life and love blesses Hagar despite her unbelief. Hagar could not see God's hands of provision, because for the past thirteen years, she had been focused on Abraham's provision. Though thirteen years earlier she had met with the All-Powerful LORD and had heard His voice, she forgot and forsook Him for what she saw in Abraham. The Father opens her eyes and her heart to the true reality. We can see that the only true, dependable One in life is the LORD OF HEAVEN—THE GOD OF LOVE.

HAGAR AND US: What "eye opening" experiences have you had, which pointed you back to the LORD of Heaven? We are very much like Hagar. The LORD blesses us with much: jobs, houses, family, and so much more. Yet, how quickly we take our focus off of the Gift-giver, and focus only on the gifts. We stop spending time with Him and become consumed by His gifts. But then, the gifts are removed—the job is lost, the house ends up in foreclosure, or the family is gone. We are then brought back to the Giver, who has been there all the time just waiting for us to return to Him. What a patient, loving LORD He is. After He opens our eyes, we can then see what He is showing us. He wants us to seek Him first, in the middle, and in the last; as He is the One who supplies all of our needs.

GOD SPEAKS: "Open my eyes to see the wonderful truths in your instructions." (Psalm 119:18 NLT) "while we do not look at the things which are seen, but at the things which are not seen. For the things which are seen are temporary, but the things which are not seen are eternal." (2 Corinthians 4:18 NKJV) "I am the LORD, and there is no other; There is no God besides Me. I will gird you, though you have not known Me," (Isaiah 45:5 NKJV)

WANDA'S PRAYER: Father, thank you for those periodic reminders that You alone are our One and only true GOD. Help us to seek only You, and not to place my faith in others.

March 21

PAPA GOD

"SO GOD WAS WITH THE LAD; AND HE GREW AND DWELT IN THE WILDERNESS, AND BECAME AN ARCHER." (GENESIS 21:20 NKJV)

This verse shows the tender side of GOD. Father God was with the lad and assumed the role of his earthly father. The "Perfect Dad" was with him watching and protecting His son. This must have been a very comforting thought to his mother, Hagar. Her heart must have overflowed with joy as she reflected on the promises God had previously made to her. They were being fulfilled before her very eyes! It shows us two things: (1) the importance of the father in a child's life; and (2) how the LORD makes up the difference. This "vignette" presents our Father in a very tender light. This reminds us as moms, especially single moms, that we are not forgotten. We have an example of how the LORD truly loves us, and no one is a second-class citizen to Him. He provides for us in every walk of life.

HAGAR AND US: Like Hagar, I remember all those years of single parenthood. Many times, I had to go out in the dead of night for diapers and pampers. I thought I was alone, and I was scared. Looking back, I see I was not alone. My kids are adults now and I am very proud of them; I love them dearly. The perfect Dad raised these kids. He provided the funds for private schools, security systems when I lived in terrible neighborhoods, kept junk cars running, and provided every morsel of food. Thank you so much Dad! You are truly Husband and Father.

GOD SPEAKS: "… Spend your energy seeking the eternal life that the Son of Man can give you. For God the Father has given me the seal of his approval." (John 6:27 NLT) Those were My kids before they were yours.

WANDA'S PRAYER: I will praise the LORD with my whole heart; His Name is glorious and wonderful! Thank you for your goodness and mercies, which have no end.

March 22

FOREVER

"AND HE (ISHMAEL) DWELT IN THE WILDERNESS OF PARAN: AND HIS MOTHER TOOK HIM A WIFE OUT OF THE LAND OF EGYPT." (GENESIS 21:21 KJV)

We can see several things in this verse. First, we see the faithfulness of GOD's forever word. Our GOD did exactly what He said. In Genesis 16:12 NKJV, God said, "He (Ishmael) shall be a wild MAN; (meaning he will grow into adulthood) …" Genesis 21:13 NKJV, (God speaking to Abraham says), "Yet I will also make a nation of the son of the bondwoman, because he is your seed." In order for the son to have a nation, the son will have to grow up, get married, and then have children. We see in this verse that the child does grow up, and his mother goes to Egypt to get him a wife. Second, we see God's forever presence; "God was with the boy as he grew up…" (Genesis 21:20 NIV) Our Eternal GOD, who exists outside of our time—space continuum, and according to Genesis 16:12 and Genesis 21:13, saw and attended to the events of the grown-up Ishmael's life, before they took place. This fact should greatly comfort us. Third, we see how the Forever Faithful GOD, had been to Hagar. He had become her husband, and they raised the boy to adulthood. Though Hagar may have had no human husband to depend on, the LORD OF HOST was always there; He did not abandon her. Finally, after being expelled from Abraham's home, Hagar is free to go back to the land of her birth to find her son a wife. Our complete GOD completes the picture for Hagar.

HAGAR AND US: Can we like Hagar, look back over our lives and see our LORD'S forever faithfulness towards us? Go back down memory lane and jot down just a few of the LORD'S fulfilled promises that you have received in the past year.

GOD SPEAKS: "The grass withers and the flowers fall, but the word of our God endures forever." (Isaiah 40:8 NIV) I am not called the ROCK OF AGES for nothing. I am the surest thing you will ever have.

WANDA'S PRAYER: As the songwriter says, "Remind me You are able; You are strong, sure, and stable… You are able to see me through it all. I will count my many blessings and name them one by one, and it will surprise me what God has done."

March 23

FULFILLED

"THIS IS THE ACCOUNT OF THE FAMILY LINE OF ABRAHAM'S SON ISHMAEL, WHOM SARAH'S SLAVE, HAGAR THE EGYPTIAN, BORE TO ABRAHAM. ...THESE WERE THE SONS OF ISHMAEL, AND THESE ARE THE NAMES OF THE TWELVE TRIBAL RULERS ACCORDING TO THEIR SETTLEMENTS AND CAMPS." (GENESIS 25:12,16 NIV)

In these verses of Scripture, we can plainly see how our LORD TOTALLY FULFILLED HIS promises to Hagar. In Genesis 21:21, we are told that Hagar and son, settled in the Wilderness of Paran. According to biblical maps of this region, the area of Paran borders Egypt. His mother goes to Egypt and gets him a wife. The above verses tell us Ishmael had a very large family—twelve sons, not counting daughters. These sons became tribal heads (rulers). This happened just as the LORD said it would. The LORD FULFILLED HIS WORD to Hagar down to the smallest detail, "His descendants settled in the area from Havilah to Shur, near the eastern border of Egypt, as you go toward Ashur. AND THEY LIVED IN HOSTILITY TOWARD ALL THE TRIBES RELATED TO THEM (THEIR BROTHER)." (Genesis 25:18 NIV) Even this seemingly minor detail given to the pregnant Hagar was fulfilled. (Genesis 16:12) We do not know how long Hagar lived. Nor do we know how many of her grandchildren she was able to see, or rock to sleep at night. However, as she watched Ishmael's family grow and grow, there was no doubt in her mind that the LIVING ONE who saw her so many years earlier had done EXACTLY what He promised; and He was still with her now.

HAGAR AND US: As we look back over our lives, can we, like Hagar, see God's fulfilled promises to us? I can! I remember having to change jobs every couple of years. I asked the LORD to give me stable employment. It seemed like such a minor detail, but my LORD wonderfully answered Wanda's prayer. I have been at my current job for over thirty years now.

GOD SPEAKS: "And now the Lord has fulfilled the promise He made..." (1 Kings 8:20 NLT) "So God has given both his promise and his oath. These two things are unchangeable because it is impossible for God to lie..." (Hebrews 6:18 NLT) Of course I, the LORD, will fulfill My Word, because I CANNOT LIE. When I say it, IT IS DONE!

WANDA'S PRAYER: Thank You LORD for that reminder. You will always keep Your Word!

March 24

HAGAR'S LEGACY (PART 1)

(The Perfect Lover)

"I WILL BE GLAD AND REJOICE IN YOUR LOVE, FOR YOU SAW MY AFFLICTION AND KNEW THE ANGUISH OF MY SOUL." PSALM 31:7 (NIV)

Hagar shows us the Perfect Lover. He is the God man. Hagar was a woman who may have never known love. Since childhood, she had been enslaved and placed in bondage. She started out as Pharaoh's slave in Egypt. She was then given to Abram and Sarai to be their slave. (Genesis 12:16, 20; 16:1) Hagar would have viewed herself as someone's property; to be used and abused at will. Under Sarai, she went from being a maidservant, to baby maker for the Patriarch and his wife. The pregnant Hagar, seeing her chance to improve her station in life, turns the tables on Sarai. (Genesis 16:1-6) Sarai strikes back at Hagar. Then, out of fear, Hagar runs away to the wilderness. (Genesis 16:6) While in her wilderness, this violated woman found the True lover. The LORD of Supreme love ran after her in this barren place. "The angel of the LORD found Hagar near a spring in the desert; it was the spring that is beside the road to Shur." (Genesis 16:7) In the middle of this barren desert near a spring, the "Eternal Well" of life finds her and fills her with Himself. This living water would fill Hagar's soul to overflowing. This Perfect lover would locate her again thirteen years later, after being cast out of her home with her son. The awesome love the Father bestowed on Hagar was a loved she had craved for all her life.

HAGAR AND US: As with Hagar, have you ever felt unloved? I have. I longed for the love that Otis Redding sang about in his song, "When a Man Loves A Woman." I did not realize I already had the Greatest Lover known to man. He alone had the kind of love my aching heart so desperately craved. He had chased after me for a long time to give it to me. He had given me things and people I thought would satisfy, yet I was still empty. One day I asked the LORD to give me this love I forever craved. I needed Him to fill my empty soul. With heart searching prayer, I began to drink from the Living Water of His Word, which was the quencher for my thirsty soul.

GOD SPEAKS: "Jesus answered, "Everyone who drinks this water will be thirsty again, but whoever drinks the water I give them will never thirst. Indeed, the water I give them will become in them a spring of water welling up to eternal life." (John 4:13-14 NIV) Seek Me with your whole heart.

WANDA'S PRAYER: Thank you Father, for the wonderful and filling love You continually show to us.

March 25

HAGAR'S LEGAGY (PART 2)

(God's Peace)

"IN PEACE I WILL LIE DOWN AND SLEEP, FOR YOU ALONE, LORD, MAKE ME DWELL IN SAFETY." (PSALM 4:8 NIV)

Hagar's second legacy she leaves for us is the peace and comfort which only God alone can give. In her first desert experience, she was young, pregnant, alone, terrified, and fleeing the wrath of an angry mistress. There was no search party dispatched to look for her. The Father of Heaven alone comes after Hagar. "Now the Angel of the LORD found her by a spring of water in the wilderness…" (Genesis 16:7) Hagar was between twenty-five to fifty miles away from the Patriarch Abram's home. "Where have you come from, and where are you going?" the LORD asks Hagar (Genesis 16:8) What great comfort and peace to know that the God of the universe, cared enough to come down and listen to a slave girl's concerns and fears. After listening to her, the LORD tells Hagar to go back home, but He first assures He would take care of her. Father God gives his daughter a future and a hope. While still pregnant, He tells her she would have an innumerable amount of descendants. The LORD conversed with Hagar as the loving, caring Dad he is. Thirteen years later, He shows up to rescue His daughter in her time of great peril. This time she was told to leave the Patriarch's home; she is put out into the desert with a thirteen-year-old. Out of water, Hagar places her son under a bush and sits at a distance, as she awaits his death. The Father shows up with His perfect peace to comfort His daughter again. "What's wrong Hagar? Do not be scared; I hear the boy crying." (Writer's paraphrase) "Dad" stops his busy schedule and swoops down from Heaven to attend to His daughter. What a wonderful display of love. He opens Hagar's eyes and gives water just in time of need. Just reading this story brings me lots of warm fuzzes.

HAGAR AND US: The Father is saying to His daughter Hagar, and to us, "You can know that I am always with you—I care for you!" Let His words to us give us peace and comfort.

GOD SPEAKS: "And the peace of God, which transcends all understanding, will guard your hearts and your minds in Christ Jesus." (Philippians 4:7 NIV) Let My peace and comfort be soothing to your heart.

WANDA'S PRAYER: May we rest and be at peace in You Dad; Your peace is so very sweet. Thank you for always looking after us.

March 26

HAGAR'S LEGACY (PART 3)

(The God Who Provides)

"YOU PROVIDED BREAD FROM HEAVEN FOR THEM FOR THEIR HUNGER, YOU BROUGHT FORTH WATER FROM A ROCK FOR THEM FOR THEIR THIRST, AND YOU TOLD THEM TO ENTER IN ORDER TO POSSESS THE LAND WHICH YOU SWORE TO GIVE THEM." (NEHEMIAH 9:15 NASB)

In the wilderness of Hagar's life, we see our GOD and Father's great provision for His children. In Hagar's first wilderness experience, Father God provides Himself. He and no one else, comes to His runaway child. (Genesis 16:7) The LORD provides Hagar with security. He says I am here, Hagar, and I will give you a future. "I will multiply your descendants exceedingly, so that they shall not be counted for multitude" (Genesis 16:10) Proof to Hagar that she is not dreaming, and she can count on His word, The LORD not only tells her of her current condition in life; "Behold, you are with child..." but He also gives her a glimpse of her future. "... You shall bear a son. You shall call His name Ishmael because I have heard your affliction." Hagar trusts the Father and returns home as He asks her to do. For thirteen years, "Dad" watches over her and keeps her safe from harm, while she lives with Abraham and Sarah. When it was time for Hagar to leave Abraham's home, the Great Provider was there with Hagar and son, to provide and protect them from all harm. Father God ultimately provides a permanent place for Hagar to live out her life as a free woman with her son. (Genesis 21:20-21)

HAGAR AND US: Have you seen our LORD'S great provisions in your life? I have. I was divorced and alone with two babies; one at three years old, and the other one was only six months, at the time. I had not finished Nursing School yet, so I had nothing. The LORD provided mightily! He kept me in a house, allowed me to get my transcript from a previous school, so I could finish Nursing School. My "Dad" was there—I felt Him, and I experienced His care and concern for me.

GOD SPEAKS: "But first, be concerned about His kingdom and what has His approval. Then all these things will be provided for you." (Matthew 6:33 GWT) Take just five minutes and reflect on My awesome care and concern for you. Do you know I am always here for you? Do you know how much I love you?

WANDA'S PRAYER: Father, You alone are God! You are past finding out. I have seen glimpses of Your love and care, which You have shown to me and my kids. I just want to say thank You for loving me, taking care of me, and for showing me pieces of Your glory.

March 27

GREATEST DAD

"DO YOU THUS REPAY THE LORD, O FOOLISH AND UNWISE PEOPLE? IS NOT HE YOUR FATHER WHO HAS BOUGHT YOU? HE HAS MADE YOU AND ESTABLISHED YOU." (DEUTERONOMY 32:6 NASB)

Our Father in Heaven is the perfect Dad. The Greek word for father is "Pater." This word means protector or provider. The God of Heaven shows Himself to be a very active Dad in Hagar and Ishmael's lives. When she fled Sarai's abuse as a young pregnant woman to the Wilderness of Shur, her Heavenly Father was there. She was alone and had no one to care for her, except her Heavenly Dad and LORD. He not only provided for her needs (Genesis 16:6-14), but He overextended Himself in both her life and in the life of her son, Ishmael. The Father knew Ishmael in detail and reveals this to Hagar before his birth. To show His tender compassion for His daughter Hagar, the LORD named this child; "call him Ishmael." (Genesis 16:11) Every time she called her son's name, it reminded Hagar of her Savior and LORD's care for her. In her second wilderness encounter with her "Dad," Hagar is homeless and alone with a thirteen-year-old. Out of water and resigning herself to imminent death, the perfect Dad shows up and rescues her. As the boy Ishmael grows up, God is with his son and Hagar; showering the boy with skills. (Genesis 21:20) The LORD made the Wilderness of Paran their home.

HAGAR AND US: In looking at the story of Hagar, we see the Father of fathers. We see a Dad who is all GOD and all Man—we see Jesus!

GOD SPEAKS: "Praise be to the God and Father of our Lord Jesus Christ, the Father of compassion and the God of all comfort," (2 Corinthians 1:3 NIV) You can praise Me with your whole heart. As you look through the pages of your life, you can know I have met all of your needs and then some.

WANDA'S PRAYER: And for that precious Father, we sing praises to Your name! You are so worthy—truly worthy to be praised.

March 28

TRUE HUSBANDMAN

"HUSBANDS, LOVE YOUR WIVES, JUST AS CHRIST ALSO LOVED THE CHURCH AND GAVE HIMSELF FOR HER, THAT HE MIGHT SANCTIFY AND CLEANSE HER WITH THE WASHING OF WATER BY THE WORD," (EPHESIANS 5:25-26 NKJV)

As I was writing about Hagar's life, the question as to whether she had a husband occurred to me. The answer is yes and yes. First, she had a human husband, Abraham. Sarai gave her as a surrogate second wife to her husband for procreation. (Genesis 16:3) That was a marriage of abuse from the pit of hell. She was a surrogate wife to be used at will. But when Hagar encountered the LORD OF GLORY in the Wilderness, this Holy union with her Maker left her singing all sorts of love songs. (Genesis 16:13-14) Heaven sanctions this marriage. She is His wife for life! Hagar's Maker showed her what a true Husband looks like. So, what does He look like? Hagar's LORD/Husband became a servant in that He met her needs. In their first wilderness meeting, "The Angel of the LORD found Hagar…" The implication is that He pursued after this woman. Of course, the LORD knew where she was; but the statement describes someone in pursuit with deep care and concern. The LORD loved Hagar, as He loved Himself, and as He gives Himself over to meet her needs. He takes time from the cares of a busy universe to talk with her and listen to her concerns. Her first husband, Abram, did no such thing. Also, he did not bother to send out any search and rescue to look for Hagar as he had done for his nephew Lot. The LORD/Husband cleansed her with His words. Those powerful words also brought comfort and trust to a weary soul. He took away the shame of abuse and the pain it brought. The Husband God says, "Name the child Ishmael, because I see your hurt and I've dealt with it." (Writer's paraphrase)

HAGAR AND US: Thanks Hagar, for showing us what a REAL Husband looks like; now we know what to look and pray for.

GOD SPEAKS: "For your Maker is your husband, The LORD of hosts is His name; And your Redeemer is the Holy One of Israel; He is called the God of the whole earth." (Isaiah 54:5 NKJV) You already know that everything said in this verse is true. Now, let My words have their home in you.

WANDA'S PRAYER: Thank you Father for reminding us again of Your wonderful love that never lets go.

March 29

ROCK TOWER

"THE NAME OF THE LORD IS A STRONG TOWER; THE RIGHTEOUS RUN TO IT AND ARE SAFE." (PROVERBS 18:10 NKJV) "…THE LORD IS MY ROCK AND MY FORTRESS AND MY DELIVERER;" (2 SAMUEL 22:2 NKJV)

From just one glance at Hagar's life, one can see the above verses are so very true. From birth, the Father surrounded Hagar with His arms of protection. He saw her through the years of slavery in Egypt and in the land of Canaan. But nothing is so striking as when the Father was with her through two wilderness experiences. Hagar's strong tower showed up in wonderful ways. While He is keeping her from physical harm, the Father deals with every other need and concern she has. In this way, GOD provides his daughter security from the inside out. Father God proved to be her Rock Tower when she needed Him the most. When she is cast out into the wilderness after thirteen years, with a son, the Heavenly Father is there to shield her with Himself. He reminds her of the precious promises He gave her thirteen years earlier. He opens her eyes and comforts her heart. He goes on to make a home for her in the desert and assumes the role of father to her son. The Rock of Ages was her foundation. He who formed Hagar in her mother's womb was her Rock Tower of care and protection in every aspect of her life.

HAGAR AND US: Hagar found Christ was her strong tower and in Him, she was very safe. I found that to be true as well. I see the wonderful fortress He has built to protect me. Thank You Lord! How about you? Has the God of Heaven been your Rock Tower? Let Him be your strong tower. Ask Him into your heart and life today.

GOD SPEAKS: "Then they remembered that God was their rock, and the Most High God their Redeemer." (Psalm 78:35 NKJV) Am I your Rock Tower? I would like to be.

WANDA'S PRAYER: Wanda's prayer is one of praise! "The God of my strength, in whom I will trust; My shield and the horn of my salvation, My stronghold and my refuge; My Savior, You save me from violence. I will call upon the LORD, who is worthy to be praised; So shall I be saved from my enemies." (2 Samuel 22:3-4 NKJV)

March 30

CHRIST'S FREEDOM

"BUT WHEN THE FULLNESS OF TIME HAD COME, GOD SENT FORTH HIS SON, BORN OF A WOMAN, BORN UNDER THE LAW, TO REDEEM THOSE WHO WERE UNDER THE LAW, THAT WE MIGHT RECEIVE THE ADOPTION AS SONS (CHILDREN)."
(GALATIANS 4:4-5 NKJV)

The Father saw Hagar before she was formed and destined her for greatness. From Creation, He knew how her life would speak volumes to us about our LORD'S goodness and mercy, for millenniums to come. Only the Creator GOD could have brought Hagar from slavery to being a "queen of women." She was the Grandmother of "twelve princes according to their nations." (Genesis 25:16). In the end, Hagar was set free from both her physical and spiritual bondage. Though Hagar was born in bondage, the beauty of her life is that we can now see how the God of Heaven gave her true freedom! This is the freedom our LORD wants to give us all. Hagar is a SLAVE NO MORE!

HAGAR AND US: Hagar's life is a beautiful illustration of being set free by Christ Jesus. As Hagar could no more deliver herself from bondage, neither can we. Before I came to Christ, I was in slavery also.

GOD SPEAKS: "So if the Son sets you free, you are truly free." (John 8:36 NLT) Every child of God is truly free.

WANDA'S PRAYER: I am Your child, and I am free! Thank You for paying the price for us all.

March 31

CHRIST THE GREAT EMANCIPATOR

"BUT THE SCRIPTURES DECLARE THAT WE ARE ALL PRISONERS OF SIN, SO WE RECEIVE GOD'S PROMISE OF FREEDOM ONLY BY BELIEVING IN JESUS CHRIST."
(GALATIANS 3:22 NLT)

Before Hagar was formed, the Father saw her and destined her for greatness. He knew from creation that she would speak volumes to us about our LORD'S goodness and mercy for millennia to come. Only a Creator GOD could have brought Hagar from slavery to being a princess of women. She was the grandmother of "12 princes according to their nations." (Genesis 25:16). In the end, Hagar was set free from her physical bondage. Her life, however, was used to illustrate a higher truth. This higher truth is that real freedom is never achieved through human efforts; it is only found in Jesus. Every day of my life, He stands before and offers me freedom in Him. There are days when I willingly accept it. Then there are other days when I feel I must do something to earn this freedom—to show my worthiness—to GOD; as if to say, "I've earned your goodness today!" WRONG! The person who the Son of GOD sets free, they are free indeed. (John 8:36) Abraham had two sons, one by a slave and one by a free woman. The slave woman's son came first—it was human invention—a flesh "thang." Hagar's son represents the good deeds I do to earn GOD'S favor. But without a relationship with the Father, it means nothing. Like Ishmael, Hagar's son, who was put out into the wilderness, my good deeds are put out of GOD'S sight. To the Father they are dirty rags and are of no use to Him. On the other hand, when I surrender my poor miserable self to my Dad for His use, great things happen. Unattainable feats are done. It is Christ in me—working His righteous acts in me, despite a very sinful me. This is what gets the job done and thus, Christ gets the glory. Hagar's life is a beautiful illustration of these principles. As Hagar could no more deliver herself from bondage—neither can I.

HAGAR AND US: All my life, I have been in bondage to my sharp tongue. I could slice your head off and serve it to you on a platter. I have tried to change and even tried fasting from speech. (It lasted about five minutes). Now, in looking at Hagar's story, I see I must serve myself up to Jesus—go under His knife, and allow Him to cut away this sin.

GOD SPEAKS: "I appeal to you therefore, brethren, and beg of you in view of [all] the mercies of God, to make a decisive dedication of your bodies [presenting all your members and faculties] as a living sacrifice, holy (devoted, consecrated) and well pleasing to God, which is your reasonable (rational, intelligent) service and spiritual worship." (Romans 12:1 AMPC) With no questions asked, just give Me all of you! You know that I only have your perfect good in mind. Now, just leave your tongue and every other body part to the Master surgeon.

WANDA'S PRAYER: LORD, have your complete way in me; I surrender mine to You.

Notes

April

INTRODUCTION

REBEKAH

Rebekah is a close relative of Sarah and Abraham, and will be the wife to their son Isaac.

Rebekah's life offers us a clear choice of which nature we will choose. We can choose faithful obedience to the God of heaven and receive life, or we can choose a self-serving nature of our flesh, which brings death. As we journey through Rebekah's life, we must decide which we will choose.

The legacy Rebekah's early life leaves for us is a true representation of what a godly wife should be. She is a standard among women. She so beautifully answered the call. Leaving all behind, she surrendered completely to the will of the Father, and traveled a great distance to become Isaac's wife. Rebekah also shows me that when I am in the center of the Father's will, He will do miraculous things in my life for His glory. She shows me that submission need not be a dirty word. It is a wonderful word of trust and complete reliance on the All-Knowing and All-Powerful God of the Universe. In looking at her life, I see how the LORD Himself was her husband—before He gave her an earthly man. Rebekah teaches me that in every area of my life, I must seek the LORD for His perfect will—His answers to my problems and difficult questions. When I do as she did, as in the case of when she was pregnant with her sons (Genesis 25:22-23), the Father will be as real to me as I need Him to be. She also shows me the tragedies of going my own way without God. In the case of deceiving her husband, she lost both of her sons. This tells me that without the Perfect Dad's guidance, I lose, and the loss is very great. Finally, this woman of God shows me the Father in Heaven will ultimately take care of me. He restored her relationship with her husband, and they were entombed together. Though not in her lifetime, the LORD also reconciled her son's strained relationship.

Notes

April 1

WRONG PLACE

"...PUT YOUR HAND UNDER MY THIGH. I WANT YOU TO SWEAR BY THE LORD, THE GOD OF HEAVEN AND THE GOD OF EARTH, THAT YOU WILL NOT GET A WIFE FOR MY SON FROM THE DAUGHTERS OF THE CANAANITES, AMONG WHOM I AM LIVING." (GENESIS 24:2-3 NIV)

The old patriarch Abraham has buried the wife of his life, Sarah. Genesis 24:1 says, "… the LORD had blessed him in every way." As Abraham looked back over his life, he realized the Father had totally taken care of him. Now the time had come for him to care for his son, Isaac. First, he would find Isaac a wife. The monumental task was done with much forethought and planning on Abraham's part. He knew that "Unless the LORD builds the house, They labor in vain who build it; …" (Psalm 127:1 NKJV). As he did in many aspects of his life, he trusted the LORD'S leading in this situation. He says as much to the chief servant in the above text. Abraham also knew the neighborhood women in Canaan were not the right women for his son. Abraham was looking for a suitable helper as a bride for his forty-year-old son, Isaac. Having lived around the Canaanites more than half of his life, he was well aware of their evil ways and practices. Father Abraham knew there was nothing suitable about these women. So, he commissioned his chief servant not to choose a wife from the Canaanites. Though they inhabited the same land, the world of Abraham and the world of the Canaanites were millions of miles apart. The Canaanites were carnal and worldly; with only thoughts of satisfying the craving of their flesh. Abraham sought for a Heavenly city, whose builder and maker was GOD. He knew that marriage was hard enough under the best of circumstances. More importantly, he also knew that being unequally yoked would make a difficult marriage an impossible one.

REBEKAH AND US: If you have known the difficulties of being in an unequally yoked, failed marriage, you are well aware of its heartaches and pain. I suffered such a fate, and it left me clinging to the LORD. I knew I was not wise enough to pick the next one. To find my next husband, I had to turn to Christ, and not look to Canaan (the world). I would have to totally rely upon the LORD and His Word. I certainly did not want to make that mistake again.

GOD SPEAKS: "Can two walk together, unless they are agreed?" (Amos 3:3 NKJV) I know what is best for you. Bring every decision of your life to Me. I will lead and guide you onto the right paths. Come walk with Me and agree.

WANDA'S PRAYER: Father, keep us in the hollow of your hands. Help us to give you every decision in life; big and small. Teach us to know that Your love for us has our best interest at heart.

April 2

THE FATHER'S WISDOM

"BUT YOU SHALL GO TO MY COUNTRY AND TO MY FAMILY, AND TAKE A WIFE FOR MY SON ISAAC." (GENESIS 24:4 NKJV)

There are interesting similarities between the preparation for the "wives to be" Eve and Rebekah. Their fathers-to-be provided very well for these would be brides prior to their arrival. The Garden of Eden, Eve's perfect paradise home, was created before she was. (Genesis 1-2) Abraham did not do too badly either with his provisions for Rebekah. He was blessed in all things; Rebekah would lack for nothing upon her arrival to Canaan. I also noticed how Father GOD and father Abraham both wanted the life partner for their sons to be closely related. God used one of Adam's own ribs to make his bride. Father Abraham did the next best thing for Isaac's wife. She would come from Isaac's own family. Isaac's wife would be from his "genetic rib." Since she came from Abraham's family, they would be related. You could say Rebekah was, genetically speaking, "bone of Isaac's bone and flesh of his flesh." Last, both fathers (God and Abraham), did not need or desire input from their sons as to the choosing of suitable mates for them. This speaks volumes about the Father's idea of marriage. The lessons are: Look for someone who has their house in order; especially financially. As I am a child of God, it is only logical that my spouse should also be a child of God. In other words, if I am a Christian, I should marry a Christian, "like with like." Abraham understood these principles and thus commissioned his chief servant to go to "his country and take a wife for his son."

REBEKAH AND US: The parallels are crystal clear. Marriage, the Lord's way, is man and woman walking in close harmony. The man and his wife are from the same spiritual tribe. That tribe is Christ.

GOD SPEAKS: "Then the rib which the LORD God had taken from man He made into a woman, and He brought her to the man. And Adam said: 'This is now bone of my bones And flesh of my flesh; She shall be called Woman, Because she was taken out of Man.' Therefore a man shall leave his father and mother and be joined to his wife, and they shall become one flesh." (Genesis 2:22-24 NKJV) My original design for marriage is a oneness of mind and purpose. In the middle of the "oneness" is Me.

WANDA'S PRAYER: Father GOD, we give ourselves to You. LORD GOD, keep us in the hollow of your hand and in the center of Your will, for our lives. Bless our marriages, and may they also be in the center of Your will.

April 3

WILLING HEART

"THE SERVANT SAID TO HIM, 'SUPPOSE THE WOMAN IS NOT WILLING TO FOLLOW ME TO THIS LAND; SHOULD I TAKE YOUR SON BACK TO THE LAND FROM WHERE YOU CAME?' THEN ABRAHAM SAID TO HIM, 'BEWARE THAT YOU DO NOT TAKE MY SON BACK THERE!'" (GENESIS 24:5-6 NASB)

I was told of a very eligible, elderly gentleman who once remarked as to why he had married none of the many women which flooded his life. His answer was, "there are many women, but very few wives." As we continue to look at Abraham's trek to find a wife for Isaac, we see two qualities reign supreme. First, she had to be in the family; and second, possess a willing heart. She must be willing to leave all behind and follow his son in marriage. Abraham was adamant; his son must not leave the land of promise to follow his bride, she must be willing to follow his leading. Now, before I get beaten up by every woman on the planet for reducing women to mindless robots, just hear me out. Abraham and Isaac were men after GOD'S heart. "The LORD, the GOD of heaven, who took me from my father's house and from the land of my birth, and who spoke to me…" (Genesis 24:7 NASB). Ladies, the men you want as husbands are those who HEAR AND FOLLOW after GOD'S heart. **You will know because he follows God's Word.** Abraham made every provision for his son's wife in the way of earthly comfort and financial security. In return, he looks for a wife to rest in these provisions and trust him. The fruit of that trust is a willing heart to follow. The analogy of Abraham to Christ is striking. Jesus offers every woman (and man) a chance to be his bride. He has lavished His love on us on this planet, and is preparing a beautiful eternity for us. In return, He asks us to follow Him.

REBEKAH AND US: Rebekah was getting a good deal in return for what she would have to give up. What our LORD asks us to give up for Him is so small, compared to what we will receive.

GOD SPEAKS: "If you are willing and obedient, You shall eat the good of the land; But if you refuse and rebel, You shall be devoured by the sword; …" (Isaiah 1:19-20 NKJV) You have the capacity to choose love, and serve Me freely. Will you choose Me as your LORD and Savior?

WANDA'S PRAYER: A thousand times, YES LORD! Fill us with Your Spirit, and energize us to walk after your will. Help us spend time with You daily, learning of You.

April 4

A GOD THING

"THE LORD GOD OF HEAVEN, WHO TOOK ME FROM MY FATHER'S HOUSE AND FROM THE LAND OF MY FAMILY, AND WHO SPOKE TO ME AND SWORE TO ME, SAYING, 'TO YOUR DESCENANTS I WILL GIVE THIS LAND,' HE WILL SEND HIS ANGEL BEFORE YOU, AND YOUR SHALL TAKE A WIFE FOR MY SON THERE."
(GENESIS 24:7 NKJV)

Abraham knows that this "wife finding" venture must be God-led and God-directed. In short, it is a "God thing." As He sends his servant to find a wife for his son Isaac, he is totally relying on God to work out all the details. Just prior to sending his servant back to his homeland to find Isaac's bride, Abraham says, "… He (the LORD) will send His angel before you, and you SHALL take a wife for my son there." (Genesis 24:7) At 140 years old, Abraham has seen GOD do so many wonders in his life. The crowning act was when God asked him to sacrifice his son (Isaac); and then at the last moment the LORD provided a ram in the bush. (Genesis 22) At this point in the old patriarch's life, he is certain the LORD could and would provide a bride for Isaac and he gives this assurance to his chief servant as he dispatches him. Abraham completely trusts his LORD. This story speaks volumes to us. From Rebekah's perspective, all of this was done without her input. The application for us is clear. Father God loves us supremely and always has our best interest at heart. We like Rebekah can rest in that love. Our only job is to follow His leading through trust and obedience.

REBEKAH AND US: Like Rebekah, GOD does not need us in His face dictating to Him the kind of man we need to make us happy. Our lives are given over to Him. He knows us intimately and is very aware of our needs and wants. He just wants our obedience as the Bride of Christ. We are to follow as He instructs us through His Word (the Bible) and His Holy Spirit. Then leave the details of the job of finding a mate up to Him.

GOD SPEAKS: "For I know the thoughts that I think toward you, says the LORD, thoughts of peace and not of evil, to give you a future and a hope. Then you will call upon Me and go and pray to Me, and I will listen to you." (Jeremiah 29:11-12 NKJV) Notice how Rebekah's love story starts with the LORD of love. This story is not how a man loves a woman, but it is how much the GOD of the universe loves mankind. It is as if the LORD was saying on each page, "I love you."

WANDA'S PRAYER: Father, never let us forget the tender love You have for us.

April 5

WHAT'S IN YOUR WALLET!

"THEN THE SERVANT LEFT, TAKING WITH HIM TEN OF HIS MASTER'S CAMELS LOADED WITH ALL KINDS OF GOOD THINGS FROM HIS MASTER..."
(GENESIS 24:10 NIV)

It is probably safe to say that Abraham's marriage to Sarah lasted many decades. He was one hundred and thirty-seven years old when she died. Based on that analysis, it is also safe to say he knew what would turn a girl's head and the head of her father. Leaving nothing to chance and wanting to impress the "would-be Mrs. Isaac," Abraham opened the vault and sent a small fortune with his chief servant. He sends ten camels with "all kinds of good things from his master." He would spare no expense to win the hand of "Ms. Right" for Isaac. Our Heavenly Father shows love like this to us as well. He spared no expense in giving us Heaven's best—His Son, Jesus. In giving us His spotless Son, Father GOD opened the Heavenly Bank of Glory, to lavish upon us a blessing, which we did not have room enough to receive.

REBEKAH AND US: Rebekah had no idea what was in store for her. The father of the promised son was preparing an oasis in the desert for his would-be daughter-in-law. Like Rebekah, our Father is preparing for us a home in glory land which will outshine the sun. This place is filled with riches untold, and we will walk on streets of gold. He will clothe us in His beautiful robe of righteousness. Unlike Rebekah, the Son of the Everlasting Father will Himself come for me, and not send one of His servants.

GOD SPEAKS: "But as it is written: 'eye has not seen, nor ear heard, Nor have entered into the heart of man The things which God has prepared for those who love him.'" (1 Corinthians 2:9 NKJV) The things I have prepared just for you is mind-blowing!

WANDA'S PRAYER: Father, we thank You for what you have already given us: Perfect, unwavering love to start. You also provide food, shelter, health, husband, kids, job, finances, and the list goes on and on. Help us show our appreciation to You, in how we walk before you.

April 6

SEEK GOD FIRST

"AND HE (ABRAHAM'S CHIEF SERVANT) MADE HIS CAMELS KNEEL DOWN OUTSIDE THE CITY (NAHOR) BY A WELL OF WATER AT EVENING TIME, THE TIME WHEN WOMEN GO OUT TO DRAW WATER. THEN HE SAID, 'O LORD GOD OF MY MASTER ABRAHAM, PLEASE GIVE ME SUCCESS THIS DAY, AND SHOW KINDNESS TO MY MASTER ABRAHAM.'" (GENESIS 24:11-12 NKJV)

This is a beautiful illustration of how the effect of a true godly man can have on his entire household. The chief servant is praying to his master's God for direction. This servant has watched the life of his master. Abraham's life, though not perfect, but a believer in God, speaks volumes to this servant. So much so that even in being many miles away from his master, the servant prays to his master's God. The servant saw this as God's mission; and would therefore seek God's perfect leading. Isaac's wife would be the one the LORD would provide.

REBEKAH AND US: Unlike the above situation, how often have I gone my own way and made bad choices, without ever consulting the All-Knowing God first. The funny thing is, I know so much better. On those occasions when I did consult the All-Wise God first (they used to be rare, but I have gotten much better now), He provided for me in wonderful ways I had never dreamed of

GOD SPEAKS: "I call on you, my God, for you will answer me; turn your ear to me and hear my prayer." (Psalm 17:6 NIV) You daughters are My precious children; and I (your LORD), cannot wait to hear from you! Now come to Me and pour out your heart. I am waiting for you.

WANDA'S PRAYER: Thank You, Father, for loving us with Your forever love. Forgive us for all our sins and shortcomings. Teach us to seek You always and in every way. We know Your ways are the best!

April 7

A REQUEST

"THEN HE PRAYED, 'LORD, GOD … MAY IT BE THAT WHEN I SAY TO A YOUNG WOMAN, 'PLEASE LET DOWN YOUR JAR THAT I MAY HAVE A DRINK,' AND SHE SAYS, 'DRINK, AND I'LL WATER YOUR CAMELS TOO'—LET HER BE THE ONE YOU HAVE CHOSEN FOR YOUR SERVANT ISAAC..."
(GENESIS 24:12-14 NIV)

Abraham's servant took his task of finding a wife for Isaac very seriously. He knew he had no way of determining who would make a good wife. So, He remembered the two things his master told him: (1) The LORD GOD would "send His angel before you, so that you can get a wife for my son from there." (2) The woman must have a willing spirit; thus symbolizing a submitting heart. With these two things in mind, the servant believes and prays to the GOD of Heaven. He thinks of a test to show him which woman would demonstrate a servant's heart. This servant sees His master's God, as a God who can do massive things. This was no small request. This man had ten camels. One camel can hold up to one hundred gallons of water. This man had traveled well over two-hundred miles over desert terrain. Translation—there were a lot of hot, thirsty camels and Rebekah would be carrying a lot of water jugs. Here is a clear lesson we can learn from these verses. We must trust that God sends his angels before us in every situation to answer our prayers. Also, more than anything, He wants our complete surrender to His leading. We see this through our obedience to His commands. Considering all He has done; the cost is not too high.

REBEKAH AND US: For most of my life, I thought submission, especially in marriage, was a dirty word. I remember once telling my ex-husband, "I'll submit, if you will love me, and love yourself." Needless to say, our marriage did not go very far. I am happy to report that twenty years later… I am still learning the art of submission, as I put it into practice.

GOD SPEAKS: "But seek first his kingdom and his righteousness, and all these things will be given to you as well." (Matthew 6:33 NIV) The operative words in that phrase are HIS (MY) Kingdom and HIS (MY) righteousness. I, your LORD, and Savior can say this because I AM, All-Knowing, and I AM, All-Powerful. On this you can trust—submit to Me.

WANDA'S PRAYER: Father, help us to "trust in You with all of our heart, and to not lean to our own understanding; but in all our ways acknowledge You, and let You direct our paths." (Proverbs 3:5-6)

April 8

INSTANT ANSWER

"BEFORE HE HAD FINISHED PRAYING, REBEKAH CAME OUT WITH HER JAR ON HER SHOULDER. SHE WAS THE DAUGHTER OF BETHUEL SON OF MILKAH, WHO WAS THE WIFE OF ABRAHAM'S BROTHER NAHOR." (GENESIS 24:15 NIV)

Often times the Father asks us to wait on Him for answers to prayer; but sometimes, as in this case, our prayers may be answered instantly. The servant must have been amazed. The LORD responded to his prayer at lightning speed. The Father did not just answer one prayer; He fulfilled the complete request in Rebekah. Abraham did not just want a wife from the people of his homeland; he specifically wanted the wife to come from his brother's family. The servant did not have a photo of Nahor or his family; how would he find the right girl? Also, remember, this was the time when women of the town would go out to draw water (Genesis 24:11). So, Rebekah would be just one of the many women in town. What were the chances of her standing before the servant with a water jug in hand? The chances were slim to none. This is a testament that nothing is too hard for the LORD our GOD. Rebekah comes out and follows the script flawlessly. The servant made his requests to Rebekah (verse 17) and with the graciousness of a southern bell; she is more than happy to fulfill his request (verses 18-20). In looking at this story, we see how GOD'S timing, plus our obedience, equals our blessings. The Father's timing is always perfect, and we receive His blessings when we obey.

REBEKAH AND US: Rebekah is to be admired. It is one thing to give a cup of water to a stranger, but to agree to give water to ten camels! Boy, did she hit a home run with the LORD.

GOD SPEAKS: "… There is only One who is good. If you want to enter life, keep the commandments." (Matthew 19:17 NIV) "If you love me, obey my commandments." (John 14:15 NLT) Dead Christians are disobedient Christians. Did you say you love me? Then just do what I tell you to do. Look in My Word and seek me out—I will reveal Myself to you.

WANDA'S PRAYER: Lord, give me a heart, hands, and feet to obey You.

April 9

WEIGHT IN GOLD

"WHEN THE CAMELS HAD FINISHED DRINKING, THE MAN TOOK OUT A GOLD NOSE RING WEIGHING A BEKA AND TWO GOLD BRACELETS WEIGHING TEN SHEKELS." (GENESIS 24: 22 NIV)

The servant of Abraham sat quietly, watching as Rebekah gave water to his camels. He wanted to know for sure if this was the LORD, making his journey a successful one. (verse 21). As he watched this woman go back-and-forth pouring water in the trough for the camels, he must have marveled at her energy and diligence to her task. He did not hear a complaining word grace those beautiful lips about the job she had signed on for. Rebekah did not waste much needed energy on that; she just did what she had to do. She certainly was not expecting the handsome reward she received. No, she was simply performing her duty and a simple thank you might have sufficed. So impressed by her work performance, the servant gave Rebekah a nose ring weighing a Beka, and two gold bracelets, weighing ten shekels. Based on today's calculations, a Beka is ½ shekel, or a little over five grams of gold (1/4 ounce). The bracelets weighed roughly fifty ounces in gold. That was a lot of gold in that day, and in this one! She may have earned a year's wage in one day; but Rebekah was worth every "Beka." The rewards our Heavenly Husband and Father wants to give us may not be monetary. Yet, the rewards from our obedience to Him are worth far more than their weight in gold, and are longer lasting. He has prepared a Heaven for those who love and obey Him.

REBEKAH AND US: Two things stand out in this story. First, as Christians, we are being watched to see if our walk matches our talk. Rebekah agreed and watered all the camels without complaint. Second, Rebekah shows us how hard work can produce great rewards. Always keep in mind that we are a work in progress. Our Lord wants to do wonderful things in and through us.

GOD SPEAKS: "Now to Him who is able to do exceedingly abundantly above all that we ask or think, according to the power that works in us," (Ephesians 3:20 NKJV) I have brought you a long way. I started this good work in you, and I will see it through to completion. (Philippians 1:6) Do you believe that?

WANDA'S PRAYER: LORD, we believe… please help our unbelief. Father, may we continue to grow in You. Help us display our love to You, by living a life of obedience and complete surrender to Your plans.

April 10

WHO YO' PEOPLE?

"THEN HE ASKED, 'WHOSE DAUGHTER ARE YOU? PLEASE TELL ME, IS THERE ROOM IN YOUR FATHER'S HOUSE FOR US TO SPEND THE NIGHT?'" (GENESIS 24:23 NIV)

I grew up in a time and place that when you met pleasant strangers, one of the first questions asked was, "who yo' people be?" You wanted to know if you were "kinfolk"—related to them in some way. Another reason for asking about each other's relatives was because you saw in each other something attractive or likeable in character. I believe this was the case in Abraham's servant's question when he asked Rebekah, "Whose daughter are you?" Rebekah had displayed such poise and charm as she performed her duties for this man. In essence, the servant was saying, "Lady, I would really love to meet the father that produced this kind of Godly daughter." The question can also be asked of us, "How well do we represent our Heavenly Father?" When others see our work and manner toward our daily tasks, does it invite them to want to meet Him? Or do we show that we have another father—the devil? Look back at the text with me (Genesis 24:17-20). The man asks for a drink of water. Rebekah gives him the utmost respect by calling him "lord" or sir. She quickly gives him a drink. Then she offers to draw water for his camels. Verse 20 says, "She quickly emptied her jar into the trough, ran back to the well to draw more water, and drew enough for all (ten) of his camels". The man sat in silence, taking in the beauty of Rebekah's grace in motion. It must have been a sight to behold.

REBEKAH AND US: Though Rebekah had outward beauty, her most impressive beauty was her inward character. The beauty of her character is what really impressed Abraham's servant, who was "wife shopping." What beauty are you putting on display?

GOD SPEAKS: "Charm is deceptive, and beauty is fleeting; but a woman who fears the Lord is to be praised." (Proverbs 31:30 NIV) External beauty is great but fleeing; internal beauty is Eternal. That Is what the Eternal God is after.

WANDA'S PRAYER: Father, teach us how to live for You. Fill us with Your Spirit so that others who do not know You will become part of the Family of GOD.

April 11

PRAISE TIME!

"THEN THE MAN BOWED DOWN AND WORSHIPED THE LORD, SAYING, 'PRAISE BE TO THE LORD, THE GOD OF MY MASTER ABRAHAM, WHO HAS NOT ABANDONED HIS KINDNESS AND FAITHFULNESS TO MY MASTER. AS FOR ME, THE LORD HAS LED ME ON THE JOURNEY TO THE HOUSE OF MY MASTER'S RELATIVES.'"
(GENESIS 24:26-27 NIV)

Have you ever had a set of God-led circumstances that worked perfectly? This was that kind of situation. It was like listening to a symphony; every note played in perfect pitch, at just the right time. In Genesis 24:24, Rebekah answers the question about her relative. She tells the man that she is Abraham's great niece; Milcah (Abraham's sister-in-law), is her grandmother. A little earlier, in Genesis 24:3-4, you will recall how these were the very instructions Abraham gave to his servant. In giving these instructions, he assured the servant that God would send His angel before him, so that he can get a wife for Isaac. (Latter part of Genesis 24:7) The Heavenly Father worked out every detail with exact precision. The servant is astounded as he observes deity in action. This man's faith went from infancy to adult faith in one afternoon. The only thing left to do was just go crazy with praise to the LORD; and that is just what he did.

REBEKAH AND US: God used Rebekah as an instrument of praise. Through her great act of kindness in giving the servant and his ten camels' water, God's love and tender care was wonderfully seen. Our Lord would like us all to display this kind of care and compassion to the strangers we meet.

GOD SPEAKS: "Praise the Lord, all his heavenly Hosts, you His servants who do His will." (Psalm 103:21 NIV) Will you be my servant, and do My will?

WANDA'S PRAYER: Father, we want to be one of Your servants. Help us do Your wonderful will.

April 12

MI CASA, SU CASA

"COME, YOU WHO ARE BLESSED BY THE LORD," HE SAID. "WHY ARE YOU STANDNG OUT HERE? I HAVE PREPARED THE HOUSE AND A PLACE FOR THE CAMELS." (GENESIS 24:31 NIV)

Rebekah's brother, Laban, comes and extends hospitality to Abraham's servant. The servant could see the hand of the LORD working in this entire situation. He would receive royal treatment. Even the camels were treated well. From this regal treatment he received at Nahor's home (Rebekah's father), it was clear this beautiful fruit (called Rebekah) came from a lovely tree. Why was the regal treatment given to a servant? Because of whom his master was! This was Abraham's servant, and this gave him not just access, but special favor. Abraham was Nahor's brother. Nahor was the head of the clan. So, a special envoy of Abraham would be very welcomed by his brother's family. This story imperfectly reflects our relationship with Father God. We are children of God because we now have access to Him, through His Son, Jesus. Our sins created an impassable gulf between Him and us; a gulf that could never be breached through any efforts of our own. We needed a Savior. The LORD Jesus, through His spotless life and sacrificial death, was the only ACCEPTABLE payment for our sins. Now we can come boldly before the Father of Heaven. We have direct access into His throne room. I can come before Him with praise, ask for forgiveness, and place at the feet of God of the Universe, my every need and care. Jesus, my LORD, gave me access to all of these riches and promised more to come.

REBEKAH AND US: Rebekah has a lovely family. From a human standpoint, it is the best. But the family Jesus has given us through a new birth in Him is so much better. Our Dad owns everything and His love for us is beyond anything we could ever understand. His dwelling in us gives us qualities to love and serve, just as Rebekah did. When our earthly life is over, He has already prepared an eternity for us to be with Him forever!

GOD SPEAKS: "Don't let your hearts be troubled. Trust in God, and trust also in me. There is more than enough room in my Father's home. If this were not so, would I have told you that I am going to prepare a place for you? When everything is ready, I will come and get you, so that you will always be with me where I am." (John 14:1-3 NLT) I need you to believe this statement with your entire heart. Allow Me to live in you now, by way of My Holy Spirit. We start now—you and I—to spend an eternity together, forever!

WANDA'S PRAYER: Father, thank You for your wonderful and perfect love You have for us. Come now and always live in us forever. Help us live as You please.

April 13

TESTIMONY

"SO HE SAID, 'I AM ABRAHAM'S SERVANT. THE LORD HAS BLESSED MY MASTER ABUNDANTLY,…'
THEN I PUT THE RING IN HER NOSE AND THE BRACELETS ON HER ARMS, AND I BOWED DOWN
AND WORSHIPED THE LORD. I PRAISED THE LORD, THE GOD OF MY MASTER ABRAHAM, WHO
HAD LED ME ON THE RIGHT ROAD TO GET THE GRANDDAUGHTER OF MY MASTER'S BROTHER
FOR HIS SON."
(GENESIS 24:34-48 NIV)

In Genesis 24:34-48, the servant of Abraham gives his testimony of how the LORD, so lavishly blessed him. He starts out telling of his master, Abraham; and how Father God had greatly blessed him. He mentions some of Abraham's wealth, and talks about the master's family. The servant continues by recounting the oath he made to Abraham. The story becomes a tearjerker when he tells how Father God so graciously answered his prayer in Rebekah. He speaks of how he prayed a simple prayer to God, and how the answer came in such a beautiful package. Rebekah displayed beauty from the inside out, through her very generous acts to him and the animals. When he found out she was from the same clan as his master, he was certain the LORD had more than answered his prayers. Just reading the story, I can hear and feel the passionate gratitude of this man to Father God, and of the blessing he received on his trip.

REBEKAH AND US: I am sure Rebekah was touched by the servant's testimony and may have cried a tear or two. She was to be the blessing in his life. Reflect on your life and ask yourself how you have been, or can be, a blessing in the lives of those around you.

GOD SPEAKS: "I have testimony weightier than that of John. For the works that the Father has given me to finish—the very works that I am doing—testify that the Father has sent me." (John 5:36 NIV) Your works, good or bad, are your testimony; they speak volumes to others in your world.

WANDA'S PRAYER: Help us speak for You, LORD, in how we live our lives.

April 14

CHOOSE

"NOW IF YOU WILL SHOW KINDNESS AND FAITH FULNESS TO MY MASTER, TELL ME; AND IF NOT, TELL ME, SO I MAY KNOW WHICH WAY TO TURN." (GENESIS 24:49 NIV)

After having given his testimony to Rebekah's family about how and why he had come to their town, the servant of Abraham now pops the question. Will Rebekah be the wife of his master, Isaac? The choice is presented to Rebekah's family. Will they, as a family, display God's "kindness and faithfulness to Abraham?" This part of the story shows us we are all presented with a choice to choose the LORD'S WAYS or not. Notice there is no forcing here. Our LORD is not the God of force. But choices must be made, and we do not have forever to make them. The servant says, "Tell me; and if not, tell me; so that I may know which way to turn." In other words, "It is your choice (family) and only you can make it. But remember, your choice will determine what other choices will be made." Rebekah's family responds with a "Yes!" "This is from the LORD; we can say nothing to you one way or the other. Here is Rebekah; take her and go, and let her become the wife of your master's son, as the LORD has directed." (Genesis 24:50-51) The servant's response is classic; he bows and worships the LORD! Father God may that be my response to You and Your blessings. After worshiping the LORD, it was time to get down to business. The servant pulled out the costly gifts of gold and silver for Rebekah. Girlfriend would know that wherever she was going, and whoever he was, he had lots of money and she would be very well cared for. She could "bank" on this. He also gave costly gifts to her brother and mother.

REBEKAH AND US: Rebekah's family shows us what a loving LORD we have. He wants to shower great and wonderful blessings on us. But these blessing are never forced. Our LORD'S blessing are "time sensitive." We must choose "yes or no."

GOD SPEAKS: "And if it seems evil to you to serve the Lord, choose for yourselves this day whom you will serve, … But as for me and my house, we will serve the Lord." (Joshua 24:15 NKJV)

WANDA'S PRAYER: Father, I choose Your Son Jesus, as my LORD. Thank You for giving us that choice so many years ago, and for giving us the choice to daily spend time with You.

April 15

"YES" HAS PRIVILEGES

"THEN THE SERVANT BROUGHT OUT JEWELRY OF SILVER, JEWELRY OF GOLD, AND CLOTHING, AND GAVE THEM TO REBEKAH. HE ALSO GAVE PRECIOUS THINGS TO HER BROTHER AND TO HER MOTHER." (GENESIS 24:53 NJKV)

On receiving a response of "yes" from the family that Rebekah would become Isaac's wife, the gifts came "pouring out" from the servant. He opens his treasure chest and showers Rebekah, who had already received gifts shortly after watering the camels. Now she receives even more gifts! She gets more gold and silver, plus clothing too. Her family, mom and brother also received gifts. Saying "yes" surely had its privileges in this case. Father Abraham certainly knew how to give good gifts to those who said yes to him. Spiritually and sometime physically, this is a small illustration of what our Heavenly Father wants to do for those who say "yes" to Him. He would love nothing more than to open the windows of Heaven and pour out gifts to us—gifts too big to be received.

REBEKAH AND US: Rebekah shows us that while living a life of integrity has a lot of challenges, saying "yes" to God's will, can have great rewards. What rewards have you received when you said "yes" to the LORD?

GOD SPEAKS: "Yes, Lord," she told him. "I have always believed you are the Messiah, the Son of God, the one who has come into the world from God." (John 11:27 NLT)

WANDA'S PRAYER: Father God, help us show You we believe You, by doing what You ask us to do.

April 16

BLESSINGS

"AND THEY BLESSED REBEKAH AND SAID TO HER, 'OUR SISTER, MAY YOU INCREASE TO THOUSANDS UPON THOUSANDS; MAY YOUR OFFSPRING POSSESS THE CITIES OF THEIR ENEMIES.'" (GENESIS 24:60 NIV)

Rebekah was going to Isaac with much wealth and fanfare; but the family knew something was missing. Before her final parting from her family, they wanted to make sure she received it. The precious commodity Rebekah needed more than anything else was the blessings of her LORD. This gift would keep on giving and was something she could not leave home without. So, they blessed their sister with a wonder blessing. They spoke wonderful words of prosperity regarding having children and victory over her enemies. They could not have known how prophetic these words were. Through her lineage would come the nation of Israel, and through that nation would come the CHRIST, the Savior of the world. Rebekah's family would give her the 'gold card' of life—they would give her the Father. He would always love and protect her. This just goes to show how very important prayer is in every aspect of life. We must always lift others up to the LORD in prayer.

REBEKAH AND US: We too have godly prayers that are continually prayed over us. Jesus is in Heaven right now, offering up prayers and interceding for us to Father God. And we KNOW the Father listens to His Son.

GOD SPEAKS: "Praise be to the God and Father of our Lord Jesus Christ, who has blessed us in the heavenly realms with every spiritual blessing in Christ." (Ephesians 1:3 NIV)

WANDA'S PRAYER: Father, thank you for all Your blessings in our lives. Live through us, the kind of life, You want others to see.

April 17

SURRENDERED BRIDE!

"THEN REBEKAH AND HER ATTENDANTS (MAIDS) GOT READY AND MOUNTED THE CAMELS AND WENT BACK WITH THE MAN. SO THE SERVANT TOOK REBEKAH AND LEFT." (GENESIS 24:61 NIV)

Rebekah's parting must have been a very touching scene. This bride-to-be and her family were aware this would probably be the last time they would see each other. I did some crude estimation of the distance from Ur, Abraham's homeland, to where he currently lived, which was somewhere near Bethel. If I am correct, the one-way trip was well over a thousand miles. Now, that is nothing for today's airlines and ocean liners, but on a camel? Now, that was quite a different story. I am sure that there was much crying on everyone's part about Rebekah's departure. After all, she was leaving the only family and lifestyle she had ever known to go and marry a wealthy stranger. She had no clue what was in store for her. Doubts must have entered her mind. What if he was weird or evil? It was not like she could catch the next camel going back to Ur. Should she trust her heart? NO! NO! A thousand times NO! What she, you, and I must rely on are God's words and His Spirit. The two will match up. What was God's word to Rebekah? "Laban and Bethuel answered, 'This (word) is from the LORD...'" The Heavenly Father had spoken to her earthly father words of confirmation. The Holy Spirit quieted Rebekah's spirit, as He spoke to her heart the same confirming words. Her final answer was, "I will go." She was in the Father's perfect will, and He would take ultimate responsibility for her care. Rebekah's submission was to her Heavenly Father; that surrender was demonstrated in how she fully obeyed Him in this circumstance.

REBEKAH AND US: We may never travel on a thousand-mile, one-way journey to meet our future spouse. However, our journey in this life is one-way, with few opportunities for a do-over. Like Rebekah, we experience the fear of leaving the familiar. As Christians, like Rebekah, we have the same LORD and His Word (the Bible), that we too can trust. And, of course, we have His Holy Spirit to confirm His words and to guide us.

GOD SPEAKS: "Surrender yourself to the LORD, and wait patiently for him. Do not be preoccupied with an evildoer who succeeds in his way when he carries out his schemes." (Psalm 37:7 GW) I am asking you to follow my instructions and My leading. Remember, your submission is important to Me.

WANDA'S PRAYER: Father, help us honor Your Word, and to know that we can fully surrender to You; being confident that You will do what is absolutely best for us.

April 18

THE HUSBAND

"AND ISAAC CAME FROM THE WAY OF THE WELL LAHAI–ROI; FOR HE DWELT IN THE SOUTH COUNTRY. AND ISAAC WENT OUT TO MEDITATE IN THE FIELD AT THE EVENTIDE: AND HE LIFTED UP HIS EYES, AND SAW, AND, BEHOLD, THE CAMELS WERE COMING." (GENESIS 24:62-63 KJV)

You can tell the heart of a man by where he spends his time. Rebekah's future husband, Isaac, is found at the Well Lahai-Roi. This special place is where Hagar met "The-God-Who-Sees-Me;" and where she gave the name "Beer Lahai-Roi" meaning, "I have seen the One who sees me." (Genesis 16:13-14) What is Rebekah's future husband doing here? He is meditating or communing with God. The Hebrew word for meditate is "Hagah," pronounced "haw-gaw." The words mean to ponder: to mourn, mutter, roar, study, talk, and to utter. Isaac could have been doing any or all of those things with his LORD. The operative words is that Isaac is found in the presence of his LORD. That is the kind of husband Rebekah was getting—a man who knew how to spend time, cry out, and commune with his LORD. It is also worth mentioning that Isaac is at home, surrendering his all to his GOD. He was the one Father Abraham was about to sacrifice on the altar, at God's request. He allowed his father to tie him down and raise the knife to slay him. (Genesis 22:1-13) This godly man was to be Rebekah's husband.

REBEKAH AND US: Rebekah's husband was a man after God's heart. Even now, he is seeking God's face. Ladies, this is the kind of man you want as your husband. To paraphrase Michelle M. Hammond, "A man who doesn't want to hurt God's heart won't want to break your heart."

GOD SPEAKS: "Husbands, love your wives, just as Christ loved the church and gave himself up for her to make her holy, cleansing her by the washing with water through the word, and to present her to himself as a radiant church, without stain or wrinkle or any other blemish, but holy and blameless. In this same way, husbands ought to love their wives as their own bodies. He who loves his wife loves himself. After all, no one ever hated their own body, but they feed and care for their body, just as Christ does the church–" (Ephesians 5:25-29 NIV)

WANDA'S PRAYER: LORD, You care so much for us; You have given men guidelines on how they are to care for their wives. You leave nothing to chance when it comes to protecting Your daughters. Thank You Father!

April 19

WHO'S THAT MAN?

"THEN REBEKAH LIFTED HER EYES, AND WHEN SHE SAW ISAAC SHE DISMOUNTED FROM HER CAMEL; FOR SHE HAD SAID TO THE SERVANT, 'WHO IS THIS MAN WALKING IN THE FIELD TO MEET US?' THE SERVANT SAID, 'IT IS MY MASTER.' SO SHE TOOK A VEIL AND COVERED HERSELF." (GENESIS 24:64-65 NKJV)

This story reads like one of the Harlequin Romance novels I read in my youth. The handsome prince anxiously awaits the coming of the princess. At a distance, he spies his long-lost love. He then swims the deep and leaps over mountains to reach his forever love. The story ends with the two of them, in a deep passionate embrace. But not so in this story; let us rewind the tape. Rebekah sees Isaac, gets off the camel, and then asks, "Who is that guy coming to meet us?" In essence, she is told, "That's the man you are going to marry." She now takes the veil and covers herself. This is something the modern woman should take note of. We liberal women expose too much, too soon, and to too many. Rebekah keeps an air of mystique until the marriage. This "bare all" concept to the first man we meet, before we are given a long-term commitment, has left us as a society of women who are very vulnerable and damaged goods. Men in the twenty-first century still love the chase when it comes to relationships with women. We as women must never forget that when we offer ourselves up so free and so quick, we are saying to men that we are so cheap. To have the "Here I am, take it," attitude to any and every man is to say we are nothing more than roadkill. We must remember that only vultures like roadkill.

REBEKAH AND US: Rebekah shows me that true love waits; and it pays a high price, because it knows it is getting something very valuable. For many years, I did not see much value in myself. To quote my mother, "Since I didn't think much of myself, others didn't think much of me either." It was a very painful lesson to learn.

GOD SPEAKS: "Since you were precious in My sight, You have been honored, And I have loved you; Therefore I will give men for you, And people for your life." (Isaiah 43:4 NKJV) You want what all women want—that is to be loved. I want you and all women to know that you are loved by the "Lover of your Souls." Believe that My love is deeper and more passionate than any man.

WANDA'S PRAYER: Father, I know it now. It is a shame that for so many years, I heard those words spoken to me, but never believed them. Help Your daughters to live as though the GOD of the Universe loves us.

April 20

I DO...MY WIFE

"AND THE SERVANT TOLD ISAAC ALL THE THINGS THAT HE HAD DONE. THEN ISAAC BROUGHT HER INTO HIS MOTHER SARAH'S TENT; AND HE TOOK REBEKAH AND SHE BECAME HIS WIFE, AND HE LOVED HER. SO ISAAC WAS COMFORTED AFTER HIS MOTHER'S DEATH." (GENESIS 24:66-67 NKJV)

Isaac listened intently as the servant told his story. The servant started with how his father Abraham had commissioned him, with God's help, to find a wife for his son from among his kinfolks. I am sure Isaac was moved as the servant recounted his prayer to the LORD at the well, as he waited for the women to draw water for their families. The servant spoke of how God answered his prayer; when before he had even finished praying, this beautiful young woman offered not only to give him water, but to water his camels also! Finally, the servant spoke of the family; how Rebekah's father also saw God's hand and gave his daughter to the servant to be a wife for this far-away stranger. This miracle of God moved Isaac's heart and confirmed in his mind that this was his wife. Isaac had spent time in God's presence just before the caravan arrived. He was certain this beautiful woman was sent from the LORD to be his wife for life. So, he took her into his mother's tent (men still want to bring the one they want to marry to Mama). There in Mama's tent, he made Rebekah his wife. In this tent, he consummated his love; the two became one flesh. This brought him great comfort, as he mourned the death of his mother.

REBEKAH AND US: As Isaac's wife, Rebekah could not take the place of Isaac's mother, yet she was a "balm to soothe the hurts of his soul." We should all strive to be the balm that soothes hurts in the lives of those around us. We should not be "salt" to the wounds of others, causing them more pain. I will make this my prayer; how about you?

GOD SPEAKS: "Life and death are in the power of the tongue, and those who love it will eat its fruit. He who finds a wife finds a good thing and obtains favor from the LORD." (Proverbs 18:21-22 BSB) Take these words to heart—let them become a part of you; and you will be a help, and not a hurt.

WANDA'S PRAYER: Thank You Father, for Your lovely words. Help us drink them in, like a thirsty man in a desert. May You and all of Your Word consume us. Change us into Your likeness, oh God.

April 21

DAD'S SINS REVISTED

"SO ISAAC STAYED IN GERAR. WHEN THE MEN WHO LIVED THERE ASKED ISAAC ABOUT HIS WIFE, REBEKAH, HE SAID, 'SHE IS MY SISTER.' HE WAS AFRAID TO SAY, 'SHE IS MY WIFE.' HE THOUGHT, 'THEY WILL KILL ME TO GET HER, BECAUSE SHE IS SO BEAUTIFUL.'" (GENESIS 26:6-7 NLT)

My mother had a very colorful way of saying things. One of her many sayings was, "A strong wind never changes." The statement meant some things would always remain—no matter how hard one may try to change them. This was the case of Abraham's lineage. For example, when the men in the town where Isaac lived noticed he had a very pretty wife, fearing for his life, he panics. His dad had that problem as well. Gripped by fear, he lies through his teeth and tosses his wife to the "wolves," just like his dad had done. "She is my sister," he says to the men. In other words, "you can have her if you want. Go ahead, take her, but spare my life." (Writer's paraphrase) What is remarkable is that Rebekah goes along with this plan just as her mother-in-law had done! This is the same story—just a different time with different people. Just like old dad, Isaac's lie is found out. The king of that town is looking out of his window, and happens to notice Isaac fondling his "sister." He confronts Isaac about his lie. Isaac repeats the same excuse his father used. He says, "I was afraid you would kill me because of her." I am struck by Rebekah's silence. She allows him to lead the family in this mess, yet trusting she will somehow be delivered out of it. Rebekah, aware of her husband's failings, stands by him in this wrong. Our ever-gracious God steps in and delivers his daughter out of this mess. What a mighty and living God we serve!

REBEKAH AND US: How would you feel if you were in that situation? I would have been very upset and do not know if I would have consented as Rebekah did. I see two lessons in this story. First, we are flawed, and those we live with are flawed as well. Because of our flaws, we need the Savior. Finally, our LORD and Savior is ready to help us in our time of need.

GOD SPEAKS: "I, even I, am the LORD, and apart from me there is no savior." (Isaiah 43:11 NIV) I am the Savior who saves.

WANDA'S PRAYER: Thank You, Lord my Savior, for constantly saving us.

April 22

BABY CARRIAGE?

**"ISAAC WAS FORTY YEARS OLD WHEN HE TOOK REBEKAH AS WIFE,...NOW ISAAC PLEADED WITH THE LORD FOR HIS WIFE, BECAUSE SHE WAS BARREN; AND THE LORD GRANTED HIS PLEA, AND REBEKAH HIS WIFE CONCEIVED...ISAAC WAS SIXTY YEARS OLD WHEN SHE BORE THEM."
(GENESIS 25:20-26 NKJV)**

For a woman, there are fewer things in life which are more devastating than the heartbreak of barrenness. The inability to produce a male heir in Rebekah's culture was considered a stroke of death, and the ultimate reproach for women. For all the wonderful qualities which made Rebekah a good wife, striking beauty, poise, and graciousness, she lacked the one most prized—she could not have children. She had left all behind and traveled many miles over a rugged desert, to meet and marry the man Isaac, and to bear his children. Now, after almost twenty years of marriage, Rebekah could not produce the one commodity most needed. At forty, Isaac was probably more than ready to start a family. Like his parents, however, children were something which did not come easily to them. So, this man of God pleaded to his LORD for help. I am struck by his patience; it would be nearly twenty years before his prayers were answered. Isaac loved Rebekah. He did not seek out another wife or concubine to have those elusive kids—he just waited and prayed to his GOD. (Oh, that more of us as children of GOD, would follow this man's way of life.) Isaac held on to the promises of his Father—to make him a nation. He had his earthly father to look to for the fulfillment of God's promises. After all, "dad" was one hundred when he was born. Isaac may have thought that at the age of forty, he still had sixty years to go. This story is a beautiful lesson on patience, especially in our instant microwave society. It tells us the Eternal God still answers prayers, but sometimes we must wait. Rebekah is also very patient; she quietly waits for the promised children. She does not offer her servants as surrogate mothers to her husband.

REBEKAH AND US: We can also admire Rebekah's patience. She does not pull a Sarah and use a surrogate to get a child. I waited five years for my first child. There are still other unanswered prayers I am learning to wait patiently for—how about you? As we remember Rebekah and Isaac's story, let us too have hope!

GOD SPEAKS: "Wait on the LORD, And keep His way..." (Psalm 37:34 NKJV) "Behold, children are a heritage from the LORD, The fruit of the womb is a reward." (Psalm 127:3 NKJV) Always remember that your LORD hears and will answer. The answer may be yes, no, or wait.

WANDA'S PRAYER: Father, thank You for all of Your gifts to us.

April 23

PROBLEM?

"...REBEKAH HIS WIFE CONCEIVED. BUT THE CHILDREN STRUGGLED TOGETHER WITHIN HER; AND SHE SAID, 'IF ALL IS WELL, WHY AM I LIKE THIS?' SO SHE WENT TO INQUIRE OF THE LORD." (GENESIS 25:21-22 NKJV)

Isaac's prayer to the LORD was answered in an incredibly big way—Rebekah is now very pregnant! However, the blessing of pregnancy for Rebekah was not problem free. The above text tells us there was a struggle in her womb. Imagine the constant twisting and tugging she must have experienced. This "war in her womb" drove her to her knees in prayer. Rebekah needed answers about this mystery from her LORD, and our ever compassionate Heavenly Dad was ready to give her an answer. He told her, "Two nations are in your womb, two peoples shall be separated from your body; One people shall be stronger than the other, And the older shall serve the younger." (Genesis 25:23) Rebekah was told she was having twins! What a strange, wonderful prophecy, she must have thought, as she pondered it in her heart. Sure enough, just like God said, she gave birth to "Hairy" (Esau) and "Heel Catcher" (Jacob). Hairy was a rugged hunter and an outdoorsman; while Heel Catcher was a mild man who liked to be around Mama. This would be the start of parental favorites. Rebekah loved Jacob because he loved being around her; and probably because of the prophetic word the LORD gave her about him. Isaac, who loved the taste of wild game, loved Esau. He was indeed the son of his father. He was a world-class hunter and an all-around sportsman. The great family divide would cause a sibling rivalry which would take decades to heal.

REBEKAH AND US: Rebekah gives us good and bad examples in this lesson. The good example is in how she goes to God when she has an overwhelming problem. The bad example is forgetting the Gift-Giver and focusing on the gift.

GOD SPEAKS: "If you then, though you are evil, know how to give good gifts to your children, how much more will your Father in heaven give the Holy Spirit to those who ask him!" (Luke 11:13 NIV) As good as the gifts of the world are, nothing compares to the Perfect Gift of God's Spirit, living inside of you. Allow Me to place My Holy Spirit in you; that we may be together forever.

WANDA'S PRAYER: Father, You are the Perfect Gift! Thank You so much!

April 24

STOLEN BLESSING?

"WHEN ISAAC WAS OLD AND HIS EYES WERE SO WEAK THAT HE COULD NO LONGER SEE, HE CALLED FOR ESAU HIS OLDER SON AND SAID TO HIM, 'MY SON.' '... GO OUT TO THE OPEN COUNTRY TO HUNT SOME WILD GAME FOR ME. PREPARE ME THE KIND OF TASTY FOOD I LIKE ... SO THAT I MAY GIVE YOU MY BLESSING BEFORE I DIE.' NOW REBEKAH WAS LISTENING AS ISAAC SPOKE TO HIS SON ESAU ..."
(GENESIS 27:1-5 NIV)

Isaac, now old and going blind, fears his impending death. He calls for his son Esau, to give him the family blessing - the coveted "Birth Right." Rebekah overhears what is going on and is very disturbed about the stolen blessing. Years earlier, when she was pregnant, the Lord told her the "older son (Esau) would serve the younger (Jacob)." (See Genesis 25:21-23) This implied the coveted blessing/birthright belonged to Jacob, not Esau. The birthright was very important for several reasons. First, it is usually given to the firstborn male of the family. Second, the inheritance of the birthright sets him up as Head of the family at the father's death. Third, as Head of the household, he gets two-thirds of the father's wealth, and last, he becomes the spiritual leader. Rebekah overhears Isaac privately planning to give this blessing/birthright to Esau, not Jacob. Was Isaac not aware of God's promise to Rebekah? I am certain he was. Yet, she feels Isaac is planning to steal the blessing from "her" son (Jacob), and give it to "his" son (Esau), which was not as the LORD had promised. Rebekah is panicking over her husband's impending actions. Is Isaac wrong? Yes! But his wrong actions are not the issue. She cannot control him, but she can control herself. She needs to STOP, and go to the Divine Promise keeper, Father-God! Many years ago, she had agonized in prayer over her turbulent pregnancy; and now is the time to agonize in prayer again over her turbulent husband. The LORD wonderfully answered her then, and He would answer her now. Is He not the All-Powerful God of the Universe? He gave her the promise, and He is more than capable of fulfilling it.

REBEKAH AND US: Rebekah (like us), finds herself at a crossroad. She (and we) feels powerless to stop the wrong. The answer is that this giant-size problem must be given to our LORD; He alone can handle it. Stay in prayer with the LORD, for as long as it takes.

GOD SPEAKS: "Blessings crown the head of the righteous, but violence overwhelms the mouth of the wicked." (Proverbs 10:6 NIV) Trust the LORD! He is over all the earth—He will ultimately "right all wrongs!"

WANDA'S PRAYER: LORD, in our times of helplessness, we, too, have been very scared. Remind us to always come to You first; trusting that "... the Judge of all the earth will do right" (Genesis 18:25)

April 25

THE FRUITS OF FEAR

"REBEKAH SAID TO HER SON JACOB, 'LOOK, I OVERHEARD YOUR FATHER SAY TO YOUR BROTHER ESAU, 'BRING ME SOME GAME ...' 'NOW, MY SON, LISTEN CAREFULLY AND DO WHAT I TELL YOU:'" (GENESIS 27:6-8 NIV)

Rebekah eavesdropped on the conversation between Isaac and Esau. In panic and desperation, she does not go to the LORD, but to her son Jacob. She figures she only has a few hours before Esau returns with the "savory meat" Isaac loves; thus, he would receive the inheritance (birthright). Her mind is going a thousand miles a minute. She decides and then tells her son, "Ok, I have a plan; Listen carefully and I'll tell you what we are going to do." (Writer's paraphrase). After all, GOD told me this was supposed to happen—He just needs me to work it out by any means necessary. She had forgotten what she needed to remember. This situation was just as stressful as when she was carrying the twins and had all the turmoil in her womb. She had a few hours to fast and pray to the Master of the Universe. Why did she not turn to her LORD, as she had years earlier? Instead, she relies on what Rebekah can do, and how Rebekah can fix things. This was a God-size problem, and it required a God-size solution. Rebekah, now acting outside of God's will, would use the weapons of Satan (lying and deceit) to solve her dilemma.

REBEKAH AND US: We need to ask ourselves, what God-size problems do we have that we feel powerless to fix? Before trying to play God, ask yourself: "Would God sanction sin in order to carry out His plans?" Since the answer is NO, go to the LORD and let Him fix the problem.

GOD SPEAKS: "The LORD foils the plans of the nations; he thwarts the purposes of the peoples. But the plans of the LORD stand firm forever, the purposes of his heart through all generations." (Psalm 33:10-11 NIV) I have a million and one ways of working out your little problems. There is nothing too hard for your God.

WANDA'S PRAYER: Help us trust in You, Lord, with all our heart; and to totally rely on Your perfect ways of working out our problems.

April 26

WICKED PLAN

"GO NOW TO THE FLOCK AND BRING ME FROM THERE TWO CHOICE KIDS OF THE GOATS, AND I WILL MAKE SAVORY FOOD FROM THEM FOR YOUR FATHER, SUCH AS HE LOVES. THEN YOU SHALL TAKE IT TO YOUR FATHER, THAT HE MAY EAT IT, AND THAT HE MAY BLESS YOU BEFORE HIS DEATH."
(GENESIS 27:9-10 NKJV)

Rebekah has cooked up a wicked plan to steal the birth from her oldest son by deceiving her husband. It is amazing how low we humans will sink to, to get our way. She figures she only has a few hours before Esau returns with the "savory meat" Isaac loves; and thus, he will receive the inheritance (birthright). Her mind is going a thousand miles a minute. "Ok," she decides, "I got it. We (Jacob and I) will trick the old blind man. He will never know the difference. After all, GOD told me this was supposed to happen; He just needs me to work it out—by any means necessary." She must have reasoned, "We all lie sometimes, right?" (Writer's paraphrase) She had forgotten what she needed to remember. This situation is just as stressful and dreadful as when she was carrying the twins, experiencing all the turmoil within her womb. Feeling helpless and hopeless, Rebekah spent that time, not scheming and plotting, but seeking and praying to the Master of the Universe. Why did she not turn to her LORD as she had years earlier? Instead, she relied on what she could do and how she could fix things. Instead of relying on God's perfect plan, which would cause no harm, she would go down this disastrous road. Rebekah, who is now outside of God's will, would use the weapons of Satan—lying and deceit—to solve her dilemma. First, she told her son to get a goat from the flock. She would cook the goat the way her husband liked. Then, she sends her son in to finish this "family killer" plan.

REBEKAH AND US: Sir Walter Scott said, "O, what a tangled web we weave when first we practice to deceive!" These "tangled webs" trap us; in the end we are caught and eventually destroyed.

GOD SPEAKS: "… And be sure your sin will find you out." (Numbers 32:23 NKJV) "They sow the wind, and reap the whirlwind…" (Hosea 8:7 NKJV). Trust Me, there is no getting away—your sin will come back to bite you.

WANDA'S PRAYER: Lord, help us to always walk in the truth of Your Word.

April 27

NO STOPPING NOW

"HIS MOTHER SAID TO HIM, 'MY SON, LET THE CURSE FALL ON ME. JUST DO WHAT I SAY; GO AND GET THEM FOR ME.'" (GENESIS 27:13 NIV)

Words out of our mouths can be so potent! Such was the case with Rebekah. She was hell bent on getting the birthright for her precious Jacob at any cost; even to the point of making herself accursed. Having taken the stand that come hell or high water, she was going to see this evil plan through. So much so, she would take a "curse" on herself in order to get her son, the promised blessing of the birthright. Oh, how we love our children. She is so consumed with her evil plan that she has not stopped to consider what the "curse" would look like. Rebekah is sowing the wind, and she would reap the world wind. Her pain would come in two forms. A completely divided house with a distant husband; and an elder son, who would want nothing more to do with her. She dressed Jacob to look and feel like Esau. She then handed him the plate of food for dad, who then goes into his father. With lies and deceit, he was able to pull off the great caper; dad gave the blessing to the younger son, Jacob. (Genesis 27:14-32) Mom and Mama's boy got what they wanted, but at what cost? A forty-year marriage built on love and trust, now shattered by a single act of deception. A divided household now permanently separated. Rebekah, was all this really worth it? I do not think so. Isaac gave Jacob the blessed birthright with all its privileges. When Esau came in, it was too late.

REBEKAH AND US: Can you relate to Rebekah? I can. I remember wanting someone so badly, I schemed, plotted, planned, and finally got my way. I had my love, but I was a miserable mess. I had sown a little ripple, but reaped a Tsunami, with 200-feet tidal waves! Why did I let pride, stupidity, and selfishness rob and leave me void?

GOD SPEAKS: "To you, LORD, I called; to the Lord I cried for mercy: What is gained if I am silenced, if I go down to the pit? Will the dust praise you? Will it proclaim your faithfulness? Hear, LORD, and be merciful to me; LORD, be my help." You turned my wailing into dancing; you removed my sackcloth and clothed me with joy, that my heart may sing your praises and not be silent. LORD my God, I will praise you forever." (Psalm 30:8-12 NIV) I will never leave or forsake you. From time to time, I will let you stew in your own mess; you are pigheaded, and not listening to Me. But before you call, I am here ready and waiting to respond.

WANDA'S PRAYER: Oh LORD, how very good and wonderful You are. Thank you for Your wonderful love and mercy.

April 28

THE STRESS

"ESAU HELD A GRUDGE AGAINST JACOB BECAUSE OF THE BLESSING HIS FATHER HAD GIVEN HIM. HE SAID TO HIMSELF, 'THE DAYS OF MOURNING FOR MY FATHER ARE NEAR; THEN I WILL KILL MY BROTHER JACOB.' WHEN REBEKAH WAS TOLD WHAT HER OLDER SON ESAU HAD SAID, SHE SENT FOR HER YOUNGER SON JACOB AND SAID TO HIM, 'YOUR BROTHER ESAU IS PLANNING TO AVENGE HIMSELF BY KILLING YOU.'" (GENESIS 27:41-42 NIV)

Rebekah hears the news of Esau wanting to kill his brother Jacob for stealing the birthright; and she is stressed about the matter. She should just go to the LORD, confess her wrong and seek His perfect wisdom. Her plans and her actions had set brother against brother. The result is now a planned murder after the father's death. This is a serious matter. Instead of seeking God for help, she acts on her "mother wit." She advises Jacob to "Run away; go and stay with my brother Laban in Haran. It will only be a little while until your brother calms down. When the anger settles down, I will send word for you to come back home. Why should I lose both of you in one day?" (Genesis 27:43-45) (Writer's paraphrase) Rebekah is totally blind to the hurt she caused her eldest son, Esau. He blamed her for her part she played in the deception. Esau's anger and rage towards his brother and mother was deep. Having chosen the love of one child over the other, she casts off Esau's feelings as small and insignificant. Had she but gone to the LORD, the Father would have opened her eyes to her deception. Instead, she is hatching another wicked plan to cover-up for the first evil; with hopes she will not lose Jacob, and later, she will regain Esau. The sad part is, she had lost both of them already, but did not realize it.

REBEKAH AND US: Rebekah shows us that when we behave as she did, no one wins—everyone loses and is left hurt.

GOD SPEAKS: "There is a way that appears to be right, but in the end it leads to death." (Proverbs 14:12 NIV) "If we confess our sins, he is faithful and just and will forgive us our sins and purify us from all unrighteousness." (1 John 1:9 NIV) You cannot fix your problems; but I can, through you. Allow Me to live in you. I will work out your every problem.

WANDA'S PRAYER: Father, come into our hearts; forgive us of our sins. Take total control of our lives, Daddy.

April 29

THE EXCUSE

"THEN REBEKAH SAID TO ISAAC, 'I'M DISGUSTED WITH LIVING BECAUSE OF THESE HITTITE WOMEN. IF JACOB TAKES A WIFE FROM AMONG THE WOMEN OF THIS LAND, FROM HITTITE WOMEN LIKE THESE, MY LIFE WILL NOT BE WORTH LIVING.'" (GENESIS 27:46 NIV)

Rebekah needs to get her son Jacob away from Esau, but does not have the authority to do so. In order to get her way, she plays the old evil Hittite woman's card. She comes to her husband with the excuse about the Hittite women Esau had married. These women had been a source of grief and disappointment to Rebekah and Isaac ever since Esau had first married them. (Genesis 26:35) "I am so disgusted with these Hittite women, honey. If Jacob gets a wife like one of these women, well, I'll just roll up and die." (Genesis 27:46) (Writer's paraphrase) Rebekah gets her wish, and her son Jacob is saved. Isaac sends Jacob back to Rebekah's homeland to get a wife from within the family. (Genesis 28:1-3) What Rebekah does not realize is this will be the last time she will see her precious Jacob alive. This will be the last time she hears his voice. She has plotted and schemed, but in the end, she loses.

REBEKAH AND US: The story of Rebekah should cut like a knife to us all. She shows us the lengths we can go to—trying to hide and cover-up the sin, of which we should just repent. Our excuses, instead of apologies, cause us to dig deeper and deeper holes, which later become harder to get out of.

GOD SPEAKS: "They will do all this to you because of me, for they have rejected the one who sent me. They would not be guilty if I had not come and spoken to them. But now they have no excuse for their sin." (John 15:21-22 NLT) Everyone who sins and offers excuses for their sin does so because they have turned from their LORD. Have you?

WANDA'S PRAYER: LORD, we come to You now. Help us follow You with all my heart.

April 30

"WEEPING"

"SOON AFTER THIS, REBEKAH'S OLD NURSE, DEBORAH, DIED. SHE WAS BURIED BENEATH THE OAK TREE IN THE VALLEY BELOW BETHEL. EVER SINCE, THE TREE HAS BEEN CALLED ALLON-BACUTH (WHICH MEANS "OAK OF WEEPING")"
(GENESIS 35:8 NLT)

The previous verse (Genesis 35:7) tells us Jacob had finally returned to his homeland of Canaan after twenty years of living in Paddan Aram, with his mother's brother. Upon sending him away, Rebekah initially thought his stay would only last for a few days, "… Until your brother's anger turns away from you, and he forgets what you have done to him; then I will send and bring you from there. Why should I be bereaved also of you both in one day?" (Genesis 27:45 NKJV) Instead, this "few day's tour" to mom's homeland turned into a difficult, two-decade journey. When Jacob finally returns to Canaan, he finds his dear mother has died. He would never see her again in this life. Now on his arrival home, one of the last vestiges of his dear mother, her nurse Deborah, has also just died. They had sent her with Rebekah when she left her home to marry Isaac. (Genesis 24:59) Deborah's death and burial appears to have caused Jacob much sorrow. The burial site was named "weeping." I believe as Jacob reflected over the death of the old nurse, he wept more at the thought of never seeing his mother again in this life. Rebekah's heart's desire for her son was for him to receive the spiritual birthright. To achieve this end, she had sacrificed both of her sons. Her deception and trickery would cause her to lose the elder son, and force her to send her younger son (her heart) away to save his life. But all was not lost. Deborah, the nurse, was buried just outside of Bethel, "The house of God." Her wayward son, now extremely wealthy, with blessings from the LORD, had made his way back to his Heavenly Father's promised land. This would make his momma proud, even though she was not there to see it.

REBEKAH AND US: Like Rebekah, there was a time in my life when my daughter and I were distant; I wept a lot over it. After some time, however, the LORD allowed me to see the mending of our relationship—in this life! Thank You, LORD, for Your wonderful gift.

GOD SPEAKS: "… Weeping may endure for a night, But joy comes in the morning." (Psalm 30:5 NKJV) I take care of My own. If you have not experienced your "joy," just remember you are experiencing a long night; your "morning" has not yet come. But you can trust in your LORD— "IT IS COMING."

WANDA'S PRAYER: Thanks Dad for the reminder! We praise You, Father, with our whole heart.

Notes

Notes

May

INTRODUCTION

LEAH

Leah is the first of Jacob's four wives. His Uncle Laban, Leah's father, tricked him into marrying her. Though she gave him six sons, scripture does not show that Jacob ever really loved her. She would spend many years trying to get his love, but without success.

Leah's life also shows us we possess many flaws and weaknesses. Therefore, many times we are often helpless, and dependent creatures. Because of our flaws and inability to help ourselves, we therefore must depend on others to get our needs met.

Leah's life shows us there are only two ways we can get our needs met. One way is by depending on other flawed and erring human beings, and the other way is we can depend on the unerring God of Heaven. Depending on the former can lead us into a life of hardship and pain. Though it has its struggles, depending on the latter, however, will lead us to a life of blessings, joy, and peace.

When Leah trusted in her earthly father, she landed in a loveless and disastrous marriage. When she turned to her Heavenly Father God, He blessed her bountifully, and gave her six sons and one daughter.

Notes

May 1

OLDER WEAKLING

"NOW LABAN HAD TWO DAUGHTERS; THE NAME OF THE OLDER WAS LEAH, AND THE NAME OF THE YOUNGER WAS RACHEL. LEAH HAD WEAK EYES, BUT RACHEL HAD A LOVELY FIGURE AND WAS BEAUTIFUL." (GENESIS 29:16-17 NIV)

Leah was the eldest daughter of Laban. It seems, according to Scripture, that she outranked her sister in birth order only. The younger sister was the one who possessed the physical attractiveness and worldly charm. "Rachel was lovely in form and beautiful." It seems her father, Laban, had genetically bestowed those womanly traits on the youngest, and left poor Leah out in the cold. Her very name means tender, frail, and weak. While the younger sister was out herding sheep and toning up that perfect figure, big sister, too fragile for such tough work, stayed home with Mama. At first glance at the above passage, it seems the writer, Moses, struggles to find positive words for Leah. If baby sister was the "Cinderella" of this family, then Leah could classify as one of the "ugly stepsisters." It was obvious Leah's looks would not carry her anywhere; she would need help from outside herself for success in life. Like Leah, we are all genetic weaklings. Sin causes genetic flaws in all of us. Every pain, hurt, and grief can be traced to the genetic flaw of sin. "For all have sinned and fall short of the glory of God" (Romans 3:23 NIV), and "… There is none righteous, no not one;" (Romans 3:10 NKJV) Our only source of help for the ails this sin defect causes is Jesus. We can go to Him for the help we need. The repair job is a lifelong process, but it is well worth it. Plus, there are the benefits of His peace and much joy in Him along the way.

LEAH AND US: Like Leah, we all come under the curse of sin; but our LORD paid the price and wants us to trade our weaknesses for His strength. We can trade our imperfections for His perfection. He is waiting for us to make the trade. Do it now.

GOD SPEAKS: "… For when I am weak, then I am strong." (2 Corinthians 12:10 NIV) That Perfect Strength is found in God alone.

WANDA'S PRAYER: Father, we need You; We are weak and frail like Leah; be our strong tower that we can run to for safety.

May 2

DADDY'S HELP

"SO LABAN BROUGHT TOGETHER ALL THE PEOPLE OF THE PLACE AND GAVE A FEAST. BUT WHEN EVENING CAME, HE TOOK HIS DAUGHTER LEAH AND BROUGHT HER TO JACOB, AND JACOB MADE LOVE TO HER." (GENESIS 29:22-23 NIV)

Jacob fell in love with Leah's baby sister at first sight (Genesis 29:9-12; 20). He agreed to work seven years for her hand in marriage. Here is where daddy's feelings come to surface, about his eldest daughter, Leah's marriage potential. Daddy Laban thought so little of her abilities to attract a husband, that he felt the only way to get her married was to deceive Jacob! (Who by the way, had agreed to work seven years for the younger sister, Rachel.) It appears old dad did not think Leah could get a husband without his help. So, he would pull the old "bait and switch" on Jacob. It would appear Leah may have agreed with this assessment of herself, and her inabilities to get a mate, because we do not read of her offering any objections to this plan. Leah would learn and teach us hard lessons of life such as trickery may get the man to the marriage bed, but love is what is needed to keep him there. She would also learn and teach us that love is given; not coerced or forced. There is a Love for all of us—He is only a prayer away. Father God loves us as no one else can; He has always loved us! He fills the hollow spaces and love-starved souls. He requires only that we seek Him with a whole and complete heart, and He does the rest.

LEAH AND US: Though not as dramatic as this, I must admit I have pulled a few tricks to get a man to notice me. My results were the same as Leah's—in the end, at first light, they also ran for the hills. How about you, reader? What schemes have you tried to command love?

GOD SPEAKS: "… I have loved you with an everlasting love; I have drawn you with unfailing kindness." (Jeremiah 31:3 NIV) "Let us then approach God's throne of grace with confidence, so that we may receive mercy and find grace to help us in our time of need." (Hebrews 4:16 NIV) Your Everlasting Dad has loved you with a perfect love. Our Perfect Dad does not use deception to bring about His perfect plans for our lives. He is always ready and willing to help us.

WANDA'S PRAYER: Father God, draw us closer and closer to You. We want to know and experience this deep abiding love You have for us.

May 3

DECEIVED

"WHEN MORNING CAME, THERE WAS LEAH! SO JACOB SAID TO LABAN, 'WHAT IS THIS YOU HAVE DONE TO ME? I SERVED YOU FOR RACHEL, DIDN'T I? WHY HAVE YOU DECEIVED ME?'" (GENESIS 29:25 NIV)

This had to have been the shortest honeymoon on record; topping the singer who was married for, I think, ninety-six hours! Jacob and Leah's honeymoon lasted from sunset the evening prior to the break of the next day. Jacob wakes up, sees Leah's face, and runs to his father-in-law with charges of deception. This was obviously no way to start a marriage. Daddy's reply was, "Oops! I must have forgotten to tell you, son; there is a clause in the contract you signed — 'the older daughter must get married first.' I am so sorry Jacob—wives are non-refundable, but I will throw in a servant girl to sweeten the deal—ok?" Poor Leah, she would spend the rest of her life playing that old Diana Ross hit, "I'm Going To Make You Love Me… yes I will… you know I will!" That broken record did not work in Leah's day, and it will not work in our day either. The Bible says that "Husbands must love their wives, just as Christ loved the church and gave Himself up for her to make her holy…" (Ephesians 5:25) We will not see this Bible verse lived out in the marriage of Leah and Jacob. What we have here is a big mess! Jacob cares truly little for Leah and loving her seems to be out of the question. The only giving he wants to do is to give her back to daddy and get Rachel. Imagine how poor Leah feels at this point.

LEAH AND US: Leah shows us the painful results deception can cause. She got the man and all the pain that comes with it. Before we enter into deception, we should ask ourselves, are we willing to suffer its painful consequences?

GOD SPEAKS: "… He will redeem their soul from oppression (deceit) and violence. Their blood will be precious in his sight." (Psalm 72:14 New Heart English Bible) Can you see what a very loving LORD we have? That He would "redeem" or buy us out of our "deceit" with His precious blood on a rugged cross so long ago.

WANDA'S PRAYER: Father, thank You for paying that extremely high cost to bring me back into a right relationship with You. Thank You for showing me how precious I am to You.

May 4

GOD SAW—GOD ACTED

"WHEN THE LORD SAW THAT LEAH WAS NOT LOVED, HE ENABLED HER TO CONCEIVE, BUT RACHEL REMAINED CHILDLESS." (GENESIS 29:31 NIV)

The rejected Leah has Jacob in name only. She is a woman who is in a loveless marriage, to a husband would eventually have four "wives." (He married the two sisters; and he was given the two sisters handmaidens, from which he fathered children.) His true love was the younger sister Rachel. Though Leah married Jacob first, she would never have his heart. Her heart must have been crushed over this ever-unfolding reality. This story teaches us that love cannot be forced or manipulated. Love must be given and received. Here is where our loving LORD steps in. In the study of the original language from the Interlinear Bible (with use of the Strong's Concordance), we gain a clearer understanding of the above text. The Eternal Father of love takes a personal interest in His unloved, unwanted daughter's plight. The word for "see" in this text is "Ra`ah." This word means to consider, gaze, perceive, or focus upon. The LORD saw Leah's hurting soul; she was in His thoughts. The LORD did not just see her pain, He acted on her behalf. He responds to Leah's loveless plight by giving her what she valued most. He opened her womb so that she could have those coveted sons for Jacob. The term here implies the Father released her from being barren like her sister Rachel.

LEAH AND US: Like Leah, many women have had the experience of unrequited love. As daughters of God, we are so loved, watched over, and cared for by Him. Spend time with the LORD by reading His Word (the Bible) and in prayer. Allow Him to love you through your pain and hurt.

GOD SPEAKS: "I will be glad and rejoice in your love, for you saw my affliction and knew the anguish of my soul. Praise be to the Lord, for he showed me the wonders of his love…" (Psalm 31:7,21 NIV) Our LORD is reminding us that His love is unending.

WANDA'S PRAYER: Lord, You are our stronghold. You are everything we need, and will ever need. Thanks Dad!

May 5

SONS CAN'T BUY LOVE (PART 1)

"SO LEAH BECAME PREGNANT AND GAVE BIRTH TO A SON. SHE NAMED HIM REUBEN, FOR SHE SAID, 'THE LORD HAS NOTICED MY MISERY, AND NOW MY HUSBAND WILL LOVE ME.'" (GENESIS 29:32 NLT)

The life of this ancient woman named Leah will teach us modern women valuable lessons about love. The LORD opened Leah's barren womb, and she gave birth to her first-born son; she names him Reuben. His name means "behold a son." Hear the words of this dejected woman. To me, the passage could read, "Look Jacob, honey; I know you don't want me, but here (as she shows the baby to Jacob), this is your first-born son." Leah then waits to hear the tender words, "I love you," from Jacob. Those words never come because he does not love her. This story speaks volumes to women today who have had babies; either to get, or to keep a man. It did not work thousands of years ago in Leah's day, and it will not work today. I am reminded of an old song by the Beetles entitled, "Money Can't Buy Me Love." Leah would learn the hard way that sons cannot buy love either. To her credit, she realizes and acknowledges, there is someone who does love her deeply and is madly in love with her—Father God!

LEAH AND US: Like Leah, many women have resorted to "bribing" or "conning" someone to love them. The end result, like Leah, is a life of much heartache and pain. But there is a Heavenly Father and Husband, who loves us deeper than we could ever imagine. In the midst of all our hurt and pain, the LORD wants to drown us in His compassionate love. He is waiting for us to come to Him.

GOD SPEAKS: "With your unfailing love you lead the people you have redeemed. In your might, you guide them to your sacred home." (Exodus 15:13 NLT) Real love cannot be bought, nor can it come from a bribe. I, your LORD, showed My love for you, by paying the ultimate cost to set you free. Now allow Me to lead you to My special place.

WANDA'S PRAYER: Thank You for Your unfailing love! Father God, lead and guide us to that special place You have prepared for us.

May 6

SONS CAN'T BUY LOVE (PART 2)

"SHE CONCEIVED AGAIN, AND WHEN SHE GAVE BIRTH TO A SON SHE SAID, 'BECAUSE THE LORD HEARD THAT I AM NOT LOVED, HE GAVE ME THIS ONE TOO.' SO SHE NAMED HIM SIMEON." (GENESIS 29:33 NIV)

Leah tries again to get Jacob's love. She gives Jacob a second son. One would think he would be a little more loving to the wife he married in deception. NOPE! Even after son number two, Jacob shows no feelings of love, or even like, for the mother of his children. This is a lesson for all of us women. Men can have intimate relations with us; we can even bear their children, and still never have their love. When I look at Leah's marriage, I sense her extreme pain and loneliness. I think while trying to ebb out a family in this loveless marriage, she is hurting deeply. But Leah teaches us how to live in the midst of all of this. Despite the pain, loneliness, and extreme hurt she feels, she goes forward in the strength of the LORD. Her hope is in GOD, and in Him alone. Leah has an active prayer life. "Because the LORD HEARD..." She names this child Simeon (which means "hears"). She knows GOD heard her every cry. The Father is close to her, and she knows it. This is the secret to her living in and through this painful part of her life. She knows without a doubt - if no one else on the face of this earth loves her, she is fully loved by her LORD.

LEAH AND US: Leah teaches us that although our husbands are commanded to love us (Ephesians 5:25), the love we need for survival will only come from the LORD of love—no one else. In His love and strength, like Leah, we can weather any distressing situation. He is our Rock and Sustainer. We can always depend on Him.

GOD SPEAKS: "The LORD is my strength and my defense; he has become my salvation. He is my God, and I will praise him, my father's God, and I will exalt him." (Exodus 15:2 NIV) Just remember my precious daughter in Christ, "I will never leave or forsake you." (Deuteronomy 31:6, 8) I am just a prayer away.

WANDA'S PRAYER: Thank You LORD for Your giant security blanket. You alone cover and protect us.

May 7

SON'S CAN'T BUY LOVE (PART 3)

"AGAIN SHE CONCEIVED, AND WHEN SHE GAVE BIRTH TO A SON SHE SAID, 'NOW AT LAST MY HUSBAND WILL BECOME ATTACHED TO ME, BECAUSE I HAVE BORNE HIM THREE SONS.' SO HE WAS NAMED LEVI." (GENESIS 29:34 NIV)

In Leah's heart of hearts, hope springs eternal. She is hoping that somewhere in the deep recesses of Jacob's heart, love for her will spring forth. With this desperate hope for love in mind, she gives birth to Jacob's third son and calls him Levi. The name Levi means "joined, attached, or connected." She has joined herself in marriage to this man; she attached herself in a sexual relationship with him also. In her mind, she was tightly connected to Jacob. After all, she was the only wife who had given him three sons. She can comfort herself in this fact. But this connection—this attachment is one-sided. Look at the verse, "… Now at last my husband will become attached to me…" Note how we NEVER read of any attachment to Leah by Jacob. We do not read, "And Jacob fell madly in love with Leah." There is no love connection in Jacob's heart for Leah. His heart is as detached from Leah's heart as it ever was; she is only his baby maker—nothing more. The LORD of Love, who allowed Leah to have children, was not distant or detached from her. He was greatly attached to His hurting daughter.

LEAH AND US: Leah paints to us two beautiful portraits. One of the painted portraits is that of pain and human rejection. The other painted portrait is the amazing love of our Eternal God. We can choose to rely on human love, or God's love. Remember, human love is fleeting, but God's love is eternal.

GOD SPEAKS: "He tends his flock like a shepherd: He gathers the lambs in his arms and carries them close to his heart; he gently leads those that have young." (Isaiah 40:11 NIV) You never have to worry—I will always be there for you.

WANDA'S PRAYER: We will praise the LORD of our salvation. We will give glory to the God of our strength. He is great and mighty in all things; and He always keeps us in the hollow of His loving hands.

May 8

JUST PRAISE

"SHE CONCEIVED AGAIN, AND WHEN SHE GAVE BIRTH TO A SON SHE SAID, 'THIS TIME I WILL PRAISE THE LORD.' SO SHE NAMED HIM JUDAH …" (GENESIS 29:35 NIV)

Leah finds her fullness in the LORD alone. "This time I will praise the LORD!" She makes a determined effort to go beyond trying to win Jacob's love at this point. With son number one, she offers Jacob his firstborn for his love. But this time she says, "I will praise the LORD!" With son number two, she realizes it is God who hears her; though her husband does not. But this time Leah says, "I will praise the LORD!" When she has son number three, she hopes Jacob will finally attach himself or connect with her; but he does not. Finally, after three failures, she gets it! Leah knows, "It's all about her LORD"—nothing more and nothing less. This epiphany comes to Leah as she gives birth to son number four. She names him Judah, which means "praise." Leah realizes that her LORD has always been there for her. At this glorious revelation, she breaks forth in a wild praise despite her circumstances. "This time I will PRAISE THE LORD!"

LEAH AND US: Leah chooses to look beyond the current gloom and doom; and all the pain it brought into her life. She knew, despite what she saw or felt, that her GOD was so worthy of all her praise. As we come to Leah's realization, we too can shout hallelujah! Thank you Jesus! You are worthy of all our praise!

GOD SPEAKS: "After this I heard what sounded like the roar of a great multitude in heaven shouting: Hallelujah! Salvation and glory and power belong to our God, for true and just are his judgements …" (Revelation 19:1-2 NIV) These saints are praising Me in Heaven as they look back; but I want you to praise me now!

WANDA'S PRAYER: (MY PRAISE): Yes Daddy! Father God and Lord, You alone are so incredibly good. Your mercies, like Your eternal grace, goes on continually—without end. We will praise You as long as we have breath. With every fiber of our being, we give You praise. There is no one who is Your equal. Words cannot express what is in our feeble, fragile hearts that You have preserved. Help us, Father, to live a life of praise to match these lips of clay.

May 9

DONE! NOW REST

"... THEN SHE (LEAH) STOPPED HAVING CHILDREN." (GENESIS 29:35 NIV)

I think this part of the story is beautiful. I picture in my mind's eye that just as the LORD had opened Leah's womb, He now shuts it to give her rest. From this reading, I also get a picture that she was ok for now, with the closing of her womb. Leah was at spiritual rest. The Father of love had completed her, and she was complete in Him. (Colossians 2:10) The wonderful thing about Leah's completeness was it was through GOD; not through a man. This speaks volumes in our day. We are not too different from the ancient women of old. We still want a man to take away our reproach. Leah allowed the God man to do for her what no human man ever could. She found her fullness in the LORD alone. She had looked, hoped, pleaded, and prayed for this fullness. He was right by her side.

LEAH AND US: Leah entered into God's complete rest for her soul; the type of rest which can only come through Him. He allowed His daughter Leah to just curl up in those giant, strong arms of love of His, and just exhale—what a wonderful relief! We have the same access to our LORD as Leah had; just come to Him as she did.

GOD SPEAKS: "There remains, then, a Sabbath-rest for the people of God; for anyone who enters God's rest also rests from their works, just as God did from his. Let us, therefore, make every effort to enter that rest, so that no one will perish by following their example of disobedience." (Hebrews 4:9-11 NIV) I have rest for you. Stop trying to work things out in your life on your own; Your rest is in Me! Let Me do the work through you while you rest. Your only labor is "to enter My rest." Everything else is disobedience.

WANDA'S PRAYER: Father God, help us to remain in Your rest. When we are tempted to leave, give us Your perfect love which constrains us to You—always.

May 10

THE BABY WAR

"WHEN LEAH SAW THAT SHE HAD STOPPED HAVING CHILDREN, SHE TOOK HER SERVANT ZILPAH AND GAVE HER TO JACOB AS A WIFE." (GENESIS 30:9 NIV)

Hebrews 4:11 NIV says, "Let us, therefore, make every effort to enter that rest, so that no one will perish …" In the last two devotionals, we see how our loving Lord offers Leah peace and contentment. She only needed to make the effort to remain in the "rest" the LORD had given her. Leah's failure to remain in God's perfect rest would result in the great baby war with her sister. She removed herself from the peaceful place Daddy God had placed her in, and now she is back on this losing battlefield. Right now, she can't have any more babies. She forgot it was the LORD who opened her womb, and, at this time, it was the LORD who shut it. He had given her this much needed rest. Fear causes Leah to take her eyes off her LORD, and look with envy and strife at her sister. Now out of place from her LORD and not listening to His voice, she listens to other strange voices in her head. Voices like, "girl, Jacob has just tossed you aside like an old rag. You know he will want you if you can give him more sons." This was utter nonsense. These were lies out of hell's pit. Leah bought the lies; hook, line, and sinker. So, she gave her maidservant, Zilpah, to Jacob as a wife in order to have more kids. Apparently, Jacob did not care where, how or through whom the kids came, only that they came. He went along with this sorry evil plan, as he had done with Rachel's maidservant. This house is totally out of order! The good news is the LORD loves them all—He will straighten out this colossal mess of things after a while, as the old folks say.

LEAH AND US: What "houses of horror" do you need the LORD to fix? For sure, it cannot be any more chaotic than this one. Nothing is too hard for our LORD. We need only to give Him our disasters, and let Him fix them.

GOD SPEAKS: "YOU have persevered and have endured hardships for my name, and have not grown weary. Yet I hold this against you: You have forsaken the love you had at first. Consider how far you have fallen! Repent and do the things you did at first …" (Revelation 2:3-5 NIV) Just remember that when you sin, I am the One you can come to. Stay in Me and let Me stay in you; I will keep you from falling.

WANDA'S PRAYER: Lord, search our heart and see if there is anything inside us, which is not of You (I know there is). Cleanse us of all of our sins—known and unknown.

May 11

GOOD FORTUNE?

"LEAH'S SERVANT ZILPAH BORE JACOB A SON. THEN LEAH SAID, 'WHAT GOOD FORTUNE!' SO SHE NAMED HIM GAD." (GENESIS 30:10-11 NIV)

Leah's servant, whom she gave as wife to Jacob, has just bore him a son. Leah calls this "good fortune." Calling evil good—is that "good fortune?" Really! It shows just how very twisted Leah's mind has become. Having turned her heart and mind from her Lord, Leah now turns to self-solutions to win Jacob's heart. Leah named this seventh son of Jacob "Gad," which means "my fortune." It was her fortune and not God's will. It was her work in the flesh. This speaks volumes to all of us. When we take our eyes off our LORD, by not spending time with Him in prayer and Bible study, the end result is our living outside of God's will. This kind of living causes us to make foolish decisions, like the one Leah made. Lead away by our feelings and emotions, we become incapable of distinguishing right from wrong. In the end, we call evil good and good evil.

LEAH AND US: We should not be too hard on Leah, though. We too have been blinded by emotion—calling evil good. As He did with Leah, our LORD brings us back into His loving fold.

GOD SPEAKS: "We all, like sheep, have gone astray, each of us has turned to our own way; and the Lord has laid on him the iniquity of us all." (Isaiah 53:6 NIV) Before I made this planet, I already knew from time to time you would stumble and fall. I knew you would walk away from Me. This is why I gave you the road map, showing how to come back. The road map is Jesus—there is no other way!

WANDA'S PRAYER: Thank You Jesus, for being the only way, truth, and life. We know we cannot come to the FATHER, except through you—Jesus the Son!

May 12

HAPPY?

"LEAH'S SERVANT ZILPAH BORE JACOB A SECOND SON. THEN LEAH SAID, 'HOW HAPPY I AM! THE WOMEN WILL CALL ME HAPPY.' SO SHE NAMED HIM ASHER." (GENESIS 30:12-13 NIV)

Who says sin does not have its pleasures? Leah is taking great delight in this foolish baby-producing war with her sister in a futile attempt to win Jacob's heart. She cannot see how very disgusting this whole situation really is. Zilpah, Leah's maid, gives Jacob son number eight. Leah, now in a state of foolish bliss, calls the child, "Asher" (which means "happy"). She does this because, as she says, "How happy I am! The women will call me happy." (Genesis 30:13) WRONG! Little does she know; they are calling this whole mess—STUPID! This is incredibly sad. Leah has totally left her one true love and turned to this self-absorb idolatry. She has now completely deluded herself into thinking she is doing a good service. Let me see if I understand Leah's reasoning. She is trying to win her husband's affections by having more children than her sister. Her sister Rachel has given her maid to Jacob as a wife. Leah does the same thing with her maid. This, Leah reasons, will cause Jacob to love her. Does any of this make sense? Yet how often do we allow ourselves to fall into this same pit Leah is in? My God, help us all.

LEAH AND US: It would be funny if it were not so sad. I, too, have done foolish acts along these lines to keep the man I never had. At times, I was just as deluded as Leah in my thinking. I am so glad I have a Savior who pulls me out of these self-dug pits I find myself in.

GOD SPEAKS: "He lifted me out of the slimy pit, out of the mud and mire; he set my feet on a rock and gave me a firm place to stand. He put a new song in my mouth, a hymn of praise to our God. Many will see and fear the LORD and put their trust in him." (Psalm 40:2-3 NIV) I think that says it all—don't you?

WANDA'S PRAYER: "Blessed is the one who trusts in the Lord, who does not look to the proud, to those who turn aside to false gods." (Psalm 40:4 NIV) Thank You Father for all You do for us.

May 13

DESPERATE

"DURING WHEAT HARVEST, REUBEN WENT OUT INTO THE FIELDS AND FOUND SOME MANDRAKE PLANTS, WHICH HE BROUGHT TO HIS MOTHER LEAH. RACHEL SAID TO LEAH, 'PLEASE GIVE ME SOME OF YOUR SON'S MANDRAKES.'"
(GENESIS 30:14 NIV)

Leah has declared an all-out war against her sister Rachel, over Jacob. She is hell bent on winning the already lost battle for his heart. Desperate, Leah is willing to use anything and anyone to achieve her pathetic desire. Now that she cannot have any more babies at this point, it seems Jacob (her husband), has no more interest in her. Leah's best option at this time is to turn to the LORD in meditation, prayer, and maybe get a hobby. She should give Him the hurt and pain of her loveless marriage, and allow Him to work on her behalf. This option would have preserved whatever dignity she had left; perhaps the Lord would change his heart. But why would she do that when she can take the most degrading option? She allows her precious babies to be placed in the middle of this despicable cat fight with her sister; over a man that was never hers to start with. It is obvious Leah had been discussing the matter with her kids because of the action of Reuben, her oldest son. "During the wheat harvest, her son brings mandrakes to his mom..." I estimate this child is about eight years old; yet he has taken on his mother's hurt and pain. He decides to give mom an edge. Coming back from the fields at harvest, I imagine him holding his little hands up and saying to her, "Here mommy, I found you some mandrakes. This will help us get daddy—huh, mommy?" Mandrake plants are thought to be a "love apple," used for exciting sexual desire and increasing procreation. Desperate Leah is hitting bottom. She has sunk even lower, as she enlists her kids to get a man.

LEAH AND US: What levels of desperation do we reach when we go outside of the LORD's will to fulfill our desires?

GOD SPEAKS: "Listen to my cry, for I am in desperate need; rescue me from those who pursue me, for they are too strong for me." (Psalm 142:6 NIV) Your Lord knows the desperation of your heart; He can rescue you from those enemies that are pursuing you.

WANDA'S PRAYER: Lord, like Leah, we need rescuing from our evil, desperate acts. Give us a heart that is only desperate to do Your will.

May 14

TWISTED FACTS

"BUT SHE (LEAH) SAID TO HER (RACHEL), 'WASN'T IT ENOUGH THAT YOU TOOK AWAY MY HUSBAND? WILL YOU TAKE MY SON'S MANDRAKES TOO? ...'"
(GENESIS 30:15 NIV)

As we look at Leah and her sister Rachel continue this "baby-making war," Rachel is still childless at this point. She wants the mandrakes that Reuben has given his mother Leah for herself, hoping she might have children. In the previous verse (Genesis 30:14), she asks Leah to share them with her. Leah uses this request to chide her sister for "stealing her husband." Our LORD must be shaking His head in utter pity over this entire situation. What a pathetic picture is painted for us. Leah's facts and mind at this point are so twisted. She is assuming a relationship with Jacob that has NEVER existed. Jacob, the husband, has always loved the younger sister—not her. Leah accused her sister of "husband stealing." Is this not a case of "the pot calling the kettle black?" But Rachel (thinking that the mandrakes will help her bare children), quickly cuts to the chase and says, "ok sis' let's trade—Jacob tonight for your mandrakes." Desperate Leah does not need the question repeated a second time—she jumps for the chance to be with Jacob. Here is how you know when love is not love. In Leah's case, she must use a gimmick or trick to get the man to be with her. In Rachel's case, she simply makes her needs known to Jacob, and they are done. Love should not have to demand, play games, or manipulate to get a positive response. Making the request known should be all that is needed.

LEAH AND US: Leah shows us that by trying to handle things through twisted facts and other manipulations, puts us in desperate situations. See how foolish and sad, to the point of groveling, Leah appears. Jacob married her thinking he was marrying her sister Rachel. It was Leah who was complicit with her dad; to trick Jacob into marrying her. This is not genuine love.

GOD SPEAKS: "Love does not delight in evil but rejoices with the truth." (1 Corinthians 13:6 NIV) When you have to twist, stretch, and bend facts, you are not showing God's love, but human lusts.

WANDA'S PRAYER: LORD, show us how to love like You love.

May 15

AIN'T TOO PROUD TO BEG

"SO WHEN JACOB CAME IN FROM THE FIELDS THAT EVENING, LEAH WENT OUT TO MEET HIM. 'YOU MUST SLEEP WITH ME,' SHE SAID. 'I HAVE HIRED YOU WITH MY SON'S MANDRAKES.' SO HE SLEPT WITH HER THAT NIGHT." (GENESIS 30:16 NIV)

There was a love song out when I was a kid called, "Ain't Too Proud to Beg." The song was about a man who would do whatever he needed to do to get the woman, which included begging or pleading for her love. Such seems to be the case here with Leah. Judging from her statement to Jacob, it seems rather obvious that he had not planned to spend the evening with her, until she approached him. I suppose we could call this discourse between Leah and Jacob, part two of "How I can know when the man doesn't love me." The man does not love me when I have to approach him. Men by nature are "hunters and gatherers," according to my husband. Translation—men like the chase! Men liked being the "chasers" of women in Leah's day, and they still like being the "chasers" today. We only degrade ourselves when we chase them. When you are in charge of the "hunt," you may get what you think you want—a warm body in bed next to you for the short term; but you will not get what you truly need—long term commitment and love. Despite what Darwin says, you cannot get order from disorder. When I am outside of God's will and order for my life, I cannot and should not expect Him to bless my mess. The answer is to always stop, turn, and seek my LORD. The Father is just where I left Him - waiting for me to return home.

LEAH AND US: I have also sought to buy a man with gifts and trinkets. This did not work for me either; it just caused me pain and embarrassment. So, reader, save your dignity and follow God's way.

GOD SPEAKS: "Why spend money on what is not bread, and your labor on what does not satisfy? Listen, listen to me, and eat what is good, and you will delight in the richest of fare. Give ear and come to me; listen, that you may live …" (Isaiah 55:2-3 NIV) Without Me in your life—filling your life, you will be as the drought of the Sahara Desert. Allow Me to fill and complete you. I am the only One who can.

WANDA'S PRAYER: Father God, come into our hearts and lives and complete us. We want to be your surrendered child. Thank you for the wonderful love You have already shown.

May 16

I HEAR YOU

"GOD LISTENED TO LEAH, AND SHE BECAME PREGNANT AND BORE JACOB A FIFTH SON."
(GENESIS 30:17 NIV)

Above the noise of the battling sisters, there was someone truly listening. It was not her double-dealing father, Laban, who had placed her in a loveless marriage. It was not the unfeeling husband who just used her as a baby factor. That listening ear belonged to the LORD. He heard the cries of this poor woman's heart. The Hebrew word for "listened" in this passage is "Shama." It means to pay careful attention to, to consider, or to regard. The King of Creation did just that for Leah. He bent His ears to listen and had regard for Leah's heartaches; He carefully considered her unloved state. He responded to her in a way by which she would know it was from Him alone; He allowed her to have a fifth son by Jacob. This speaks volumes. It tells us that there is someone listening to our hurting hearts. He hears our silent cries in the middle of the night. He not only hears, but His answers to our cries are so personal—to and for us alone. The question is not, "If God hears us?" He does! The question is, are we listening to the answers He gives us regarding life's questions?

LEAH AND US: In God's response to Leah, He shouts, "Daughter, I heard your cry, and I have answered. I care about you Leah—I have always cared." We can take comfort in knowing, our LORD feels the same way about us as well.

GOD SPEAKS: "The righteous cry out, and the Lord hears them; he delivers them from all their troubles. The Lord is close to the brokenhearted and saves those who are crushed in spirit." (Psalm 34:17-18 NIV) Remember, my Name is Savior—this is what I do! I am close to your broken heart; I am just waiting for you to come to me with all your cares.

WANDA'S PRAYER: Out of our depths, Heavenly Father, You hear and answer us.

May 17

GOD'S WAGES?

"THEN LEAH SAID, 'GOD HAS GIVEN ME MY REWARD, BECAUSE I GAVE MY SLAVE TO MY HUSBAND.' SO SHE NAMED HIM ISSACHAR." (GENESIS 30:18 NASB)

Leah's relationship with the Father God is one that challenges my heart. Though her reasoning behind the blessings she receives from the LORD is very misguided, she is clear on who gave her the gift. Her Heavenly Husband and Father provided the gift to her. She is aware that every good and perfect gift comes from God above. Leah takes no credit for the sons she bears for Jacob. She names this son "my wages (reward)" or Issachar. The Hebrew word for Issachar is "Sakar" which means "pay for services rendered." Leah thinks God paid her for giving her maid to Jacob. She supposes this is a good thing—NO! NO! The family dynamics in Jacob's household are so twisted because God is an afterthought! This family has its own warped sense of right and wrong. The LORD blessed Leah with a child because He saw she was unloved by Jacob. It was God's way of saying to Leah, "My daughter, you are loved by the perfect Lover of Souls." He especially seeks the unloved and downcast. He heard her aching heart, and He rewarded Leah with Himself. The evidence of this love was Issachar. This gift speaks against human effort. If you can recall, the LORD gave her this son after she sold the mandrakes to her sister Rachel for a night with Jacob. Rachel did not conceive, but Leah without the mandrake did. She needed nothing but her LORD.

LEAH AND US: I have two kids I gave birth to; and another who calls me mom. They are my little "Issachar's." When I look at them, I see the words, "Wanda, I love you." However, my Issachar's do not stop there; the Heavenly Father provides for me in every way. He started by giving me a new life in Him. He is preparing a place for me to live forever with Him. In the here and now, He gives me life, health, strength, food, shelter and so much more. These rewards are not rewards; they are His gifts to show me just how much He loves me.

GOD SPEAKS: "… I am… thy exceeding great reward." (Genesis 15:1 KJV). "But without faith it is impossible to please him: for he that cometh to God must believe that he is, and that he is a rewarder of them that diligently seek him." (Hebrews 11:6 KJV) Your reward is in believing that I am God! Act on that belief by completely surrendering your life over to Me. You must do it day by day and sometimes, hour by hour.

WANDA'S PRAYER: Lord, I cannot seek You unless you give me the desire to seek You; and the strength to do so.

May 18

MORE LOVE

"LEAH CONCEIVED AGAIN AND BORE JACOB A SIXTH SON." (GENESIS 30:19 NIV)

Leah had given Jacob six sons. She had also given her maid to him to bear sons and build his tribe. In a feeble attempt to win his affections, Leah had given herself to this man, in every conceivable way she knew. Jacob would never love or even offer her respect. This incredibly sad epitaph speaks volumes to us. What a loveless marriage her father, Laban, placed her in. Yet today in our modern and liberated society, how often do we women place ourselves under the same yoke as Leah? We, like Leah, give and give to men who will never love or respect us. I am told that to repeat the same process and expect different results is insanity. Leah's earthly father was not a man after Father God's heart, but after his own self-interest. She felt unloved, and she acted as the unloved act. Leah did not realize how much the Master Lover loved her; though He had yelled it out to her in every conceivable way. The more Jacob despised and dishonored her, the more the Father of Supreme love drowned her in His love. It was as if God was saying, "Look Leah, I love you; My love is real, true, and has been proven. I gave you the undesired (and some might say) the weak one, six sons." (Writer's paraphrase)

LEAH AND US: In giving child number six, God tells her again that she is His heart's desire. This provision of the Father to Leah shows her (and us) how wonderfully she was loved and cared for by the Dad of Love. We women never have to pour out our affections on a man who will never return that love.

GOD SPEAKS: "For God so loved the world that he gave his one and only Son, that whoever believes in him shall not perish but have eternal life." (John 3:16 NIV) On an old rugged cross, over two thousand years ago, I gave the best and most precious gift the world could ever receive. In that treasure is life, joy, and hope; not only in this world, but it is also the ticket for your trip to spend an eternity with Me. I cannot wait!

WANDA'S PRAYER: Father, thank You for just being you! Your gifts are nice, but the more we get to know You, the more we realize how the true Gift is really You! Help us to cherish You always. Teach us how to tell others of your gift, in how we live for you.

FATHER GOD

"AND LEAH SAID, 'GOD HAS ENDOWED ME WITH A GOOD ENDOWMENT; …'" (GENESIS 30:20 NKJV)

It is easy to look at Leah with pity. Her earthly father placed her in this loveless marriage for his own profit. He got Jacob to work seven years for him; as a price for her. No matter what she did, or how many sons she gave the man, he never expressed love or even gratitude to her. But before casting Leah off as one to be pitied, look at this woman's heart. She has a heart after the true Father of Heaven. Over and over again, she acknowledges the Lord as her provider. Leah continually praises God for His goodness, as in this case. "… God hath endowed me with a good dowry." This woman has joy unspeakable—beyond the sad circumstances of her life. She is able to rise above the pathetic hand life has dealt her, to see the face of an exceptionally good God. At the birth of the sixth son, the verse says, "Leah said…" Meaning Leah announced, or made known to all around her, that Elohim—the Supreme LORD, "endued" or conferred on her "a good dowry." The word dowry means precious, bountiful, best, beautiful gift. Leah was saying the God of Heaven chose me—the outcast; He favored me with this precious gift.

LEAH AND US: Leah did nothing to deserve it. The Lord of Love just wanted to say, "Daughter of mine, I love you; I want to show you how much, so here is your sixth son." The same God of love wants to show that same love to all of His daughters and sons. Isn't that beautiful?

GOD SPEAKS: "Every good and perfect gift is from above, coming down from the Father of the heavenly lights, who does not change like shifting shadows." (James 1:17 NIV) I am good, complete, and full of light. The only gifts I can give are ones which are good and will complete you. My gifts will never fade or grow old. What I give you, and that which I withhold from you, is for your perfect good; they are my perfect will for you. My daughter—never forget this!

WANDA'S PRAYER: Father, we know You are good and everything You give is good. We will bless the LORD with a full heart. Your praise will continually be in our mouths.

PEACE PLEASE

"... NOW MY HUSBAND WILL DWELL WITH ME, BECAUSE I HAVE BORNE HIM SIX SONS." SO SHE CALLED HIS NAME ZEBULUN." (GENESIS 30:20 NKJV)

To understand the above passage, we must consider the complete verse: "And Leah said, 'God hath endued me with a good dowry; now will my husband dwell with me, because I have born him six sons:' and she called his name Zebulun." (Genesis 30:20 KJV) In the first part, Leah speaks of God giving her a good dowry. "The dowry was a gift given to the father of the bride. It was not considered payment, but compensation for the father's loss of help as a daughter. The dowry could be money, goods or services rendered." (Nelson's New Illustrated Bible) Jacob's dowry was seven years of work to Laban with the expectation of getting Rachel, but he was tricked into getting Leah. In order to get Rachel, Jacob had to work another seven years. The deception by Laban to Jacob left him very bitter. It is obvious from her statements that Leah bore the brunt of that bitterness for her part in this arranged trickery. Since divorce was not an option, Leah spent years trying to somehow atone for this wrong and make her marriage work. With the birth of her sixth son, she finally felt the Lord had redeemed her worth as a wife. It is as if Leah is saying, "God has given me a precious gift (dowry); now I really hope my husband (this man I married) will finally see me as his wife and want to live with me." She names the child Zebulun, meaning "dwelling place or residence." Loosely translated— "home." Leah was tired of the struggle, anger, and pain all of this had caused. She saw the Lord as giving her a white flag of surrender and hoped Jacob would see this son as the one who would finally bring peace to this embattled home.

LEAH AND US: How often we, like Leah, jump through so many "hoops," in an effort to work the "unworkable." We are determined to fit that square peg into that round hole.

GOD SPEAKS: "In peace I will lie down and sleep, for you alone, Lord, make me dwell in safety." (Psalm 4:8 NIV) This verse is for you! Despite your circumstances, you can have peace and joy in Me. I Am your safe dwelling place. Come and rest in Me—give Me all your cares and woes; leave them at My feet. In peace, through faith, trust that I will work them out for your good and My glory.

WANDA'S PRAYER: Thank you Father! The load was getting a bit heavy. You can have it—it is Yours.

May 21

APPLE'S EYE

"SOME TIME LATER SHE GAVE BIRTH TO A DAUGHTER…" (GENESIS 30:21 NIV)

The life of Leah is a beautiful illustration to all of us, as to what our LORD and Father will do for His helpless ones. Leah was seen as the less desirable one—the weakest link; yet Leah is the one God is primarily using to build Jacob's family. As she gives birth to her seventh child, she is very much aware of the blessings the Father of Heaven has bestowed upon her. Though she makes no proclamations about the child's name, I believe her joy is the same as she felt for her sons. It would be easy to miss this point in a casual reading of the text. A closer look and study of the words in their original meaning best expresses her feelings. The Hebrew word for "daughter" is "Bath." It is from the word "Banah." The word "bath" means the "apple of the eye," and the word "Banah" means to "build up or to repair." I think Leah saw the Lord as having given her this precious apple of her and Jacob's eye, to perhaps build up or repair the breech in this very torn marriage. Leah is a true optimist. Despite all the failed attempts to win Jacob's heart, she is still viewing this seventh child as the one which would bridge the divide between her and Jacob. This woman is able to look at her dismal circumstances, and by God's grace, still find hope and joy.

LEAH AND US: Leah's attitude on life should put us to shame. She never gives up on trying to win Jacob's love. How like her Heavenly Father, Leah is. He continually gives us His precious "apples" (wonderful gifts), in hopes that we, too, will turn to Him and realize just how much He genuinely loves us.

GOD SPEAKS: "Keep me as the apple of your eye; hide me in the shadow of your wings…" (Psalm 17:8 NIV) Leah remembered what most seem to forget—you are the apple of My eye!

WANDA'S PRAYER: Thank you for Your love and gentle reminders of Your extreme love for us.

May 22

JUST A NAME?

"SOMETIME LATER SHE GAVE BIRTH TO A DAUGHTER AND NAMED HER DINAH." (GENESIS 30:21 NIV)

Biblical names fascinate me. Some names were picked based on the parent's hopes and dreams for their child. I believe such was the case of Leah's baby girl, "Dinah." Her name speaks of "memorializing, giving honor, or renown." Dinah literally means, "Justice, judgment, plea, or strife." Her name implies the settling of scores and making wrongs right. Maybe Leah saw her daughter, child number seven, as the one who would right the wrong in her failed marriage. If this was the case, she forgot something she should have remembered—it is GOD alone who judges justly (1 Peter 2:23). The LORD had given Leah seven children. With the birth of each child, He kept pouring His love out to His untrusting daughter. The Father chased after Leah's love by lavishing His love on her. He did this by opening her womb and giving her seven children. Leah, in turn, chased her husband's love by offering him kids. She may have thought this child would or could vindicate her cause; that Jacob would finally sweep her into his arms and profess his love for her. While it is nice to be optimistic, at some point practicality has to set in. What is really sad is that TRUE LOVE (God's love) was right in front of her face, and she could not even see it.

LEAH AND US: Like Leah, we want the wrongs to be made right. To accomplish this, we turn our focus towards the things of this world; and turn away from the loving LORD. He so wants us to seek Him. He gives and gives and keeps on giving to us— "pressed down and running over." Yet, we cannot see His love, because we are so focused on the temporal, and ignore the eternal.

GOD SPEAKS: "My people have committed two sins: they have forsaken me, the spring of living water, and have dug their own cisterns, broken cisterns that cannot hold water." (Jeremiah 2:13 NIV) If you would just turn to Me completely, you will find that I alone can truly satisfy. I really am all you need!

WANDA'S PRAYER: Father God, complete and fill us; Keep filling us and we will continue to drink in You.

May 23

WIFE NO. 2

"SO JACOB SENT WORD TO RACHEL AND LEAH TO COME OUT TO THE FIELDS WHERE HIS FLOCKS WERE. HE SAID TO THEM, 'I SEE THAT YOUR FATHER'S ATTITUDE TOWARD ME IS NOT WHAT IT WAS BEFORE, BUT THE GOD OF MY FATHER HAS BEEN WITH ME.'" (GENESIS 31:4-5 NIV)

Is it just me or should not this text read, "He sent word to Leah and Rachel," and not "Rachel and Leah?" After all, didn't he marry Leah first? (Genesis 29:22) It reads the way it does because Jacob considered Rachel the primary wife, and Leah the secondary child giver. I will give him his props—he includes her in the family meeting. He does not give this privilege to the servant mothers of his kids. Leah obeyed her husband and came without a whisper. Some may say she came because she was desperate to show her affections to Jacob, and would take him any way she could have him. Leah may have finally realized her place in Jacob's life, and her place in God's will. Maybe she accepted the fact that "I am deeply loved by the One who truly matters." Being confident in that fact, Leah's mindset may have been the following, "Lord, wherever You want to place me in Your Kingdom and in this household, is ok with me." Thoughts such as these may have brought peace to Leah's heart as being second fiddle. After all, as she looked in the face of each of her children, she could see the words "I love you," signed the LORD OF LOVE. And maybe this time she finally got the message the Father was sending her. This message was "Leah—married or single, I, your Lord, am also your Husband."

LEAH AND US: Can we, like Leah, be accepting of the place our LORD has placed us in? Or do we whine and grumble over our circumstances?

GOD SPEAKS: "Humble yourselves in the sight of the Lord, and He will lift you up." (James 4:10 NKJV) Climb yourself onto My big shoulders; let Me carry you where I need you to go.

WANDA'S PRAYER: We are ready, Daddy, let's go!

May 24

UNITY AND PEACE

"THEN RACHEL AND LEAH REPLIED, 'DO WE STILL HAVE ANY SHARE IN THE INHERITANCE OF OUR FATHER'S ESTATE? DOES HE NOT REGARD US AS FOREIGNERS? NOT ONLY HAS HE SOLD US, BUT HE HAS USED UP WHAT WAS PAID FOR US … SO DO WHATEVER GOD HAS TOLD YOU.'"
(GENESIS 31:14-16 NIV)

The white flag of peace is now raised over Jacob's household. It seems the battle between the sisters has ended. Leah had declared a truce with her sister. They now unite behind their husband, Jacob. In the above text, we are given part of a discussion. Leah and her sister agree their father has cheated and used them (Leah, Rachel, and Jacob). Now in a united front, the two sisters tell Jacob they are with him as he follows God, "… So do whatever God has told you." (Genesis 31:16) I believe Leah could end the fight for Jacob's heart, because the Father God has given her His heart! With the heart of God came His perfect peace, which was beyond Leah's limited comprehension. The peace God gave her caused her to end the "sister war," and align herself under her husband's leadership. She takes the LORD at His word in that she leaves her father and cleaves to her husband. What is remarkable is she does it, knowing she is the second wife. I think Leah can fully submit to Jacob, because she has already completely submitted to her true Husband—the God of Heaven. While she may have doubts about her earthly husband's directions, she is certain her Heavenly Husband, Lord, will always make the right call. She knows the One who has cared for her up to this point will never leave or forsake her—ever! This quiet submission by the wives brings order and rest to an otherwise chaotic home.

LEAH AND US: While Leah's family life is not ideal for marriage, her attitude of surrender to the Heavenly Husband, and uniting under His perfect plans for her life, is one worth adopting.

GOD SPEAKS: "Let the peace of Christ rule in your hearts, since as members of one body you were called to peace. And be thankful. Let the message of Christ dwell among you richly as you teach and admonish one another with all wisdom …" (Colossians 3:15-16 NIV)

WANDA'S PRAYER: Thank You Father, for being our Rock of Gibraltar.

May 25

THE JOURNEY

"THEN JACOB PUT HIS CHILDREN AND HIS WIVES ON CAMELS, AND HE DROVE ALL HIS LIVESTOCK AHEAD OF HIM, ALONG WITH ALL THE GOODS HE HAD ACCUMULATED IN PADDAN ARAM, TO GO TO HIS FATHER ISSAC IN THE LAND OF CANAAN." (GENESIS 31:17-18 NIV)

After twenty years of living in Paddan Aram, Jacob loads up his family and heads back to his home in Canaan. We are told in the above verse, "he put his twelve children (eleven boys and one girl) and his four wives (Rachel, Leah and their two servant girls), on camels …" The feuding sisters signed lasting peace treaties and lined up under Jacob's divine authority as Head of the house. The move from Paddan Aram to Canaan appears to be one of quiet order and peace. We see Jacob taking charge of his house. I envision him gently placing the little ones on camels. He gets all his stuff and heads home to the land of promise. The journey Leah had already taken with her Heavenly Father and LORD had well prepared her for this one. She could just sit back on her camel and say, "Honey, lead the way." This is Perfect peace. This peace says, "My God and my husband have things under control. Whatever problems come along, honey, you can work it out okay. I will give them to you and watch you and God fix it." The beautiful thing about this mindset is it takes the control from the flawed, erring human, and puts it into the hands of the Perfect, All-Powerful LORD.

LEAH AND US: This is the kind of peace, quiet, and trust many of us have searched for all of our lives. It is right at our fingertips; we need only to reach out our feeble hands in faith and grasp it.

GOD SPEAKS: "Trust in the LORD with all your heart, And lean not on your own understanding; In all your ways acknowledge Him, And He shall direct your paths. Do not be wise in your own eyes; Fear the LORD and depart from evil." (Proverbs 3:5-7 NKJV) Humans have 20/20 vision at best—I have infinite/infinite vision! With the blink of an eye, I see all the paths of your life; I know your thoughts before you even think them. I am Perfect—everything I do is perfect—I can do nothing less! All I need is your complete and abiding trust in Me.

WANDA'S PRAYER: Lord, we believe; strengthen those very weak muscles of unbelief.

May 26

NO GOD HERE

"AND LABAN WENT INTO JACOB'S TENT, INTO LEAH'S TENT, AND INTO THE TWO MAIDS' TENTS, BUT HE DID NOT FIND THEM (HIS GODS). THEN HE WENT OUT OF LEAH'S TENT AND ENTERED RACHEL'S TENT." (GENESIS 31:33 NKJV)

The background of this verse is found in Genesis 31. Laban, (Leah and Rachel's father), feels cheated by Jacob—despite all the cheating he had done to Jacob! Anyway, the Lord tells Jacob it is time to go home to daddy. Jacob obeys and leaves while his father-in-law is out of town. Laban finds out and catches up with Jacob's caravan. Meanwhile, Rachel had stolen her father's idol or gods. Laban is angry over all these things happening in his family and is now going from tent to tent in a frantic search for his gods. He looks in Leah's tent and does not find them. He will never find them because he is looking for the wrong God! He is looking for the man-made gods that has now led him to poverty, instead of the GOD of Heaven, who has now made her husband Jacob, rich. Leah knows well of this God; for He has blessed her with six healthy boys and one girl. Though she was considered the weakling of the two sisters, the true God has given her strength to have seven children. The abiding peace she has is from the God, who is not made with hands; He can never be lost or stolen. As she watches her earthly father panic, scrambling around in search of these clay or stick gods, she can comfort herself with the true God of Heaven who has met all of her needs.

LEAH AND US: Some time ago, I decided to put God to the test. I said to myself, "Self, you are going to trust the Lord. You are going to take your every care and concern to Him. You will follow His leadings and not your futile ways." It works … it really works! The peace you get from letting God handle things is great! It lowered by blood pressure by twenty points and dropped my pulse. I have also never slept better; despite the back pain I was having. Now, if I would just stay in the Father's hands, I will be just fine.

GOD SPEAKS: "Those who know your name trust in you, for you, Lord, have never forsaken those who seek you." (Psalm 9:10 NIV) Do you know My Name today? If you stay in the knowing of Me, you will be okay. The problems start when you stop spending time knowing I AM. You will have struggles, but I have promised to get you through them all.

WANDA'S PRAYER: Father God, always keep me in the knowing stage with You. Never take me out of your hands—ever!

May 27

I'M GLAD I KNOW WHO MY REAL HUSBAND IS

"NOW JACOB LIFTED HIS EYES AND LOOKED, AND THERE, ESAU WAS COMING, AND WITH HIM WERE FOUR HUNDRED MEN. SO HE DIVIDED THE CHILDREN AMONG LEAH, RACHEL, AND THE TWO MAIDSERVANTS. AND HE PUT THE MAIDSERVANTS AND THEIR CHILDREN IN FRONT, LEAH AND HER CHILDREN BEHIND, AND RACHEL AND JOSEPH LAST." (GENESIS 33:1-2 NKJV)

Just when you think this guy has a changed heart, he does this crazy stunt. All these people are his responsibility; these children are all his! Why doesn't he ask the LORD for a heart to love them equally? Why doesn't he ask the Father to protect them? No, he takes matters into his own hands and does this stupid, very selfish act. He places the children and their mothers in order of importance, like pieces of wood or something. The least desirable is placed in the heat of the battle—ready for the kill, while he protects precious Rachel and Joseph. This move on Jacob's part spoke volumes to his children, as well as to the women in his life. It said, "this one is important, and this one is not." I believe this act would come back to bite him later. The extreme comfort I take from this is Leah's comfort. This comfort is from her Lord. Though I am very much complaining, she did not complain one bit. She just took her place and totally trusted in her LORD. In her mind, the LORD who gave her these seven children would step in and take care of all of them. Leah knew who her real Husband was. She knew it was not Jacob—he was only the earthly husband; The LORD, her Maker, was also her Husband. He was her Protector and Provider in the past and would be so now. She would stand still and see His salvation over her, and the children He gave her.

LEAH AND US: This woman has truly grown-up in the Lord. As I look at Leah's life, I can see this is where peace really comes from. Leah trusted in the Lord and submitted to His perfect order through Jacob. I want to be a woman like this—she is a woman after the Father's heart.

GOD SPEAKS: "… submitting to one another in the fear of God. Wives, submit to your own husbands, as to the Lord. For the husband is head of the wife, as also Christ is head of the church; and He is the Savior of the body." (Ephesians 5:21-23 NKJV) Look at this verse with Me for a moment. I Am the Head and Savior of the Body—the church. I am also the Head and Savior of your body. I have been your GOD and Husband throughout your single life. Name a point in your life when you trusted and followed me, that I did not provide for you. I can meet your needs all by Myself; and I can provide for you using a million people. It is Me, your LORD, whom you are to place your ultimate trust in.

WANDA'S PRAYER: Father, help us to know that whatever provision You send our way is Your perfect provision for us.

May 28

A DAUGHTER'S HURT—MOM'S PAIN

"NOW DINAH THE DAUGHTER OF LEAH, WHOM SHE HAD BORNE TO JACOB, WENT OUT TO SEE THE DAUGHTERS OF THE LAND. AND WHEN SHECHEM THE SON OF HAMOR THE HIVITE, PRINCE OF THE COUNTRY, SAW HER, HE TOOK HER AND LAY WITH HER, AND VIOLATED HER." (GENESIS 34: 1-2 NKJV)

This is a sad chapter in the life of Leah's already wearied life. Jacob had moved his family back to the land of Canaan. Jacob and his family were to be in the land; but not of the land. They were to live in the land and be an eyewitness of God's glory to the world around them, but not to yoke themselves with the world. Leah had lived her entire life inside the clan. It never dawned on her to venture out to see what she may have been missing. This was not the case with her daughter Dinah. Perhaps bored with home life, she wanted to see something and someone new. She did not know curiosity kills and destroys. She left home an inquisitive child with her virginity intact, only to return a dejected and violated young woman. The abuser who raped her was the prince of that country. This was a terrible crime then and now. Though Leah does not speak, we can be sure she suffered in pain with her daughter over this tragedy. After all, what could she say? I would imagine as Mama held her daughter in her arms, allowing the tears to saturate her clothing, she remembered her baby girl of long ago. Remember, the word for daughter in Hebrew means "apple of the eye." This was the tainted fruit she had longed to shelter and protect. The good news is vengeance belongs to the Lord; and He does repay. Dinah's name means judgment. Shechem violates God's daughter, and the Lord allows his death at the hands of her brothers.

LEAH AND US: My heart aches for my children when I see others hurt them. Many times, because of my circumstances, like Leah, I feel there is little or nothing I can do to help, but that is not true. I can repeatedly give it to my Father—He is still in control and will repay! He can still make right all the wrongs.

GOD SPEAKS: "… Shall not the Judge of all the earth do right?" (Genesis 18:25 NKJV) This is a particularly good question, don't you think? The answer is yes! I will always do what is perfectly right and just—because that is who I Am! I am correct when you understand; and I am just, even when you do not. I must be right or correct to the victims, as well as to the violators. Your only job is to let Me do what I do best—everything perfectly well!

WANDA'S PRAYER: Ok Lord, help us to just be quiet and watch You work. You know we like to question the things you do in and around our life.

May 29

LESS + GOD = ABUNDANCE

"THESE WERE THE SONS LEAH BORE TO JACOB IN PADDAN ARAM, BESIDES HIS DAUGHTER DINAH. THESE SONS AND DAUGHTERS OF HIS WERE THIRTY-THREE IN ALL." (GENESIS 46:15 NIV)

There is a childhood song I sang in church when I was small. It goes something like this: "Count your many blessings, name them one by one … and it will surprise you what the LORD has done." No truer words were ever spoken than these when you apply them to Leah—the less desired one. As biblical history adds up the father of Israel, Jacob's sons, I am struck by the awesome power of our LORD. Our Heavenly Dad took the "weak-eyed" one who was considered so much less than her sister Rachel and produced a bumper crop of sons. Leah gave birth, directly or indirectly, to 47% of Jacob's offspring. Truly little becomes much when placed in the hands of the Master. This should speak volumes to all of us of our LORD'S power and His willingness to bless if we would just surrender our all to the KING OF KINGS. In looking back at Leah's life, as revealed in the pages of God's Holy Word, I see the words "I LOVE YOU LEAH," written across every phase of her difficult life. In our world of loving the lovely and loveable, what a refreshing contrast to behold. It is like a glass of ice-cold water in the middle of the Sahara Desert at high noon. Our Father did not just sprinkle some love on His unloved daughter, He nearly drowned her with His deep, tender compassion, which He had for her.

LEAH AND US: As I look back over my life, I see those same words too: "Wanda, I love you, I love you, I love you!" They were written in the good times and especially in the bad. I know they had to have been written in the tough times, because He brought me through them. It was during those times, He taught me the greatest lessons of life. Thank You Father, for loving me always; especially during those times when I did not love myself.

GOD SPEAKS: "I have loved you," says the Lord. "But you ask, how have you loved us? …" (Malachi 1:2 NIV) Wanda, I will answer that question as it applies just to you. I, your LORD, have loved you since before even your great-grandmother was born. Before I formed the world, I saw every step of your life. I destined you as My own, from everlasting. Words can never express the depth, width, or height of the love I have for you. By way of my Holy Spirit, just allow Me to speak to your heart, a little of the love I feel and have for you.

WANDA'S PRAYER: Speak LORD, speak; Your child is listening.

May 30

LEAH GETS HER DUE

"THERE ABRAHAM AND HIS WIFE SARAH WERE BURIED, THERE ISAAC AND HIS WIFE REBEKAH WERE BURIED, AND THERE I BURIED LEAH." (GENESIS 49:31 NIV)

Leah spent a great deal of her life's effort in a feeble attempt to get love and respect from Jacob. I have read and reread her life as given to us in God's Word, and I do not find where Jacob ever gave her that for which she most craved. However, in her death, Leah seemed to have hit a home run. She is buried in the family mausoleum right beside the grand "matriarch," Sarah herself. This was an extreme honor given by Jacob. We note he did not bury his beloved Rachel in the holy tomb; though the place of her death was probably less than a hundred miles away from there. At Leah's death, what Jacob seems to now be saying is, "I proclaim her as my wife. I now honor this woman who God used to build more than half my tribe, as my wife." "See," he says, "Grandfather Abraham buried his wife Sarah here; My dad Isaac, buried my dear mother Rebekah here; and here I buried Leah." (Genesis 49:31 Paraphrased)

LEAH AND US: There are times in my life when I, too, have felt unappreciated; and I did not receive the rewards I thought I should have received for the "good" job I had done. Like Leah, I felt the guilt and mistakes of my youth loom large, and foreboding over my life. At times, I feel these mistakes and failures may have paralyzed the blessings I believe I should have received. Father, speak to my heart on this matter.

GOD SPEAKS: "I the Lord search the heart and examine the mind, to reward each person according to their conduct, …" (Jeremiah 17:10 NIV) I know your heart better than you will ever know. I am aware of the good, bad and the ugly; I have always known. What I know about you has no bearing on My love for you. I charted your destiny well in advance of your birth. The rewards I give you are only held back by your lack of faith as you walk according to My Word.

WANDA'S PRAYER: Order all of my life after Your Holy Word.

May 31

GOD'S EPITAPH

"… MAY THE LORD MAKE THE WOMAN WHO IS COMING INTO YOUR HOME LIKE RACHEL AND LEAH, WHO TOGETHER BUILT UP THE FAMILY OF ISRAEL …"
(RUTH 4:11 NIV)

This verse speaks volumes in just a few words. In the town of Bethlehem, the Elders speak a blessing regarding Ruth, who marries Boaz, the Great Grandfather of King David. The comparison made is that she would be such a blessing to her husband to help form a nation. In looking at the life of Leah and her sister Rachel, we can see that indeed Father God did use them to build the nation of Israel through Jacob. Together, the sisters "built up the house of Israel." This tells me a lot of forgiveness must have taken place. If forgiveness and reconciliation had not happened, the verse may have read, "each of them contributed to the building of Israel's house." The sisters put away the clawing and scraping at each other for the common good—to build the House of the Lord. In the end, the sisters united to build this house, and our Lord recognized their efforts for centuries to come. Leah and Rachel are remembered not for the battles over Jacob's affections, but for their uniting to build up the family of God, through which our LORD Christ would come. This tribe of Israel was one body founded by God through these women. In our day, it speaks to us of what unity in the Body of Christ can do when differences are put aside for the common goal. This goal is to show the love of Christ to a dying and lost world.

LEAH AND US: As I look over my life these past forty-plus years, I must ask myself this question, "Have I divided, conquered, and destroyed in search of my own pleasure? Or have I sought to build up my LORD'S kingdom?" In looking at Leah's life, I see a woman who, in the end—kept the main thing, the main thing. The main thing is Christ and Him crucified. He gave His life to save me. The question I must ask is, "how am I giving my life to bring others to Him?"

GOD SPEAKS: "For we are co-workers in God's service; you are God's field, God's building." (1 Corinthians 3:9 NIV) "For no one can lay any foundation other than the one already laid, which is Jesus Christ." (1 Corinthians 3:11 NIV) Work with Me, as I work out My will, in and through your life. Together, with My other children, we will reach this dying world and save some.

WANDA'S PRAYER: Father, work out Your will for our lives. Help us to always remember—it is all about YOU, and not about us.

Notes

June

INTRODUCTION

RACHEL

Rachel is the second daughter of Laban. Blessed with beauty and poise, she was the love of Jacob's life. We learn from her life that not one of us has everything. Rachel had good looks, with a great personality and a strong work ethic. While these are all good qualities, they are not everything. In this life, we still have missing pieces.

Rachel also teaches us that because we have great qualities or traits, we may feel we don't need God's help. She shows us we will always need God's help and cannot rely on our own wits to function. Trusting in ourselves and other humans will lead us to disappointments and sadness. In the end, we will be forced to turn to and trust in the God of heaven.

I love studying Rachel's life because she teaches me how to act around the opposite sex. Her life is a brilliant study of how we as women don't need to chase men. Instead, let them chase us.

She is also an excellent case study on how and why we should involve our families in our dating lives. While these are controversial topics today, I believe a study of the ancient Rachel's life will provide answers to many of these questions.

Notes

June 1

JUST ONE LOOK!

"… YES, HE IS," THEY SAID, "AND HERE COMES HIS DAUGHTER RACHEL WITH THE SHEEP." "LOOK," HE SAID, "THE SUN IS STILL HIGH; IT IS NOT TIME FOR THE FLOCKS TO BE GATHERED. WATER THE SHEEP AND TAKE THEM BACK TO PASTURE." (GENESIS 29:6-7 NIV)

Jacob is continuing his journey to the East, in search of his father's relatives. He meets some shepherds at a well in the middle of the day. He starts a conversation with them, asking if they know Laban, his mother's brother. The shepherds say yes, and points to Laban's daughter coming to the well to water her sheep. Just the reading of this text gives you a picture of a man who has already lost his heart to a woman. If Leah is a demonstration of what it is like to be unloved, then Rachel is the icon of what it is to be truly loved. Jacob sees Rachel coming to herd sheep. He finds out she is his cousin and immediately wants to spend time with her. How do I know this? Let us look at the text. He sees her coming, and he says to the men around the well, "Hurry up; water your sheep, and go… take them back to graze, or something—ok?" (Genesis 29:6-7 Writer's paraphrase) Come on now; Sista' girl was not made up, washed up, or anything! By hanging around with those sheep, her perfume would have been called, "Ode of Sheep." What was it about her that made Jacob just flip over her? Perhaps it was too much time spent in the desert; after all, he had traveled a long way from home to get to Laban. We can see that brother-man was in love at first glance! All he wanted to do was get next to Rachel.

RACHEL AND US: As the old folk would say, "I've turned a few heads in my day." In my case, I was clad in make-up and dressed to the nines. I do not think I ever moved a man with the smell of laundry detergent, while dressing in tattered jeans.

GOD SPEAKS: "And he passed in front of Moses, proclaiming, 'the Lord, the Lord, the compassionate and gracious God, slow to anger, abounding in love and faithfulness, maintaining love to thousands, and forgiving wickedness, rebellion and sin …" (Exodus 34:6-7 NIV) Every fiber of My being just oozes with love—this is who I Am! It is a part of My nature. I do not just ooze with it, but it flows out like Niagara Falls onto you. You never have to worry about human love, for it really does not compare with the kind of love I give.

WANDA'S PRAYER: Father, let your glory pass before us like You did for Moses; show us Your wonderful glory and love.

June 2

A SHEEP THING

"WHILE HE WAS STILL TALKING WITH THEM, RACHEL CAME WITH HER FATHER'S SHEEP, FOR SHE WAS A SHEPHERD." (GENESIS 29:9 NIV)

In my research, I discovered that in those days and in that culture, men and women herded sheep. Rachel could relate to our modern world because she was a woman who worked outside the home. Besides Rachel's good looks and fine shape (Genesis 29:17), I suppose one of the reasons Jacob loved Rachel is because she reminded him of his mother. No doubt he must have loved hearing the story of how his mother met Abraham's servant. As he saw her coming with the sheep, he may have reflected on how his mother watered all those camels. I am certain Rachel reminded him of his mother, who he must have missed so very much. In any case, this sheep driving beauty was headed straight towards him, and he could not take his eyes off of her. Now this is love. Rachel does nothing but be Rachel.

RACHEL AND US: My shepherd's hat goes off to Rachel. She must have been something else to catch a man with desert swept hair and the smell of fresh sheep on her skin. I guess I have had guys look at me in that way. It really is a nice feeling.

GOD SPEAKS: "For as high as the heavens are above the earth, so great is his love for those who fear him;" (Psalm 103:11 NIV) Human love may give you the desire to want to get up in the morning, but it cannot compare to My love. My love is the love that wakes you up in the morning. My love gives you power and strength to make it through the day. My love watches over you during the night. Turn your love to Me; I will show you real love. And you will sing like Stephanie Mills, "Oh, I never knew love like this before!"

WANDA'S PRAYER: Father God, I can definitely testify to Your love. It was Your love that kept me and loved me, during the nights after the breakup of my first marriage. It was Your love that gave me a new job to take care of my children when I messed up and lost the first job. It was Your love, which later brought a wonderful man into my life. You loved me when I felt I was unlovable. It is Your love that now sustains every beat of my heart. It is Your love which supplies every breath I take. Thank You, LORD GOD, my Dad, for all the tender ways You care for me.

LOVE MOVES—LARGE STONES

"WHEN JACOB SAW RACHEL DAUGHTER OF HIS UNCLE LABAN, AND LABAN'S SHEEP, HE WENT OVER AND ROLLED THE STONE AWAY FROM THE MOUTH OF THE WELL AND WATERED HIS UNCLE'S SHEEP." (GENESIS 29:10 NIV)

Yep, I was right. Rachel reminded Jacob of his mother, Rebekah. He was a momma's boy. Now, back to the story. Jacob is what we would say—gone! The boy is so love struck that now he is moving a large stone that would normally take several men to move. (Genesis 29:3,8) Love will make a man move large stones. Not only did he move the super-sized stone, but he also watered her sheep. This was no small feat, considering the fact that this macho man was at least sixty years old at the time! If a man loves you, you will see it in how he treats you. Rachel knew she had this man. Her Hebrew name meant "lamb." Jacob had found this little lamb, scooped her up in his arms, and was not letting her go. Notice how Rachel does nothing to earn this love. Jacob loves Rachel; he cannot give or do enough for her. Men are commanded to love, and women are commanded to respect. This story points out the Father's order of things.

RACHEL AND US: The love of Our LORD moved the large stone of sin for us. He was the stone the builders rejected; He became the cornerstone. For too long, I had been out of GOD'S order. I once cared deeply for a man and felt I had to buy him things and do things for him. One day, another woman came into his life. She moved nothing; she gave nothing, and he fell head over hills in love with her. As I stood there then, and now reflect on what happened, I realized I had tried to take my disorder, and get order from it. It was a very painful lesson to learn. Later, I followed the divine handbook (the Bible) as the LORD would have me to do. It has turned out for God's glory and my good.

GOD SPEAKS: "Whoever dwells in the shelter of the Most High will rest in the shadow of the Almighty." "He will cover you with his feathers, and under his wings you will find refuge; his faithfulness will be your shield and rampart." (Psalm 91:1,4 NIV) It may be nice to find a man who can move some of My Creation around for you. But can he speak Creation into existence? Can he call forth time or make it stand still? I can do all these things and so much more. Child of mine, just stay in my secret place and watch me work.

WANDA'S PRAYER: One of the words I like in that verse is "rest." I can rest in the All-Powerful, All-Knowing GOD. I do not have to worry. Father, we give You all our problems and needs, knowing You can work them out. Thank You Father!

June 4

YEP, SHE'S THE ONE

"THEN JACOB KISSED RACHEL AND BEGAN TO WEEP ALOUD." (GENESIS 29:11 NIV)

I have turned the heads of a man or two in my direction. I even had a man stop me in the store and wanted to date me. But I must say, I have never had a man to kiss me at first and then burst out in tears. I tell you—brother man is hooked! This is the one for him; he is looking no further. I have spoken with many married women and most of them have said the same thing— "he told me he knew when he first saw me, or after a date or two, that he wanted me as his wife." This was certainly true for old Jacob. This fact blows holes in our twenty-first century thinking that says, "If I live with him, give him my all, become his door mat for five to ten years, then he will wake up one day and truly love me." Ladies, it did not work thousands of years ago, and it will not work today either. If a man loves you, he loves you. If he does not, pick up your toys, your dignity, and go your merry way. In doing so, you will save yourself much heartache. Notice that Rachel does not chase Jacob. She does not flaunt herself or the sheep in front of him to get his attention. She is going about her God-given tasks in life. She is a wonderful model for us.

RACHEL AND US: When I met my "Big Bear," I was going about my life. I had resigned myself to the fact that I may never get married again. Slowly, over a period of twenty years, the LORD was finally getting it into my head that I was complete in HIM! I was coming into the realization that He was my True Husband and would satisfy my every need. I wanted His will and His purposes for my life—that is, when it happened. I stopped working on my plans and allowed GOD to work His perfect plans for my life.

GOD SPEAKS: "The LORD foils the plans of the nations; he thwarts the purposes of the peoples. But the plans of the LORD stand firm forever, the purposes of his heart through all generations." (Psalm 33:10-11 NIV) I have you and I have wonderful things for you. As you seek My heart totally and completely, I will give you the desires of your heart. I can do this because it is My heart to give good gifts to My children. All you have to do is to stay very close to Me.

WANDA'S PRAYER: Father God, keep us so very, very close to You. We want You to be the first face we see in the morning and the last one we see at night. We want to meet with you, LORD, in our dreams.

June 5

WE ARE FAMILY

"HE HAD TOLD RACHEL THAT HE WAS A RELATIVE OF HER FATHER AND A SON OF REBEKAH. SO SHE RAN AND TOLD HER FATHER." (GENESIS 29:12 NIV)

Things could not have been any better for Jacob or Rachel at this point. Jacob was not just family; he was first cousin. (I guess it must have been ok to marry your first cousin). I am not condoning this outlawed practice, but the principle is very clear; Christians should be yoked together with other Christians, and not unbelievers. Jacob and Rachel were of the same family; "How can two walk together, except they agree?" (Amos 3:3) This was one reason Jacob was so delighted to see Rachel. He had been taught he must marry in the family. Rachel does something that I find interesting. She does not just stay there conversing with Jacob; she runs to tell her father. I will agree her father was not a believer, but again, the principle is very clear here for us today. As daughters in Christ, we must take every potential mate or casual interest to the LORD. Our Heavenly Dad has perfect discernment. He reads the thoughts and intents of the heart. He longs to protect His daughters from hurt and sorrow. We would often spare ourselves the pain of a breakup or nasty divorce, if we would just bring that rascal to our Perfect Heavenly Father.

RACHEL AND US: I know well of what I speak. My marriage ended badly because I did not bring my first husband to my Heavenly Dad. I learned the lesson, however, the second time around. I asked and asked and asked the Father again and again, "Are you sure he is the one, Lord?"

GOD SPEAKS: "For no one can lay any foundation other than the one already laid, which is Jesus Christ." (1 Corinthians 3:11 NIV) With a house as important as the marriage house, why would anyone build on anything less, than on the sure foundation of the Perfect God?

WANDA'S PRAYER: Lord, do not just lay the foundation, but put in the plumbing, the walls, the windows—everything into this marriage house that You have built.

June 6

THE BRASS TACKS

"... AFTER JACOB HAD STAYED WITH HIM FOR A WHOLE MONTH, LABAN SAID TO HIM, 'JUST BECAUSE YOU ARE A RELATIVE OF MINE, SHOULD YOU WORK FOR ME FOR NOTHING? TELL ME WHAT YOUR WAGES SHOULD BE.'" (GENESIS 29:14-15 NIV)

Jacob had been at his uncle's house for about a month. It is clear from this passage of Scripture that he had been idle, but had donated a month of free labor. What is also implied is that Jacob probably was a very good worker. Laban, Jacob's uncle, is now discussing permanent employment arrangements for a price. This speaks volumes of our LORD'S provisions for us as women. Rachel's husband-to-be was a man who knew how to provide for his family. The Lord God designed work for man since His Creation. (Genesis 2:15) Jacob, a son of GOD, would not shrink from its daunting tasks. In fact, it appears he did his work so well that Jacob would be offered to set his own price for the work he provided. I imagine as Rachel looks at his work, it must have given her much comfort. After all, if he took as much care of a woman as he did at performing his work, she knew she would be well taken care of. Do you notice we hear nothing of Rachel trying to manipulate events in order to win Jacob's love? This silence in Scripture is a lesson to me.

RACHEL AND US: When I was dating my Big Bear, I loved many things about him. Yet I was not ready to marry him. Deep down inside, I was not sure he could take care of me. Then one day, the plumbing at my house backed up into the shower and bathtub—it was a mess. I called him very early that morning. He came right over and helped to clean up all the mess. He made a few calls and by the end of the day; he made sure all was working. I saw God's provision for me through this man. Like Rachel, I knew my Father would take very good care of me.

GOD SPEAKS: "But my God shall supply all your need according to his riches in glory by Christ Jesus." (Philippians 4:19 KJV) Notice that your needs are taken care of by Me and Me alone. Cast all your cares on Me—let Me care for them. Find better ways of spending your time than wasting it on worry.

WANDA'S PRAYER: Thank You again, Father, for reminding us how much You love us; and for taking care of all of our needs.

June 7

NO-BRAINER

"LEAH WAS TENDER EYED; BUT RACHEL WAS BEAUTIFUL AND WELL FAVOURED." (GENESIS 29:17 KJV)

Since Jacob first laid eyes on Rachel, his only thought was, "the girl is mine." Now Laban's open-ended offer of wages made Jacob's answer a "no-brainer" for him. Jacob was looking for a wife to settle down and have a family. The choice was an easy one for him. Laban had two daughters, Leah the eldest and Rachel the youngest. The comparison of the two were striking. All that is said of Leah is that her eyes were tender or weak. But of Rachel, it is said she was "beautiful and well favoured." Another translation says she was "lovely in form and beautiful." The translation in our modern vernacular is the girl was a "brick house" and nice to be around. These are qualities men like—then and now. Jacob's mother was beautiful; so when he saw Rachel, it probably reminded him of his mother. Or perhaps he may have been thinking of having pretty babies. At this point, it really did not matter—it would not take a rocket scientist to guess which one of the women Jacob would choose.

RACHEL AND US: When I first met my Big Bear five years before we married, he looked through me. At that time, I was very thin and wore no make-up. Unlike Rachel, I was not naturally drop-dead-gorgeous; I needed Fashion Fair's help. When I met him again five years later, I was a little heavier and cosmetically enhanced. (I was made up) This time he could not take his eyes off of me.

GOD SPEAKS: "He has made everything beautiful in its time. Also He has put eternity in their hearts …" (Ecclesiastes 3:11 NKJV) My timing is always right. Despite what you may feel or think, I am always on time. I make everything perfectly beautiful because I am Perfect. Just allow Me to do what I do best—EVERYTHING!

WANDA'S PRAYER: Teach us how to wait patiently for You with joy, knowing that You will work everything out for our good and Your glory.

June 8

CLEAR CHOICE

"NOW JACOB LOVED RACHEL; SO HE SAID, 'I WILL SERVE YOU SEVEN YEARS FOR RACHEL YOUR YOUNGER DAUGHTER.'" (GENESIS 29:18 NKJV)

Well, while Jacob's choice of a wife was not a surprise, the price he paid was remarkable. In those days, a dowry was given to the father of the woman you wanted to marry. It was not payment for the woman, but it was a token to the father. In some way, the dowry was given to compensate the father for his loss, so to speak. The husband-to-be was taking away one of the helping hands in the father's household. Rachel was a shepherdess and an immense help to Laban. Jacob, in offering such a generous gift of seven years of service, was acknowledging this fact, and also showing the world just how much he loved her. Scholars say Jacob was between sixty to eighty years old at this time; so this was not a small gift or small task for him. This is a real lesson to me about love. It tells me that love will pay a high price to have me, because it knows I am worth it. I do not have to try, buy, beg, or plead for it. Rachel shows all of us as women, that in God's eyes we are all pearls of great price. We do not have to buy love—love wants to purchase us. This is the Father's will and plan for us girls. To do otherwise is like "trying to catch the right bus, standing on the wrong street" (Michelle McKinney Hammond)—it will never happen.

RACHEL AND US: I learned this lesson in a very painful way. Before I met my second husband, I knew a man of whom I tried my hardest to win his affections. All the many efforts I put forth were futile. I had the Diana Ross philosophy when she sings, "I'm going to make you love me; yes I will, you know I will." This was very STUPID! He cared little for me. I was out of GOD'S order for my life; and I was missing the blessings He had for me. When this man's Rachel came along, I knew I had been standing "at the wrong bus stop." That bus was never coming!

GOD SPEAKS: "Husbands, love your wives, just as Christ loved the church and gave himself up for her ..." (Ephesians 5:25 NIV) I am the standard of perfection; everyone is measured by Me. If you have Me, then you have all you need. Let me complete you in every way. Lavish all of your love and affection on Me, instead of on the earthly—I will never let you down. Give me your heart, over and over again; only I can fill it to the brim.

WANDA'S PRAYER: Lord, just fill us up now and forever. I know we will have to come to the well—over and over again.

June 9

JUST DO IT

"AND JACOB SERVED SEVEN YEARS FOR RACHEL; AND THEY SEEMED UNTO HIM BUT A FEW DAYS, ..." (GENESIS 29:20 KJV)

This is a true love story; man sees woman, man falls in love with woman, and now man hurdles through obstacles to be with woman. Brother man is in love. He is so in love that seven years to him seemed like only a few days. Tell me when has seven years of your life seemed like a few days? Not in my life—at times it has seemed like an eternity! It was that way to Jacob because all he thought of was his precious Rachel. She was the coal that gave energy to his work engine. Jacob kept his eyes on his prized Rachel. This is the kind of love the Father has for us. This is the kind of love He expects His sons (the men) to give His daughters (us women). Jacob was more than happy to give this love in order to receive his lovely bride. A friend once told me her dad said this to her, "You want the man who loves you to love you more than you love him." This was certainly true in Jacob's case.

RACHEL AND US: My Big Bear loves me this way; he shows it in many ways. Recently, we were invited to a close friend's wedding. My husband wore a suit. After the wedding, I was to help serve the food at the reception. When we arrived at the Reception Hall, however, to our surprise we found nothing was set-up. He took off his coat and quietly began to help get the rest of the place ready for the reception. We never made it to the wedding, but he never complained—not before, during, or after.

GOD SPEAKS: "Looking unto Jesus the author and finisher of our faith; who for the joy that was set before him endured the cross, despising the shame,..." (Hebrews 12:2 KJV) My daughter, "Love"—this is one of My names. It shuts up and just gets the job done. It was for the pure pleasure of knowing you would be with Me in Paradise, that I paid the price for your sins. I would do it again and again.

WANDA'S PRAYER: Lord, meager words of thanks are not enough; but it is all we can truly say. We will praise You with our complete heart.

June 10

MY WIFE, PLEASE

"AND JACOB SAID UNTO LABAN, 'GIVE ME MY WIFE, FOR MY DAYS ARE FULFILLED, THAT I MAY GO IN UNTO HER.'" (GENESIS 29:21 KJV)

I think this text speaks for itself, don't you? This is a man who has worked for seven years with the great expectation of getting his lovely bride. For seven years, he dreamed of nothing else but his bride Rachel. Now the time had finally come. "I've paid my price. Now give me my wife so that I can have and hold her forever." (Writer's paraphrase) This seems to be the thought of Jacob, as he is speaking to Laban. He could not wait a moment longer to have her. He wanted all the world to know—this is the one! This is how our LORD sees us. We are His bride. He bought us with His own blood. Now He awaits the time when He can come and take us home. In a marriage, it is to be between a man and a woman. The man makes his preparations for his bride. When all is ready, he takes her as his own. In this setting, Rachel gives us such a beautiful illustration of the Bride of Christ. She continues to function in the role her father placed her in. You do not read of her attempting to help Jacob win her heart. She is in position, and she stays in her position, as she awaits directions from her father. This is the position we are to be in as we await the Father's instructions for our lives.

RACHEL AND US: Rachel can be at peace because she trusts her father will do what is best and correct for her. She can trust and rest in knowing her father has her best interest at heart. Though in her case, it was not true. We, however, can rest and trust in our Heavenly Father, who is the All-Wise and Perfect GOD. We can be confident in knowing He will always have our best interest at heart, and will never hurt us. He always wants to protect us from harm.

GOD SPEAKS: "But now, this is what the LORD says—he who created you, Jacob, he who formed you, Israel: 'Do not fear, for I have redeemed you; I have summoned you by name; you are mine.'" (Isaiah 43:1 NIV) You are Mine; You will always be Mine. I love you too much to ever let you go.

WANDA'S PRAYER: Now that is real security! We have a love from You that will never let go. Thank You, Father, for Your unfailing love.

June 11

GREAT DECEPTION

"SO LABAN BROUGHT TOGETHER ALL THE PEOPLE OF THE PLACE AND GAVE A FEAST. BUT WHEN EVENING CAME, HE TOOK HIS DAUGHTER LEAH AND BROUGHT HER TO JACOB, ..."
(GENESIS 29:22-23 NIV)

Here is where this earthly father shows no characteristics of our Heavenly Dad. Our Father never deals in deceit as this man does. Remember, the original agreement was for Rachel, not Leah. Jacob was very clear on this point. (Genesis 29:18) Laban apparently agreed with Jacob. (Genesis 29:19) So what is he doing? How did Rachel feel when she knew she would not be the bride? But again, Scripture is silent about her response. She must have revered her father; though I am sure she did not like this situation at all. But what could she have done about it, anyway? Rachel does nothing—she must trust the twisted judgment of her father. It has no rhyme or reason to her, but her only option is to wait patiently. Though Rachel's father has evil and demented motives for giving his first-born daughter, instead of the agreed upon second-born, the principle of waiting on the Father is the same. Our LORD and Dad only knows love; He deals only in truth. We, like Rachel, can fully trust in Him. Unlike Laban, He is looking out for our best interests, and not just His own. After all, He is called the LORD OF LOVE.

RACHEL AND US: There was a time when I really loved a man. I thought he was the one for me. I even felt the Father was telling me he was the one. It was also very clear to me he did not measure up in Scripture as to what the Father said His husband would look like. That did not matter to me. I continued to follow my emotions, and turned them into a delusion. I waited, I hoped, I even prepared—all in vain. The wedding to that man never came. Now, years later, I jump for extreme joy and praise to my GOD! He alone knew what was truly best for me. He did not give me what I wanted at that time—He gave me so much more! I am so glad He does what is best for us, despite us, aren't you?

GOD SPEAKS: "... but those who hope in the LORD will renew their strength. They will soar on wings like eagles; they will run and not grow weary, they will walk and not be faint." (Isaiah 40:31 NIV) As you put the weight of your full self in My hands, it will blow your mind when you see the things I have in store for you. I know how to give good and perfect gifts.

WANDA'S PRAYER: Lord, we believe this! Help us act and live like we believe it. You will always do what is best for us.

June 12

TRICKS CAN'T KILL LOVE

"WHEN MORNING CAME, THERE WAS LEAH! SO JACOB SAID TO LABAN, 'WHAT IS THIS YOU HAVE DONE TO ME? I SERVED YOU FOR RACHEL, DIDN'T I? WHY HAVE YOU DECEIVED ME?'" (GENESIS 29:25 NIV)

Poor Jacob! He woke up expecting to look into the face of his beautiful Rachel, and to his awful surprise, it was the weak-eyed sister, Leah. Jacob wasted no time confronting his father-in-law. There must have been some mistake, Jacob thought. He knew he had agreed to Rachel. There was no mistake on Laban's behalf. He tells Jacob the older daughter must first marry before the younger. "Well, thanks dad! Why didn't you reveal that tiny little disclosure before I locked down seven years of service?" (Writer's paraphrase) You would think Jacob had a right to know that small detail before signing the contract, right? But notice, Rachel does not confront her dad, or even her sister Leah. Her silence shows me she trusts the situation will still work out in her favor. She allows Jacob to handle things, and he does.

RACHEL AND US: This woman shows a lot more faith and restraint in her youth than I have in my forty-plus years of living. I know my Father cares and always has my best interest at heart, but I do not act like it. When I was "waiting" on a husband, I really was not waiting at all. I was complaining, crying, and whining to the LORD and others about my plight. I am very ashamed.

GOD SPEAKS: "Truly my soul finds rest in God; my salvation comes from him. Truly he is my rock and my salvation; he is my fortress, I will never be shaken." (Psalm 62:1-2 NIV) Make Me your aim; find everything you need in Me. I will supply your needs, out of My abundant riches. The things I give you, as well as things I withhold from you, are all for your perfect good. Never forget this!

WANDA'S PRAYER: Father, our souls find rest in You alone! You alone have the perfect plan for our lives—You alone have the power to carry it out. Thank you Father!

June 13

I WILL DO IT AGAIN

"FINISH THIS DAUGHTER'S BRIDAL WEEK; THEN WE WILL GIVE YOU THE YOUNGER ONE ALSO, IN RETURN FOR ANOTHER SEVEN YEARS OF WORK." AND JACOB DID SO. HE FINISHED THE WEEK WITH LEAH, AND THEN LABAN GAVE HIM HIS DAUGHTER RACHEL TO BE HIS WIFE." (GENESIS 29:27-28 NIV)

This is a very sad thing we humans, made in God's image, do to each other. This father sells his daughters like cattle. They are traded on the auction block like brute beasts. He seemingly has little emotion for his daughters. Jacob quickly agrees because of his deep love for Rachel. He is driven and will not give her up now. Again, I am struck by the silence of both of these women. Maybe it is a product of the times or something more. Maybe it is an extreme reverence and trust in their father. I am not sure, but again, it teaches a very valuable lesson in trust. If they can trust in a very twisted and flawed man, why can't we trust in the All-Knowing and All-Powerful LORD OF LOVE? I do not have an answer for that either.

RACHEL AND US: This story is teaching me to trust in the Lord with all of my heart and not to lean to my own ways. My Father gives me so much more reason to trust Him. He has never lied or deceived me. I find a sad epitaph about myself; I sometimes have more trust in flawed humans than in the perfect God.

GOD SPEAKS: "This is what God the LORD says—the Creator of the heavens, who stretches them out, who spreads out the earth with all that springs from it, who gives breath to its people, and life to those who walk on it: "I, the LORD, have called you in righteousness; I will take hold of your hand. I will keep you…" (Isaiah 42:5-6 NIV) This is just a reminder of who I am. You never have to worry if I am not big enough, or strong enough, to handle your little problems; they are no problem to Me.

WANDA'S PRAYER: Father, thank You for the daily reminders; we need them so much.

June 14

AHHH...FOR THIS I WORKED

**"JACOB MADE LOVE TO RACHEL ALSO, AND HIS LOVE FOR RACHEL WAS GREATER THAN HIS LOVE FOR LEAH. AND HE WORKED FOR LABAN ANOTHER SEVEN YEARS.
(GENESIS 29:30 NIV)**

I think this statement is one of the biggest understatements found in Scripture. "… He loved Rachel more than Leah." I say this because if you read Chapter 29, you realized that a better rendering of the text would be, "He adored Rachel, but he liked Leah". Let me recount to you some events. He does heroic feats to win her attention and spend time with her. Next, he runs up to her, kisses her, and then breaks down in tears. At the family home, he cannot wait to name Rachel, as the wages for seven years of hard labor. Finally, he agrees to give another seven years of labor for this woman. Nothing alters or diminishes Jacob's love for Rachel. His love for her is not affected by changing circumstances, situations, people, or time; it only grows stronger. Many women would envy that kind of love, but we do not need to. We have a Man who lives outside of space and time; a Man who loves us deeper than the deepest love Jacob had for Rachel. He created us to be the object of such a love; with the hope we would love Him in return. He started our great-great grandmother out in the lap of luxury and perfection. When the first family blew it miserably, He sent His own Son to pay the awful price to bring us back to Him. Why, even now, He is preparing mansions in the heavenly paradise for us to live in. In the here and now, He gives us our every breath and keeps our hearts beating at a steady pace. Yes, our LORD has done all of these things and more, just to say to you and me, "I LOVE YOU SO MUCH!" Can you hear it? I can. Next time you open up His Word, or go out in nature, be very quiet and listen to Him speak—I LOVE YOU _____, (put your name in this blank).

RACHEL AND US: While Rachel may have had a very good thing in old Jacob, between the two of us, I have the best deal! Our Dad sure knows how to provide for His girls, don't you think?

GOD SPEAKS: "See, the Sovereign LORD comes with power, and he rules with a mighty arm. See, his reward is with him, and his recompense accompanies him. He tends his flock like a shepherd: He gathers the lambs in his arms and carries them close to his heart; he gently leads those that have young." (Isaiah 40:10-11 NIV) See, I can be tough and gentle too. Do not let the fact that because you do not see flesh, cause you to doubt My love for you, or My power to take care of you.

WANDA'S PRAYER: What can we say LORD; You are the Man—the GOD MAN!

June 15

EVERYONE MUST BE LOVED—RIGHT

"WHEN THE LORD SAW THAT LEAH WAS UNLOVED, HE OPENED HER WOMB; BUT RACHEL WAS BARREN." (GENESIS 29:31 NKJV)

This is an interesting verse of Scripture, don't you think? I do. This Scripture implies several things to me. First, both women were, or would have been, barren, were it not for our LORD'S intervention. Second, it says to me—everyone must be loved. In fact, GOD stepped into Leah's world to say this very thing. In giving the unloved Leah all her children, the Father was saying to her, "Leah, don't worry and don't fret over this man; I love you girl—now let Me show it to you." Let us discuss these two points. When I did some research on the lineage of Rachel and Leah, I found there seemed to be a history of barrenness in their family. The beautiful Grandma Sarah struggled with childlessness. (Genesis 11:30) In fact, she was barren for almost ninety years until God intervened. (Genesis 21:1-5) Then there was Aunt Rebekah; she too was very beautiful, yet she struggled with not being able to have children. (Genesis 25:21) She remained barren for twenty years, finally giving birth when her husband was sixty years old. (Genesis 25:26) So what is the point of this brief history lesson? One is that both women were barren, and two, God showed His divine favor on them both—in different ways. To the one who received no human love, God Himself became love. Is GOD unfair—NO! What GOD is, among many things, is faithful. He was faithful and loving to Rachel by giving her Jacob, who lavished her with untold amounts of love. He was also faithful and loving to Leah, who received no love from her husband. GOD stepped in and became the Perfect Husband; to provide Leah with what she needed love.

RACHEL AND US: I can relate well to both women. The Perfect LORD has met my needs on both levels. He gave me Himself and His divine love, and He provided a man to love me deeply. Father, I just want to stop now and say how much I love and thank You for your wonderful gifts to me.

GOD SPEAKS: "He who does not love does not know God, for God is love." (1 John 4:8 NKJV) I AM the very essence of pure love. I do not have to go anywhere to get it—it is just who I am. So, when I give Myself to you, I give you love. When you give love, you take on Me and display My glory. Go and give some of Me away today.

WANDA'S PRAYER: Father GOD, help us do that today and every day. Clean out all the spaces we have filled with other things. Fill us completely with You and Your perfect love. Then we will gladly give some away. Thank You for your wonderful love.

June 16

WHEN HUMAN LOVE IS NOT ENOUGH

"WHEN RACHEL SAW THAT SHE WAS NOT BEARING JACOB ANY CHILDREN, SHE BECAME JEALOUS OF HER SISTER. SO SHE SAID TO JACOB, 'GIVE ME CHILDREN, OR I'LL DIE!'" (GENESIS 30:1 NIV)

Verses like the one above teach one thing. I do not care who you are or what you may have, one thing reigns true—none of us have it all! We all have missing pieces; holes we cannot fill or close. We have a part in our lives which cannot be fixed by human invention and/or ingenuity. Rachel possessed beauty beyond compare. Even in the middle of the desert, while herding sheep, she was deemed beautiful. Not only was she beautiful in any weather, with that beauty she carried poise and grace. She was what women hoped and dreamed they could be. She had a man who worshipped the ground she walked on—one who stopped at nothing to show it. In this clan of four women, she ran the show. On the surface, Rachel seems flawless, but let's look a little closer at the text. The verse tells us she looked at herself, and she looked at her sister. She then noted she had a missing piece—she could not have children. This was not just a tiny pinhole, but a huge pit. After all, not having children, then or now, was considered shameful at best, and a downright scandal at worst. This open crater in Rachel's life was a source of deep hurt and pain for her. What grew out of this hole was equally more devastating. For deep inside her was the spirit of envy; she envied her sister. To envy means to resent or want to possess someone else's achievements as your own. (Random House College Dictionary) This was Rachel's problem—she was envious of her sister. Leah was able to give Jacob children, and Rachel could not. So Sista' girl discovered what the rest of us (less than beautiful women) already know—we all have missing pieces. Where could she or we go to fill in the gap? Rachel has a large wound in her life, and it needs healing.

RACHEL AND US: Like Rachel, the issue is not that she had problems or flaws, but where could she (or we) go for relief or healing? Is the healing from our scrapes and wounds found in this world only? Or is there another source of complete relief?

GOD SPEAKS: "But I will restore you to health and heal your wounds,' declares the Lord, 'because you are called an outcast …" (Jeremiah 30:17 NIV) I AM the Ever-Present, All GOD of the universe! Therefore, not you, Rachel, or anyone, have any holes I alone cannot fill. Name your broken or missing piece and give it to Me. Then seek Me with all of your heart, mind, and soul. I will complete you with Me. Just do it!

WANDA'S PRAYER: Lord, we bring every shattered and missing piece of our lives before you. Heal and fill us completely with Yourself. Thank You for making us whole!

June 17

WOMAN, I CAN'T HELP YOU

"JACOB BECAME ANGRY WITH HER AND SAID, 'AM I IN THE PLACE OF GOD, WHO HAS KEPT YOU FROM HAVING CHILDREN?'" (GENESIS 30:2 NIV)

Human love can do a lot of things. It can motivate a man to move a large stone in order to attract a love interest. That same love can motivate a man to work fourteen years for his bride. It can even motivate a man to amass a fortune in order to take care of his family. But human love cannot produce life, only God can! Rachel had watched her beloved Jacob pull one rabbit after another out of his turban to win her love. She saw him, and not the LORD as the supplier of her needs. When she could not have children, she saw Jacob as the problem and the solution. So, she railed to her aging husband; "Give me children or I'll die." This caused their first recorded fight. We can see in the above verse Jacob became angry with his wife; and then speaks words of deep truth. In essence, he says to her, "Listen here woman, it is the LORD who has blessed your sister to have children, not me. I cannot give you kids—only sperm. It is GOD who has kept you from having kids; and you need to ask Him why you cannot have them." (Writer's paraphrase) This is exactly what Rachel needed to do. She needed to take all of her ego and pride, and cast them along with a complete heart at the feet of Jesus. While at His feet, she needed to ask Him the reason and the solution to her infertility. She did not. Why? I think it was because her many blessings became a curse. When it came to the world's standards, Rachel had it all. She was in perfect health. As a shepherdess, she could herd a thousand sheep around any man in her town. She was incredibly beautiful and graceful; this made her the envy of her sister. All of these natural "gifts" had taken her far in life, but they would not get her children. Having children was withheld from her, and she needed to go to the source to find out WHY!

RACHEL AND US: I can relate to Rachel when it comes to feeling like I have been denied something I felt should have been mine. Can you? I can also relate to the anger over the denial of that thing to me. Thoughts such as, "It's not fair, LORD! Why can I not have this or that?" Unlike Rachel, you and I must ask the Lord, "why don't we have…?"

GOD SPEAKS: "But he gives us more grace. that is why Scripture says: 'God opposes the proud but shows favor to the humble.'" (James 4:6 NIV) Always remember, this is My world; I run it and everything that is in it. Come to Me, submit your complete life to My perfect will, and I will supply all of your needs and many of your wants.

WANDA'S PRAYER: Father, You alone are the God of the universe and our LORD. Give us a heart totally submitted to You alone.

June 18

NO… LORD, I WON'T PRAY—I GOT THIS

"SO SHE (RACHEL) SAID, 'HERE IS MY HAND MAID BILHAH; GO IN TO HER, AND SHE WILL BEAR A CHILD ON MY KNEES, THAT I ALSO MAY HAVE CHILDREN BY HER.'" (GENESIS 30: 3 NKJV)

This verse is, to excuse my expression, "pregnant" with food-for-thought. First, I am amazed to see the stubborn, pigheadedness of this woman. All she needed to have done was pray to her GOD for help. After all, she had already seen how the Father worked in the life of her sister. God was no respecter of persons, and He could have done the same for her. But no, Rachel would have no such thing. She must have been Frank Sinatra's Great-Great Grandmother because she was definitely going to do it her way. The next thought I get from this text is the women in this family were not too bright at times. It is said that insanity is doing the same thing, but expecting different results. This is truly the case here. You would think she must have known about Grandma Sarah's brilliant plan with Hagar (Sarah's handmaid), and the disaster it caused. It seems all we learn from history is how to repeat it. In any case, this apparently was a common method of starting a family when the mistress of the house was barren. How about that? And I thought surrogate motherhood was a new concept—obviously not! What also strikes me as odd is that while Rachel may not have been aware of the family sins, Jacob had full knowledge of them. Despite this knowledge, he went along with this foolish scheme and impregnated the slave girl. So where is the Heavenly Father in all this mess? He is there observing this whole ugly thing, which He will have to clean up later. But why, one might ask? Well, one reason is that since He gave us as humans the power to choose, He must also allow us to experience the consequences of our choices. Even though those consequences are devastating at times.

RACHEL AND US: I honestly wish I could tell you I was smarter than Rachel, but I cannot. If I had a nickel for every time "I did it my way," I would be a very, very rich woman now. Like Rachel, after doing it my way, I can now look back on my life and see the messes I have made in doing it "my way." I have shed many tears over my life's, "shoulda,' coulda,' woulda's."

GOD SPEAKS: "Some trust in chariots, and some in horses; But we will remember the name of the LORD our God. They have bowed down and fallen; …" (Psalm 20:7-8 NKJV) When you trust in anything but Me, the end is a great fall.

WANDA'S PRAYER: LORD, today we say, "O my God, I trust in You; Let me not be ashamed; Let not my enemies triumph over me." (Psalm 25:2 NKJV)

June 19

THIS WAS A "HUMAN THANG"

"THEN RACHEL SAID, 'GOD HAS JUDGED MY CASE; AND HE HAS ALSO HEARD MY VOICE AND GIVEN ME A SON.' THEREFORE SHE CALLED HIS NAME DAN."
(GENESIS 30:6 NKJV)

I laughed when I read this verse. God is so very good, despite all of our foolishness. He shows us how pathetic our human plight really is. In looking at the above verse, we see a woman and her husband, who are totally out of the will of God. This shows me just how sin can twist our thinking. Rachel did a very wrong act in giving her husband to the slave girl. Because she is not punished for this evil deed, she now has the nerve to call this evil a blessing from GOD. Let us look at what Rachel does. She cannot have children. She prays to the Lord; then she says, "Ok God, here is what I am going to do—this is how You are going to answer my prayer. Trust me, Lord, I know what is best for my life." She goes against God's laws of marriage. The man already had two women and now he has a third. Someone once said, "if you want to make God laugh, tell Him your plans about your life." If this is true, then our LORD was probably doubled over in laughter. If this situation were not so sad, it would be laughable. No, this was not God's will for this family. Yes, He allowed the conception of the baby, but it was not His design that His chosen people would be produced through a harem and polygamy. This was Rachel, who is now her own god, who judged what she did to be right. This brings up a point of discussion. There are those in our day who say, "this must have been an act from God, because the outcome was a good one." Good is only defined as a good GOD defines it. Our loving Father acts according to His Word. He will not contradict His Word; not for Rachel, me, or anyone. Therefore, if what I am doing does not match His perfect Word, then what I am doing is of human invention and it is sin. The fact that I am not always punished as my sins deserve does not take away from the sinfulness of my sins; it only magnifies His grace to me. We would do well to remember that in the Father's case, silence does not mean consent.

RACHEL AND US: I say "ditto," to Sista' girl. I have made my own decisions and then wanted God to bless my messes as well. So, I can only let the LORD speak to all of us.

GOD SPEAKS: "But God demonstrates His own love toward us, in that while we were still sinners, Christ died for us." (Romans 5:8 NKJV) Do you really believe that any of this crazy behavior came as a surprise to Me? Remember, I was killed as a sin offering from earth's foundation. (Revelation 13:8) I love you and knew what it would take to save you. I would do it all over again to save My precious daughters.

WANDA'S PRAYER: LORD, we know what is Holy and what is right. Give us the will, the heart, and the mind to do what You say.

June 20

THIS IS PERSONAL

"RACHEL'S SERVANT BILHAH CONCEIVED AGAIN AND BORE JACOB A SECOND SON. THEN RACHEL SAID, 'I HAVE HAD A GREAT STRUGGLE WITH MY SISTER, AND I HAVE WON.' SO SHE NAMED HIM NAPHTALI." (GENESIS 30:7-8 NIV)

Listen closely and you can hear the deep hurt and pain Rachel is feeling. While we do not know where all of these emotions are coming from, we can hear them loud and clear in her statement. It is as if she says, "I have been battling with my sister. In fact, it has been a long and bitter fight. My struggle with her is great, but now I've won! So, I will name my trophy— 'struggle'." What would cause so much hurt and pain in this young woman's life at this point? Perhaps she was angry and resentful at her sister for marrying Jacob to begin with. Certainly, if that were not bad enough, at this point, her sister had now given him four sons, to her zero. This must have been heart-wrenching for Rachel on many levels. As a woman who seemed to have it all before, this barrenness was a bitter pill to swallow. She must have endured the taunts of the older sister as she waved the babies in her face. Life is peculiar at times. Rachel possessed beauty, charm, and all the social graces, plus a man who was willing to drink her dirty bath water. Yet, this was not enough! She wanted what she could not now have. This want left a gaping hole inside, which was tearing her apart. Having children was the all-consuming factor. Rachel's true resentment was not really at her sister—no, it was at her GOD. In her mind she was saying, "God, I do not know why you are holding this wonderful gift from me, but I WON'T HAVE IT! I WILL HAVE KIDS AND I WILL WIN!"

RACHEL AND US: I can certainly relate to Rachel. There are many times in my life when I get so hung up on that one missing piece. A better job, more money, a bigger house, a nicer car, and the list goes on and on. I think the fight is with my sisters, but it really is not. It is between my "wants," and my "have not's."

GOD SPEAKS: "The Spirit of the Sovereign LORD is on me, because the LORD has anointed me to proclaim good news to the poor. He has sent me to bind up the brokenhearted, to proclaim freedom for the captives and release from darkness for the prisoners, to proclaim the year of the LORD's favor and the day of vengeance of our God, to comfort all who mourn, and provide for those who grieve in Zion—to bestow on them a crown of beauty instead of ashes, the oil of joy instead of mourning, and a garment of praise instead of a spirit of despair. They will be called oaks of righteousness, a planting of the LORD for the display of his splendor." (Isaiah 61:1-3 NIV) My daughter, when you read these verses, there should be no doubt—I am all you need! Come to Me with all that fight. I am the only one who can deal with all the anger and hurt.

WANDA'S PRAYER: No doubt, LORD.

June 21

WELL, IT WAS A COMPLETE KNOCK OUT

"DURING WHEAT HARVEST, REUBEN WENT OUT INTO THE FIELDS AND FOUND SOME MANDRAKE PLANTS, WHICH HE BROUGHT TO HIS MOTHER LEAH. RACHEL SAID TO LEAH, 'PLEASE GIVE ME SOME OF YOUR SON'S MANDRAKES.'"
(GENESIS 30:14 NIV)

Even though the servant girl of Rachel had given Jacob two sons in "her" name, it was not the same as having her own kids, so she would not give up the battle. In Rachel's mind, she was fighting the battle on two fronts: (1) She wanted to have more kids than her sister at any cost. (2) She wanted to give Jacob a son from her own womb. To reach this end, nothing was off limits—not servants, children, or even her husband. She would use Leah's own son in this heated battle as we see in the above verse. She was so eager to have those all-important mandrakes that she threw her beloved Jacob in the pot. She tells her sister, "I want the mandrakes, you want the man, so let us make a trade, ok?" (Genesis 30:15-16) (Writer's paraphrase) What was so important about those mandrakes that she would bargain away her husband to the enemy (Leah), to get them? Well, this mandrake plant produced a yellow, sweetly fragrant fruit, which was considered a love potion and used for fertility purposes. Rachel would leave no stone unturned in her elusive pursuit of children. It is ok to be stressed and depressed over a helpless or seemingly hopeless situation; but Rachel was sampling the wrong fruit. The plant she needed was the root out of dry ground; that root was her LORD, the Christ. He had already fought and won this battle for her, and she did not even know it.

RACHEL AND US: I, like Rachel, do not look up to God for help in the midst of my deepest struggles. I feel I must fight them all by myself; with my "no power" self; stupid, huh? I guess my reason for this exercise in stupidity is that in the back of my mind, He was not quite big enough to fix my problems without my help.

GOD SPEAKS: "A shoot will come up from the stump of Jesse; from his roots a Branch will bear fruit." (Isaiah 11:1 NIV) Daughter, this fruit has all the nutrients you will ever need. I, your LORD, am that fruit. My fruit has healing from all that hurt, and it is life everlasting. Take a bite of My Word today.

WANDA'S PRAYER: Father, I will taste and see that You are so very good!

June 22

GOD MAKES A POINT

"SO WHEN JACOB CAME IN FROM THE FIELDS THAT EVENING, LEAH WENT OUT TO MEET HIM. 'YOU MUST SLEEP WITH ME,' SHE SAID. 'I HAVE HIRED YOU WITH MY SON'S MANDRAKES.' SO HE SLEPT WITH HER THAT NIGHT. GOD LISTENED TO LEAH, AND SHE BECAME PREGNANT..."
(GENESIS 30:16-17 NIV)

It would seem Leah got the better end of the deal; she got Jacob, two more sons, and a daughter (Genesis 30:17-21). Rachel got mandrakes, but no children. It would appear our LORD wanted to make a huge point. To me, He is saying, "I, and I alone, am calling the shots!" He seems to want to say to Rachel, you have been going everywhere and doing everything to have children, but you have not really come to Me. You, my daughter, have prayed at Me, but you have not had a heart-to-heart discussion with Me. I will keep your womb closed until you realize that I alone am the answer to your prayers. Our Father and Lord is just waiting on Rachel to really come to Him and pour out her heart. But still in Rachel's mind, she is saying, "I'll try this one last thing, then maybe I'll try prayer." Rachel is at the point of near desperation. This is a very good thing. When she finally gets to the end of her rope, she will find that her LORD was already there, holding the other end. There is a question we should ask ourselves: Where will deep adversity and pain drive us?

RACHEL AND US: When I look at Rachel, I see myself. I believed, (though I never said it), that I should try everything else. Then, when all my silly plans failed, I should try God. Looking back over my life, I realize how foolish this self-counsel was. If I had only listened to the words of a childhood hymn: "Are you weak and heavy laden, cumbered with a load of care? Precious Savior, still our refuge, take it to the LORD in prayer." He would have taken the burden so long ago; but no, I continued to carry the load until I dropped.

GOD SPEAKS: "I, even I, am he who comforts you. Who are you that you fear mere mortals, human beings who are but grass," (Isaiah 51:12 NIV) "When you pass through the waters, I will be with you; and when you pass through the rivers, they will not sweep over you. When you walk through the fire, you will not be burned; the flames will not set you ablaze. (Isaiah 43:2 NIV)" My daughters, you may never know the answers to your "why's," in life, but to quote a song by Babbie Mason, "... When you don't understand, when you don't see His plan, when you can't trace His hand—trust His (My) heart." You can be sure My heart is always good and loving.

WANDA'S PRAYER: Father God, help us do just that!

June 23

GOD'S TIMING IS NEVER LATE—TO GOD

"THEN GOD REMEMBERED RACHEL; HE LISTENED TO HER AND ENABLED HER TO CONCEIVE. SHE BECAME PREGNANT AND GAVE BIRTH TO A SON ...."
(GENESIS 30:22-23 NIV)

This is one of those verses I love to read. It speaks not only of the Father's love but also of His strength and absolute authority over our lives. Rachel could do nothing but wait on the LORD. She had tried everything she knew to have children, and nothing worked. Finally, after all the failed efforts, God stepped in and He "remembered." The word "remember" in Hebrew means to turn and recognize; or to make mention of. The word "listen" in Hebrew means to give consideration with intent to obey. The word "opened" in this text means to loosen or to plow. Before we put all these words together, we must realize that God is never unmindful or forgetful. He did not have to say, "Oh… I forgot about Rachel, what's her name, and her prayer." When we put all of these words together, we see our LORD marked out a set time where He would address Rachel's infertility and fix her problem. It would not be a moment before, or after, His set timing. This answers the questions we may have concerning our prayers; as to whether or not our Heavenly Father truly hears us. He answers each and every one of them. Sometimes He says "yes," sometimes "no," and sometimes "wait." In Rachel's case, He was saying, "wait." Notice the text says that He (God) opened her womb. There would be no mistaking who caused the pregnancy and who gave her the son.

RACHEL AND US: I remember once I needed some financial funds badly; or should I say, some quick cash! I prayed and cried to the LORD. No answer! Bills were piling up and my cash had dwindled very low. Then, just when I was going under for the last time, the Lord paid the bills; though I do not remember how. It happened so many times when the kids were young. Like Rachel, I had (and still have) no control over when or how the LORD answers my prayers. I am just so thankful to Him He does.

GOD SPEAKS: "I lift up my eyes to the mountains—where does my help come from? My help comes from the LORD, the Maker of heaven and earth." (Psalm 121:1-2 NIV) The next time you look at your problems and they look higher than the San Bernardino Mountains, just remember who made those mountains. If I can make a mountain, then to Me, your problems are not a problem.

WANDA'S PRAYER: Father, as the man on the radio once said, "I want to tell my problems how big my God is, and not tell You how big my problems are."

June 24

IN A LEAGUE ALL BY HIMSELF

"... 'GOD HAS TAKEN AWAY MY DISGRACE.' SHE NAMED HIM JOSEPH, AND SAID, 'MAY THE LORD ADD TO ME ANOTHER SON.'" (GENESIS 30:23-24 NIV)

Rachel now speaks words of wisdom for all to hear. She speaks of the stain of disgrace because she could not have children. For her, there was a bright, red scarlet letter "B" for barrenness, branded across her chest and back, for everyone in her day to see. There was nothing she could do to remove this letter, or the stigma that came with it. On her own, she tried to rid herself of it, using everything from servant girl surrogates to plants; but nothing helped. Only our LORD could remove this stain. He opened her womb and took away her disgrace. She would name her son, "Yacaph," which means, "He (the LORD) will add to me another son." She now recognized that God alone was the "giver" and "taker" of life. In naming her son, she believed her LORD would also give her another son. She no longer depended on Rachel to be the maker, mover, and shaker of her life. She was now crying out, "uncle," or "I give up." She recognized she was God's property, and that He was not her whipping boy. For those of us who are dull of hearing, she shouts out, "this is our Father's world! He does whatever He pleases, to whomever He pleases, and whenever He pleases."

RACHEL AND US: I do not have any problem learning that lesson. The problem I have is forgetting it when the next big trial comes. If the lesson could just stick with me, then I would be ok.

GOD SPEAKS: "You, through your commandments, make me wiser than my enemies; For they are ever with me." (Psalm 119:98 NKJV) The answer, my daughters, is to keep My commands with you forever. Learn to love My law and meditate on them all day long. (Psalm 119:97)

WANDA'S PRAYER: Hide Your Word in my heart Lord, so that I do not sin against You. (Psalm 119:11)

June 25

IT IS TIME FOR A TRUCE

"SO JACOB SENT WORD TO RACHEL AND LEAH TO COME OUT TO THE FIELDS WHERE HIS FLOCKS WERE. ... THEN RACHEL AND LEAH REPLIED, '...SO DO WHATEVER GOD HAS TOLD YOU.'" (GENESIS 31:4-16 NIV)

This verse of Scripture is long, so I did not quote it. When you read it, however, you will find the LORD telling Jacob, it is time to go. He calls Rachel and Leah in for a family discussion. They both come in with a fuss; yet they conclude in a peaceful agreement to support all God tells him to do. The man must have thought he had died and gone to heaven. He finally had peace in the house. God had settled Rachel's soul. When He opened her womb, He also opened her heart. He filled it with Himself and left her with room to have compassion and love for others. Also, she learned what she knew deep down inside; that God has order in His kingdom, and that she had been out of order for a long time. It had forced her to submit to the LORD. She could now allow her husband to head their home, as he should have all along. Where GOD rules, there is joy, perfect order, and peace. Here is an illustration of this.

RACHEL AND US: Like Rachel, when I finally let go, and let GOD do what He does best, I too experienced that same joy and peace. I want those times in my life to be daily occurrences.

GOD SPEAKS: "The Lord bless you and keep you; the Lord make his face shine on you and be gracious to you; the lord turn his face toward you and give you peace." (Numbers 6:24-26 NIV) My face is always turned towards you. You need to keep your face and the rest of you always turned towards Me.

WANDA'S PRAYER: Father, keep us in the center of Your will for our lives.

June 26

THE THRILL IS GONE

"WHEN LABAN HAD GONE TO SHEAR HIS SHEEP, RACHEL STOLE HER FATHER'S HOUSEHOLD GODS." (GENESIS 31:19 NIV)

My question is, Rachel, why? Was the thrill and peace of the loving LORD gone? Did you not just see an awesome display of His power on your behalf? Have you forgotten the disgrace of childlessness that only the LORD could take away? It was He who opened your dry, empty womb. And now you are going on a long trip, far away from home, and you turn to idol gods that you must carry? Are these gods, carved by sinful man, going to protect and keep you? Do you choose to rely on them in place of the Omnipotent LORD of the universe? Rach, Rach, Rach, does that make any sense at all? Or maybe you were angry at your daddy for stealing your husband from you and giving him to your sister first? Did you just want to see him suffer, or make him pay—huh? Was that your motive for such a very foolish act? Listen to me girlfriend—you cannot get any bigger, wiser, stronger, or more loving than the Eternal KING OF KINGS AND LORD OF LORDS. Everything you need, or will ever need, for every problem or situation in your life, our Father already has the solution. Where were your idols when you were trying to get pregnant? They did not help you then and they will not help you now. If it was vengeance on your father you were seeking, those sticks and stones, cannot help with that either. Vengeance belongs to the LORD alone—He will repay! Girl, God's payback is so much sweeter; trust me on that one. Not only will He do what is right regarding daddy, and whoever else has hurt you, He will take away your pain in the process. Put away those gods which are just stuffed pieces of wood or stone.

RACHEL AND US: At first glance, I did not think there was anything I could relate to Rachel on about this one, but I was wrong. Every time I have tried to fix my own problems, or attempted to handle my own issues after seeing God's magnificent display of power on my behalf, I have done the same thing. I, like Rachel, have picked up idols and carried them with me—thinking and hoping they will protect me.

GOD SPEAKS: "Do you not know? Have you not heard? The Lord is the everlasting God, the Creator of the ends of the earth. He will not grow tired or weary, and his understanding no one can fathom." (Isaiah 40:28 NIV) It hurts Me when you do not trust that I love you enough to care for all of your needs. I just need you to believe that I am all you need.

WANDA'S PRAYER: Lord, help our unbelief. Give us a steadfast heart that is always set on You.

June 27

POOR THING, NOW YOU'VE GOT TO HIDE GOD

"NOW RACHEL HAD TAKEN THE HOUSEHOLD GODS AND PUT THEM INSIDE HER CAMEL'S SADDLE AND WAS SITTING ON THEM. LABAN SEARCHED THROUGH EVERYTHING IN THE TENT BUT FOUND NOTHING." (GENESIS 31:34 NIV)

This is a pitiful site. Rachel has to protect her stolen gods. You would think if the stolen gods had any power, they would protect themselves. The narrative, as found in Genesis 31:22-55, is almost laughable. Laban has discovered his daughters and grandchildren are gone with Jacob. But what upsets him the most is that someone has made off with his gods! At this point in the story, he is going bankrupt; so his gods have not done well by him either. Anyway, daddy Laban catches up with the runaway family with the stolen gods, and is now going from tent to tent to look for his "good luck charms." Jacob has even threatened death to the man who has the stolen idols. Everyone allows him free access to their tents. Well, I guess I should say, almost everyone has given him free rein to look for his gods; everyone except his precious Rachel. In the next verse, she tells a bald-faced lie that she is on her period and cannot get up to greet him properly. She tells such a tale because she is sitting on the idols to hide them from her father. This is the pathetic part of this story. Rachel feels she has to steal, lie, and protect the god who is supposed to protect her. Think with me Rachel, if you have to hide your god from danger, how can this god protect you? How great can this god be if you have to protect and carry it? After doing all of this for your immobile, non-seeing, non-hearing god, he requires that you pray to it? Give me a break!

RACHEL AND US: Again the LORD has shown me that though I do not bow to sticks or stones, there have been gods I put on pedestals before the Eternal, Everlasting LORD. I bowed to and gave my life over for these gods. These were gods of money and men, which really did nothing for me. Like Rachel, they were old habits I could not break.

GOD SPEAKS: "... Ignorant are those who carry about idols of wood, who pray to gods that cannot save. Declare what is to be, present it—let them take counsel together. Who foretold this long ago, who declared it from the distant past? Was it not I, the LORD? And there is no God apart from me, a righteous God and a Savior; there is none but me." (Isaiah 45:20-21 NIV) Just settle it in your little mind, I AM GOD—end of story!

WANDA'S PRAYER: LORD, this settles it in our pea brains; but just in case, Father, please remind us again when troubles come.

June 28

OK, THE GODS HAVE GOT TO GO!

"SO JACOB SAID TO HIS HOUSEHOLD AND TO ALL WHO WERE WITH HIM, 'GET RID OF THE FOREIGN GODS YOU HAVE WITH YOU, AND PURIFY YOURSELVES AND CHANGE YOUR CLOTHES.'"
(GENESIS 35:2 NIV)

A lot has happened in Rachel's life. The family is now in Canaan; her husband's homeland. Her niece Dinah was raped in Shechem, and Dinah's brothers had killed the perpetrators. Now the family is on the run. The Loving LORD steps in at this point. He calls his son Jacob and his family back into TRUE WORSHIP, with the TRUE GOD. Jacob obeys and takes the family to Bethel, which means the house of worship. Before going to Bethel where they can worship the real GOD, Jacob knows they must rid themselves of the false gods. He tells his household to "get rid of the foreign gods, purify yourselves, and change your clothes." It is at this point Rachel finally lets go of the "darling gods" she had kept for so long. She gives him the foreign gods and the rings in the ears. When she left her father's house, she only had the household god, so she may have picked up these new earring gods along the way. If this is so, it just goes to show how if we hold on to the little "sins," they will multiply. Her husband buries the gods in Shechem. This was fitting since this was the place of pain. They were starting fresh with GOD, and all things were becoming new.

RACHEL AND US: As I go through the closets of my mind and heart, I wonder if there are any "darling gods" I am holding on to. Like Rachel, these little gods hinder my worship with the true and living GOD.

GOD SPEAKS: "'In that day,' declares the LORD Almighty, 'I will break the yoke off their necks and will tear off their bonds; no longer will foreigners enslave them. Instead, they will serve the LORD their God ...'" (Jeremiah 30:8-9 NIV) Again I say, make Me your one and only GOD for life!

WANDA'S PRAYER: DONE Father! Be our one and only GOD for life!

June 29

A TRAGIC ENDING TO A WONDERFUL LIFE

"... RACHEL BEGAN TO GIVE BIRTH AND HAD GREAT DIFFICULTY. AND AS SHE WAS HAVING GREAT DIFFICULTY IN CHILDBIRTH, THE MIDWIFE SAID TO HER, 'DON'T DESPAIR, FOR YOU HAVE ANOTHER SON.'" (GENESIS 35:16-17 NIV)

This was a tragic end to a wonderful life. Rachel truly lived her life to the fullest. She was outgoing and so full of vigor. Looking back at Rachel's life, it seems almost ironic she would die this way. She seemed the stronger of the two sisters; she herded sheep while her weak-eyed sister stayed at home. We are not told what caused this difficult, life ending labor. We only know the family was on their way to Bethlehem, so it could have been the stress of moving, but it is hard to say. The process of this childbirth would end her life. While dying, the midwife tells her she is having the coveted baby boy. Though this is what she had hoped for and dreamt of, she did not find joy in these very sad moments. So in her last breath, she names the child, "Ben-Oni" which means, "son of my sorrow." But the father names the child "Benjamin," which means, "son of my right hand." Jacob changed the name because he knew she had spoken out of her pain, and not from her heart. Had she lived, he knew she would have treasured this son. He also recognized this was the child GOD had added to her, as she prophesied He would. (Genesis 30:24) Rachel was buried in Bethlehem, where she died. "Over her tomb Jacob set up a pillar, and to this day that pillar marks Rachel's tomb." (Genesis 35:20 NIV) Rachel's legacy far exceeded her brief life span on this planet. Her tomb is still a visitor's attraction to this day, thousands of years later. Jacob grieved the loss of his lovely Rachel until his own death. (Genesis 48:7) A testament of his extreme love for her is shown in how he loved the two children she gave him above the other ten. Every time he looked at Joseph and Benjamin, he saw her, and was reminded of the passionate love he forever held for her.

RACHEL AND US: As I look at Rachel's death, I wonder what markers I will leave on the lives that I touch every day. Will I, like Rachel, leave a legacy that will remain long after I am gone?

GOD SPEAKS: "So we fix our eyes not on what is seen, but on what is unseen, since what is seen is temporary, but what is unseen is eternal." (2 Corinthians 4:18 NIV) Fix your eyes on ME; I AM the Eternal God, and I will take care of the rest.

WANDA'S PRAYER: Father, help us live a life totally sold out to You for all the days of our lives. I want to always walk with You in my mind's eye.

June 30

A TESTAMENT TO A GREAT LADY

"THEN THE ELDERS AND ALL THE PEOPLE AT THE GATE SAID, 'WE ARE WITNESSES. MAY THE LORD MAKE THE WOMAN WHO IS COMING INTO YOUR HOME LIKE RACHEL AND LEAH, WHO TOGETHER BUILT UP THE FAMILY OF ISRAEL."
(RUTH 4:11 NIV)

It is interesting that when you read of Jacob's wives, Rachel's name always comes first. In fact, though he had four women in his life, Rachel is the only one he calls his wife. I think it is because in his mind; she was supposed to be the only wife. Since because of trickery, she was not the only wife, then she would always be the primary wife. This fact is cemented all throughout Scripture. Her name is always mentioned first, which tells us of her place of importance. In the time of Ruth, she is praised with Rachel and Leah as having built the house of Israel. (Ruth 4:11) Rachel was, and always will be, synonymous with "mother of Israel." By the time you get to Jeremiah's day, Rachel's name alone is used to represent the children of Israel. "This is what the LORD says: "A voice is heard in Ramah, mourning and great weeping, Rachel (not Leah) weeping for her children and refusing to be comforted, because they are no more." (Jeremiah 31:15 NIV) Written many centuries later, Matthew points to the persecution and suffering of Israel's infants under the cruel hand of King Herod. (Matthew 2:16-18) In looking back at our Scripture verse, we see the LORD does not remember Rachel's flaws. I see no discussion of her idol worship, the catfights with her sister, or the barrenness. She is only seen in God's eyes as the woman who was foremost in building the house of Israel. This is one of the wonderful things about our GOD; He does not see us as we are in the flesh. Our GOD sees us through His blood-washed, sanctified-colored glasses.

RACHEL AND US: Like Rachel, I know I am saved; I rejoice in that hope. The world may see and vividly remember all of my faults and sins. Who knows, they may even be written down in a book somewhere. The good news is that my Savior, Jesus Christ, paid the price for my sins on Calvary's cross. I have been washed, cleaned, and my sins were cast into the depths of the sea; never to be seen or heard of again.

GOD SPEAKS: "Therefore, if anyone is in Christ, the new creation has come: The old has gone, the new is here!" (2 Corinthians 5:17 NIV) My daughters, I see you as you are in Me. What I see is the true reality of your life. Keep your eyes forever fastened on Me, and day by day you will be changed into the image I see you to be.

WANDA'S PRAYER: Father, keep our eyes forever beholding Your face, until the day we meet face to face.

Notes

Notes

INTRODUCTION

HANNAH

Hannah is a woman who lived during the time period of the judges. This period in Israel's history can be categorized as ancient "moral relativism." The people of that time period did what was "right in their own eyes." They lived their lives based on their feelings and personal perceptions. Hannah married a spiritual man who would take a second wife. This decision made by her husband caused Hannah much suffering and pain.

Hannah's life teaches us the effect others can have on us and how their poor decisions can cause us much heartache and pain. As it was with Hannah, we will see how we, too, can go through years of suffering and heartache because of our pain. However, Hannah also shows us what to do with this pain and who we should take our pain to.

Hannah's life is a beautiful illustration of the power of agonizing prayer. She also shows us we ought to pray despite the hindrances and distractions placed in our path. Hannah's life also shows us that having placed our pain at the foot of our Lord, we can leave it there. We have a Savior and Lord to whom we can take our pains and heartaches to. In doing so, we can know He has heard our cry and will answer it. We can come to Him any time of the day or night, and, like Hannah, He will hear us, and He will answer our prayers.

Notes

July 1

NOW THAT'S A NAME

"THERE WAS A CERTAIN MAN FROM RAMATHAIM, A ZUPHITE FROM THE HILL COUNTRY OF EPHRAIM, WHOSE NAME WAS ELKANAH SON OF JEROHAM, THE SON OF ELIHU, THE SON OF TOHU, THE SON OF ZUPH, AN EPHRAIMITE. HE HAD TWO WIVES; ..." (1 SAMUEL 1:1-2 NIV)

The beginning of Hannah's story, as we know it, begins in 1 Samuel, Chapter 1, with her husband, Elkanah. Since Scripture starts with him, this is where we will start. The first verse goes into great detail about this man. Not only are we told exactly where he lives, but it gave us his complete lineage all the way back to his great-great-grandfather. As we read the glowing ancestry of this man, we get the feeling he is quite proud of his genealogy, as well as he should be. Elkanah had descended from the priestly tribe of Levi. God had chosen this tribe and had given it the high honor of ministering before the LORD, in His sanctuary. So special was this man that his name literally meant, "God has possessed." Yes sir, this was a true man of God, if ever there were one. But this true man of God had a glaring flaw; he had two wives. Being a Levite, who ministered in, and before, the very presence of the God of Heaven, he was very aware of God's laws concerning marriage. This man of God knew very well what the Word of God said about marriage; that it was to be a monogamous relationship, and that our Father made no exceptions. So why would this man of God so boldly defy his LORD and Maker? Perhaps it was the times in which he lived; which was during the period of the Judges of Israel. This was a time of "ancient moral relativism." Everyone did what was "right" in their own eyes. Right and wrong were based on popular opinion and not on God's perfect law of liberty. So, the times swept this holy man of God up. Unfortunately, he did not live in a vacuum. Elkanah's decision to disobey his LORD would have ill effects for the rest of the family. Hannah would have to live a life of pain because of her husband's disobedience.

HANNAH AND US: Even though this story was written thousands of years ago, it still speaks loudly to us today. I, too, am also affected by the decisions of others. Sometimes the suffering seems hardest when I did nothing to contribute to it. Father, speak to our hearts on this matter.

GOD SPEAKS: "... He has sent me to bind up the brokenhearted ..." (Isaiah 61:1 NIV) My daughters, My name is "Wonderful Counselor, Mighty God, Everlasting Father, and the Prince of Peace." I am here to bind and heal all the wounds of this sin sickened world. I just need you to bring them to Me continually. Let us trade—My forever joy for your temporary pain, ok?

WANDA'S PRAYER: Father, you can have all the pain and suffering; we lay it all at Your feet. Give us Your joy and may we rest in You. Thank You Lord!

July 2

A GOOD REASON FOR A BAD DECISION

"HE (ELKANAH) HAD TWO WIVES; ONE WAS CALLED HANNAH AND THE OTHER PENINNAH. PENINNAH HAD CHILDREN, BUT HANNAH HAD NONE." (1 SAMUEL 1:2 NIV)

I will start by giving you my paraphrase of the above text. This is a story of a family who lived during the time of the Judges. The husband's name was Elkanah, and he was a Levite. His name meant 'possessed of God or created by God.' He was a man of God and he had two wives. The first (or primary) wife's name was Hannah. Her name meant 'grace or highly favored one.' He had a second wife named Peninnah; her name meant 'Pearl.' Pearl had given Elkanah a lot of children; but the 'highly favored one' could have none. Thus, here we can see this man's reason for sinning against his LORD. He wanted children to carry on this good name and lineage. On a human level, we can understand this man's dilemma over not having children. If we add to that the times in which he lived, we understand why he would have two wives. One he loved, and the other he used to bear his children. However, this was a priest—a preacher who knew God's Holy law very well. So how he justified his actions to himself, and his LORD is beyond me. Also, I would think that of all men, he would know how to go to the LORD for children, instead of following the times in which he lived for answers. Our Father and LORD, whose name is Holy, does not share this viewpoint of compromise for a good cause. In God's eyes, it is never ok to disobey His laws to keep up with the popular culture. To do so is to roll out the red carpet to heartache and sorrow.

HANNAH AND US: Hannah may not have had much say in the matter; but in my life, I can think of having done just as her husband did. I invited sin and the pain it brought with my willful disobedience "for a good reason."

GOD SPEAKS: "My people have committed two sins: They have forsaken me, the spring of living water, and have dug their own cisterns, broken cisterns that cannot hold water." (Jeremiah 2:13 NIV) This happens when you try to do things your own way. Remember, "I am the way, the truth, and the life…" (John 14:6 NKJV) So if you want to know the perfect way to go, then come to the Perfect God for answers.

WANDA'S PRAYER: LORD, constantly remind us that Your commands are not suggestions.

July 3

PLAYING FAVORITES

"WHENEVER THE DAY CAME FOR ELKANAH TO SACRIFICE, HE WOULD GIVE PORTIONS OF THE MEAT TO HIS WIFE PENINNAH AND TO ALL HER SONS AND DAUGHTERS. BUT TO HANNAH HE GAVE A DOUBLE PORTION BECAUSE HE LOVED HER, AND THE LORD HAD CLOSED HER WOMB." (1 SAMUEL 1:4-5 NIV)

On the surface, this sounds like such a beautiful and noble jester on Elkanah's part. After all, He loved Hannah, and she could not have any children because "big bad God" had closed her womb. He was just showing her love in her unloved state—right? So he showers Hannah with love, and tosses a bone at the work horse/child producer (Peninnah) and her kids. This does not sit well with me because of what they are supposed to represent, based on their names. Elkanah's name loosely translated means, "man of God." Hannah's name means, "highly favored one." If anyone in this story knew God's word, His promises, and the miracles He had performed, it would be the man of God—correct? So why isn't Elkanah, the man of God, who faithfully attends church and worships his Lord, (1Samuel 1:3) going to his GOD on behalf of the beloved wife's infertility? Or why isn't Hannah, the "Highly Favored One," praying to her LORD about her own problem? Of course, I do not know. However, if Elkanah had recalled his Jewish history the way he recalled his family heritage so well, he would have remembered how God gave children to women such as Sarah, Rebekah, and Rachel, just to name a few. But instead of praying to his GOD, I believe Elkanah just makes an unpleasant situation even worse. Five thousand years later, we, as children of God, do the same thing. As Christians today, we have many problems and issues in this life. But do we go to GOD for His solutions? No. Instead, we prefer to find our own pitiful answers to the giant problems of life. As a result, we continue to suffer needlessly. We try to patch up our massive, hemorrhaging wound with a mere Band-Aid. While still bleeding to death, we take our very anemic, pale selves to church. Should someone call to mind our diseased, sickened state, we are quick to answer and let them know we are true men and women of God—blessed and highly favored. The more things change, the more they stay the same.

HANNAH AND US: Like Hannah, I do the same thing. I know I should go to the LORD. I know He is waiting for me to come and unload the very heavy burden. LORD... HELP!

GOD SPEAKS: "Cast all your anxiety on him because he cares for you." (1 Peter 5:7 NIV) When will you realize that I, your GOD, am LOVE! Love always wants what is best. Give Me your burdens; I will not pry them out of your hands.

WANDA'S PRAYER: Lord, may we remember to bring everything to you first! We trust You!

July 4

WHAT'S IN A NAME

"BECAUSE THE LORD HAD CLOSED HANNAH'S WOMB, HER RIVAL (PENINNAH) KEPT PROVOKING HER IN ORDER TO IRRITATE HER." (1 SAMUEL 1:6 NIV)

Hannah's name means, "grace or highly favored one." She must have had issues about being childless, especially considering the meaning of her name. I imagine she asked herself, "How can I be both favored and barren?" Peninnah's name meant "Pearl." When you think of how pearls are made, this name did not fit this woman. Oysters make pearls as a natural defense against an irritant, usually a grain of sand or parasite. The oyster cannot get rid of the irritant, so it secretes a chemical that surrounds the irritant. Over time, the end product is a pearl. In this story, Peninnah was misnamed, because she was Hannah's irritant. Pearl was jealous of the love the husband, Elkanah, had for the 'highly favored one.' Pearl knew she would never receive the love she so desperately craved from this man. So, the next best thing was to make Hannah's life miserable. What do we do when we have an irritant which makes our lives a living hell? The answer is to take lessons from the oyster. Hannah was the highly favored one, and she needed to remember that. She was a God-fearing woman and needed to take her irritant to the Lord. He had the perfect chemical mixture for the healing of her wounded soul. Then, over time, that irritant would gleam like pearls. So how does this look in a life? How do we approach our loving Lord and receive answers to our hurting hearts? Remember the ACTS acronym: The letter "**A**" is for **Adoration**. We are to let our Heavenly Father know He is so worthy to be praised for being the God of the universe. He is a very good, and wonderful Dad. We praise Him for who He is—the KING OF KINGS AND LORD OF LORDS. Next is the letter "**C**" which stands for **Confession**. We confess all of our sins—known and unknown. We confess our faithlessness to Him and His mighty power to answer our prayers. The third letter "**T**" stands for **Thanksgiving**. We thank our LORD for the blessings we have already received. We have life, health, food, shelter, employment, and the list goes on and on. The last letter is "**S**," which stands for **Supplication**. We make our needs known to our loving Dad. He will answer us. Sometimes He says "yes," sometimes He says, "no," and sometimes He will say, "wait."

HANNAH AND US: During my storms and deep heartaches of life, I forget to pray. I think, like Hannah, I forget I am my Father's "highly favored one." As children of the Heavenly King, we all are His highly favored ones. When I forget that fact, I just sit around and allow myself to be tortured.

GOD SPEAKS: "This poor man called, and the LORD heard him; he saved him out of all his troubles. The angel of the LORD encamps around those who fear him, and he delivers them." (Psalm 34:6-7 NIV) I am just a whisper away; just call upon Me, and I will hear you.

WANDA'S PRAYER: Lord, thank you for saving us.

July 5

THE HOLIDAY BLUES

"THIS WENT ON YEAR AFTER YEAR. WHENEVER HANNAH WENT UP TO THE HOUSE OF THE LORD, HER RIVAL PROVOKED HER TILL SHE WEPT AND WOULD NOT EAT."
(1 SAMUEL 1:7 NIV)

Peninnah was miserable, and she made everyone else's life a living hell. Pearl was especially a nag during the holidays or "holy days." I suspect her vicious attacks on Hannah were because of Elkanah's giving Hannah double portions. (1 Samuel 1:5) This served as a further reminder to Pearl that her only function in this household was to produce children. It told her she would never reach the highly favored status Hannah had. So, if she could not be "the highly favored one," she would make the "highly favored one" feel like a terrible wretch. For Hannah, this resulted in heartache and tears. She even experienced anorexia over her circumstances. Hannah's pain was real, and it sent her into periods of depression. As far as we are told, Hannah did not have clinical depression brought on by a chemical imbalance; it was because of her childless state. So her solution was to go to the Source for answers. Hannah did not need to just cry, she needed to cry out to the LORD. Praying to God gives us all the things the secular world says we need to deal with our problems. God gives us a safe environment to vent, and He gives us real solutions to the problems of life. I will repeat the acronym I gave yesterday for prayer and how it relates to Hannah's life. The **"A"** is for **Adoration**. Hannah needed to remind herself that in God's eyes, she was highly favored. She also needed to remind herself that she served the All-Powerful LORD, who has limitless resources. This takes the pressure off of her and puts it on the one who cannot fail. The **"C"** is for **Confession** of sins. This clears the air of things that would prevent Him from hearing her prayers. (Isaiah 59:2) The **"T"** is for giving the Lord **Thanksgiving** for her present and future blessings. Last, the **"S"** is for **Supplication**. This is the safe place where she can give her every emotional and physical issue to her LORD; and trust Him not to tell anyone. In return, He will give her peace, rest, and silence her enemies. God has promised to answer His children. Remember, the answer may be yes, no, or wait. So drop that load at the feet of Jesus and leave it there.

HANNAH AND US: Like Hannah, I have suffered through and endured the painful situations of life. During those times, I knew I should have gone to the Father for help, but I just waited, cried, and did not eat. (This was in the past—I eat too much now!)

GOD SPEAKS: "Sing the praises of the LORD, you his faithful people; praise his holy name. For his anger lasts only a moment, but his favor lasts a lifetime; weeping may stay for the night, but rejoicing comes in the morning." (Psalm 30:4-5 NIV) Remember that being favored does not mean you will not have pain. It does mean, however, that when you give it to Me, your night will end, and your day will come.

WANDA'S PRAYER: Lord, we would go crazy if we did not have You to deal with our many issues.

July 6

KIND BUT CLUELESS

"HER HUSBAND ELKANAH WOULD SAY TO HER, 'HANNAH, WHY ARE YOU WEEPING? WHY DON'T YOU EAT? WHY ARE YOU DOWNHEARTED? DON'T I MEAN MORE TO YOU THAN TEN SONS?'" (1 SAMUEL 1:8 NIV)

People (started to say men, but changed it) can be so two-dimensional when it comes to dealing with problems. For example, they say, "You have a problem—I will fix the problem—so there!" Elkanah, in showing concern for his wife's hurt, tries to console her by asking her to not dwell on the pain, but to think about the good. He feels the good in her life is that his love for her is better than having ten sons. In doing so, he thinks the pain will just "magically" go away, though Scripture has made it clear in previous verses that Hannah's problems are because "the LORD has closed her womb." This was a LORD-sized problem, but her husband was attempting to fix the problem with a human-sized solution. From a human standpoint, it seems like good advice, but it does not deal with the heart of the problem. "Grace," as Hannah's name means, has an elephant size hurt in her life because of her barrenness. Pretending the problems did not exist would solve nothing. It was God's problem and only He could solve it. Our LORD Jesus gives us the model prayer to the Father in Matthew 6. Hannah and I would do well to apply this model in every area of our lives. First, to recognize that God is our Perfect Father, our Heavenly Dad. His name is Holy. This statement tells me I am communicating with someone who loves me so much. It also says to me He is the loving person who has all the power needed to fix my "unfixable" problem. I do not cover up the hurt, but instead I lay everything at His loving feet. The prayer goes on to say that when I have sinned, I need to confess the wrong and clear the air. There is also a need for me to forgive those who have hurt me. I then must also ask my Father to help me not to sin, by keeping me away from the things which might cause me to sin. I can ask this because He is the King and has all power.

HANNAH AND US: I realize Hannah and I are the same. We go to humans when we should always go to the Higher Source. When we go to the wrong source, it just prolongs the hurt and pain.

GOD SPEAKS: "I have seen their ways, but I will heal them; I will guide them and restore comfort to Israel's mourners, creating praise on their lips. Peace, peace, to those far and near," says the LORD. "And I will heal them." (Isaiah 57:18-19 NIV) I create praise on the lips of the mourners, because I give Myself to them. I am the Wonderful Counselor, the Mighty God, the Everlasting Father, and the Prince of Peace. (Isaiah 9:6) When you have Me, I have healing in My hands; I am the complete package.

WANDA'S PRAYER: Father God, you are the complete package, and we have everything we need when we have You.

July 7

HERE IS THE PLACE—NOW IS THE TIME

"ONCE WHEN THEY HAD FINISHED EATING AND DRINKING IN SHILOH, HANNAH STOOD UP. NOW ELI THE PRIEST WAS SITTING ON HIS CHAIR BY THE DOORPOST OF THE LORD'S HOUSE. IN HER DEEP ANGUISH HANNAH PRAYED TO THE LORD, WEEPING BITTERLY." (1 SAMUEL 1:9-10 NIV)

There are times in our lives when we are presented with many opportunities. How many times have we read of a housewife who had a great idea, acted on it, and now she is a multi-millionaire? Such was the case for Hannah. How many times had she carried her burden of a sad and broken heart like an old suitcase to Shiloh, only to go home the same way? Why would she do such a thing? Shiloh was the Temple of the LORD. This was the place to go into the presence of God. The meaning for Shiloh is tranquil, secure, or success. It also means to be happy, prosperous, and safe. Finally, the light came on in Hannah's mind and she asked herself, "girl, why are you carrying this two-ton load, when you do not have to?" Hannah, or the "highly favored one," finally realized the "who," "where," and "when" about her life. The "who" was that she was the beloved daughter of the Heavenly King. The "where" of her life was that she was in the presence of her loving LORD. This is the place of safety, tranquility, and peace; He is the Prince of Peace. The "when" was now! I can be at peace and know that I am in a place of safety. It is here and now that I will lay down all my deep hurts and pain before You. I am choosing to carry them no more. Take away the hurt and pain of my barren state. Father, take all the pain away right now, please! It is here and now, in this very safe and secure place, she would lay herself bare before her Daddy. She tells Him of all her bitterness of soul and weeps. At the feet of Jesus, she unleashed a flood of dammed up emotions. She would not leave this place until she had given her all to her LORD. On this day, Hannah would not leave this place the same way she came.

HANNAH AND US: What Hannah does speaks volumes. I, too, have carried my burdens, sometimes neatly packed and sometimes all jumbled up in my old case. I brought them to God and took them home again. It is only when I, like Hannah, left them at the feet of Jesus, were the problems dealt with.

GOD SPEAKS: "Cast all your anxiety on him because he cares for you." (1 Peter 5:7 NIV) I am the "Him," referred to in this verse. I care about everything which concerns you. I am the only one with the like yoke. Give Me yours and take Mine.

WANDA'S PRAYER: Father, you would think by now we would know or remember some of the things You have been trying to teach us.

July 8

TAKE THIS BURDEN AND KEEP IT

"AND SHE MADE A VOW, SAYING, 'LORD ALMIGHTY, IF YOU WILL ONLY LOOK ON YOUR SERVANT'S MISERY AND REMEMBER ME, AND NOT FORGET YOUR SERVANT BUT GIVE HER A SON, THEN I WILL GIVE HIM TO THE LORD FOR ALL THE DAYS OF HIS LIFE, AND NO RAZOR WILL EVER BE USED ON HIS HEAD.'" (1 SAMUEL 1:11 NIV)

When I read this part of Hannah's prayer, I can almost hear the heartbreak in her voice, and I can feel the misery of her soul. If I were to paraphrase what she is saying, it would sound like this to me: "LORD GOD, You can do anything. I just need You to turn Your attention to me for just a little while. Here I am, LORD, and I need for You to remember me! I have been hurting a long time and I just need for You to answer this one request, LORD. Give me a son… please! The pain of not having children has been almost unbearable. I feel like such an outcast. If You would give me a son and take away my shame, then I will give him right back to You all the days of his life—I promise!" This is the prayer of a woman who has put all of her hopes in God, and in Him alone. With that thought in mind, Hannah laid her all on the altar before her LORD. Did she have to bargain with God in order to receive a son? No! The Father gave Sarah, Rebekah, and Rachel children without them giving away their firstborn. Our Dad is just waiting to give wonderful gifts to His kids. Hannah suffered for many years in pain and heartbreak, but this is the first time we read of her pouring out her soul to God and asking the Father for His help.

HANNAH AND US: I can remember wanting God to answer a certain prayer. I even talked to friends and church members about what I wanted the Father to do on my behalf, but I never took it to Him personally. Never did I really pour out my soul over the matter. When I finally did, the LORD gave me such a peace in the middle of the problem. The solution was not instant, but He lifted and took away the heavy load. He allowed me a time to get in position to receive His perfect answer to Wanda's prayer.

GOD SPEAKS: "If you, then, though you are evil, know how to give good gifts to your children, how much more will your Father in heaven give good gifts to those who ask him!" (Matthew 7:11 NIV) I am Perfectly Holy and Perfectly Good. Always keep that in mind. If you do, then you know that even when I say "no," "wait," or "yes," they are all for your perfect good.

WANDA'S PRAYER: Thank You, LORD, for the reminder. Now we know that whatever Your answers are to our prayers, they are for our good and Your glory.

July 9

JUDGING A BOOK BY ITS COVER

"AS SHE KEPT ON PRAYING TO THE LORD, ELI OBSERVED HER MOUTH. HANNAH WAS PRAYING IN HER HEART, AND HER LIPS WERE MOVING BUT HER VOICE WAS NOT HEARD. ELI THOUGHT SHE WAS DRUNK AND SAID TO HER, 'HOW LONG ARE YOU GOING TO STAY DRUNK? PUT AWAY YOUR WINE.'" (1 SAMUEL 1:12-14 NIV)

Hannah's heart was so heavy at this point that she could not even speak audibly. All she could do was utter groans that only her Father in Heaven understood. So because of this, Eli, the high priest, assumed she was drunk. This is a very sad commentary on his day and on him. It is sad if his parishioners had a habit of coming to church falling out drunk. Even sadder, to think the High Priest did not have the spiritual insight to discern the hurting hearts of his congregation. Either way, he completely misjudged this poor woman and pronounced a sentence on her case. But, before I criticize Eli's actions, I am reminded of how many times I have done the same thing. A hurting young woman comes into church—scantily dressed and exposing enticing body parts. What have I done? Instead of asking God to show me His child's hurt and pain, I have gotten very offended. At that point, I am not an instrument of helping and healing as I ought to be. Like Eli, I inflict more pain and attempt to chase away the child of God from the only Source of true healing and relief. Father, help us—Your poor, pathetic children. Little do we know that one day, we too will have to give an account of our inappropriate reactions to His little ones.

HANNAH AND US: At times, I have been misjudged by some as I entered God's house, but most of the time, I have been the one doing the misjudging, overreacting, and chasing away of the "undesirable ones." Once I was in a church and a scantily dressed woman came in. My friends and I asked her not to attend anymore. We were so afraid of our husbands being tempted. Boy was I an idiot! I have asked the LORD a thousand times to forgive me for my very foolish sin.

GOD SPEAKS: "Stop judging by mere appearances, but instead judge correctly." (John 7:24 NIV) "And I heard the altar respond: 'Yes, Lord God Almighty, true and just are your judgments.'" (Revelation 16:7 NIV) I am the only Righteous Judge. I am the only One who knows everything all the time. You would do wisely to consult Me, before making any judgment calls, don't you think?

WANDA'S PRAYER: Father God, give us a heart like Yours. We want to see what You see. Help us look past the appearance and see the hurt and pain of others. Help us be an instrument of healing, and not an object that inflicts pain.

July 10

SINCE YOU DIDN'T ASK, I'LL TELL YOU

"NOT SO, MY LORD," HANNAH REPLIED, "I AM A WOMAN WHO IS DEEPLY TROUBLED. I HAVE NOT BEEN DRINKING WINE OR BEER; I WAS POURING OUT MY SOUL TO THE LORD. DO NOT TAKE YOUR SERVANT FOR A WICKED WOMAN; I HAVE BEEN PRAYING HERE OUT OF MY GREAT ANGUISH AND GRIEF." ELI ANSWERED, 'GO IN PEACE, AND MAY THE GOD OF ISRAEL GRANT YOU WHAT YOU HAVE ASKED OF HIM.'" (1 SAMUEL 1:15-17 NIV)

Hannah was a bigger woman than I would have been at this point. She knew she was acting out of a pure heart, and that even men of God have flaws. She would gently correct this erring man of God and set the record straight. Hannah tells Eli about her hurt and pain; how she was not drunk as he supposed, but in agony — pouring her soul out to her LORD. This brings up a good point on what to do when you have a brother or sister that shows up at the church door, dressed or acting inappropriately. First thing, stop to pray for God's perfect wisdom and discernment. Next, listen to the complete story while continuing to pray for God's will to be done. Then, apply God's Word to the subject while again continuing to pray for wisdom and judgment. When we do these things, it might pleasantly surprise us as to what the Father will do for them and for you (myself included). In the above discourse, when Eli hears the whole matter, he is blessed as well. He now becomes a tool for God's blessing, and not the hammer to beat down the child of God. Hannah also shows to hurting souls what should be done with the hurt. She knows without a doubt that this is where she should be, and she will not lose her blessing because of someone else's offense. No matter what, she will have her time with her Father. She is determined that hurt feelings and the misunderstanding of others will not deter her from coming into the presence of her LORD.

HANNAH AND US: Like Hannah, sometimes I have said, "I will not quit until I hear from my LORD." In those moments, the Father has made Himself very real to me. I found I do not have to grovel before God. I must only believe He has heard me and will answer me according to His perfect will for my life.

GOD SPEAKS: "Whoever would foster love covers over an offense, but whoever repeats the matter separates close friends." (Proverbs 17:9 NIV) When I died on that cross over two thousand years ago, I covered all of your offenses. When I see you, I do not see your sins—I only see my perfect righteousness.

WANDA'S PRAYER: Jesus, the covering of our sin has filled our hearts with an overwhelming love for You. Thank You for loving Your unlovable children.

July 11

BABY IS ON THE WAY

"SHE SAID, 'MAY YOUR SERVANT FIND FAVOR IN YOUR EYES.' THEN SHE WENT HER WAY AND ATE SOMETHING, AND HER FACE WAS NO LONGER DOWNCAST."
(1 SAMUEL 1:18 NIV)

Hannah had gotten her breakthrough. No, she was not pregnant yet, but she knew the Lord God of Heaven had heard every word and utterance of her prayer. Hannah knew it was not a matter of if, but when, she would get pregnant. She did not have to be downcast anymore. She could now eat, because her Father was working on the problem; the answer was on its way. The Lord had made the great exchange! He had given her a crown of beauty, for her ashes of shame; the oil of gladness instead of mourning. (Isaiah 61:3) When she got off of her knees that day, she was certain she was "grace," or God's unmerited favor. She was now soaring on God's wings. She could sing the song, "This joy I have, the world didn't give it to me… the world didn't give it and the world can't take it away." Hannah was now ready to face all the thorns in her side because she had her Lord on the inside. At this point she may have thought, "So bring it on Pearl! I'm not worried about your insults—my GOD has got this one and you cannot shake me."

HANNAH AND US: In those moments of my life when I am totally assured that my Dad has complete control, an unexplainable peace comes with it. That peace stays, and it keeps me. The insomnia is gone, along with any associated worries and fear. I am not sure how the particular problem will be resolved, but I am certain of who will resolve it.

GOD SPEAKS: "Instead of your shame you will receive a double portion, and instead of disgrace you will rejoice in your inheritance…" (Isaiah 61:7 NIV) I am just waiting to make the great exchange with you. Give Me all of your junk, and I will give you all of Me and My joy—ok?

WANDA'S PRAYER: Deal! Father, take our all for Your all.

July 12

PRAISE ON CREDIT

"EARLY THE NEXT MORNING THEY AROSE AND WORSHIPED BEFORE THE LORD AND THEN WENT BACK TO THEIR HOME AT RAMAH. ELKANAH MADE LOVE TO HIS WIFE HANNAH, AND THE LORD REMEMBERED HER." (1 SAMUEL 1:19 NIV)

One of my favorite pastors, Dr. Peeler, had a great phrase I loved. He would say, "we should praise God already and on credit." What I felt he meant is we should praise God for blessings in advance, as if they were already answered. This is just what Hannah, and her husband did. Elkanah was probably so happy to see his wife's joy and peace that he too had to give his Father some praise! They could worship the Father unhindered because He had removed Hannah's chains and set her free from everything that kept her bound. She was totally free. Not only was she free to praise her LORD, but she was also free to give and receive love from her husband. The next part of that verse says that God remembered. The question then becomes, "does our God forget or is he senile?" NO! That phrase could be more properly written to say, "God turned His attention to Hannah and her problem." God inhabits or dwells in our praises. As we give total praise to Him, we do at least two things: First, we take the burden off of us weak, flawed human beings, who are powerless to do anything. Second, with confidence, knowing the problem will be solved, we place the burden onto a limitless GOD. The breakthrough for Hannah was not the child, because she was just now getting pregnant. Her breakthrough was in the releasing of her complete self, to the Sovereign will of her perfect Father's love. The testament of her releasing was total praise to Poppa God.

HANNAH AND US: A while back, I read over some of my old prayer journals. They reminded me of the deep distress I was in many years ago—even as of that previous week. They seemed so pressing and urgent at the time. Then, I read of how the Holy Spirit urged me to praise my Daddy for His goodness and mercy, and to the problems at His feet. I am amazed at just how thoroughly the Father worked out my problems. Yes, are still in process, but He has given me peace to know that they too, are a done deal.

D SPEAKS: "Yet you are enthroned as the Holy One; you are the one Israel praises. In you our ancestors their trust; they trusted and you delivered them." (Psalm 22:3-4 NIV) I am not only the trust of Israel, but I the trust of the entire world. Continue to make Me the Source of your trust and watch Me work.

WANDA'S PRAYER: "I will extol the LORD at all times; his praise will always be on my lips." (Psalm 34:1 NIV)

July 13

TIMING

"AND IN DUE TIME SHE GAVE BIRTH TO A SON. SHE NAMED HIM SAMUEL, FOR SHE SAID, 'I ASKED THE LORD FOR HIM.'" (I SAMUEL 1:20 NLT)

In reading this text, one word jumps out and grabs me by the throat; that word is "timing." I have a good friend who, in every situation, would always say to me, "Wanda, my dear, timing is everything." When I look at Hannah's life in the light of this verse, I can say this is very true. The LORD gave her a son at just the right time. So I have asked Dad, why did He wait so long to give her a son? The answer He showed me was that it took time to get to the heart of their matters—which was the matter of their hearts. This is what I mean: This chapter presented us with a very godly family. We see they love the LORD; they attend church regularly to worship God. Yet, these righteous people have a big problem—the wife cannot have children. There is a verse in Scripture which says, "The righteous person may have many troubles, but the LORD delivers him from them all;" (Psalm 34:19 NIV) We can see this family does not really believe in God; or they doubt He will fix their problem. Instead, the husband attempts to fix the problem by getting a second wife, Peninnah. The second wife tortures the first wife, Hannah, who drives her into a deep depression and almost insane. It was not until Hannah, whose name means, "highly favored one," goes beyond just going to church—she goes directly into the presence of the LORD ALMIGHTY. This is where she receives answers to her prayers. In seeing God for who He is, she comes to realize that He is the answer to her every question, problem, or situation in life. At the Temple in Shiloh that day, it was just Hannah and her LORD. When she believed that He alone had the answers to her every need, and had cried out to Him from the pit of her soul, this is when her breakthrough came. It was on that day Dad gave her a new spiritual heart. After He fixed the spiritual, her heart and soul, then He repaired her physical body and gave her a son. He did this because she went to Him with everything and asked. His answer to her was a son, and she called him, "Samuel—asked of God."

HANNAH AND US: This story is so full of application for me. With all my "spirituality" and pretense of holiness, I lack the simple faith to believe God for who He is. He is the All-Powerful LORD. When I spend time in His presence as Hannah did, then everything else falls into place.

GOD SPEAKS: "For in Christ all the fullness of the Deity lives in bodily form, and in Christ you have been brought to fullness. He is the head over every power and authority." (Colossians 2:9-10 NIV) I am GOD and all that it means. I am POWER beyond measure. I alone can complete you. What is your issue? What is your need? I am "completeness and fullness" overflowing. Allow Me to complete and fill you with Myself. I will take control and reign over the powers and authorities that control your life.

WANDA'S PRAYER: LORD, hurry—rule and reign in our lives! As we spend time with You in prayer and study of Your word, constantly fill us with You.

July 14

LORD, I SAID IT AND I MEANT IT

"WHEN HER HUSBAND ELKANAH WENT UP WITH ALL HIS FAMILY TO OFFER THE ANNUAL SACRIFICE TO THE LORD AND TO FULFILL HIS VOW, HANNAH DID NOT GO. SHE SAID TO HER HUSBAND, 'AFTER THE BOY IS WEANED, I WILL TAKE HIM AND PRESENT HIM BEFORE THE LORD, AND HE WILL LIVE THERE ALWAYS.'"
(1 SAMUEL 1:21-22 NIV)

In Hannah's mind, a promise made is a promise kept! She had promised the LORD that if He gave her a son, she would return the child to Him. Now we see she is making good on that promise. I really admire this woman. I think at this point I would have wanted to play the game, "Let's Make A Deal," with God. Personally, it would be very hard for me to keep my vow to the LORD on giving up my only son. In those days and still today, in countries besides the United States, mothers will usually breastfeed their babies for up to five years old, before weaning them. It was time for the annual offering and worship of God at Shiloh. The man of God, Elkanah, was getting the family together for this event. Hannah informs her husband she is not going; she will wait until she weaned the boy off of the breast and possibly, had fully potty trained him. Then she will present him to the LORD, as she had vowed. This dynamic is also amazing—the husband goes along with this plan. Why? He, according to the Levitical Laws, could have overruled his wife's plans. The answer is in the text itself. Elkanah was a man that kept his word to God, and he would have his wife do nothing less. The verse says he was going "to offer annual sacrifices and to fulfill his vow to the LORD." He was a man of principle and those principles filtered out to his entire household. He tells his wife in the next verse, "Do what seems best to you. Stay here until you have weaned him… So the woman stayed at home and nursed her son until she had weaned him." (1 Samuel 1:23) This woman would keep her promise no matter what. This man also shows a deep love and respect for his wife's judgment in this matter. This speaks volumes about the character of Hannah.

HANNAH AND US: O LORD, my prayer is that I would emulate this woman's resolve to keep her word. I fall short in this. LORD, I say many things and make many promises which I fail to carry out. Help me be a woman of my word.

GOD SPEAKS: "And whatever you do, whether in word or deed, do it all in the name of the Lord Jesus, giving thanks to God the Father through him." (Colossians 3:17 NIV) The answer to keeping your word is by letting the WORD (ME) live in you continually.

WANDA'S PRAYER: "Let the words of my mouth and the meditation of my heart be acceptable in YOUR sight, O LORD, my strength and my redeemer." (Psalm 19:14 NKJV)

July 15

A PROMISE MADE IS A PROMISE KEPT

"AFTER HE WAS WEANED, SHE TOOK THE BOY WITH HER, YOUNG AS HE WAS, ALONG WITH A THREE-YEAR-OLD BULL, AN EPHAH OF FLOUR AND A SKIN OF WINE, AND BROUGHT HIM TO THE HOUSE OF THE LORD AT SHILOH." (1 SAMUEL 1:24 NIV)

This is very interesting to me. Hannah takes her only child, who is now about three to five years old, to the Lord as fulfillment of the pledge she had made. We do not read of the boy kicking, screaming, or crying, which is remarkable to me. He seems to have just calmly accepted his lot in life at a very young age. Hannah and Elkanah are remarkable parents, and this says something about their child-rearing. By the time he reached the Temple at Shiloh (which means peace), the whole family was at peace about the decision which had been made. After they slayed the animal offering, she goes to Eli and reminds him of the other, and more important, offering vow she made to the LORD. To jar his memory, she recants her story and does what she has pledged: "So now I give him to the LORD. For his whole life he will be given over to the LORD. And he worshipped there." (1 Samuel 1:25-28) This story is an illustration of what the Father did in giving His Son, Jesus. Dad gave His one and only Son to save you and me from sin and to give us eternal life. When Hannah gave Samuel over to the LORD, what did that mean? From birth, she instilled into her son the love and knowledge of our Savior and LORD, through Word and deed. She set aside moments of worship and prayer with praise to her GOD with the child. She attempted to use every moment with him to teach him the love, care, and compassion of the Father. How do I know? Because by the time this child reached Shiloh, he was totally sold-out and dedicated to his LORD. The Word says, "… And he worshipped there." Samuel worshipped God in Shiloh, beginning as a child. Hannah's mindset was that this child was God's son, and not hers. He was only on loan to her—to be trained in the LORD'S service, and not for her own purposes.

HANNAH AND US: I salute this woman. Though I took my kids to church weekly and had Bible studies with them, but the training of my kids did not come anywhere near Hannah's.

GOD SPEAKS: "Fix these words of mine in your hearts and minds; …Teach them to your children, talking about them when you sit at home and when you walk along the road, when you lie down and when you get up." (Deuteronomy 11:18-19 NIV) This means your job, all the time, is to tell your kids about Me.

WANDA'S PRAYER: LORD, we really need some help in this area. At times, we feel like we are boring them to death. Show us how You do it.

July 16

NOW LET'S BREAK OUT IN PRAISE

"... MY HEART REJOICES IN THE LORD; IN THE LORD MY HORN IS LIFTED HIGH. MY MOUTH BOASTS OVER MY ENEMIES, FOR I DELIGHT IN YOUR DELIVERANCE."
(1 SAMUEL 2:1 NIV)

Looking at this verse, one would think Hannah had just won the Lotto by giving her son away. In a very real sense, this is exactly what she had just won. I will use a "Wanda's paraphrase" of this verse to show you what I mean. (I know it's a little sappy, but bear with me.) "In the innermost part of my being, deep down in my soul, I am jumping for absolute joy! I cannot help myself or contain these feelings. Why? Because the LORD—the Almighty God, the King of Creation gave me this boy. You know I was barren, but He gave him to me as a showpiece. So, I will praise the LORD on High, as I show him off to the world. In fact, I am gonna brag on God and tell all the haters in my life that this is what the LORD does for His children when they ask. I am so excited that I am going to throw a block party and tell everybody I see just how good the LORD has been to me." I could see from this verse the Father had given her 3 P's—His Peace, a Present, and His Presence. The first P is for Peace. She remembers a time when she could not rejoice. Go back and re-read chapter one and see how torn down Hannah was. For years, the shackles of deep depression held her captive. Now the Father had set her completely free, and she would praise him forever. The second P is for a Present. The present is actually the gift of her son, Samuel. There was no doubt in her mind that Samuel was a gift from the LORD, and Him alone. The last P the Father gave her was His Presence. God gave Hannah Himself. She said He was her Savior. He had given her freedom to live, move, and praise Him.

HANNAH AND US: It is good sometimes to remember just how good GOD has been to us. I will take time to thank Him for food, shelter, strength, sanity, a job, children, a husband, and the list will continue forever. He is so worthy of my praise. In my complaints, I often forget to just stop and give Him thanks.

GOD SPEAKS: "O give thanks unto the Lord; for he is good: ..." (Psalm 136:1 KJV) My goodness knows no end. I am good when things are going well, and I am still good when you think things are falling apart. Always remember that.

WANDA'S PRAYER: Lord, You alone are so worthy of all our praise. Our prayer is that our praise will be ten times more than our complaints.

July 17

IN A CATEGORY OF HIS OWN

"THERE IS NO ONE HOLY LIKE THE LORD; THERE IS NO ONE BESIDES YOU; THERE IS NO ROCK LIKE OUR GOD." (1 SAMUEL 2:2 NIV)

I can see that Hannah is doing some praise—preaching in this verse! She puts the Father in a category all by Himself. She tells us He alone is Holy; that He alone was her only stronghold breaker. This woman had known strongholds in her life. In 1 Samuel, Chapter 1, we see a woman trapped in a deep depression because of her inability to have children. For years, she could not break free from the reproach of being barren. But when she encountered her LORD, her chains of depression and despair fell off like shredded paper. Until that day at Shiloh, she was stained with the shame of reproach—of being childless. But when Hannah came into the presence of the Father, He removed the old, ragged garments of mourning and despair. He then washed His daughter in the oil of His gladness. Now made pure by the Father's righteousness, He clothed her with His beautiful garments of praise. He gave her a sure foundation in Himself, and He was more solid than the Rock of Gibraltar. That Rock, the foundation of her salvation, now gives her another name. He called His daughter a solid oak of righteousness. (Isaiah 61:3 paraphrased) She was His hardwood, made tough by the circumstances the Father brought her through. On the solid Rock, she stood with her head held high. This was the ROCK which would never move. He was her LORD of love.

HANNAH AND US: I can relate to Hannah. There are many storms and struggles in life the Father has brought me through. Having gone through the fire and flood, I have been a little singed and waterlogged, but not consumed. When I look back over those experiences, there is no doubt in my mind who brought me through—it was the ROCK of my salvation. Without Him, I would have burned to a crisp, or drowned long ago.

GOD SPEAKS: "And from Jesus Christ, who is the faithful witness, and the first begotten of the dead, and the prince of the kings of the earth. Unto him that loved us, and washed us from our sins in his own blood," (Revelation 1:5 KJV) I am the King of the Universe; yet I humbled Myself enough to wash away all your sins and flaws with My blood. Never forget how much I love you.

WANDA'S PRAYER: Lord, we will never forget it took 100% of Your spotless blood to take away our sins. You paid the price without a second thought. Thank You LORD!

July 18

BONDAGE AND FREEDOM

"DO NOT KEEP TALKING SO PROUDLY OR LET YOUR MOUTH SPEAK SUCH ARROGANCE, FOR THE LORD IS A GOD WHO KNOWS, AND BY HIM DEEDS ARE WEIGHED." (1 SAMUEL 2:3 NIV)

In this country, we pride ourselves on having freedom of all sorts, particularly speech. What we fail to realize is that we are all slaves to sin and its dictates. If I have a habit or an addiction, I am subject to the cravings of my flesh, and will do what the habit tells me to. True freedom only comes through the LORD Jesus Christ. As we have seen in Samuel Chapter One, Hannah's depression held her captive because she could not have children. This taskmaster exacted a heavy toll on Hannah's life. She was in such bondage that the only freedom she had was to feel miserable and cry incessantly. (1 Samuel 1:6-9) Her rival reigned such terror over her that not only was she in emotional bondage, but she was also physically bound as well. So much so, she did not even want to eat. It was not Hannah's sin, but the sin of others which held her captive because of her childless condition. The freedom that Christ brought to Hannah when she met with Him in the Temple was the true liberation of the total Hannah. The freed Hannah cowered to no one; now she could speak boldly in the LORD, and put her enemies in their place. She, through Christ, could speak up and speak out. The LORD has silenced her enemies. To me, she is saying, "You can shut your mouth now—with all the proud bragging you were doing. Just be quiet because you do not know—anything! Only God knows what is true and He alone gives true justice." (Writer's paraphrase)

HANNAH AND US: Like Hannah, I can look back over my life and see where old habits have stood like Mount Everest over my life. As I stood at the base of the colossal giants, I shuttered in fear and shame because I felt powerless to overcome. But when Christ set me free and allowed me to die to these destructive habits, I, like Hannah, could not help but sing like a bird.

GOD SPEAKS: "You will not have to fight this battle. Take up your positions; stand firm and see the deliverance the Lord will give you, Judah and Jerusalem. Do not be afraid; do not be discouraged. Go out to face them tomorrow, and the Lord will be with you." (2 Chronicles 20:17 NIV) Let Me make it very simple—this fight is Mine and I always win! Make yourself a Judah. As you know, Judah means praise. Jerusalem is My city. Your only job is to let Me have total control over you; and for you to give Me praise.

WANDA'S PRAYER: Father, thank You for once again letting us know You are always in total control; and all we need to do is to get in the place You put us and just praise You!

July 19

I'VE GOT THE POWER

"THE BOWS OF THE WARRIORS ARE BROKEN, BUT THOSE WHO STUMBLED ARE ARMED WITH STRENGTH." (1 SAMUEL 2:4 NIV)

In this verse, Hannah speaks of where the real power comes from. She makes a simple comparison and contrast between human power and the power of God. In speaking of human power, she says, the warrior's bows are broken. A warrior is one who engages in and is experienced at warfare. (Random House Dictionary) In Hannah's day, bows and arrows were the "smart bombs" of choice. Peninnah, the second wife of Elkanah, warred against Hannah (Grace). She was a formidable foe. This highly skilled archer used her weapons well to destroy her enemy, Hannah. She caused Grace (Hannah) to stumble into a deep depression. The "bow and arrows" in her arsenal were painful; she used wounding words to tear into the marrow of Hannah's soul. Yes, Grace was stumbled, but not fallen. Hannah (Grace) now contrasts the human stronghold with the deliverance of the LORD Almighty. The delivered Hannah, strengthened by her Omnipotent LORD, was now standing upright with praise for the God of her salvation. She did not need bow or arrow or any human weapon of mass destruction because, "The LORD was the strength of her life and whom should she fear." (Psalm 27:1) From the day she went into the Temple and poured out her soul to the LORD, He became her Light and salvation. The LORD was all Grace needed.

HANNAH AND US: Like Hannah, as I reflect on the many things the Father has delivered me in, from, and through, I have to say like the Psalmist, "If it had not been for the LORD on my side ...," I do not know where I would be now. He has been my strength and firm stronghold. Thanks Dad.

GOD SPEAKS: "One thing I ask from the LORD, this only do I seek: that I may dwell in the house of the LORD all the days of my life, to gaze on the beauty of the LORD and to seek him in his temple." (Psalm 27:4 NIV) I have all the power in this universe. When you live in Me, and let Me live in you, you will have all you need—understand?

WANDA'S PRAYER: Father, we want to live and be in Your Holy presence forever.

July 20

GOD FLIPS THE SWITCH

"THOSE WHO WERE FULL HIRE THEMSELVES OUT FOR FOOD, BUT THOSE WHO WERE HUNGRY ARE HUNGRY NO MORE. SHE WHO WAS BARREN HAS BORNE SEVEN CHILDREN, BUT SHE WHO HAS MANY SONS PINES AWAY." (1 SAMUEL 2:5 NIV)

In my humble opinion, praising and complaining have only one thing in common. Their commonality is that when the faucet of either is turned on, it becomes like the Hoover Dam, not easily turned off. Hannah is a great example of this. The more she thinks of her LORD, the more she is reminded of His goodness. This then results in her unrestrained praise poured out to Him. In this verse, she continues to remind us of the Father's goodness as He flips the switch on behalf of His children. She makes the comparison between herself and the second wife, Peninnah. Peninnah, or Pearl, was full of food and children; but now she is left in want. Before the LORD blessed Hannah with a son, Pearl sparkled and shone like the sun in the house of Elkanah. Hannah, on the other hand, was dying of starvation and was as barren as an old, dried twig. But GOD! He stepped in and made all the difference in the world. Pearl still holds the title of the most sons born to Elkanah, but this brings no satisfaction to her now. In fact, she is still hungering—starving; she has hired herself out for food. Despite all the trophies called children, she is pining away. (1Samuel 2:5) This is the case for all of us who drink from the well of human successes and human accomplishment. Those cisterns will never fill. It is like drinking salty water from the ocean—the more we drink, the thirstier we get, until finally, we die of dehydration while surrounded by a sea of water.

HANNAH AND US: There was a time in my life when "things" meant everything. I had just bought a nice house in a great neighborhood. I had a good job, but my time with my LORD was nothing. Despite my things, I was still very hollow and dry, so much so that I echoed from the inside out. It was only when I returned to my Father, and He filled me with Himself, that the emptiness went away.

GOD SPEAKS: "Why spend money on what is not bread, and your labor on what does not satisfy? Listen, listen to me, and eat what is good, and you will delight in the richest of fare. Give ear and come to me; listen, that you may live …" (Isaiah 55:2-3 NIV) I alone can fill the empty, unsatisfied heart. Everything outside of Me is only death. I AM life— more than you will ever need. Come, eat of Me, and be filled completely.

WANDA'S PRAYER: LORD, we are hungry now; We sit at the table with bib, plate, and fork. Father, feel free to start the feeding.

July 21

CAN'T STOP PRAISING HIS NAME

"THE LORD BRINGS DEATH AND MAKES ALIVE; HE BRINGS DOWN TO THE GRAVE AND RAISES UP." (1 SAMUEL 2:6 NIV)

Praise is the gift that keeps on giving. We give praises to our LORD; He is so worthy of them. The Father comes to receive our praises; and thus, by His mere presence, the blessings continue to flow. The blessings received are not always tangible like money, but they are things which our spirits desperately need, such as joy and peace. These intangible, costly jewels money cannot buy, but they are of great value. As Hannah continues her praise, she realizes this truth. She also realizes there is so much more to say about His goodness and mercy. The more she gives Him worship, the more He reveals Himself to her. She tells us here that He brings death, and He makes alive. This verse is so rich; it is a parody of hers and ours. Our LORD needed to kill in Hannah, what was killing her—the pent-up bitterness and depression of her barrenness. In this stagnate cesspool, nothing could breed and live, but death. When she came into the presence of her Holy Father, He killed this infestation of death. Dad then gave her His new life. Gone were those grave clothes of depression and sadness. Now she sported His new life of peace and hope. When people have a certain rare blood disorder, they need to have an exchange—a transfusion. The old blood products causing death and destruction must be removed, and new, life-giving ones are put in. This is what Dad did for His daughter. He removed the bad (evil) spirit that coursed through her veins with death. Then He infused His new Spirit—this life-giving blood, which quickened her soul! Hannah now has energy from on High, and she is praising the LORD with all her might. The Father also brought death to the taunts and torture of her foe; and this gave her more to shout about.

HANNAH AND US: I, too, have so much to praise my LORD for. I was on my way to hell in a handbasket, and the Father reached out and saved me. He took away the deadness of my depression and anger over the many hurts and injuries life had given me. He gave me His joy, peace and, well, some tangible gifts, too. I have a new life! Yes, problems still come, but with them come His perfect solutions.

GOD SPEAKS: "Very truly I tell you, whoever hears my word and believes him who sent me has eternal life and will not be judged but has crossed over from death to life." (John 5:24 NIV) New life begins here and now with ME. Allow Me in, and I will do the rest.

WANDA'S PRAYER: Come into our hearts, LORD Jesus. Come today and stay always.

July 22

GOD CALLS THE SHOTS

"THE LORD SENDS POVERTY AND WEALTH; HE HUMBLES AND HE EXALTS."
(1 SAMUEL 2:7 NIV)

The Word says that by beholding the glory of the Lord; we become changed. (2 Corinthians 3:18) This is a very true statement as it relates to Hannah. The more she beholds Him, the more she clearly sees His hand in every aspect of Creation, especially as He relates to her life. She sees the Father not only as the LORD of all but also LORD in all things. In this verse, she tells how the LORD sends poverty and wealth. How well she knew of this. She was desperately poor in childbearing; she could not have a single child. The Scripture says that "The LORD had closed her womb." (1 Samuel 1:5-6) Why would the LORD of love allow Hannah to experience poverty of childbearing? We are not told. We know, however, that we live in a world racked and stricken by the plague of sin, and we live in its fallout. But in Hannah's case, we only see the results of her poverty state. This woman, impoverished of children and debilitated in spirit, was led to seek the Father—her God, who was filthy rich in both. Jesus says, "Blessed are the poor in spirit, For theirs is the kingdom of Heaven." (Matthew 5:3 NKJV) Hannah had reached the point of bankruptcy when she approached her LORD in His temple. She walked into the Kingdom of Heaven as a penniless popper and walked out filled with riches untold. What was she filled with? Him! He filled her with Himself and that was all she needed. After all, He owns the cattle on a thousand hills, does He not? In all of its fullness, this earth is the Lord's, and everything in it, the world, and we who live in it (Psalm 24:1). Because of His filling, Hannah produced. First, He produced in her His Spirit of peace, joy, and love. Then came the physical children. She came to the King humble and brokenhearted, and He lifted her up to Himself, for all the world to see.

HANNAH AND US: I tell you—Sista' girl is speaking to my soul! I was poor of so many things. The Father changed my life when I was an emotional wreck. The world cannot make enough paper to record what all the LORD of love has done to and for me.

GOD SPEAKS: "Humble yourselves in the sight of the Lord, and he will lift you up." (James 4:10 NKJV) All I have ever wanted was you completely. Just let go—give all of yourself to Me, and I will do the rest. I AM high and lifted up; and you will be right up here with Me.

WANDA'S PRAYER: Father, take us now and use us for Your good pleasure.

July 23

LOVE LIFTED ME

"HE RAISES THE POOR FROM THE DUST AND LIFTS THE NEEDY FROM THE ASH HEAP; HE SEATS THEM WITH PRINCES AND HAS THEM INHERIT A THRONE OF HONOR …" (1 SAMUEL 2:8 NIV)

I wonder when Hannah spoke these words if she was thinking of the patriarch Job? As I read this verse, this comes to my mind. Job was a man rich in all things, but suddenly became poor through no fault of his own. In the end, after experiencing all the hurt and pain, the Father restored to him double. From Hannah's viewpoint, she had lived the life of Job. She had suffered the poverty of childlessness and the reproach that came with it. The depression and anguish of it all reduced Hannah to a pile of emotional dust. It reduced her shattered esteem to an "ash heap," which her rival shoveled up daily. One encounter with her LORD and her ongoing relationship with Him changed all that. He took the dust called Hannah, put His Spirit into her, and fashioned this woman into a thing of beauty for His glory. He then seated her in a place of honor, as His princess. It took Hannah from the proverbial "out house to the White House." The saying was now true, "It was LOVE that had lifted her." LOVE (GOD) wants to lift us. His only requirement is our coming to Him, just as we are. In His perfect care, we will never be the same. Sometimes in our lives, we feel empty and barren. Those expected hopes and dreams have crumbled into dust. The best thing we can do is to give them and ourselves to Him—the One who created man from dust. Hannah's verse reminds me I serve the LORD GOD, who is Creator and King.

HANNAH AND US: As I write this, I am experiencing one of those moments of poverty and emptiness. The cupboard lays bare, with no resources left. If the focus is on me with my meager purse, then I should just curl up as a speck of dust, to be blown away. But I will look beyond Wanda and her itty-bitty self. I will look to the Maker of the hills because I know my help, my hope, and my ALL come from Him. He will never disappoint. I will do so while pouring out praise to the God who never fails. I will remember where He has brought me from, and I will trust where He is taking me.

GOD SPEAKS: "Everyone who is called by My name, whom I have created for my glory; I have formed him, yes, I have made him." (Isaiah 43:7 NKJV) You call Me your Father; allow Me to be your LORD. Surrender all you have to My care. I will take care of My own—always.

WANDA'S PRAYER: Thank you, Father, for restoring peace, joy, and order to our wobbly hearts.

July 24

I STAND ON A SOLID ROCK

"… FOR THE FOUNDATIONS OF THE EARTH ARE THE LORD'S; ON THEM HE HAS SET THE WORLD." (1 SAMUEL 2:8 NIV)

Though Hannah was not a carpenter or a builder of homes, she must have known something about how they were made. She knew enough to know that nothing could stand without a firm foundation. From this knowledge is where I think she gets this verse. A foundation is a strong stable base from which buildings are constructed. (Nelson's New Illustrated Bible Dictionary) The foundation of anything must be strong and stable, or else whatever is placed on top of it will fall and break into pieces. Hannah informs us that the earth's foundation—its powerful support is the LORD. She goes on to say that He (God) has set the entire world upon Himself. This implies several things to me: (1) He, our LORD, is the immovable force; (2) Our LORD has the power and might enough to sustain the earth and the world; and (3) He needs no assistance in holding up the earth and the world. So what did this mean to Hannah? It meant (1) Her loving LORD was the only One she needed; (2) She could place her worry, fear, and sorrow, which she had carried for so long, on the ROCK—He would work them out perfectly, and in His perfect timing; (3) This Rock was solid and dependable. Since He held the earth and the world in its place, then surely He could, and would, care for her little problems.

HANNAH AND US: When I think of how my LORD keeps our planet in orbit, or how He sustains human life so effortlessly, my faith increases in Him. Sister Hannah reminds me I serve a God who cannot fail. She also reminds me that in trying to "fix it" myself, I only make a bigger mess of things. I can submit to His way and do things as He commands; trusting He will work it all out. Finally, she reminds me I can rest in the strong, immovable God who is the same—yesterday, today, and forever. Now that is peace!

GOD SPEAKS: "He is the Rock, his works are perfect, and all his ways are just. a faithful God who does no wrong, upright and just is he." (Deuteronomy 32:4 NIV) Do you believe this? You must believe it when all is going well, and when all hell is breaking loose. You must hold on to Me, with all of your strength and might.

WANDA'S PRAYER: LORD, we rarely have a problem believing when all is going well. It is when all hell breaks loose; we tend to falter. Do a work in us which will help us believe, no matter the circumstance.

A CONTINUED REMINDER

"HE WILL GUARD THE FEET OF HIS SAINTS, BUT THE WICKED SHALL BE SILENT IN DARKNESS…"
(1 SAMUEL 2:9 NKJV)

I once heard a story of how people climbed a certain high mountain. It is said the path was so narrow and the drop so steep, that to travel by day caused many losses of life. The answer was to travel at night, under the cover of darkness. Also, the hiker must follow close to his guide. I think rope linked them as they traveled. Finally, the hiker had to walk in the footsteps of the guide to guarantee safety up the mountain. Hannah may not have known this story, but she knew well of the lessons it contained. She continues praising our LORD for how He guards the feet of His saints, to keep them in a safe place. Using our feet is usually the method by which we travel up mountains. Our Heavenly Mountain Guide does the things this earthly guide does, and so much more. We do not have to travel by night. We are children of the day. He is that perfect light who directs our way. We also do not need a rope to hold us. Instead, He holds us with His strong arms. We need not fear in the most rugged mountain areas of our lives, because in those times, He will carry us on His shoulders. He is the continual guard who keeps our feet from falling. He gladly does this for His children, but the wicked are left in the hollow silence of darkness, because they do not have His illuminating presence. Hannah could testify that all of these things were true; including her rival, whom she thought wicked, was now silenced.

HANNAH AND US: Sometimes it is just good for me to reflect on the goodness of my God. In life, when I am in the middle of a hard climb, sometimes I think I will never reach the top. But as I glance back at the hills and valleys the Father has brought me through, I can be sure He will take me to the top. Nothing will stop Him from completing the journey in me.

GOD SPEAKS: "He will not let your foot slip—he who watches over you will not slumber;" (Psalm 121:3 NIV) I do not just watch over your feet, but I watch over all of you. The constant reminder to you is to keep your feet in My feet.

WANDA'S PRAYER: Father, help us to always keep our feet in Your feet.

July 26

POWERLESSNESS

"... IT IS NOT BY STRENGTH THAT ONE PREVAILS;" (1 SAMUEL 2:9 NIV)

As Hannah continues in her praise to the Father, He continues to show her more of Him. The more she sees of her beautiful Dad, the more she gives Him glory and the praise continued. On this side of glory, we see Christ and the Father through the dim glass of Scripture; but in Heaven, when we are face to face before the throne of God, we will see what we can now only imagine. It is then that we too will praise the LORD our God continually. Hannah gives us a little crash course in praise. So let us listen in as Sista' girl tells us just a little about our Dad's power. The Hebrew word for strength is "Koach" or "Kowach." This word has a literal and figurative meaning. To be firm or to have vigor is the general meaning of the word. The literal meaning is force, to good or bad. The figurative meaning is capacity, means, or to produce—to have substance or wealth. The word prevail means to exceed; to be great and mighty or valiant. Hannah well understood the meaning of these words as they applied to her life. Though it is not written, this verse implies Hannah may have tried many things to have children. I was told if a couple had intercourse in a certain, very contorted position, it would increase their chances of having a male child. I do not know what Hannah's fertility methods were, but we are told they worked for her. Going back to the meaning of the two words: strength and prevail. Hannah seems to say she used her energies—her "strength" in a firm way for the good—to have a child. She may have also used some means or money to buy things to help her get pregnant. Through these human efforts, the end result was that she did not prevail. Nothing she did "exceeded" or was "valiant" enough to win the battle of having children. Hannah speaks to our modern world of the do-it-yourself woman. It did not work 5,000 years ago and guess what? It will not work now.

HANNAH AND US: In my attempts to have my first child, I tried all sorts of things. Herbs, seasons, and spices—nothing worked. The end results were only five years of frustration, heartache, and tears. Like Hannah, I had to give my reproductive organs and myself wholly over to my Dad; the King of the Universe. He alone gave me the two beautiful birth children I have.

GOD SPEAKS: "So he said to me, 'This is the word of the Lord to Zerubbabel: 'Not by might nor by power, but by my Spirit,' says the Lord Almighty." (Zechariah 4:6 NIV) What I say to Zerubbabel, I say to you and Hannah. Human power and might are only puffs of smoke to Me. The power, strength and might to get the job done is in Me alone.

WANDA'S PRAYER: Father, we know the words as head knowledge. Help us to apply the words to every part of our lives. When we apply Your Word, that is when You get the glory.

July 27

DON'T EVEN THINK ABOUT IT

"THOSE WHO OPPOSE THE LORD WILL BE SHATTERED; HE WILL THUNDER IN THE HEAVENS AGAINST THEM. THE LORD WILL JUDGE THE ENDS OF THE EARTH ..."
(1 SAMUEL 2:10 CSB)

As Hannah is closing her praise psalm, she reminds us—it really is all about JESUS! She has told us that her rejoicing is from the LORD. (1 Samuel 2:1) She now speaks of the GOD who is unstoppable. If I were to paraphrase what Hannah is saying to me, it would sound like this: "You ain't got no power at all against My LORD, no sir! If you mess with Him, you-just-fixin' to get broken into itty-bitty pieces. He makes a noise from His big ole' Heaven, which rocks this little earth; so you better go somewhere and sit down. You cannot beat God, or do nothin' to Him. He is gonna judge you and everyone else on this planet." Hannah is saying loud and clear, "This is God's world, and He rules." This is an unpopular statement in today's society, but it is the absolute truth. She has seen it in her own life. She looked at the twin tower of opposition—a closed womb and a relentless rival who had beaten her down with evil words. With child in hand, she looks back and sees how her LORD toppled these foes like a house of cards. Neither of those foes prevented her from getting what her LORD had destined for her. She speaks to me and says, "What God has for me—it is for me." Therefore, I can and will praise the LORD with all my might. Hannah offers us the needed rest for our souls. She shows us our Father is the only GOD who has no equal; and our foes are no match for Him.

HANNAH AND US: In looking at Hannah's psalm of praise, I see the awesomeness of our GOD; He is so worthy of our praise. I also see how praise lifts my spirit—as my focus is on the LORD, and not my problems. As I seek You, LORD, and Your righteousness, You will fight and win the battles for Your glory. Praise brings rest and peace to my troubled soul. Thank you, Father.

GOD SPEAKS: "Your right hand, LORD, was majestic in power. Your right hand, LORD, shattered the enemy. In the greatness of your majesty you threw down those who opposed you. You unleashed your burning anger; it consumed them like stubble." (Exodus 15:6-7 NIV) You do not need to fear anyone but Me. I AM the only One who can keep you out of Heaven, or place you in hell. But I will not, because you are Mine. I will always keep what is Mine.

WANDA'S PRAYER: Thanks Dad, for Your wonderful words of comfort, and for the true rest only You can provide.

A SPECIAL GIFT FOR HIS "HIGHLY FAVORED ONE"

"... HE WILL GIVE STRENGTH TO HIS KING AND EXALT THE HORN OF HIS ANOINTED." (1 SAMUEL 2:10 NIV)

As previously mentioned, Hannah's name can be translated "Grace or Highly Favored one." At the end of her praising, our LORD shows up and gives her a sweet taste of His favor. He gives her more "grace" and honor. Scholars believe this text to be one of the Messianic prophesies foretold. Here she speaks of the Father giving strength to His king (David) and exalting the horn of his Anointed (the Christ). This is the first mention of the "Anointed One" or the Messiah. The word "anointed" in this verse means Messiah in Hebrew. As she wraps up her praises to the LORD, Dad gives the complete picture of this world's salvation. The Son of God will come to our planet to judge the world by His life and His death on the Cross. This is the prophetic word of His Son's victory over Satan. Now, ain't that very good news? Father God gave this special gift of mankind's salvation to a woman who was barren. What makes this so special is that He gave her this Word of truth before Israel even had kings! At the time Hannah was given this prophetic word, judges ruled Israel. Our Dad just loves to give good gifts to His kids. Aren't you glad you belong to Him?

HANNAH AND US: Reading this gives me goose bumps. After all the heartache and pain, our LORD blesses His daughter beyond measure. He gives her a gift we all can unwrap. This is the gift of His Son Jesus. He was her Savior, and today, He is our Savior. He is the settler of scores; He is the righter of wrongs.

GOD SPEAKS: "Praise be to the Lord, the God of Israel, because he has come to his people and redeemed them. He has raised up a horn of salvation for us in the house of his servant David." (Luke 1:68-69 NIV) What you are now reading is how I kept My word when I sent My Son to die for your sins. This is proof of My unfailing love for you.

WANDA'S PRAYER: You are right, LORD. You have done more than we could have ever hoped or dreamt of. This is Love beyond anything we have ever seen! Thank you Father.

July 29

THAT'S MY BABY

"BUT SAMUEL WAS MINISTERING BEFORE THE LORD—A BOY WEARING A LINEN EPHOD. EACH YEAR HIS MOTHER MADE HIM A LITTLE ROBE AND TOOK IT TO HIM WHEN SHE WENT UP WITH HER HUSBAND TO OFFER THE ANNUAL SACRIFICE."
(1 SAMUEL 2:18-19 NIV)

For Hannah, the LORD had given her something to praise His name about. Priests who served in the temple had to be at least 30 years of age, according to the Levitical Law. But the LORD had done a special thing for His daughter. He made a baby a priest, at about five or six years of age! He is the only baby priest we know of in Scripture. This was her "horn"—Hannah's shining star. God had given this woman, who was called barren and tortured for her plight, a zenith for all the world to see. Each year, as she and her family went to the temple, there was her boy, ministering before the LORD. He had his own cut little priest robe, the ephod, just like the men priests. This site must have made Peninnah, the second wife, green with envy. Hannah's son performed the sacrifices to pardon the sins of his mother and for himself. Little did she know that her little son, who ministered before his LORD, was a type of the Son who would later come, to take away the sins of the entire world. Year after year, she was glad to sacrifice to the KING OF KINGS AND LORD OF LORDS. As Hannah reflects on the goodness the Father had bestowed upon her, no sacrifice was too much to give. We also notice Hannah is completely cured of her depression, although she has no other children as of yet. When the LORD takes over a life, He totally overhauls it from the inside out.

HANNAH AND US: Hannah's life demonstrates to me one that is totally given over to the LORD. He takes and makes it a wonder to behold! I know this is what He wants of me. LORD, make me completely sold out to You—every day, in every way.

GOD SPEAKS: "For to us a child is born, to us a son is given, and the government will be on his shoulders. And he will be called Wonderful Counselor, Mighty God, Everlasting Father, Prince of Peace. (Isaiah 9:6 NIV) I gave you My most precious gift; what will you do with Him?

WANDA'S PRAYER: Father God, we want to cherish You and Your Son all the days of our lives. Then, when we reach eternity, we want to worship Him and You forever!

July 30

YOUR KIDS WILL BLESS YOU

"ELI WOULD BLESS ELKANAH AND HIS WIFE, SAYING 'MAY THE LORD GIVE YOU CHILDREN BY THIS WOMAN TO TAKE THE PLACE OF THE ONE SHE PRAYED FOR AND GAVE TO THE LORD' … MEANWHILE, THE BOY SAMUEL GREW UP IN THE PRESENCE OF THE LORD." (1 SAMUEL 2:20-21 NIV)

When I was a kid, I was told to watch how I behaved myself, because I represented the Thomas family. If I were to misbehave, it would reflect poorly on our family name and give a bad impression. I could also expect corporal punishment. That was ok because I did not act up much, and I am still around to tell of it. Hannah's son was not just a blessing to her, but also to Eli, the High Priest. His own sons were wicked, and our LORD would deal with them later. Hannah, Elkanah and Samuel, Hannah's boy, must have been a breath of fresh air at the Temple. Samuel grew up in God's presence. This child knew his Father God was ever before his face. So, more than just not embarrassing his earthly parents, neither would he shame his Heavenly Father. This testimony spoke volumes to Eli, especially in view of his own evil sons. Therefore, he could not help but to bless this couple, and to praise Hannah for her wonderful act of sacrifice in giving her son to the LORD. The family of Elkanah and Hannah would do in a few years with the boy Samuel, what Eli could not do in a lifetime with his sons—train them in the fear of the LORD.

HANNAH AND US: My children are now adults. It is so nice when people tell me how respectful they are. I take no credit for the successes—they belong only to the LORD. I can, however, take credit for any shortcomings they may possess—it comes from flawed human genes. I want to give praise and thanks to my LORD. He was there with me during those very tough times, when I had a three-year-old and a six-month-old to raise. He was my Husband, as well as my LORD.

GOD SPEAKS: "Those who trust in the Lord are like Mount Zion, which cannot be shaken, but endures forever. As the mountains surround Jerusalem, so the Lord surrounds his people both now and forevermore." (Psalm 125:1-2 NIV) As My child, know that you are in protective care. Nothing can touch you unless I allow it. If I allow it, then it is for your good. It may not seem like it at first, but it all works out for good because I am GOOD.

WANDA'S PRAYER: Father, You are not only GOOD, but You are PERFECT. Thank You for being everything we have ever needed.

July 31

A MEGA DOSE OF GRACE

"... THEN THEY (ELKANAH AND HANNAH) WOULD GO HOME. AND THE LORD WAS GRACIOUS TO HANNAH; SHE GAVE BIRTH TO THREE SONS AND TWO DAUGHTERS ..." (1 SAMUEL 2:20-21 NIV)

I love happy endings. The ending to this story is indeed a tearjerker. Hannah only wanted one son to take away her reproach. But because of her very generous offering to her LORD, He gave to her gifts she does not have room enough to receive. She gets five for the price of one. She gave the first fruit of her womb to the LORD. The Father honors Hannah's name. The verse says that "The LORD was gracious to Hannah..." What exactly does this mean? Grace means, "Favor or kindness shown without regard to the worth or merit of the one who receives it and in spite of what that person deserves." (Nelson's New Illustrated Bible Dictionary) The Father opened the window of Hannah's womb and poured out upon her, a blessing beyond anything she could have ever imagined. Did Hannah do anything to warrant such a gift? No! She just simply came to her Father and emptied herself to Him. In return, He filled her with Himself. The fruit of being filled with Christ was joy and peace, which were the best and lasting fruits. Because of her now being filled with Her LORD, He could now work to give to her beyond the desires of her heart. He could do this because her desires were His desires. This screams to all of us who may wonder at times if God hears and answers prayer. The answer is YES HE DOES! His will is not my will—it is so far beyond. And His will is so much better! This story also tells us we can trust the heart of the Wonderful God we cannot always see. His heart is very good, and He so longs to bless us with His wonderful gifts.

HANNAH AND US: As I reflect on my life, I, too, can see how He has given me many things I did not deserve. Salvation and a place in His Kingdom for one: healthy children, a good husband, a steady job, a place to stay, clothes to wear. I will stop now because I am running out of paper, but the list is endless. Thank You, Lord, for your mercy and grace. I do not get what I deserve, punishment for my sins; and I get favor all in one package.

GOD SPEAKS: "For it is by grace you have been saved, through faith—and this is not from yourselves, it is the gift of God—not by works, so that no one can boast." (Ephesians 2:8-9 NIV) I love you and I want the absolute best for you, always. My best is so far beyond what your best will ever be. I want you to believe Me and believe in Me. You demonstrate that by following Me with your complete heart. Your only job is to come to Me and receive what I have for you. Ok?

WANDA'S PRAYER: Father, we give all of ourselves to You. Take our life and use it as You see fit. Speak loudly to our hearts because we are tone deaf. Give us the power through Your Spirit to obey and to receive what You have for us.

HANNAH'S TESTIMONY

"THEREFORE, THERE IS NOW NO CONDEMNATION FOR THOSE WHO ARE IN CHRIST JESUS, BECAUSE THROUGH CHRIST JESUS THE LAW OF THE SPIRIT WHO GIVES LIFE HAS SET YOU FREE FROM THE LAW OF SIN AND DEATH." (ROMANS 8:1-2 NIV)

Wow! What can I say about this remarkable woman and what her life says to me? I certainly cannot put on one piece of paper the many lessons learned. So, I will focus on three things I have learned from Hannah. I will call them the three "S's." The first "S" is for submission. Hannah was a godly, faithful wife to her husband, Elkanah. I know of very few women, (I, being among them), who would live in, much less put up with, a second wife in the home for any reason! This daughter of God knew the importance of giving her husband children for a heritage. She submitted to this "surrogate—second wife ordeal," in order to allow him to have children. In the end, the Lord rewarded her for her obedience. The next "S" is for suffering. Hannah suffered severely because of her inability to have children and the jealousy of the second wife, Peninnah. Year after year, she was persecuted and beaten down by Peninnah; the suffering was merciless. This speaks loudly to us today who despise the slightest of discomforts. Hannah was a woman of God, yet she suffered. "All who live godly will suffer persecution." (2 Timothy 3:12) As children of the Heavenly Father, we are not promised a life of ease. No, in fact, just the opposite. Most importantly, Hannah teaches me where I am to take my suffering. I am to take it to the Father and Jesus, His Son, as she did. In doing so, He gave her the best of the "S's"—His Spirit. At His feet, He allowed her to empty herself of all the stagnant hurts and pains of the years gone by. When emptied of self, He filled her with Himself through His Spirit. This filling of the Spirit of God brought with it wonderful fruit: "Love, joy, peace, patience, kindness, goodness, gentleness, and self-control." (Galatians 5:22-23) With such luscious non-fat fruit, she was now filled to overflowing, and would never hunger or thirst again.

HANNAH AND US: This woman teaches me of the Father's constant love and faithfulness. Through her life, I see that I, too, am loved with an everlasting, long-suffering (putting up with a lot of Wanda's mess) love. When I look at both Hannah's life and my own, I can see the Father never leaves or forsakes me.

GOD SPEAKS: "Now the Lord is the Spirit, and where the Spirit of the Lord is, there is freedom. And we all, who with unveiled faces contemplate the Lord's glory, are being transformed into his image with ever-increasing glory, which comes from the Lord, who is the Spirit." (2 Corinthians 3:17-18 NIV) You are My canvas; let Me create a masterpiece in you.

WANDA'S PRAYER: LORD, we are a blank page for You to paint whatever You wish.

Notes

Notes

August

INTRODUCTION

ELIZABETH

Our devotional study now takes us into the New Testament, where we will explore the lives of five women, beginning with Elizabeth. Like Hannah, Elizabeth teaches us that though we may serve God with all of our heart and soul, we may suffer because of unmet needs.

Elizabeth was the wife of a priest, and she was a descendant of Aaron. She and her husband were called "blameless." They would have been highly respected in their community. We read of no scandals in the lives of this godly couple, yet they were childless.

Elizabeth's life further confirms to us that in this world of sin, we will all go through hurt and pain. Yet, during these times, she shows us we do not have to lose our faith in God. Her life also tells us that our LORD has no time limit on when He can and will answer our prayer.

Most importantly, Elizabeth shows us we are God's masterpieces—His trophies to be displayed for His glory and praise. In her case, she would give birth to John the Baptist in her old age, and he would introduce us to Jesus the Christ.

Notes

August 1

ANCESTRY

"IN THE TIME OF HEROD KING OF JUDEA THERE WAS A PRIEST NAMED ZECHARIAH, WHO BELONGED TO THE PRIESTLY DIVISION OF ABIJAH; HIS WIFE ELIZABETH WAS ALSO A DESCENDANT OF AARON." (LUKE 1:5 NIV)

Ancestry means a line of descent or lineage. It could also mean a form or stock from which an organism has developed or descended. The word ancestry is similar to the word pedigree. A pedigree is a genealogical record or a distinguished, pure ancestry of animal or people. Elizabeth could trace her lineage back to Aaron, the first High Priest of Israel. This was Jewish nobility. Talk about good stock! The Jewish social structure centered primarily on religion. This meant they considered the High Priest as royalty. Great-great grandfather Aaron was God's handpicked man; chosen by name to be His special minister. He alone was the only man in Israel permitted to go directly into the presence of the Most High God. This was a very prestigious position, to say the least. The text tells us Elizabeth was Aaron's descendant. This meant she was not just a preacher's kid; she was the "preacher's, preacher's, preacher's kid" from about twenty or more generations back. Why is this so important? It was important because Elizabeth was considered "spiritual blue blood or spiritual royalty." Imagine growing up under such a wonderful lineage and how her heritage must have shaped her life. To add to all of this "spiritual heritage," this daughter of God was given the name of the wife of Aaron, the High Priest. This woman was set up for success from birth. To top it all off, this preacher's kid married a preacher man.

ELIZABETH AND US: I certainly cannot compare myself to this woman in any shape, form, or fashion. I can only trace my lineage back to my grandparents. As far as I know, I do not know of any royal pedigree in my lineage. My grandparents were descendants of slaves and brought to this country in chains.

GOD SPEAKS: "But you are a chosen people, a royal priesthood, a holy nation, God's special possession, that you may declare the praises of him who called you out of darkness into his wonderful light." (1 Peter 2:9 NIV) It is one thing to be a descendant of a king whose glory fades away; but you are a descendant of Holy blood, and My Kingdom will never end. I have washed and made you clean! You belong to Me—forever. Sing My praise, for you are a precious child of the Light.

WANDA'S PRAYER: Thank You Father, for reminding us of our precious heritage in You. Our prayer is that we will always give You praise and bring You glory, for the wonderful salvation You have given us.

August 2

ELIZABETH—THE NAME

"... AND HER NAME WAS ELIZABETH." (LUKE 1:5 NKJV)

An advertising company started a popular phrase to sell credit cards; the phrase is, "What's in your wallet?" I will parody that phrase by asking, "Elizabeth—What's in your name?" In search to find out what was in her name, I found deep spiritual truths. Her name means, "God is my oath." This says a mouth full on its own. We can break the name Elizabeth down into "Eli" and "Sheba." Eli means Jehovah (GOD) is high. "Sheba" means oath or covenant. When I put the two words together, I get, "The most high God is my covenant. He is the one I give my complete allegiance to." In modern day vernacular, the phrase would loosely translate, "I'm totally sold out to Jesus, the KING OF KINGS." In giving this child the name Elizabeth, it tells us her parents were so in love with, and totally dedicated to, their LORD. The name displays the passions of their heart. So what does all of this background about Elizabeth mean and what does it have to do with me? I think it means that from birth she was to be wholly dedicated to the LORD. After all, she had come from the "spiritual blue blood" of Aaron, the first High Priest of Israel. The question now is, would she elect to live out her name's sake? We will see as we study her life—so stay tuned. Names are important to our LORD because they say something about the character of our lives. We who have given our hearts and lives to Jesus are called "Christians." We are followers of the Christ, the Messiah. He is God who became flesh to save us from our sins. When we say we are Christians, I think we are saying God is our oath and pledge our allegiance to Him alone. That gives me a lot to think about and to live out.

ELIZABETH AND US: My name is Wanda. The name Wanda means "Wanderer." Until I met my LORD JESUS CHRIST, I was an aimless wanderer, always going here, there, and everywhere. He changed my name to Child of the Most High God, Christian for short. It seems I still move a lot, but now I have purpose and meaning—to and for my life and movements. I, like Elizabeth, want to live out my name as a Christian, to give Him glory and not bring Him shame.

GOD SPEAKS: "Ascribe to the Lord the glory due his name; worship the Lord in the splendor of his holiness." (Psalm 29:2 NIV) As you allow My Spirit to indwell your heart daily; as you follow Me in every aspect of your life, you "Ascribe" to Me the glory due My name.

WANDA'S PRAYER: Father, today we give you our whole life. "We will praise You with a complete heart." As You live in us, with You in control, we will show forth Your perfect works.

August 3

A SOLD-OUT LIFE

"BOTH (AARON AND ELIZABETH) WERE RIGHTEOUS IN GOD'S SIGHT, LIVING WITHOUT BLAME ACCORDING TO ALL THE COMMANDS AND REQUIREMENTS OF THE LORD." (LUKE 1:6 CSB)

The compliment the LORD gives this couple is awesome! Now, it is one thing for a human to say of another human, "that's a good person," but for the LORD to say that of His children—is mind blowing. The Father calls this couplet "righteous" in His sight. They were so righteous that they kept all six hundred plus laws in the Levitical Code of justice (read it for yourself in the above text). I cannot top what Elizabeth did. I have a hard enough time just trying and failing to keep the ten commandments the LORD gave on Mt. Sinai. This woman was truly sold out to her LORD. Her life speaks volumes about that fact. The question to ask is, was she perfect? You know, did she walk on water also? NO! Notice the text says they were "blameless," it doesn't say "sinless." Yep, Elizabeth was a sinner; in need of a Savior, just like little ole me. Although she was born in sin, her blameless lifestyle cuts my heart like a razor-sharp knife. What is said of her in our text is she gave her best, and all, to her LORD. Her life causes me to look at my life and ask, "am I (a Christian woman), living my life righteous in God's sight?" Elizabeth lived as she did before the time of the indwelling of the Holy Spirit's power. Her exemplary life leaves me without excuse for not living a righteous life; when God in Spirit form waits for the asking to give me the power to overcome sin. In my shame, I would want to excuse my behavior by saying, "Well, the time she lived in was better and that's why she could live such a life." NOT! Looking back at Luke 1:5, we find this woman lived in horrible times. According to Nelson's New Illustrated Bible Dictionary, Herod the Great was a very ruthless man. The man killed his first wife and two sons. He was also a politician's—politician. He was able to maintain good relations with Rome (his bosses), and the Jews at the same time. Because he was a king, he could not be voted out of office—ever. Try living holy under those evil conditions—Elizabeth did.

ELIZABETH AND US: I must admit that girlfriend's life puts me to shame. "LORD, what is Your solution to my problem?"

GOD SPEAKS: "Remain in me, as I also remain in you. No branch can bear fruit by itself; it must remain in the vine. Neither can you bear fruit unless you remain in me." (John 15:4 NIV) The fruit is a righteous life. What that fruit looks like to the world is: "Love, joy, peace, patience, kindness, goodness, faithfulness, gentleness, and self-control. Against such things there is no law." (Galatians 5:22-23 NIV) The answer to your dilemma is to always keep Me in you—through constant communication (prayer and Bible study).

WANDA'S PRAYER: Well LORD, let's get started.

August 4

A GODLY LIFE, BUT NOT PAIN FREE

"BUT THEY HAD NO CHILD, BECAUSE ELIZABETH WAS BARREN, AND THEY WERE BOTH WELL ADVANCED IN YEARS." (LUKE 1:7 NKJV)

When I selected these women to write about, I did not realize so many of them had been barren. I just thought I would say that, in case anyone thinks I may have chosen these women for their conditions, I did not. Going back to our subject, we see Elizabeth, for all of her "holiness," could not have children. Our LORD tells us the "rain falls on the just and the unjust" alike. (Matthew 5:45) For all the wonderful things we may have in this life, all of us have missing pieces—empty spaces. Elizabeth's missing piece was her inability to have children. This must have been very heart wrenching for her. She has this perfect marriage to a wonderful husband, and she cannot "give him children," because she is barren. This was her scandal and her shame. Though the text does not mention it, I am sure this couple prayed to the LORD for children. The answer they seemingly got was NO. This story speaks not only to women in our society, but it speaks to us all. We have the perfect marriage, nice jobs, beautiful homes, live in good neighborhoods, and yet, we are barren and have missing pieces. Those missing pieces in our lives prevent us from a life of perfection on planet Earth. So, we try to fill it with other things or people. The key is filling our lives with the right Person. That Person is Jesus our LORD, as Elizabeth apparently did. How do I know? Shh... Listen—do you hear her whining or complaining about the missing pieces in her life? No! She is totally sold out to her LORD. She and her husband know where to take the hurt, pain, and disappointment of being childless. They take it to the LORD; they wait and try His perfect answer. I am sure she would love to have kids, but if she does not, "that's all right." Her love for her LORD does not diminish. She knows GOD loves her, even though she does not have everything she wants. This is a wonderful lesson for me. The lesson I see in her life is I cannot expect a world flawed by sin to bring perfection. I am thankful to my LORD for His salvation and the Heavenly perfect home He has prepared for me.

ELIZABETH AND US: There are things I want, and yet do not have. Because of the lusts of my flesh, I would want a bigger house, a better car, or a cushier job. Like Elizabeth, I will praise and thank my Father for the many, many blessings I do have—starting with life, health, strength, family, food, shelter, clothing, a sound mind, just to name a few.

GOD SPEAKS: "But we have this treasure (Christ in our hearts) in jars of clay to show that this all-surpassing power is from God and not from us. For our light and momentary troubles are achieving for us an eternal glory that far outweighs them all." (2 Corinthians 4:7,17 NIV) Keep your eyes on the TRUE prize—I AM that prize.

WANDA'S PRAYER: Father, never let us forget You are the TRUE PRIZE—You and You alone!

August 5

I'M WAITING TO BLESS YOU

"THEN AN ANGEL OF THE LORD APPEARED TO HIM, STANDING AT THE RIGHT SIDE OF THE ALTAR OF INCENSE. WHEN ZECHARIAH SAW HIM, HE WAS STARTLED AND WAS GRIPPED WITH FEAR." (LUKE 1:11-12 NIV)

What greatly interests me is Luke 1:11. I gained some very interesting insight while looking up the meanings of several of the words in the original text. The word "Appeared" or "there appeared" (Optanomai), means a prolonged watching at a distance with intensity. The word "Angelos" (angle) means messenger. "Of the LORD" (Kuriou) means one of supreme authority. The word "Standing" (Histemi) means remaining in place or a fixed covenant. "Right side" (dexios) means feminine or gentle posture. When I put all the words together, the text says something beautiful to me. It says the angel of the LORD had been in the Holy Place, waiting for Zechariah for some time. He had a marvelous blessing for Elizabeth and Zechariah, which Dad wanted to give to His kids. The angel approached the priest in a very gentle way (standing at the right or feminine side of the altar), while Zechariah was at the altar of incense. This was fitting because the incense represented the prayers of the saints. It was as if the Father was saying, "My son, for years you have been praying for children, and My answer to those prayers my boy is, 'yes!' I am giving you your heart's desire." Luke 1:12 is intriguing, especially in light of verse eleven. According to the text, the angel had been there for a while, but it took some time for Zechariah to become aware of his presence. When he became aware, the old priest was gripped with fear. The angel of the LORD was there to give blessings, and not punishment, as Zechariah may have feared. This shows the Father is always with me, even though I may not see Him or feel His presence. I have someone in high authority who is constantly watching me, and watching over me. Elizabeth had a husband who could go into the Father's presence, offer up prayers, and commune with Him. The fact that the text says the angel appeared standing says to me the Father does not have to work me into His schedule; He is here in my presence, listening to my needs.

ELIZABETH AND US: My husband is also a minister; a pastor of a local church. This is where the comparison ends. To my knowledge, he has never seen an angel, nor have I. Neither of us have ever seen angels in person. However, we are certain of the presence of the Father's special messengers. We are also certain that Dad is forever watching over us with His loving care. He has covenanted to take excellent care of our family.

GOD SPEAKS: "… I delight to sit in his shade, and his fruit is sweet to my taste." (Song of Solomon 2:3 NIV) I cannot wait to spend time with you. I long for you to sit and dwell in My presence. Taste and see that I am good.

WANDA'S PRAYER: Father, the times we spend with You are always sweet and fruitful. The covering You place over our lives keeps us from so much harm and danger. Thank you for loving, loving, and loving us, Father.

August 6

I HEARD YOUR PRAYERS—I ANSWERED

"BUT THE ANGEL SAID TO HIM: 'DO NOT BE AFRAID, ZECHARIAH; YOUR PRAYER HAS BEEN HEARD. YOUR WIFE ELIZABETH WILL BEAR YOU A SON, AND YOU ARE TO CALL HIM JOHN.'"
(LUKE 1:13 NIV)

The background of this story is that it was time for Elizabeth's husband's division to serve as priests before God. It was the priest's responsibility to keep the incense burning on the altar, in front of the Most Holy Place (The HOLY OF HOLIES) continually. (Exodus 30:6-8) The chance to go into the Holy of HOLIES was so rare that they cast lots (similar to throwing dice), to decide who would serve. On this occasion, the lots fell on Elizabeth's husband, Zechariah, (whose name means "Jehovah remembers)." This time, he would have this great honor of service. While in the Most Holy Place, Gabriel, an angel of the Lord, had been sent to tell Zechariah the Father had heard and was now answering his prayers; and that his wife would have a son. (Luke 1:8-17) Dad loved His kids and to show them, He would give them a son. We are not told why Dad waited to answer their prayers, nor do we need to know. What we need to know is that in the midst of waiting, many times we are faced with the question regarding our commitment to our LORD. Will God remain my oath? Will I love and obey Him even when my most coveted prayers are not answered? Elizabeth and Zechariah did. The delay in answered prayer teaches me to continue praying to my LORD for seemingly unanswered prayers. We see in this verse, the LORD heard. The Father then turned and answered their cries. Truthfully, the Father answered their prayers before now—the answer was "wait." It was as if God was saying to this couple and to me, "Trust Me—I know what to do and when to do it." Elizabeth's response was, "LORD, I love You and will be faithful to You, no matter what."

ELIZABETH AND US: I am awed by this woman's unwavering faith in her LORD. How often do I whine and complain when things don't go my way? Father, forgive me for my sins. Help me learn to wait joyfully. I can do that because I have an unwavering faith that says, "You absolutely know what is perfectly best for me, in all situations of my life."

GOD SPEAKS: "The eyes of the Lord are on the righteous, and his ears are attentive to their cry;" (Psalm 34:15 NIV) I've got my eye on you—I will never let you go.

WANDA'S PRAYER: Well LORD, this makes more than two of us because we are never letting go either.

August 7

I'M GIVING A SON TO ENJOY

"HE (JOHN) WILL BE A JOY AND DELIGHT TO YOU ..." (LUKE 1:14 NIV)

The background for this verse starts in Luke 1:11. The old priest, Zechariah, has been chosen to minister before his LORD. While at the altar of incense, the angel of the Most High God tells Zechariah that he and his wife, Elizabeth, are going to have a son. Zechariah is speechless and terrified at this point. (Luke 1:12) After telling the old man not to fear, the angel Gabriel further eases his fears as he unveils to Zechariah this wonderful gift from the Father. The big blue bow on the gift was the child's name— "… and you are to call him John." John (Yehowchanan) means "Jehovah favored." This is a child favored by the LORD. This favored one of God is going to bring the old couple joy and delight. Regarding this verse, "Joy" means a "calm delight." Imagine that. I am well past my forty's and while I love kids, I cannot imagine finding a calm delight in full-time care of a newborn at my age. That next word "delight" in the verse means "extreme exultation, exceeding gladness." Dad was giving his faithful kids a happiness that will knock their socks off! Should this surprise us? Not at all! Our LORD sets the standard for what is good, and He loves to give good gifts to his kids. He proves His love and goodness to His children by giving them "calm delight and extreme gladness" in one package. He knows they will love this gift because he (John) is "favored by Jehovah."

ELIZABETH AND US: Looking at this verse causes me to reflect on the birth of my kids. My Perfect Dad gave me, "Anointed One and Enduring one" (that is the meaning of their names). I can recall their births and much of their childhood. I remember their first steps and when they walked across the stage to receive their high school diplomas. Some ups and some downs, but looking back, I am certain of just how blessed I am with the joy and delight He gave me through my children.

GOD SPEAKS: "Trust in the LORD and do good; dwell in the land and enjoy safe pasture. Take delight in the LORD, and he will give you the desires of your heart." (Psalm 37:3-4 NIV) Delighting yourself in Me is trusting that I love you too much, to ever hurt you. What I have for you is totally good and perfect. So enjoy My good pleasures now, and trust Me with your future. I will never let you down.

WANDA'S PRAYER: LORD, we do trust You. Our problem at times is that we keep letting go of Your hands, or we take our eyes off of You, and turn them on to ourselves. As long as we keep looking at You and Your perfect love for us, we know everything will be fine.

August 8

REJOICE WITH ME

"... AND MANY WILL REJOICE WITH YOU BECAUSE OF HIS BIRTH," (LUKE 1:14 NIV)

As I read this verse, I am reminded of Sarah and Abraham at the birth of Isaac (laughter). She made a similar statement about her friends laughing with her, instead of at her, about the birth of the promised child. (Genesis 20:6) Laughter is infectious—it spreads; and rejoicing does so as well. This rejoicing would not be limited to this couple and their household only; no, there would be "many," a lot of folks, who will be happy and rejoice with the couple, over the birth of this child. I think as Gabriel spoke this prophecy to the old priest at the altar of incense, this is what the LORD had in mind. To me, the text could read, "I am giving you My favored one (the meaning of John is Jehovah's Favored). He will give you a calm delight and extreme happiness. Others will see your joy, your laughter and gladness; they will rejoice and be glad with you." (Writer's paraphrase) The fact that others would rejoice with them instead of scolding the old couple for having kids so late in life, would be of great comfort to the aging couple. When family and friends who knew the hurt and pain of this couple for many years, and would now see the miracle the LORD had given His faithful couple in the form of a baby boy, the end result would be rejoicing! There would be few "haters" at the birth of this baby. Many would say that it couldn't have happened to a more deserving couple; our LORD thought so too!

ELIZABETH AND US: When our LORD gives His wonderful gifts, they are pressed down and running over. This was the case in the giving of little John. I started having kids at twenty-six years old. As previously mentioned, it took five years to have my first, and three years to have my second. Though the wait was not as long as Elizabeth's, any wait is too long.

GOD SPEAKS: "Sing the praises of the LORD, you his faithful people; praise his holy name. For his anger lasts only a moment, but his favor lasts a lifetime; weeping may stay for the night, but rejoicing comes in the morning." (Psalm 30:4-5 NIV) You can praise Me now—for past and future blessings.

WANDA'S PRAYER: Our prayer to You, Father, is praise! We will praise You, Oh LORD, with a complete and perfect heart. You alone are fully righteous and true. In You, there is no shadow of turning. You alone are very good, and Your mercies and goodness last forever.

August 9

MORE ABOUT YOUR BOY

"FOR HE WILL BE GREAT IN THE SIGHT OF THE LORD..." (LUKE 1:15 NIV)

As the aging priest stood listening to the angel tell him what sort of child was now being formed in Elizabeth's womb, he must have been amazed and spellbound. The words, "He will be great in the sight of God," must have conjured up all sorts of grandiose thoughts of his son, perhaps becoming royalty. As the LORD bragged about the parents, so He is now bragging about this unborn child. But what does greatness, "in the sight of the LORD" mean? As I prayed and looked up parallel verses of this Scripture, one thing came to mind. Greatness in God's sight is one who would live, move, and breathe to give God glory. The Father was telling the aging Zechariah his boy would succeed at giving God the utmost glory. The life he lives and the message he proclaims would cause his world, and ours, to look for a better hope for our dreary existence. Just as he has caught our attention, he would be given the special privilege of announcing to us, "The Lamb of God who would take away all of our sins." This was not just Israel's hope, but the hope of a lost and dying world. The KING OF THE UNIVERSE was coming to our lost planet to bridge the way back home. This is the ultimate in greatness. Through his life and word, John would be the one who would point to us sinners, the way out of sin. That way is Jesus, and nothing in life or eternity was more important than this. I believe that this is what the above verse was referring to. Our LORD would give the honor of rearing such a child for His glory to this aging, blameless couple. What a sacred privilege this couple was receiving! It would be the child-rearing by these godly parents, which would help mold this child into a vessel to be used by the Father. Elizabeth's name meant "oath to God," and her complete allegiance was to her Heavenly Father. Thus, the child He gave her would be no less loyal to his God. John's faithfulness to his LORD would not be left as a thing of chance, or happenstance, it would directly result from a Divine blessing from the Father, and strong godly discipline from his home. This combination would produce a child who would be great in the sight of the LORD.

ELIZABETH AND US: I attempted to pour much Scripture and discipline into the lives of my kids as they were growing up. Time will tell if it was enough. When I look back, I see my failings and shortcomings while child-rearing. I was not a perfect mom by any stretch of the imagination. As the LORD'S hands were on John, I know the Father has His hands on these. So with prayer and praise, I give them totally over to Him for His keeping and care.

GOD SPEAKS: "These commandments that I give you today are to be upon your hearts. Impress them on your children. Talk about them when you sit at home and when you walk along the road, when you lie down and when you get up." (Deuteronomy 6:6-7 NIV) Give your kids and everything else in your life to Me. Leave it all at My feet.

WANDA'S PRAYER: Father, forgive us for all of our sins and shortcomings; especially concerning the children You gave to us on loan.

August 10

HOLINESS IN, HOLINESS OUT

"… HE IS NEVER TO TAKE WINE OR OTHER FERMENTED DRINK, AND HE WILL BE FILLED WITH THE HOLY SPIRIT EVEN BEFORE HE IS BORN." (LUKE 1:15 NIV)

It is interesting to note that only John the Baptist and Jesus Christ were filled with the Holy Spirit from birth. With that said, we can see how the verse is complete: "For he will be great in the sight of the Lord, he will never take wine or other fermented drink, and he will be filled with the Holy Spirit even before he is born." How would he be great in the sight of the Lord? Answer: This child would be set apart from the womb for his LORD's use alone. The LORD proclaimed this child a Nazirite from birth. (Numbers 6) The idea of being a Nazirite was being one who was totally set apart and consecrated for the LORD's service. This text has literal and spiritual implications. Alcohol, the component which comes from ferment drinks as it decays, is a mind-altering, mood-altering substance. The consumption of this substance would cause him to think and act in ways contrary to his LORD's will. In abstaining from wine or other fermented drink, John's mind would always be clear and focused. John's actions and life would say, "I will not have any dead or decaying thing to have influence over me. Instead, I will drink from the Living Holy Spirit, which has indwelt me from my mother's womb." This leading of the Spirit would cause him to reign in the greatest revival in history. John's intoxication with the Spirit of Life would cause him to herald in the One who divides not only our earth time—AD from BC, but Eternal life from hell's damnation. The same is to be said of all of us who are born of God and filled with His Spirit. We are not to have decaying, intoxicating earthly "spirits" to have sway over our lives. Instead, we are to be filled with the Holy Spirit of God, which we received at our spiritual birth. This gives the Father glory and makes us great in His sight. John's parents well understood the meaning of this verse and the application it would have to us all.

ELIZABETH AND US: Elizabeth well understood the meaning of purity to God and being completely given over for His glory. I would do well to sit up and pay attention.

GOD SPEAKS: "Do not get drunk on wine, which leads to debauchery (excessive indulgence in sensual pleasures; intemperance or a seduction from allegiance or duty). Instead, be filled with the Spirit," (Ephesians 5:18 NIV) I think the difference is crystal clear, don't you? The line is drawn—where do you stand?

WANDA'S PRAYER: LORD, we stand on Your side. Now, with the power of Your Spirit, we want to live like it.

August 11

HOLY POWER PURIFIES COMPLETELY

"HE WILL BRING BACK MANY OF THE PEOPLE OF ISRAEL TO THE LORD THEIR GOD." (LUKE 1:16 NIV)

There is a saying used today which goes; "Absolute power corrupts absolutely!" This is true in our sin-saturated world. But what is even more true is that Holy Ghost power purifies more completely than sin can corrupt. This is illustrated in our verse for today. Before discussing the verse, I would like to point out a very important fact. We have the angel of God, with revelation from God. The words the angel Gabriel speaks are what our LORD has already seen come to pass. This is not guesswork—it is what will take place. Dad shows us how this child will be great in His sight. This Spirit-filled child will grow up to be a holy man of God. Through his preaching and living, "Many of the people of Israel will he bring back to the LORD their God." When will I get this point? Our LORD is not looking so much for the half-hearted commitment of the "many," as He is the faithfulness of the "one." Elizabeth's baby would be the faithfulness of one who would turn the hearts of many to the Father of all. This baby boy was definitely a chip off the "spiritual blue bloods" block. His name may as well have been "Elizabeth Junior" because, like his mother, John's oath was to his God. He would live a life that would preach purity and love, and when the time came, he would give an audible sermon, and many would repent and turn back to their God.

ELIZABETH AND US: As I look at this story, I think to myself that no life is unimportant to Jesus. He can take our lives and make them a thing of beauty and bring glory to His name. I want Him to use my life for His glory. Lord, get me out of my fear of telling others about You.

GOD SPEAKS: "In the year that King Uzziah died, I saw the Lord, high and exalted, seated on a throne; and the train of his robe filled the temple." (Isaiah 6:1 NIV) What in your life needs to die before you can see Me for who I really am—the EXALTED ONE WHO INHABITS ETERNITY? Allow Me to show you. Let that thing die in you. When it does, then I will take the entire stages of your life, and you will never be the same again.

WANDA'S PRAYER: Father, as we draw ever close to You, more and more pieces of us fall away. Purge us in You. We want there to be no more "us," but all of YOU.

August 12

YOUR GREATEST GIFT TO HUMANITY

"AND HE WILL GO ON BEFORE THE LORD, IN THE SPIRIT AND POWER OF ELIJAH, TO TURN THE HEARTS OF THE PARENTS TO THEIR CHILDREN AND THE DISOBEDIENT TO THE WISDOM OF THE RIGHTEOUS—TO MAKE READY A PEOPLE PREPARED FOR THE LORD." (LUKE 1:17 NIV)

So many things are "running around in my head," as I read this text. I think, if I had one chance to impact history, what would I like to contribute? What would be my greatest gift to sinful humanity? Answer: A way out of the sins and plagues that rack our world; and a pathway back to perfection—that would be my tribute. Our LORD gives Elizabeth's son this opportunity. Look at the text with me: "He will go before the LORD in the SPIRIT AND POWER OF ELIJAH…" What does that mean? Elijah was a mighty prophet of God. He called down fire from Heaven. He raised people from the dead. He turned idolatrous Israel back to their God (for a brief time, anyway). Then he rode to Heaven on a chariot of fire. This is what our LORD was giving to Beth's baby boy. This child would run the whole gambit. He would get families in order by refocusing the father's attention back to their children. Then he would give the disobedient, wisdom of the Righteous and Holy God; because "A fool has said in his heart there is no God." (Psalm 14:1) Finally, after he has set the family in order and given wisdom to disobedient fools, this would make ready a people prepared for the LORD. All this our Loving LORD would give to one old, seemingly forgotten couple, who remained faithful to their LORD. The amazing thing is Dad would do this wonderful feat through one man—John. The question I ask myself is, what could the Father do through me and my children? He shows me He can do at least what He did for Zechariah and Elizabeth.

ELIZABETH AND US: The picture is clear to me now. Dad wants nothing less than a surrendered life to Him. I struggle with this. My flesh always wants to come out and get its own glory. What do I do to win this fight?

GOD SPEAKS: "Thanks be to God, who delivers me through Jesus Christ our Lord! So then, I myself in my mind am a slave to God's law, but in my sinful nature a slave to the law of sin. Therefore, there is now no condemnation for those who are in Christ Jesus, because through Christ Jesus the law of the Spirit who gives life has set you free from the law of sin and death." (Romans 7:25–8:2 NIV) The struggle ends when you sell out to Me. Just become Mine in your mind, and I will control your body.

WANDA'S PRAYER: Father, help us do this—to let go …

August 13

THE DUMBEST QUESTION

"ZECHARIAH ASKED THE ANGEL, 'HOW CAN I BE SURE OF THIS? I AM AN OLD MAN AND MY WIFE IS WELL ALONG IN YEARS.'" (LUKE 1:18 NIV)

I remember once when I was very young, about ten or eleven years old, listening to my brother-in-law discuss deer hunting with his friends. He mentioned, "treeing a deer." Instead of just listening to the story and perhaps learning the meaning, I blurted out my very silly question, "I didn't know deer could climb trees?" I said this with the seriousness of a mad scientist. Everyone laughed, except my brother-in-law; I had unknowingly spoiled the punch line. Still, I did not know what all the fun was about and anyway, I still wanted to know about deer climbing trees. This was the case of Zechariah, Elizabeth's husband. Father God, through His authoritative angel Gabriel, has just revealed tomorrow's headlines about the child they had long prayed for. He and his barren wife would be given a miracle child and this miracle child would be filled with the Holy Ghost from conception! He would single-handedly cause personal and national revival in his nation. Finally, after doing all those things, this precious child would usher in the reign and rule of the Messiah. The Messiah was not only for Israel, but He would be the world's last and best hope. After being told all of this, the first words out of his mouth are: "Are you sure? We are old, you know? I just do not see how this can be." This must have floored the angel. His first thoughts might have been, "You old goat, you've got to be kidding me—are you for real? Do you think I would just show up in this place, at this time, to play some silly game? Get a grip, old man." But Zechariah was serious—it was no joke to him. Still, Zechariah asked this question despite all he had heard and knew about his Jewish history. He knew of the patriarch Abraham and Sarah. He was not one-hundred years old as Abraham was, and Elizabeth was not ninety-years old, as Sarah was. So why would he doubt? Since he doubted, would his wife doubt also?

ELIZABETH AND US: While I might marvel at this man's unbelief, I am reminded that I suffer from the same ill. Lord, what is the remedy?

GOD SPEAKS: "Now faith is the substance of things hoped for, the evidence of things not seen." (Hebrews 11:1 NKJV) Remember, faith is not an airy, puffy fleeing feeling; faith is substance. Wrap your arms around, and take hold of that substance of what you hoped for; your hope is in Christ! As you grab hold of the substance of faith, you will have the evidence not seen.

WANDA'S PRAYER: Father, we will do just that. We know You are all Your word says You are, and so, so… much more.

August 14

HE WAS RIGHTEOUS, BUT NOT SINLESS

"AND NOW YOU WILL BE SILENT AND NOT ABLE TO SPEAK UNTIL THE DAY THIS HAPPENS, BECAUSE YOU DID NOT BELIEVE MY WORDS, WHICH WILL COME TRUE AT THEIR APPOINTED TIME." (LUKE 1:20 NIV)

The background of this verse is interesting. As I said in an earlier text, Zechariah, whose name meant, "God remembers," has a few flaws. One of them is he seems to have forgotten the meaning of his name. In Luke 1:18, Zechariah is disputing with the angel of the LORD about the birth of the child John, whose name means, "God is gracious." The scene would be comical if it were not so sad. I laugh because I am the same way. The man of God is arguing with the angel who the LORD Himself, had dispatched. He is telling this angel, "No, you must be mistaken about our having a child. You see, my wife and I are too old for God to do this miracle." (Writer's paraphrase) The angel Gabriel puts the priest in his place. He tells Zechariah who he is and reminds the old priest that he has just come from the throne room of GOD! Gabriel is upset at this man of God because of his unbelief. Why? Here are three reasons I think the angel might have been upset with the priest. (1) The old priest forgot "who" he was (Zechariah—the one whom God remembers), and he forgot "whose" he was. He forgot he belonged to the Most High GOD. (2) He had forgotten the word of the LORD; "Is anything too hard for the LORD?" He also forgot his national history and he forgot its founders (Abraham and his wife Sarah). They had kids at the young age of one hundred (Abraham) and ninety (Sarah) years of age. (3) In his forgetfulness, he questions the integrity of the messenger and, most importantly, he questions the LORD Himself. The scene is amazing. Picture Zechariah in the temple worshiping the All-powerful God and offering up prayers to His name. Yet, he questions the graciousness of God and refused to believe the Father loved him enough to give him this wonderful gift. This hurts the Father's heart. We, too, doubt Him, as Zechariah did. He was head of the home and priest of the LORD. If he doubted God, then what of his wife, Elizabeth?

ELIZABETH AND US: I cannot really blame Elizabeth or her husband for not believing. They had waited many years for children; and it seemed as if their hopes were all but gone. This story shows me God's faithfulness, even in the midst of my doubting.

GOD SPEAKS: "God is not a man, that He should lie, Nor a son of man, that He should repent. Has He said, and will he not do? Or has He spoken, and will He not make it good?" (Numbers 23:19 NKJV) It hurts Me when you do not believe Me. To coin a phrase, when you cannot see My hands in your life—you can always trust My heart of love for you.

WANDA'S PRAYER: Father, all we can say is, please forgive us for the doubt and distrust.

August 15

YOU MAY FORGET, BUT I DON'T

"WHEN HIS TIME OF SERVICE WAS COMPLETED, HE RETURNED HOME. AFTER THIS HIS WIFE ELIZABETH BECAME PREGNANT AND FOR FIVE MONTHS REMAINED IN SECLUSION." (LUKE 1:23-24 NIV)

This verse once again shows the faithfulness of our Dad. His goodness is not dependent on our faithfulness. God is good because that is who He is! So Zechariah goes home to his wife, unable to speak. They make love, and the LORD opens Elizabeth's closed womb. She is pregnant with baby John. Zechariah, smitten with a mute tongue by Gabriel for his unbelief, watches in wonder as the Father carries out His Divine plan. I wonder if he told Elizabeth about his angelic encounter at first. I doubt it, because of her reaction to the pregnancy. Elizabeth hid herself for five months. Perhaps at first, she was unsure this was the Father's prophetic will for her life. Other answers are: She really wanted to be sure she was pregnant. Maybe she had gotten her hopes up before about the pregnancy, only to be disappointed. Or maybe she knew she was pregnant through missed menstrual cycles, and did not want to receive the scorn of friends and family who would not believe her miracle. After five months, she would be "showing," and a protruding abdomen would be hard to deny. One look at her in the fifth month of her conception, and everyone would say, "Yep, that old lady is really pregnant." Then she could say, "See, I told you so!" But in the home of this old faithful couple, there must have been much joy, even though Zechariah was speechless. This was a woman's dream; to have a husband you can babble on to, and he cannot answer you a word. His speechlessness was also a sign of the Father's amazing love for them. It says to me God was guaranteeing a healthy pregnancy. The old priest was told, "And now you will be silent and not able to speak until the day this happens, because you did not believe my words, which will come true at their proper time." (Luke 1:20 NIV) As he observed his wife's ever increasing waist size, he was sure the Father's words were true. Elizabeth must have been beside herself with joy and praise to her Dad.

ELIZABETH AND US: As I mentioned previously, it took me five years to conceive my first child (a daughter), and three years to get pregnant with my second (a son). I, too, remember the ups and downs of that period; the hoping, only to be let down. Then when I was finally really pregnant—the bulging stomach, "Humpty-Dumpty" looking pregnant, I was so happy! I wobbled like a walrus everywhere I went. Those were great times.

GOD SPEAKS: "All creatures look to you to give them their food at the proper time. When you give it to them, they gather it up; when you open your hand, they are satisfied with good things." (Psalm 104:27-28 NIV) Allow Me to satisfy you with Myself. I am satisfaction to the fullest.

WANDA'S PRAYER: Father, You are beyond satisfaction!

August 16

MOVE AND LET ME PRAISE HIM

"THE LORD HAS DONE THIS FOR ME," SHE SAID. 'IN THESE DAYS HE HAS SHOWN HIS FAVOR AND TAKEN AWAY MY DISGRACE AMONG THE PEOPLE.'" (LUKE 1:25 NIV)

There is a song recorded by CeCe Winans called "Hallelujah." As she is singing about all the things to praise our LORD for, she comes to a verse in the song I love. The verse says, "Move and let me praise Him!" When I read this verse, this is what I envisioned Elizabeth saying as she gives praise to her LORD for His wonderful act of grace to her. In this verse, Elizabeth speaks from her heart. Her surrender and total submission has always been and will always be, to her LORD. But in those days, barrenness meant uselessness. I can just hear the whispers of the townsfolk; "Her husband is a priest; I wonder why she cannot get pregnant—what's wrong with her, anyway?" Those evil taunts must have stung like a viper's bite. The disgrace or disfavor among her people is obviously a painful experience, as she expresses here. Her loving LORD saw the whole wicked scene. He watched His daughter endure like a true woman after His heart. In His perfect time, He showed His beautiful, undeserving favor to the daughter of His heart. What I like about Elizabeth is that she worshipped Him "before" the blessing, and she praised Him "after" she received His wonderful gift. She let all of us know the blessing was from God and Him alone. She knows it was a gift from her LORD, and not an entitlement. Her name means, "God is my oath"—my life is dedicated to Him. He is LORD, and I am not. This makes the gift even more special—the fact that her Father, "… showed His favor and took away her disgrace from among the people."

ELIZABETH AND US: Elizabeth's life speaks to all of us. It reminds us that the Father never forgets; neither is He ever far away from us. Just as He heard His daughter Elizabeth, He hears and will answer our prayers, too.

GOD SPEAKS: "Praise the LORD, my soul; all my inmost being, praise his holy name. Praise the LORD, my soul, and forget not all his benefits—who forgives all your sins and heals all your diseases, who redeems your life from the pit and crowns you with love and compassion, who satisfies your desires with good things so that your youth is renewed like the eagle's." (Psalm 103:1-5 NIV) I know all about you. I AM your only help; I enjoy helping you. I AM your all. Just praise Me because you know that I AM GOOD.

WANDA'S PRAYER: You LORD, are VERY GOOD—You truly are!

August 17

BLESSED TO BE A BLESSING

"NOW INDEED, ELIZABETH YOUR RELATIVE HAS ALSO CONCEIVED A SON IN HER OLD AGE; AND THIS IS NOW THE SIXTH MONTH FOR HER WHO WAS CALLED BARREN. FOR WITH GOD NOTHING WILL BE IMPOSSIBLE." (LUKE 1:36-37 NKJV)

We all go through tough times in our lives. During those times, we wonder, "why do I have to go through all of these problems? Why must I endure all of this suffering?" The LORD brings us through the struggle and gets us through the difficult times. Then, months or years after the event, we meet someone who is (figuratively speaking) driving our same car—taking our same trip. They are perplexed and troubled. This struggling child in Christ has the same fears and distress you had when you went through your troubled times. As you listen to their story, you recall your time of pain; but now you know of your deliverance. At this point, it hits you like a ton of bricks. Yes, the purpose of your pain and hurt was so you would know and believe in God; but also that you would be a wonderful blessing to someone else. This is the case in this verse. The background is the angel Gabriel is speaking to Mary. He is telling her she is going to have a child fathered by the HOLY SPIRIT OF GOD. Mary questions in her heart if she is imagining things—could such a thing really happen? The assurance He gives her is to look at her relative Elizabeth. In my "Writer's paraphrase," the verse sounds something like this: "As a testimony to you Mary, and to show you my words are true, just look at your cousin Elizabeth. She is a very old woman. Remember, she was called 'barren.' Now she is six months pregnant. WITH GOD! NOTHING—not Elizabeth's barrenness or God supernaturally giving you a child, is IMPOSSIBLE FOR HIM!" Elizabeth's life and experiences were not just for Elizabeth and her husband. They were also meant to bless and strengthen all who would hear her testimony about the power of her LORD.

ELIZABETH AND US: The breakup and divorce of my first marriage was very painful and tragic to me. I wondered for years how it would ever be a blessing to anyone. Then, years later, I met a woman who was going through the same problems the LORD had brought me through. I knew at that point, like Elizabeth, my victory was not just for me, but so I could bless someone else along the way. Unlike Elizabeth, some of my problems were of my own making; yet my LORD was gracious and blessed me through them all.

GOD SPEAKS: "The angel of the LORD encamps around those who fear him, and he delivers them. Taste and see that the LORD is good; blessed is the one who takes refuge in him." (Psalm 34:7-8 NIV) I allow rainstorms so a flower garden can grow. The beauty of the flower garden is not just for you, but for your neighbors and friends to admire as well.

WANDA'S PRAYER: As the songwriter says, I thank You for mountains and valleys; joys and pain. If I had not had sorrow, then I could not contrast it with the joy You give on the other side of pain.

August 18

I'VE GOT TO SEE THIS FOR MYSELF

"... THEN THE ANGEL LEFT HER. AT THAT TIME MARY GOT READY AND HURRIED TO A TOWN IN THE HILL COUNTRY OF JUDEA," (LUKE 1:38-39 NIV)

The testimony about Elizabeth, given to her by the angel, stirred up Mary's troubled heart and caused such a rumble in her soul that she was driven to see this act of God for herself. This points out a very important principle about the Christian life. Since we as Christians are crucified with Christ, we are dead to self and self-seeking. We live to give Him glory in everything we do. One way we do this is by sharing our testimony of how He has blessed us. We live our lives to showcase His goodness and mercy. Elizabeth's blessing from her LORD was the salve Mary needed. Hearing and seeing how the Father had worked His marvel for Elizabeth was just what she needed to see, to continue on her calling. Her story is a testament of God's great love for His child. Elizabeth had gone through the valley of despair, and came out blessed beyond anything she could ever imagine. Mary was just starting her journey. Having seen her cousin's victory would strengthen her for the long, painful journey ahead of her. Had Elizabeth not gone through her years of barrenness with the pain it brought, she would never have been able to bless the young mother of our LORD so incredibly. It also shows us how our loving LORD and Father uses every trial, problem, and circumstance for our good, and for His glory.

ELIZABETH AND US: As I look at how magnificently Elizabeth was used for God's glory to bless her young cousin, it gives me a new vigor to be totally sold out to Him. In Liz's story, I see I should not complain when I go through trials and tribulations. Instead, I need to fall down in "crazy praise" to my LORD, as I give Him all the hurts and pains. As I give them to Him, I know for certain that for every tear I cry, and for every affliction I experience, He will mix them into His perfect recipe for my life. This delightful dish, when fully cooked, will not only be a delicious delicacy for me, but for all who sample my testimony of praise.

GOD SPEAKS: "And we know that in all things God works for the good of those who love him, who have been called according to his purpose. For those God foreknew he also predestined to be conformed to the image of his Son, that he might be the firstborn among many brothers and sisters." (Romans 8:28-29 NIV) You are My beautiful work in progress. Believe it, know it, and live it! This will give ME, MY glory.

WANDA'S PRAYER: Our response is: "If God is for us (me), who can be against us (me)? He who did not spare his own Son, but gave him up for us all—how will he not also, along with him, graciously give us all things?" (Romans 8:31-32 NIV)

August 19

JUMPING FOR JOY!

"WHEN ELIZABETH HEARD MARY'S GREETING, THE BABY LEAPED IN HER WOMB…" (LUKE 1:41 NIV)

I almost skipped this part of the story; had I done so, the significant loss would have been mine. In getting into the story, we see that Mary, the mother of Christ, has just entered the home of Zechariah and Elizabeth. She is newly pregnant with the Christ child, probably less than three months' gestation. Mary greets her elder relative as she enters the home. Elizabeth's unborn son, in utero form, hears the mother of our LORD'S voice and leaps for joy. When I read this verse, I envision the baby John doing violent somersaults in Elizabeth's womb. What was so special about this voice? What would put the son of Elizabeth in such a stir? The unborn child in Elizabeth's womb immediately recognizes the presence of his King. Mary was carrying the Messiah of Creation in her womb! Elizabeth's unborn son was filled with God's Holy Spirit. The Spirit of God, in the fetus John, reacted to the Holy child in Mary's womb. The embryo John was aware he was in the presence of the Holy Creator, so he worshipped Him. This gestating John did a praise dance to his LORD. This story reveals several things to me: (1) The unborn fetus can hear and be aware of their surroundings. They can hear and distinguish voices (This scientific fact given in the Word, predates by centuries, our human discoveries.) (2) The Spirit of God will lead us to the Truth of God. (3) Being aware of our Lord's presence brings worship and praise.

ELIZABETH AND US: As I listen and learn from this lesson, I am given a new awareness of His presence. The Spirit of the Living God is in me; I am His temple. This fact alone is a cause for worship with tongue and praise, everywhere I go, and in every situation of life.

GOD SPEAKS: "After they prayed, the place where they were meeting was shaken. And they were all filled with the Holy Spirit and spoke the word of God boldly." (Acts 4:31 NIV) When it comes to speaking My Word while at work, I know you are timid. Pray and allow Me to give you My Holy boldness.

WANDA'S PRAYER: Father, forgive us for our sin in this area. Fill us fully with You! We want to proclaim Your Word to everyone we meet. We never want to be ashamed of the gospel. It is the power to change a life. The "Good News" is the only thing that truly saves.

August 20

THE INFECTIOUS SPIRIT

"WHEN ELIZABETH HEARD MARY'S GREETING, THE BABY LEAPED IN HER WOMB, AND ELIZABETH WAS FILLED WITH THE HOLY SPIRIT." (LUKE 1:41 NIV)

Did you catch the last part of Luke 1:41? Let's read it again: "… And Elizabeth was filled with the Holy Spirit." It seems now we have a fire season in California yearly. Every summer for the past four or five years, fires break out only to destroy thousands of acres; at a cost of millions of dollars in property damage. I am told these mega damages can stem from only a tiny spark. Well, something like this happened at the home of Elizabeth and Zechariah—the spark was Jesus Christ, coming through, via Mary's womb! Inside of baby John was the Holy Spirit, and it was like smoldering embers awaiting that Spark, which lightens every man. When the Spark of the world came in contact with the embers of the Holy Ghost, an explosion happened. The fire of the Holy Spirit consuming baby John crossed the placenta and lit inside his mother. This infectious Spirit now consumed mother and child. The presence of the LORD had filled this place. On the surface, this seems like an abnormal phenomenon—having two persons of the Godhead in one place. But this is what our LORD longs to do for each of us. Jesus says, "I will not leave you as orphans; I will come to you." (John 14:18) So how is He going to come to us? By way of the Holy Spirit; "And I will ask the Father, and he will give you another advocate to help you and be with you forever—the Spirit of truth…" (John 14:16-17 NIV) This indwelling of our God within us is to be a daily occurrence of the Christ, and not a special event. Dad, via His Spirit, wants free and total reign of our hearts and lives. Elizabeth, whose name means, "God is my oath," was that willing vessel. Her life is a picture of what happens when we give Him full control over our lives—a spiritual plaque ensues and infects everyone in His path.

ELIZABETH AND US: I love this part of the story because it shows me what the Father wants to do in my heart and life. He took an ordinary woman and did an extraordinary thing in her life. The story shows us that our LORD loves us and wants us to have His absolute best. His best is Himself!

GOD SPEAKS: "Do you not know that your bodies are temples of the Holy Spirit, who is in you, whom you have received from God? You are not your own; you were bought at a price. Therefore honor God with your bodies." (1 Corinthians 6:19-20 NIV) Since Creation, I have wanted to occupy mankind. Allow Me to live in every cell of your body. With Me in control of your life, we can do wonders!

WANDA'S PRAYER: Father, take complete control of our lives and heart. When we have the urge to try and fly by ourselves, remind us of the many times we have crashed and burned.

August 21

THE COMFORTER

"IN A LOUD VOICE SHE (ELIZABETH) EXCLAIMED: 'BLESSED ARE YOU AMONG WOMEN ...'" (LUKE 1:42 NIV)

Yesterday, we discussed what happens to a life that is totally given over to the Master. That life becomes a place where the Spirit of God can run wild with His perfect will. Elizabeth is our example of this. The Spirit of the LORD uses her mightily for His divine purposes. He, the Spirit of the Living LORD, can display one of His characteristics—the Comforter. Mary, at only a few months pregnant with the Christ, needed comfort and understanding. She did not understand what was going on inside of her, or how to explain it to anyone else. She only knew what the angel Gabriel had said to her. Mary knows she is pregnant by divine design—sounds crazy, huh? The Spirit, who had impregnated her, was now going to console His precious one with Himself. As this weary soul walks in the door of Elizabeth's house, she speaks greetings to her elder relative. She is not met with condemnation or accusation. Instead, Dad drowns her with His adoration and commendation. He does what only He does best—He comforts His child with a trumpet blast of blessings. Elizabeth screams these "well done" (blessings) to Mary at the top of her voice. These are words Mary's fainting soul desperately needs to hear. I will paraphrase what the Spirit may have said to her struggling soul. "You have done very well (blessed), My precious child. I chose you out from among every woman ever created. You will carry My Son. There is no shame in this. In fact, I am yelling from the mountaintops for all to hear. Comfort yourself in these words, from My heart to your troubled soul." The Spirit-filled Elizabeth could give what had been given to her. She was now the conduit of our LORD; used to pour out blessings and confirmation to Mary's thirsting soul. This is what the Father wants to do in each of the lives of all of His children.

ELIZABETH AND US: Elizabeth paints a beautiful portrait of what the LORD wants to do in and through my life, as I totally yield myself for His glory and to His plans. I am far from being there; but I am His wonderful work in progress.

GOD SPEAKS: "… whom I created for my glory, whom I formed and made." (Isaiah 43:7 NIV) I created you to display My beauty. Again I say to you—you are My masterpiece. Allow Me to display My glorious splendor. Allow Me to live in you. I bring with Me wonderful food. I bring peace, joy, patience, love, kindness, faithfulness, gentleness, and self-control. This food is very satisfying, and it will not add unwanted pounds. You will never get in trouble for having these fruits.

WANDA'S PRAYER: Lord, feed us from Your table.

August 22

THE CONFIRMER

"... AND BLESSED IS THE CHILD YOU WILL BEAR!" (LUKE 1:42 NIV)

Gabriel had spoken the words of our LORD to Mary in Nazareth. He told her she was "highly favored." Elizabeth, under the influence of the Holy Spirit, now confirms the Father's words in the first part of Luke 1:42, "blessed are you among women..." In other words, our LORD gives this unique opportunity to you alone. The LORD'S megaphone (the Holy Spirit) continues in the latter part of the same verse, "... And blessed is the child you will bear!" This statement is also a confirmation of what the angel Gabriel had spoken to Mary; "You will conceive and give birth to a son, and you are to call him Jesus. He will be great and will be called the Son of the Most High..." (Luke 1:31-32 NIV) Elizabeth calls this child blessed (one to be praised; well done Mary, or good job). How did she know anything about Mary from her one greeting, much less that she was going to have a child, or that this child was someone to be praised? Luke 1:38 tells us Mary was alone with the angel. Luke 1:39 says that shortly after receiving the revelation of her pregnancy, and her acceptance of God's will, she hurried to Elizabeth's house. This left no time for anyone to know about the pregnancy. Elizabeth lived in the mountains, and they did not have telephones, so how was she to know? But as soon as Mary entered the house and spoke, the Holy Ghost stole the show. It was the Spirit of God—the Spirit of Truth, in Elizabeth's heart who confirmed Mary's role and revealed that the Child Mary was carrying, was the "blessed one." The Spirit had told her the truth, and Elizabeth could not contain herself. She had to let it out. In obedience to her LORD, she was able to hold up and strengthen her younger relative. This speaks to me. I have the truth of Christ. Am I letting it out in word and deed? Am I strengthening and holding up my sisters with the Words of our LORD?

ELIZABETH AND US: Elizabeth's life is very inspiring. I see how her Spirit-filled life was used to bless others in the family of God. She was the first to proclaim the coming King. In doing so, she confirmed the message of the LORD sent by Gabriel, and was also a great source of strength to Mary. She shows me that my job is to know Him and make Him known. Lord, I want this as one of my prime directives in life.

GOD SPEAKS: "I proclaim your saving acts in the great assembly; I do not seal my lips, LORD, as you know. I do not hide your righteousness in my heart; I speak of your faithfulness and your saving help ..." (Psalm 40:9-10 NIV) Ponder on just how good your LORD has been to you. Then, out of all of that goodness, open your mouth to all you see, and give Me praise.

WANDA'S PRAYER: Father God, we will give You praise in word and in deed.

August 23

A PLACE OF HONOR

"BUT WHY AM I SO FAVORED, THAT THE MOTHER OF MY LORD SHOULD COME TO ME?" (LUKE 1:43 NIV)

This verse is so rich in content. Devouring it would be like eating a four or five-course meal. So, let us dig in and sample some of its delicacies. First, Elizabeth speaks of her "favor" from her LORD. A definition of favor in Hebrew is "Chanan." This word means to stoop in kindness to an inferior; to "favor" by petition. To deal, give or grant, to be gracious to entreat, to have pity upon. (The New Strong's Exhaustive Concordance) Elizabeth could have been thinking of one or all of these definitions. The Spirit of our LORD, through His revelation of the Christ child, had "floored" this woman. Dad, through the inspiration of His Spirit, had told His child Lizzy, "this is the Messiah—God coming to earth in human form." Mary's arrival totally humbled Elizabeth. Here Mary thought she would get much needed encouragement, and she did; but look at the honor Elizabeth was getting in return. When she reflected on everything which had happened in her life until now, she knew without a doubt, she had been favored. She must have remembered the many long years of her barrenness. After all those lonely heart-breaking years, Dad had given her a child. Then, while still pregnant with the miracle child, she is privileged to host the "Holy of Holies" and His mother in her humble home. The Savior of the World would make one of His first stops on planet earth, at her home. Again, Elizabeth's statement was further confirmation to the young Mary's heart of what the angel had said to her. Elizabeth realized she was receiving a direct revelation of the Christ from the Spirit of God. This giant package of blessing must have overwhelmed this old woman. She realized her blessing came not because of her goodness, but only through the Father's faithfulness to His daughter.

ELIZABETH AND US: As I look at my life, I too, have received many wonderful revelations from our LORD. Just to think about the process of salvation is mind-boggling. Imagine, the Spotless Son of God, coming as a frail, human child, to save filthy me from my sins. Not only did He save me from sin, but He raised me in thought, lifestyle, and into a newness of life, where He is. Then, when it is all said and done, He has prepared a glorious home for me in His kingdom. As I think on these things, as well as the temporal perks of life, health, strength, soundness of mind, employment, food, shelter, family, etc., I too am "floored" by the goodness of my LORD.

GOD SPEAKS: "LORD, our Lord, how majestic is your name in all the earth! You have set your glory in the heavens. When I consider your heavens, the work of your fingers, the moon and the stars, which you have set in place, what is mankind that you are mindful of them, human beings that you care for them?" (Psalm 8:1,3-4 NIV) Your job is to never take your eyes off of Me. As you behold Me continually, I will change you into a reflection of Me.

WANDA'S PRAYER: Father, we want to reflect Your beauty and glory; may others only see You through us.

August 24

GIRL, I GOTTA TELL IT!

"AS SOON AS THE SOUND OF YOUR GREETING REACHED MY EARS, THE BABY IN MY WOMB LEAPED FOR JOY." (LUKE 1:44 NIV)

In this part of the story, Elizabeth recounts to Mary what the spark was that kindled this Spirit fest she is now having. Can you hear the excitement in her voice? This is what I hear Elizabeth saying with bated breath, as she tells Mary the story. "Girl, when you walked in the door, called my name, and greeted me, my baby went crazy with joy! The baby heard your voice and started doing 'flips and turns' inside of me, and just would not stop. After that, girl, the Spirit of the LORD just took over and filled me up. Now, I cannot stop praising GOD and blessing you—Hallelujah!" (Writer's paraphrase) This lesson teaches the benefits of witnessing for our LORD. Let us discuss a two-fold blessing that comes from giving our testimony to others. Testifying to others of what our LORD has done in our lives gives confirmation and courage to both the giver and the receiver of the testimony. By nature, testimonies are a form of praise to our LORD, for His many blessings to us. In Elizabeth's testimony to her young cousin, she speaks from a heart that has been filled with God's Spirit. Then, while listening, the Spirit of Truth (The Holy Spirit) confirms to Mary something God had revealed to her previously. The "something" was that our LORD had indeed chosen her to bear His Son. Mary reflects on her confirmation, as Elizabeth praises God. (Luke 1:46-56) The result is mutual rejoicing and continual praise. Courage is the second blessing received from giving our testimony to what our LORD has done in our lives. As the words drop from Elizabeth's lips, they are like Kryptonite falling onto Mary's limp and weary soul. Strengthened with her new infusion of courage, she is refreshed and able to complete the task God has given her to do.

ELIZABETH AND US: This Sista's life just continues to pour spiritual nourishment into mine. Looking at her life teaches me lessons about giving my testimony. I am learning how my life is to be a blessing and a hope for those around me. Father God, teach me how to live and testify to Your glory.

GOD SPEAKS: "I will praise You, O LORD, with my whole heart; I will tell of all Your marvelous works. I will be glad and rejoice in You; I will sing praise to Your name, O Most High." (Psalm 9:1-2 NKJV) "For My glory, you were created." As you allow Me to fill your heart continually and completely with Me, I will bring glory to My name.

WANDA'S PRAYER: LORD, thank You for the love and goodness You continually give to us. Empty us of self, and fill our hearts with You.

August 25

YOU'RE MY HERO

"BLESSED IS SHE WHO HAS BELIEVED THAT THE LORD WOULD FULFILL HIS PROMISES TO HER!"
(LUKE 1:45 NIV)

Under the influence of the Holy Spirit, Elizabeth has given her young cousin three great blessings from the LORD. The first two "blessed" stems from the word "Eulogeo." Eulogeo is a combination of two words, meaning, "to speak well of." They are a form of praise to Mary for her glad acceptance of what God was doing for and in her. She is to be praised because Father God had chosen her for His special mission, and she said "yes." He took her out from among every other female on the planet, and allowed her the honor of bringing His Son to earth in human form. She is saying, "I speak well of you," or, "you ought to be complimented because of what my LORD has done for you." (Writer's Paraphrase) The last "blessing" she gives to her young relative is a supreme or super blessing. The root word for the blessing given in the above text is "Makarous." Makarous means, "supremely blest, extremely fortunate, happy." Elizabeth is saying to Mary, "Our LORD has placed in your womb riches untold. The total hope of humanity is gestating in your womb. Realizing the magnitude of this gift will make you extremely happy." Elizabeth continues by telling Mary that her fortune (wealth) and happiness stems from her complete trust that God had spoken to her through the angel Gabriel. Because she was certain it was God who spoke, she knew His words were going to come true. This unwavering faith in the Sovereign LORD is worth incalculable riches. Elizabeth realized this was a great act of faith. She reflected on the momentary doubts both she and her husband had when Gabriel told her husband he would father a child in his old age. Yet, Mary fully accepted this conception from Divine origin.

ELIZABETH AND US: "Wow!" That is all I can say when I look at the insight Father God, our wonderful Dad, gave this woman through the Holy Spirit. I look at this story and see how our LORD gives us the opportunity to exercise the same faith in Him as these women did. He wants the chance to birth great things through us, as He did through these women.

GOD SPEAKS: "Let us hold unswervingly to the hope we profess, for he who promised is faithful. And let us consider how we may spur one another on toward love and good deeds," (Hebrews 10:23-24 NIV) Child of Mine, translate this to your mindset; "hold on to Me with a vise grip," and to the promises, in My Word, concerning you. Know for certain that what I say, I am fully able to do. As you chew and digest My blessings in your life, turn and strengthen your sister—help them make it through their journey.

WANDA'S PRAYER: Lord, give us the wisdom and strength to do what You want us to do.

August 26

I WILL SING OVER YOU NOW

"AND MARY SAID: 'MY SOUL GLORIFIES THE LORD AND MY SPIRIT REJOICES IN GOD MY SAVIOR,'" (LUKE 1:46-47 NIV)

Though Mary believed the angel and had accepted the plan of God in her life, the challenge and stigma of unwed motherhood would be a great burden to bear. This is why the Father, our loving LORD, sent the "elder sister" (who was actually a cousin) Elizabeth. Father God used her to offer strength and encouragement to His young daughter. As the Spirit of God filled her soul, Elizabeth could do nothing less than empty this "living water" into the soul of her thirsting younger sister. The soul of little Mary is bursting at the seams with torrents of blessings given to her by the Holy Spirit. From this fullness, her mouth speaks. From a saturated heart filled with blessings, encouragement, and strength for her life's journey, she gives back something special to her elder sister in the form of praise. In Luke 1:46-56, Mary bellows out songs of joy to her God and King. In Elizabeth's house, Mary gives praise to her LORD for His salvation, His personal care of her, His mercy, and His awesome deeds. (I will deal more in-depth with Mary's praise later in her chapter.) As Elizabeth listens to this young woman, she receives a tremendous blessing. It must have been like having company for dinner. After having fed them, they get up from the table, clean your kitchen, and then they cook you your favorite meal, including dessert. As Elizabeth feasted on Mary's words of praise, she was blessed. Young Mary's spiritual feast nourished her. This brings up a very important principle. Our lives are not little "Christian islands" to be lived separately from each other. Instead, our lives are to be totally intertwined with others. Our triumphs and defeats can be used to help and lift up our sisters and brothers in the LORD. As they are built up, they will in turn build up others, until our LORD (through us) builds His impregnable fortress.

ELIZABETH AND US: Elizabeth's life shines like a blinding light on mine, as to the kind of witness I am to be for my LORD. In reading this, I am brought to much shame as I see the standard I fall so short of. Father, what will You say to my heart?

GOD SPEAKS: "Do you feel like a lowly worm, Jacob? Don't be afraid. Feel like a fragile insect, Israel? I'll help you. I, GOD, want to reassure you. The God who buys you back, The Holy of Israel. I'm transforming you from worm to harrow, from insect to iron. As a sharp-toothed harrow you'll smooth out the mountains, turn those tough old hills into loamy soil. You'll open the rough ground to the weather, to the blasts of sun and wind and rain …" (Isaiah 41:14-17 MSG) These are My plans for you. I need you to allow Me to occupy every part of your heart all the time; and you will be able to freely pour out My blessings to others, like Elizabeth.

WANDA'S PRAYER: Ok, LORD, we are ready to get started, since You are willing.

August 27

DON'T JUST COME FOR A VISIT—STAY!

"MARY STAYED WITH ELIZABETH FOR ABOUT THREE MONTHS AND THEN RETURNED HOME."
(LUKE 1:56 NIV)

Mary staying in Elizabeth's home for three months was a great honor for the elder woman of God. At Mary's entrance into her home, she cried out, "But who am I that the mother of MY LORD should come to me?" (Luke 1:43) You might ask, why such joy and jubilation? It is because the Creator God had entered her home as a babe inside of Mary, and Elizabeth was beside herself with awe and adulation. Israel's hope, the KING OF KINGS and LORD OF LORDS, is in her house and not showing any signs of leaving her home. He would spend the next three months with the lowly daughter of Aaron. This was quite an honor! Every day for the next three months, Elizabeth could sit and visit with the gestating LORD OF HOST, Jesus Christ! She could talk to the Promised One. She could reach out and touch Him by putting her hands on Mary's stomach. The Eternal Son of Glory was continually in her presence for three straight months. Day or night she could visit with Mary and have fellowship with Him. The Father truly honored Elizabeth to have such access to His precious Son. At first, I was envious, even a bit jealous, of the privilege the Holy woman of God enjoyed. Then I realized I have an even greater honor. Before Jesus went to the Cross of Calvary, He promised He would send His Spirit to live in me forever—24/7 (John 16). As a child of the KING, I have access to the personal touch of God. When I asked Him to come into my heart as LORD and Savior, He promised never to leave me. The Comforter is as close as the whisper of His name. I do not need the stomach of Mary near me to be in the presence of God. I can house His presence inside of me, in Spirit form, just as Mary did in bodily form. If that were not enough, I also have His precious words called the Bible, to speak to me. What could be more of a privilege than that?

ELIZABETH AND US: In this section, Elizabeth is teaching me to appreciate how much Father God truly loves me and wants to spend time with me. I see when I do not feel Him near, those are times when I have not sat in His presence and had our special time together.

GOD SPEAKS: "And I will ask the Father, and he will give you another advocate to help you and be with you forever—I will not leave you as orphans; I will come to you." (John 14:16,18 NIV) I do not have orphan children. I always take care of My own. I AM the perfect Father. My words are worth their weight in gold—you can bank that statement, make deposits and withdrawals on it as well.

WANDA'S PRAYER: LORD, we will continue to do just that.

August 28

LOVE'S PERFECT TIMING

"NOW THE TIME HAD COME FOR ELIZABETH TO GIVE BIRTH, AND SHE GAVE BIRTH TO A SON." (LUKE 1:57 NASB)

The time has finally come. It has been nearly ten months of pregnancy and Elizabeth is about to pop. According to our Father's perfect schedule, she goes into labor. I wonder how she knew she was in labor. Did her bag of waters break? Or did she have the excruciating death grip pains of labor? You know, the ones that cause us to twist and contort into four different positions at once. Whether her labor was fast or slow, difficult, or easy, the one thing that screams out to Elizabeth, and to our minds, is the PERFECT TIMING OF OUR ETERNAL GOD. The Father had promised Elizabeth's unbelieving husband, Zechariah, that his wife would have a son. Now at full term, John was born right on schedule—not premature or post term. This was not just a fulfillment of promise to an old barren woman and her aged husband; this was the fulfilling of a promise made to us all. Our Father God promised from the beginning that our LORD was coming to fix the mess made by Adam's fall. We read in Isaiah 40:3 of the forerunner's proclamation of our precious LORD. In the last book of the Old Testament, the very last words of that book we read, "Behold, I will send you Elijah the prophet before the coming of the great and dreadful day of the LORD. And he will turn the hearts of the fathers to the children, And the hearts of the children to their fathers …" (Malachi 4:5-6 NKJV) With each contraction Elizabeth felt, and with each urge to push during delivery, until baby John had squeezed through the birth canal, these were all reminders that their God was not only awesome, but truly faithful to His word. Like clockwork, our God delivered this baby right on time and not a moment too soon. What makes this story even more remarkable is the gift was not dependent on the old couple's faith, but on the Father's love.

ELIZABETH AND US: I am in awe of our heavenly Dad's great love for us. The faithfulness of our Father has little to do with our faithfulness. When we are not faithful, He is. He does these wonderful things to not only demonstrate, but to strengthen our love for Him. He is the only one that will never change.

GOD SPEAKS: "God is not a man, that He should lie, Nor a son of man, that He should repent. Has He said, and will He not do? Or has He spoken, and will He not make it good?" (Numbers 23:19 NKJV) I always do what I say I will do. You never have to worry that I cannot keep My word to you—I can! You just need to first, stay in My word and next, be sure you are correctly understanding what I say. After you do those two things, then just patiently wait on Me to do what I do.

WANDA'S PRAYER: Father, give us the faith to just rest, and completely rely on Your perfect and unfailing word!

August 29

GOD'S GOODNESS ON DISPLAY

"HER NEIGHBORS AND RELATIVES HEARD HOW WONDERFULLY GOOD THE LORD HAD BEEN TO HER, AND THEY ALL REJOICED WITH HER." (LUKE 1:58 GNT)

God's perfect plan has always been to present His children as beautiful ornaments, to display His excellent glory. The life of Elizabeth and Zechariah are examples of what the Father wants us all to be. The text says, "Her neighbors and relatives 'heard' how good the LORD had been to her…" The question to be asked is, "how and what did they hear?" "They" heard about God's goodness to Elizabeth through observation of her life. "They" observed a life that was totally sold out to her Maker and LORD, despite her circumstances. "They" observed a woman too full of God's love to be bitter over the missing pieces in her life. And "they" observed this woman's strength, which stemmed from her commitment to prayer and constant communion with the LORD. In short, "they" saw a life primed for the blessing of God to flow through. Then, in God's timing, "they" saw the hand of the loving God pour out a blessing that nearly drowned this old couple. He sent a special delivery from Heaven by the angel Gabriel to give to His kids. The message to His babes was this, "Zach, Dad has heard your and Lizzy's heart's cry. He has seen your dedicated life, and now He has a gift for you—a bouncing baby boy!" (Writer's paraphrase) This blessing was etched on the mountains of Judea, and was hard to miss. Elizabeth was very old and barren. An old woman getting pregnant, going full term, then enduring the rigorous labor process. It must have been mind-blowing as the friends and relatives watched the process unfold. The spectators beholding this site had just one thing to say: "God is good to Elizabeth." As "they" observed God's goodness, their response was to rejoice with her. This is important because Elizabeth says in verse twenty-five of this chapter, "My people were ashamed of me, but now the LORD has taken away that shame." The Father had said this would be the result of this blessing: "He will be a joy and delight to you, and many will rejoice because of his birth," (Luke 1:14 NIV) Isn't it beautiful to watch God's goodness unfold before our very eyes?

ELIZABETH AND US: As I reflect on Elizabeth's life, I am forced to take the magnifying glass and look into my own life. I say I am a servant of Christ, but what does my life say of the Father's goodness during the trials, as well as in times of success? Sadly, I know every aspect of my life does not give Him the glory it should. Father, speak to my heart concerning these matters; what do You want to say?

GOD SPEAKS: "The LORD is good to those whose hope is in him, to the one who seeks him;" (Lamentations 3:25 NIV) As you focus on My goodness, the way you praise Me is with a life sold out to Me. I get My glory when I am free to live, move, and breathe through you.

WANDA'S PRAYER: Father God, we are Yours—take the reins of our life.

August 30

I'M DOING WHAT GOD SAID!

"ON THE EIGHTH DAY THEY CAME TO CIRCUMCISE THE CHILD, AND THEY WERE GOING TO NAME HIM AFTER HIS FATHER ZECHARIAH, BUT HIS MOTHER SPOKE UP AND SAID, 'NO! HE IS TO BE CALLED JOHN.'" (LUKE 1:59-60 NIV)

This part of the story is so touching. As I read it, I can see the immediate family and close friends rallying around the old couple, as they are adjusting to their new role as parents. The child is now eight days old and is to be circumcised and named. Hebrew culture considered the rite of circumcision to be a special event. The act itself signified an agreement between them and God. It told the world He was their God, and they were His chosen people. (Genesis 17:11-12; 21:4, and Philippians 3:5) In their zeal to help the old couple with things, "they" thought it smart to name the child after his father, Zechariah; this seemed like a good thing. After all, the father, Zechariah, was still mute and could not talk, so "they" thought they were just helping the couple out a little. (Luke 1:19-22,62) Good suggestion or not, Elizabeth would have no part in this. She knew what her LORD had told her to do, and she was sticking to her guns. "Nope, people, I do not think so! God gave him the name John, and that is his name—thank you very much!" (Writer's paraphrase) So, what is the big deal? What was so important about giving this child this name? Simple—it was what the LORD had instructed Zechariah to do, and this couple was being obedient to God's Word. It did not matter what others thought or felt, the old couple had God's mandate, and that was enough! This was a household which served the LORD! Just as a sidebar, John derives his name from the Hebrew word (Yehawchanan). This word is a compound name comprising two words, meaning "Jehovah-Favored." By naming the child John, this would forever remind the couple that the LORD and Father had shown them much favor (grace). The appreciation of the Father's unmerited favor (Grace) is seen in the face of Elizabeth's obedience.

ELIZABETH AND US: This woman continues to teach me. LORD, every day, every morning, Your lessons are new to me—Great is Your faithfulness! (Lamentations 3:23) If I were to count the faithfulness of my LORD, I could do nothing else. So, I will praise Him all the days of my life with the way I live.

GOD SPEAKS: "The LORD's love never ends; his mercies never stop. They are new every morning; LORD, your loyalty is great." (Lamentations 3:22-23 NCV) Remember, My love always has your best interest at the center of My heart. My love is perfect LOVE—in good times and bad.

WANDA'S PRAYER: Father, thank You for loving us with a FOREVER LOVE—which is You.

August 31

HONEY, I GOT THIS

"THE PEOPLE SAID TO ELIZABETH, 'BUT NO ONE IN YOUR FAMILY HAS THIS NAME.' THEN THEY MADE SIGNS TO HIS FATHER TO FIND OUT WHAT HE WOULD LIKE TO NAME HIM. ZECHARIAH ASKED FOR A WRITING TABLET AND WROTE, 'HIS NAME IS JOHN,' AND EVERYONE WAS SURPRISED." (LUKE 1:61-63 NCV)

This part of the story, though cute and somewhat comical, illustrates a wonderful point about life lived in the kingdom of God. The point shown in the above verse is that there can be strong opposition to our walk of faith. Here is such a case. Elizabeth speaks for her mute husband and names the child. She is sternly chided for this, as though she is a foolish old woman, void of common sense. The people then start to re-educate her on her obviously forgotten family history. I'm sure they thought her hormones were unbalanced or something. But Lizzy (Elizabeth) had taken her unwavering stand. The opposition did not stop there. In an attempt to circumvent her decision in favor of their own, they would turn to ask the head of the house, Zechariah, to straighten out his somewhat deluded wife. This manly man takes a manly stand in defense of his LORD, and his wife. He does not argue with the crowd, he is just a "matter of fact" with his answer. "His name is John." (Luke 1:63) That's the child's name—no questions and no discussion. This vignette in Luke Chapter 1 is the way our Father God would have us deal with temptation and opposition to our living out a righteous life. He says to let our "Yes be yes, and our no be no." We are to have the Father's word imbedded in our hearts and mind. When alternate suggestions or difficult antagonism cross our paths, we are to stand on God's word alone. We are not to argue, fret, or get into a discussion with the enemy. We just stand on the Word of God alone and go forward as this couple did. Our LORD rewards such absolute obedience. The end result is the LORD gave Zechariah back his voice as promised. He used his new voice to praise the God of his salvation!

ELIZABETH AND US: This story is definitely a tear-jerker. I can see through Elizabeth what our Father has for the life of a believer. In life, there will always be ups and downs. Despite whatever comes, however, I am to always remember—my Father loves me! When I am fully convinced of this, I am in the place of blessings. I must remember that the true blessing is the opportunity to serve the KING OF KINGS AND LORD OF LORDS.

GOD SPEAKS: "The LORD has told you, human, what is good; he has told you what he wants from you: to do what is right to other people, love being kind to others, and live humbly, obeying your God." (Micah 6:8 NCV) If you did this little thing for Me, that would be more than enough.

WANDA'S PRAYER: LORD, as we continue to sit at Your feet, do in and through us, Your perfect will.

Notes

September

INTRODUCTION

MARTHA

Martha, her sister Mary, and their brother Lazarus lived in the town of Bethany, just two to five miles outside of Jerusalem. She is a woman of strength and possibly a woman of means. They were all very close friends of Jesus.

Martha shows us that to be a friend to our LORD is to open ourselves up to Him. We see her opening up her home to Jesus at a moment's notice. Martha's heart is one that was always available to her LORD. She was always ready and willing to serve Him. In fact, Martha has a heart of service. Her life also presents us with a great lesson on trusting our LORD despite what we see or how we feel.

While Martha has this wonderful heart of service, she would learn and teach us that time spent at the feet of Jesus should always precede earthly service. She shows us that service, absent of worship, will leave us empty and dry. Finally, Martha shows us we can and should take every need, care, and concern to our LORD. Having given Him our requests, we then trust and obey Him, as we patiently wait to see how He will answer us.

Notes

September 1

HELLO, I'M MARTHA

"WHILE JESUS AND HIS FOLLOWERS WERE TRAVELING, JESUS WENT INTO A TOWN. A WOMAN NAMED MARTHA LET JESUS STAY AT HER HOUSE." (LUKE 10:38 NCV)

Words are never wasted in God's Word, the Bible. Here is a good example of this. Packed in this one verse are volumes of teachings. As we start the text, we see Jesus traveling from town to town, preaching the life-changing news of His salvation. He enters the town of Bethany (John 11:1) where Martha lives. Immediately, we are told that she freely opens her home to Jesus. Martha's name means "lady or mistress" according to Nelson's Bible Dictionary. The word mistress according to Random House College Dictionary means, "a woman in authority, as over a household, an institution, or a servant. A woman who has the power of controlling or disposing of something." When I re-read the above verse, I got the feeling that Martha lived up to her name. Notice the verse says, "she let Jesus stay at her house." This residence was her house, and she made the decisions about her house. We don't read of a Mr. Martha in Scripture, but I get the impression that even if there were one, it was still her house. The Bible implies Martha was a woman of means. Few women in the Bible are described as having their own homes. If she was single, then it really says something, since widows and single women were usually poor unless they earned money in illicit ways. Martha was also a believer in Jesus, so much so that she opened her home to Him and His traveling companions. We know there were at least twelve hungry men (the twelve disciples) and possibly more. Again, this speaks of her wealth in being able to provide adequately for her guests. Jesus also loved Martha. The fact that He wanted to dine in her home said much about Him. Eating in someone's home in those days was considered a very intimate affair, since they did not use many eating utensils and most food was handled by hand. Attending a dinner in those days was thus a way of saying, "let us develop a closer relationship with each other." As she allowed Jesus into her home and into her life, this high-powered woman of God would learn the true meaning of servanthood.

MARTHA AND US: When my adopted grandson comes to our home, he always says, "This is grandma's house." My bossy attitude must be so overwhelming that a four-year-old kid can see it! (How pathetic on my part). Like Martha, I try to run my home.

GOD SPEAKS: "You are God's children whom he loves, so try to be like him. Live a life of love just as Christ loved us and gave himself for us as a sweet-smelling offering and sacrifice to God." (Ephesians 5:1-2 NCV) What kind of odor are you giving off? If I am not controlling your life, the odor is foul.

WANDA'S PRAYER: We do not know LORD; what we do know, however, is that we want to smell more like You. Father, take control.

September 2

I DON'T HAVE TIME TO SIT

"MARTHA HAD A SISTER NAMED MARY, WHO WAS SITTING AT JESUS' FEET AND LISTENING TO HIM TEACH." (LUKE 10:39 NCV)

I love how God's Word reads. In this verse, we are told Martha has a sister. We are also told the sister was sitting at Jesus' feet, literally inhaling His every word. (Writer's paraphrase) We are not told Martha is sitting, so we can rightly assume she is not just standing, but swiftly moving about the house. I picture Martha with a haggard look, hair flying all over her head, and sweat popping out of every pore, as she is running around the house preparing things. She is not at Jesus' feet, or even thinking about Jesus. All she can see is a sea of mouths to feed. Since it was her house, she was responsible to take care of all these people. All those eyes, with all those stomachs to feed, were looking at her, she thought. She does not have time to sit with Jesus—this girl's got a job to do! Now, what makes matters worse is that her sister is just sitting with Jesus and seems totally unaware of the needs of the people. This means she now has to do all of this work, all by herself. Yes, Martha is very much aware of who Jesus is—the Messiah, her LORD. Martha knows this is an opportunity of a lifetime. She, too, would like to spend time at His feet and listen to His every word, but someone has to feed all these people, and the lot has fallen on her. She has too much to do, and does not have time to sit and listen to the Master right now. Martha's attitude and behavior is a burn out waiting to happen. You might ask, "but, what is so wrong with working for the LORD? After all, someone has to do the work. If everybody just sat, how would the work get done? The "what is so wrong? …" in this picture is Martha's priorities are misplaced. Our first priority should always be to start and remain with Jesus because He alone is the power source. Martha has her eyes in the wrong place. She is looking at the things of this world, instead of focusing on the LORD.

MARTHA AND US: I can well relate to Martha's situation. I like to have people from church over to my house for dinner, as well. If I had a nickel for every time I pulled out my little twigs I call hair, I would be filthy rich by now.

GOD SPEAKS: "For in him we live and move and have our being… We are his offspring." (Acts 17:28 NIV) I want you to get this—In ME, you live; without Me, you die. In Me, you move. I control every organ in your little body. I wake you up every morning, and put you to sleep every night. Your very essence is in Me. You came from Me—I did not come from you. When you start with Me first, I supply everything else—you got that?

WANDA'S PRAYER: Yes, LORD, we got it! Keeping it, however, is the problem. We need to stay better connected to You Father.

September 3

DRIVEN TO DISTRACTION

"BUT MARTHA WAS DISTRACTED BY ALL THE PREPARATIONS THAT HAD TO BE MADE..." (LUKE 10:40 NIV)

Any woman who has ever had a party in their home can well relate to Martha's dilemma. The verse says, "Martha was distracted by all the preparations that had to be made." It was these preparations which had her focus, and not Jesus. But before we judge Martha too harshly, let us look at what she may have been dealing with. First, it is Jesus the Christ in her home. At this point in Jesus' life, He was a major celebrity. It would be like having Denzel Washington at my house. Let's say He has an entourage of twelve to fifteen men with Him. A good Jewish host in those days would first wash their guest's feet. So, she needed to be sure there was enough water and basins for that purpose. Not to mention the time it required doing the actual work. Plus, let us not forget before eating you had to do some sort of ceremonial washing. This would require more water, which had to be set up and performed, thus requiring more work. Whew! I am getting tired just thinking about all these chores. Anyway, and since it was Jesus, and not your husband Joe with a couple of his work buddies, you would want to serve something nice. How about a rack of Lamb, with aged cheese, bread, and something to drink? Now Sista' girl has to slave over a hot "stove" or "open pit"—something to get all of that meat cooked. Let us also not forget, she had to keep the food coming—the girl was feeding hungry men. I need a mental vacation after all the work Martha had to do. No wonder she was driven to distraction.

MARTHA AND US: This woman is a true sister of my soul. I am also one of those people who can get so bogged down into details that I lose sight of the bigger picture. I was that way about everything from housekeeping, work, politics; you name it. The result? I was always going off on some wild rabbit trail, and not really getting much done.

GOD SPEAKS: "In the beginning God created the heavens and the earth. Now the earth was formless and empty, darkness was over the surface of the deep, and the Spirit of God was hovering over the waters." (Genesis 1:1-2 NIV) Let Me school you on a few things about Me. First, I AM the BEGINNING. I start and finish everything. I AM GOD! Yours and Martha's life is a big gunk of formless glob without Me. I am in your midst "hovering"—just waiting for the chance to speak light, life, joy, and peace. As it was with Martha, I need you to also be still long enough for me to create My glory in you.

WANDA'S PRAYER: Father God, we so desperately need You to create in us a clean heart. We want a heart that continually pants to know Your will. We also need the strength to do it.

September 4

DRIVEN FROM DISTRACTION TO THE FEET OF JESUS

"… SHE CAME TO HIM (JESUS)…" (LUKE 10:40 NIV)

When I was a kid, I used to ride around town with my older sister a lot. This was a treat since most of my travels were on foot. Back then, her motto was that a quarter tank of gas could take you everywhere. So, she would put her $1.50 worth of gas into the tank and expect to travel cross-country. After riding on fumes for the first block, we would end up walking the next two miles or so to our destination or to a gas station. As I baked to a crisp from the sweltering heat, I would angrily think to myself, "Why didn't she just fill up the car before we started?" This was Martha's problem. She did not go to the "FILLING STATION" of GOD, and now she is running on fumes. The Spiritual oil well of heaven was in her house and she refused to "gas up" before starting her day. The poor woman's spiritual tank was on empty, but she was convinced she had enough to do a work for God. After running around all day like a chicken with its head cut off, she now tires and has come to Jesus. Everyone in this world will eventually end up at the foot of the Savior, Jesus Christ. The Word says that every knee will bow, and every tongue is going to confess that JESUS IS LORD, to the glory of the Father. (Philippians 2:10-11) Martha's sister was driven and knew the necessity of coming to sit at Jesus' feet first, before starting her day. Martha's car was a little slow, but her car of many distractions would inevitably bring her to the LORD, Jesus. Our LORD has a way of getting us to His Holy Service Station—one way or another. Some come sooner and some come later, but they will come.

MARTHA AND US: Unfortunately, most of my life I have been like Martha. I have had to be flat on my back before I ever looked up. I am ashamed it took such drastic measures for me to surrender to such a loving LORD. But I praise the LORD for those times, because at least He allowed me the chance to come to Him. He could have given up on me, but He did not. Thanks Dad!

GOD SPEAKS: "Give ear and come to me; listen, that you may live… Seek the LORD while he may be found; call on him while he is near. Let the wicked forsake their ways and the unrighteous their thoughts. Let them turn to the LORD, and he will have mercy on them, and to our God, for he will freely pardon." (Isaiah 55:3,6-7 NIV) Why are you running around in circles chasing the wind? Girl, just sit down at My feet and rest.

WANDA'S PRAYER: Lord, we do not really know. However, what we do know is we are now going to sit because we are exhausted!

September 5

OK LORD, I'VE GOT SOMETHING TO SAY

"... SHE CAME TO HIM AND ASKED, 'LORD, DON'T YOU CARE THAT MY SISTER HAS LEFT ME TO DO THE WORK BY MYSELF?...'" (LUKE 10:40 NIV)

Boy, this is a loaded question if ever I have read one. There are several ways to look at this question she poses to Jesus. One way is her question was an indirect statement, "LORD! You do not care that my sister is not helping me, and I have to do all this work all by myself." Another way to view Martha's words is she was tattling on her sister, "LORD, you may not know there is all this work to do; and I'm doing it all by myself—my sister is not helping." Either way, Martha's focus is on Martha. So, what is wrong with that? Isn't she doing a good thing, feeding the LORD, and those who came with Him? Why should she not get some help? Answer: It is not about Martha. From the time Jesus, the Creator of the Universe, stepped foot in Martha's home, she made it all about her. Martha had taken the focus off of the Savior of the world, Jesus Christ, to what good thing Martha can do for Jesus. Oh, I am sure her actions and purposes were well meaning, but she lost sight of the fact that it is all about Jesus, and not Martha. Jesus was the only One who could bring life, and that more abundantly. Perhaps she had forgotten or did not yet know that it was Jesus who fed five thousand with two fish and five barley loaves. In another instance, He fed four thousand. Both times He had lots of leftovers. If He could feed that many people, then could He not have fed the little crowd at Martha's place? The focus should have been on God in the flesh. He is at Martha's house wanting to impart to her His precious words of eternal life. Here was the Bread of Life in her home. He was serving an eternal meal, to give her eternal life, and she was upset because she could not get the temporal bread on the table — bread that would quickly pass away.

MARTHA AND US: In looking at Martha, I can see how I too am so focused on the here and now that I quickly forget I will soon pass away. My life is really just a puff of smoke.

GOD SPEAKS: "He rained down manna for the people to eat, he gave them the grain of heaven. Human beings ate the bread of angels; he sent them all the food they could eat. He let loose the east wind from the heavens and by his power made the south wind blow. He rained meat down on them like dust, birds like sand on the seashore. He made them come down inside their camp, all around their tents." (Psalm 78:24-28 NIV) Just look at Me and My awesome power. As you behold Me, you will realize you will always need Me. I am the One who came to save you—I do not need you to save Me.

WANDA'S PRAYER: Lord, forgive us for not keeping You as our main focus; help us keep our eyes always on You alone!

September 6

MARTHA'S MAD MELTDOWN

"LORD, …TELL HER TO HELP ME!" (LUKE 10:40 NIV)

We can see from this statement Martha makes to her LORD, that she is spiritually burned out and has hit her meltdown. Her burnout is because she has reached the point of holy frustration. I am glad you asked me to define that term. Holy frustrations are those uncomfortable situations our loving Father allows us to reach, or at times, places us in, to bring us to Himself. This is a part of His divine plan for our lives. But what good purposes could come from such a place of frustration you might ask? The holy frustration clearly reveals to us our inabilities to deal with the problems without God's help. We are then drawn to fall at the feet of Jesus and plead for His help. Martha is in holy frustration over the way things are going in her home. She is not just frustrated; she is mad. How do I know this? Her anger-madness is seen in the snippy words she uses to our LORD. Who in their right mind would turn and bark out instructions to the LORD and Creator? As a child, I lived with the threat of death if I even thought about talking back to my earthly parents, and here this woman is raising her voice to God! She is blessed to still have breath at all after that statement. Doesn't she know that with just a mere thought, He could in an instant end her earthly existence? She must be suffering from temporary insanity. Martha knows she needs help, and that is good; but she thinks the help should come from her sister, and not from her LORD. Insanity is looking in the face of omnipotent power, then turning to frail humanity for help.

MARTHA AND US: I am so glad the LORD loves His little insane ones, like me. I remember really liking this guy who cared absolutely nothing for me. My prayer at that time was, "LORD, if You could just make him love me." How stupid was that? Looking back on that experience, I realized that Holy, perfect Love was staring me in the face; and I was as blind as a bat, and could not see Him.

GOD SPEAKS: "With your (GOD'S) help I can advance against a troop; with my GOD I can scale a wall. As for God, his way is perfect: The Lord's word is flawless; he shields all who take refuge in him." (Psalm 18:29-30 NIV) I am the only true HELP. Know that My way is without flaws; it is perfect just like ME.

WANDA'S PRAYER: LORD, Your ways and acts are without fault. Help us store Your Word in our hearts continually, so that we live by You alone.

September 7

IT'S ALRIGHT BABY

"MARTHA, MARTHA," THE LORD ANSWERED, … (LUKE 10:41 NIV)

Just two carefully chosen words from Jesus are all that was needed for Martha. Ok, here comes another one of those "when I was a kid" stories. As a kid, one of my "aunts" (who were actually second cousins) would use the words, "it's alright baby." She was always so calm in her manner, no matter what problems came up. It did not matter how tragic the event, she always had the same words, "It's alright baby." This is the picture presented here by our LORD. He gently calms His baby girl down. I think she may have deserved a little pat on the lips to get her quiet if you asked me. (Of course, no one asked me though). But picture the scene if you can. Jesus is preaching to the crowd in the house. Martha is running helter-skelter throughout the home with sweat slinging and hair flying in a fruitless attempt to serve everyone at once. In her utter frustration, she bellows out jaw-dropping words to her LORD. At this point, I imagine you could hear a pin drop; even on a dirt floor. If I were her Lord, I would have been, at the very least, extremely disappointed with her, possibly even angry. (It shows you why I am not the LORD!) But our Father looks at His frustrated daughter with love and says, "Martha … Martha …" I can see Him putting those strong arms of love around her worn out body. I can almost hear the words, "Calm down, it is all right baby… just settle down now. I am right here with you." Jesus is Comforter (2 Corinthians 1:3); He demonstrates this fact in how He deals with the holy frustration of His daughter Martha. Those words to her must have been a cup of ice-cold water to her thirsty soul.

MARTHA AND US: I do not like to brag, but there is one skill I have mastered; in fact, in this art, I am working on my PhD. That art is getting in way over my head! It does not take me long to do it. I can dive out in rough waters and start drowning in a few seconds. Then, like Martha, in an oxygen deprived—brain dead state, I have the nerve to blame my LORD and bark out orders to Him as well. Thank God, literally, He just says, "I love you so much, My very silly child. Come to Me and let Me fix your wounds."

GOD SPEAKS: "The soothing tongue is a tree of life, but a perverse tongue crushes the spirit." (Proverbs 15:4 NIV) I AM the Tree of Life everlasting. Eat of Me, and not only will I heal your heart and mind, sometimes I will heal your body too!

WANDA'S PRAYER: Father, thank You for being the Great Healer; as well as a Comforter.

September 8

TOO STRESSED TO FEEL BLESSED

"... (MARTHA) YOU ARE WORRIED AND UPSET ABOUT MANY THINGS, ..."
(LUKE 10:41 NIV)

In this section of Scripture, Jesus is speaking to His "worried and upset" daughter. Let us recall again why Ms. Martha may be just a little stressed. Where shall we start? Martha has at least a dozen or more invited guests in her home. She is under a lot of pressure to serve them, feed them, and make them feel comfortable. Next, she has the social graces of her time to contend with, like washing the feet of the visitors, making sure they are provided with enough water for the ceremonial washing before a meal. Then, there is the cooking and serving of the food, and making sure the supply of the food does not run out. To top it all off, poor Martha has to do it all by herself. In her mind, she sees her sister just sitting there doing nothing! At this point Martha may think that perhaps her sister wants to be served too? At the height of the stress, she goes to Jesus to get him to make her sister help her (Luke 10:40). But look at how the Master (Jesus) handles Martha's problem. Martha thought her problem was Mary's laziness. She was not helping her, Martha said. (Luke 10:40) But Mary was not Martha's problem; Martha was Martha's problem. Jesus says to her, "You are worried, and you (Martha) are upset about many things." This statement to Martha seems to point out the obvious. But Jesus wants Martha to see herself, as He sees her. A fresh look at herself would cause her to rethink her situation. She could think, "Wait a minute; Ok LORD, I am very upset. My blood pressure is 1000/500 at this point. My neck veins are so distended that they are sitting on my shoulder. I have a two-ton headache right now, and a massive stroke is knocking at my door as I speak. But as I look at my sister, I see her sitting at Your feet, sucking up Your every word. She is completely calm without a care in the world. But my stress is about to put me 10-feet under". Then her response could have been, "LORD, I need some major help. You just fed five thousand; this little crowd is nothing for You.

MARTHA AND US: Looking at Martha has caused me to rethink many of my crazy prayers to the LORD. Crazy prayer #2110 goes something like this: "LORD, please let that check I wrote for those new shoes (I didn't need) get lost before it gets to the bank." Instead of praying before I go to the store, or reminding myself I cannot live in those shoes, so I should pay the rent first. Or, after I have sinned, confessing it to the Lord, and asking Him to take over, no matter the consequences. (They cannot be any worse than the ones I have made).

GOD SPEAKS: "Be careful, or your hearts will be weighed down with carousing, drunkenness and the anxieties of life, and that day will close on you suddenly like a trap." (Luke 21:34 NIV) You and Martha have allowed the world to entice you away from Me. Your focus on it has caused you to become scattered and wasteful. This causes you to be anxious and stressed.

WANDA'S PRAYER: Father God, give us eyes for You only. Take total control.

September 9

KEEP THE MAIN THING THE MAIN THING

"BUT (ONLY) ONE THING IS NEEDED, ..." (LUKE 10:42 NKJV)

Jesus packs a solid punch in His statement to Martha. He says to her, "Girl, you are worried about too much stuff! You have missed the main thing! You need only one thing—just one." He has to say this to her because Martha's got that "duh" look on her face at this point. All she can see is her huge "to-do" list. The girl is on another planet and completely unaware of what she really needs. Who she needs is Jesus! Omnipotent (Jesus) had walked out of Heaven, into her home, and was staring her in the face. She could touch God in human flesh, and she was totally oblivious to this. He was all she needed now and would ever need. Let us look at her possible needs list again, shall we? (1) Water and servants to help her wash the visitor's feet. This was not a problem for the God who spoke oceans into place. An ocean! Now, that ought to be enough water, huh? Oh, and what about those servants for foot washing? Not a problem. He made man from dust, and his wife from one of the man's bones; so people production is not a big thing to Him either. What about her need for plenty of food for the crowd in her home? Ok, didn't He give her fore parents bread from heaven and quail to go with it? Didn't He take two small fish and five little loaves and feed five thousand on one occasion, and four thousand on another, with food left to spare? He says He is "WONDERFUL, COUNSELOR, MIGHTY GOD, EVERLASTING FATHER, PRINCE OF PEACE. (Isaiah 9:6) Yep! All Martha needed was JESUS! He says to her and to us, "I'll give you everything you need and so much more." Had she taken the time to sit at His feet, she would have discovered what her needful things really were. Then, as with Adam when God showed her the need—He would meet it.

MARTHA AND US: Like Martha, I waste so much time chasing my tail—going around in circles, because I am not sitting at Jesus' feet. I know what to do; I just need to do it.

GOD SPEAKS: "One thing I ask from the LORD, this only do I seek: that I may dwell in the house of the LORD all the days of my life, to gaze on the beauty of the LORD and to seek him in his temple. For in the day of trouble he will keep me safe in his dwelling; he will hide me in the shelter of his sacred tent and set me high upon a rock." (Psalm 27:4-5 NIV) Just ask Me to give you a desire to seek Me; I will not only give you the desire, but everything else that goes with it.

WANDA'S PRAYER: Yes LORD! Give us a desire to seek You every moment of every day.

September 10

MARTHA, THERE'S A BETTER WAY

"MARY HAS CHOSEN WHAT IS BETTER ..." (LUKE 10:42 NIV)

I like how our LORD is so gentle in dealing with Martha. Notice He says Mary has chosen what is better. There is a saying that is so very true, "We make choices and choices make us." Mary made a deliberate choice to sit at Jesus' feet. Martha made a deliberate choice "not" to sit at the feet of Jesus. I know for all the huffing and puffing she does in Luke 10:40, one could lose sight of that fact. She puts on the "poor me" act and implies she is forced to feed all these people, all by herself. The truth is, she allowed the earthly (providing for people—a good thing) to overshadow the heavenly (spending time with God incarnate—a great thing). Martha is looking at Jesus' presence in her home, as a social gathering and nothing more. Starting out with this mindset, she ends up in burnout. While it is true, our LORD Jesus enjoys social gatherings, He never loses sight, however, of His primary focus of every occasion—to seek and save lost souls. He uses everything at His disposal to accomplish this purpose. Martha's wanting to attend to human needs is a good thing. Work is good, for "... if a man does not work, he should not eat." (2 Thessalonians 3:10) But sitting at the feet of Jesus and consuming His life saving words, is the absolute best and better thing. Jesus' words to Martha to choose the better thing, speaks to us all. The primary thing in life is becoming filled with Jesus—the Son of God. Nothing should come before this. Jesus gently clarified something else to her. He was telling her He was her LORD, and should be worshipped as such. As her LORD, He was to have the highest seat of honor in her life. He is also telling Martha that He was her true satisfaction.

MARTHA AND US: How I relate to Ms. Martha! I too, often drown myself in the sea of "busyness" for my LORD. I have to remember He has prepared the meal and set the table. He is just waiting for me to come and eat. Then, after having gotten a good spiritual breakfast, I now have much energy to complete the tasks He has given me for the day.

GOD SPEAKS: "The poor will eat and be satisfied; Those who seek the Lord will praise him—may your hearts live forever!" (Psalm 22:26 NIV) Without Me, you are poor and needy—but that is a wonderful thing! I can, and will, satisfy you with Myself. As you consume Me, you will see that I alone will fill you. The outflow of a filled heart is praise.

WANDA'S PRAYER: Lord, today as we sit before You, fill us with You; stuff us to the gills! You alone are the only one who can complete us.

September 11

MARTHA, YOU CAN REFUSE YOUR MEAL BUT I'M NOT TAKING HERS

"… AND IT WILL NOT BE TAKEN FROM HER." (LUKE 10:42 NIV)

The question I ask myself is, what is this "it" that will not be taken from her (Mary)? Why is this "it" so very valuable that even our LORD Jesus Christ would not pry it out of her hands? More importantly, why didn't Martha seek or want this most important "it"? The "it" is actually a "Who" and the "Who" is Jesus, the Spotless Son of God. Mary craved to be in the presence of Jesus like a drowning man gasps for air. Her very heartbeat was for her LORD Jesus, and she sought every opportunity to be near Him. While Martha had a love for Jesus, her true passion was in performing human acts of care and compassion. Her noble task of caring for others, and not putting our LORD Jesus first, left her soul dry and empty. She was starving spiritually because she had not eaten from the banquet table of our LORD Jesus. Meanwhile, her sister Mary sat at our LORD'S feet devouring His every word and became fat in Him. Jesus, fully aware of Martha's hungry soul, turns to His spiritually emaciated daughter to confirm this fact to her. This is what I see Jesus saying to Martha, "My child, your sister Mary, is feasting on the true food and is full. She has chosen to hook up with Me, the true source of life. From this source, I will never disconnect her." The implication to Martha is; "If you want the true connection, it is yours. If not, that's your choice, too."

MARTHA AND US: I relate so well to Martha in this passage. Many times, in much of my well doing, I become so tired, drained, and empty. This hollow space is not filled by, nor even by doing, "things of God." My soul cries out, "LORD, I need a filling and right away."

GOD SPEAKS: "Let them give thanks to the Lord for his unfailing love and his wonderful deeds for mankind, for he satisfies the thirsty and fills the hungry with good things." (Psalm 107:8-9 NIV) Look at that verse and see what I am saying to you. It says, you are to thank Me because My love never ends—it never stops. It keeps going and going and going. Since My love is ever ongoing, My wonderful deeds flow out to you and My other creatures. I alone can satisfy your thirsty soul because I placed the thirst in you. This spiritual thirst and hunger of yours is like a locked door and I have the only key. I will satisfy you with good things because I am good! Drink and eat of Me, My word, the Bible, and prayer with praise, and you will never be hungry; but you will want more. I am the endless supply to meet your every need.

WANDA'S PRAYER: Father God, our Savior, as we empty ourselves of self, fill us with Your presence by way of your Holy Spirit. We want to drink and eat of You, moment by moment. Remind us during those times when we feel hollow and lonely, that it is because we have not stopped to dine with You. After eating at Your table in the morning, remind us to come back for snacks during the day.

September 12

STANDING STILL

"NOW A MAN NAMED LAZARUS WAS SICK. HE WAS FROM BETHANY, THE VILLAGE OF MARTHA AND HER SISTER MARY." (JOHN 11:1 NIV)

Let us look at this verse through Martha's eyes. Martha was a committed follower of Jesus. She loved Him and supported His ministry. (Luke 10:38-42; John 11:2-5; 12:1-3) The ill man, Lazarus, in this verse, was not just some man living in Bethany; he was Martha's own brother. (John 11:2) She watched helplessly as her beloved brother's fragile life slipped away before her very eyes. She must have experienced extreme frustration and pain over her powerlessness to do anything about his critical illness. The word "sick" in this verse suggests that Lazarus' illness was harsh and crippling. Sickness, like an unwanted guest, was living comfortably in her home and she did not have the power to evict him. All she could do was to just stand helplessly by and watch as this sickness ravaged her poor brother. I do not know which is the hardest; being very ill, or having to watch the malady slowly eat away the life out of the one you love. About now, questions like "why me?" could have entered her mind. Or how could this be happening to our family? Do we not, as a family, love and serve the Jesus that calmed seas with a word, and fed thousands with just a few fish and pieces of bread? Surely, would not Jesus keep those He loved from sickness and disease? The answer is He can, but sometimes in His Sovereignty, He chooses not to. We must never forget we live in a world totally consumed by sin and its evil effects. Therefore, disease and sickness are to be expected. The old songwriter put it best when she said, "Into every life some rain must fall." Martha was having her downpour at this moment.

MARTHA AND US: As I write this, I recall the sudden, unexplained illness and death of my oldest sister. The afternoon prior to her death, she laughed and chided with me over the phone from her hospital bed. We looked forward to seeing each other at our first family reunion. Early the next morning, I received a call from one of my brothers of her very untimely, sudden death. I am still stunned to this day. Father, please speak to my confused and shattered heart on this matter.

GOD SPEAKS: "When you pass through the waters, I will be with you; and when you pass through the rivers, they will not sweep over you. When you walk through the fire, you will not be burned (consumed); the flames will not set you ablaze. For I am the LORD your God, the Holy One of Israel, your Savior; …" (Isaiah 43:2-3 NIV) You and Martha need to know that life on this planet of sin is just a vapor, a brief span of time to eternity. As My child, I will take you through raging waters. I will take you through torrent rivers and I will take you through blistering heat. In the midst of all the trials, struggles, heartaches, and pain, I am with you. I will love you through it all. I speak these words of comfort to you in your confused, shattered state. "Be still and know (be absolutely certain) that I AM GOD." (Psalm 46:10)

WANDA'S PRAYER: WOW! I am silenced.

September 13

IT'S ALL YOURS AND YOU CAN HAVE IT

"SO THE SISTERS SENT WORD TO JESUS, 'LORD, THE ONE YOU LOVE IS SICK.'"
(JOHN 11:3 NIV)

Volumes have been preached and written about this one text of Scripture, and I am going to write one more—just kidding. But what is true of this text speaks volumes to us. Let us look back at verse two for a moment. This verse tells us these women had a very personal relationship with their LORD, Jesus. (Take a moment to read the verse for yourself—I'll wait.) Now that you've read it, you'll see that because of their intimate friendship with their Master, Jesus, these women felt very comfortable going to Him without hesitation. Notice they went to Jesus first—not last. Also, notice the complete confidence and boldness of these women. They "sent word…" You can do this when you are "in the know." The word which was sent says, "the one You love is sick." Now this is bold confidence. They were completely certain of Jesus' love for their brother. Actually, this statement indirectly says the women were certain also of Jesus' love for them too! How else could they have been so bold as to approach the Creator of the Universe as they did? I am left with the question, "how confident am I in my relationship with the LORD Jesus?" Can I too come boldly to His throne for help, knowing with total certainty that He loves me, and that I will receive help in my time of need?

MARTHA AND US: Martha hits this one out of the park. She has problems beyond her, and without hesitation, she knows just what to do with this overwhelming circumstance. It has taken me years to learn this simple truth.

GOD SPEAKS: "Cast all your anxiety on him because he cares for you." (1 Peter 5:7 NIV) Take all of your problems, anxieties—every issue you have, and know I care for you. Then, just rest in Me.

WANDA'S PRAYER: LORD, we give You everything—kids, man, job, house; what else? Sickness, pain, heartaches, presidential election, etc., Father take it all! Now LORD, please teach us to just leave it there with You—it is YOURS!

September 14

IN ALL YOUR GETTING, GET GOD'S PERSPECTIVE

"WHEN HE HEARD THIS, JESUS SAID, 'THIS SICKNESS WILL NOT END IN DEATH. NO, IT IS FOR GOD'S GLORY SO THAT GOD'S SON MAY BE GLORIFIED THROUGH IT.'" (JOHN 11:4 NIV)

This is a refreshing verse amidst a very gloomy circumstance. Lazarus is sick to the point of death. The sisters have sent word to our LORD about the sickness, and are no doubt waiting on His rapid response. Our LORD, Jesus, does respond, but He does it from a Divine point of view. He sends word that this sickness will not end in death, but will give the Godhead glory. Jesus, who is God, in the flesh, sees Lazarus' illness not as a grave infirmity, but as a wonderful opportunity to display His matchless glory. He alone knows this single event will establish Him as God in the minds of not only the Jews, but the entire world. This verse speaks to us in our day as well. The One who hushed storms into silence, and fed five thousand with a few fish, is about to show us He is truly God. What does this say to you and me? It says all of our problems, pains, and distresses are not life ending tragedies, but are life-changing opportunities in the hands of Master Jesus.

MARTHA AND US: Martha did not yet know Jesus' thoughts concerning her brother's illness, but I do. Knowing this speaks peace and security to my soul. Just like Martha, my momentary hurts and pain are not the end of my existence. Nor am I condemned to a perpetual life of misery. I can take my problems to my loving LORD Jesus and leave them at His feet. I can walk away knowing with absolute assurance they (the hurts and heartache of life) will be used for my good and His glory.

GOD SPEAKS: "For I know the plans I have for you," declares the LORD, "plans to prosper you and not to harm you, plans to give you hope and a future. Then you will call on me and come and pray to me, and I will listen to you." (Jeremiah 29:11-12 NIV) Notice these verses are written to a people in captivity. I know their adversity and pain, and yet, because I alone know and have determined their future, I can and will bless them. I want to do the same for you. I did not promise you would be problem free; but I have promised to see you through all of them. Will you trust Me and hold on to My hand?

WANDA'S PRAYER: Yes, LORD! Help us to always hold on to Your strong, unchanging hands. Hold us close, and never let go.

September 15

MARTHA, DON'T FORGET WHAT YA' KNOW

"NOW JESUS LOVED MARTHA AND HER SISTER AND LAZARUS. SO WHEN HE HEARD THAT LAZARUS WAS SICK, HE STAYED WHERE HE WAS TWO MORE DAYS,"
(JOHN 11:5-6 NIV)

On the surface, the above text does not appear to make much sense. The first part of the verse tells us how much Jesus, the King of the Universe who has all power, truly loved this family. Yet, the next part of this verse says, He waited two more days after having received word of Lazarus' debilitating illness. (Please explain this to my mind.) I imagine Martha, not having privy to Jesus' thoughts or plans, must have been an emotional wreck, as death hovered like a dark cloud over her brother. Where is her LORD in her hour of deep agony? Millions of questions must have raced through her mind. "Where is He? Didn't He get the urgent message? Does He know how sick my brother is? Does He care? And why… is He taking so… long?" I am sure all of these questions and many more must have flooded her thoughts, drowning her in bitter despair. Is Jesus not aware of Martha's distress? The answer is yes; He is very much aware. We must remember God is Infinite and Eternal. So His decisions are based on eternal effects, and not necessarily temporal ones. His thoughts, ways and actions fill galaxies. Our meaningful thoughts may fill half a page on one sheet of paper. His ways are past finding out. We are pretty shallow. Poor Martha has poured out her soul to the Master and God of the Universe. Yet, it would seem as though He has closed the windows and doors to her prayers. And He is not responding to phone calls or emails either. So, what should she do? Should she lose faith and lose heart? No! Martha must hold on to what she knows. She knows without a doubt, her LORD loves her and her family. She knows He has her best interest at hand, despite what she may see or feel. Martha needs to do the challenging thing at this point—she must wrap herself in His complete love, and trust that her LORD has everything under control. She must believe, despite her emotions, that His decisions for her life are for her good and His glory. She can rest in perfect peace, having left the outcome in His loving, capable hands.

MARTHA AND US: Martha's dilemmas of faith are mine. A little over a month prior to the time of this writing, my sister entered the hospital for chest pain and never came out. Since that time, it has plagued my mind with the "whys" and "how comes." Father, speak a word to my heart.

GOD SPEAKS: "But the eyes of the LORD are on those who fear him, on those whose hope is in his unfailing love, to deliver them from death and keep them alive in famine." (Psalm 33:18-19 NIV) Hold on to My love for you, with a vise grip—a love that will never fail. I am bringing you through. You may hurt for a while, but don't let go.

WANDA'S PRAYER: Father God, we need You to hold us and carry us through.

September 16

IN THE COMPANY OF FRIENDS

"ON HIS ARRIVAL, JESUS FOUND THAT LAZARUS HAD ALREADY BEEN IN THE TOMB FOR FOUR DAYS. NOW BETHANY WAS LESS THAN TWO MILES FROM JERUSALEM, AND MANY JEWS HAD COME TO MARTHA AND MARY TO COMFORT THEM IN THE LOSS OF THEIR BROTHER." (JOHN 11:17-19 NIV)

The days just before my sister's funeral, many people were in and out of their home. The place was so packed at one point, there was barely standing room. People were everywhere. Here is the scene pictured in this very verse. In reading, we can see this family is loved very much. Lazarus, Martha, and Mary were "good people," and their community came out in droves to support them. Martha was known for opening up her home and heart, to serve her community. Now, in her time of need, she was receiving love and support in return. It is nice and comforting to know that when tragedy hits, we do not have to face it alone. Bible scholars tell us that in those days, there were hired mourners to grieve for the departed. There may have been some of those in this crowd, but most of the guests came to comfort these dear sisters. Lazarus had been dead for four days; yet the comfort given to the sisters remained. This crowd of friends and family were dedicated to caring for these two sisters for days to come.

MARTHA AND US: My daughter traveled to Michigan to attend the funeral. She was of great comfort to me during this time. When I returned home, a loving husband and son were there to meet me, and provide even more comfort in my time of grief. There were also more friends, family, and co-workers who provided great comfort. The most comfort I received, however, was from my LORD. As I write, I realize I also must comfort others, as I have received it.

GOD SPEAKS: "The LORD will surely comfort Zion and will look with compassion on all her ruins; he will make her deserts like Eden, her wastelands like the garden of the LORD. Joy and gladness will be found in her, thanksgiving and the sound of singing." (Isaiah 51:3 NIV) I am the "God of all comfort." I will give you inner peace and comfort with Myself in this life; and I will give eternal rest, peace, and joy in the one to come. Hold on to My words and never let them go.

WANDA'S PRAYER: Father, thank You for being our God of comfort, peace, rest, joy and so much more—in this life and throughout eternity!

September 17

JESUS, AREN'T YOU JUST A LITTLE LATE?

"WHEN MARTHA HEARD THAT JESUS WAS COMING, SHE WENT OUT TO MEET HIM, BUT MARY STAYED AT HOME. 'LORD,' MARTHA SAID TO JESUS, 'IF YOU HAD BEEN HERE, MY BROTHER WOULD NOT HAVE DIED.'" (JOHN 11:20-21 NIV)

When I read this text, I laughed because I recalled the movie, "The Color Purple." There is a scene in the movie where Oprah Winfrey marches to what seems like miles, through tall grassy fields to boldly confront her mother-in-law with sharp, harsh words. This is how I picture Martha's confrontation with Jesus, as she learns He has come to town four days after her brother has died. With arms swinging, "she went out to meet Him." I picture her with either arms crossed or hands on her hips and head bobbing. I hear her heart saying as she speaks, "LORD, what took you so long? It's too late now." Before we get angry with sister Martha, I think we can all sympathize with her plight. We know God loves us. We know He has all-power to fix the broken stuff in our lives and He just does not. Then to top it all off, He shows up late—or does He? Here in this story, our LORD Jesus teaches us a great lesson. John 11:4 says, "Jesus said, 'this sickness will not end in death. No, it is for God's glory so that God's Son may be glorified through it.'" So, we find in the next couple of verses, Jesus makes a deliberate decision to wait. (John 11:6) Then later He says, "Then after he had said this, he went on to tell them, 'Our friend Lazarus has fallen asleep; but I am going there to wake him up.'" (John 11:11) We see in these verses God's plans and God's power. God's plans are for His glory and always will ultimately result in our good. Our circumstances do not stop, nor do they hinder God's power! Whether four days, or four hundred days—neither are an obstacle to Jesus. Because He knows what He is going to do, He quietly listens to His stressed-out daughters' complaints.

MARTHA AND US: I continue smiling because I am made more aware of how much my LORD loves me. He wants me, like Martha, to come to Him for everything. He does not even mind my whining.

GOD SPEAKS: "Answer me when I call to you, my righteous God. Give me relief from my distress; have mercy on me and hear my prayer." (Psalm 4:1 NIV) "I call out to the LORD, and he answers me from his holy mountain." (Psalm 3:4 NIV) I want you to come to Me in any and every way—just come! Come with praises of joy and with the deep-felt agony of your soul. I just want you to come to Me with all you have. I am waiting for you.

WANDA'S PRAYER: Lord, we come rushing to You—just as we are!

September 18

A CHANGE OF HEART

"BUT I KNOW THAT EVEN NOW GOD WILL GIVE YOU WHATEVER YOU ASK." JESUS SAID TO HER, 'YOUR BROTHER WILL RISE AGAIN.'" (JOHN 11:22-23 NIV)

Martha's last comment before Jesus speaks is interesting. She starts out chiding her LORD for tardiness and ends up humbled and broken. At this point in her discourse with Jesus, she is pleading for just a morsel of a miracle of some kind. It is almost as if she is saying, "LORD, just ask Father God to do a miracle or something—He'll do whatever You ask Him to." (Writer's paraphrase) She realizes what we all must realize—that Jesus alone is in charge of everything, including life and eternity. Jesus takes control of this situation and says to her. "Your brother will rise again." In other words, "Martha, this is only a temporary separation—it's not permanent—not at all!" He answers her prayer according to His perfect will and her unspoken desire. Martha teaches me I can come to Jesus just as I am, but He will not leave me as I came. Martha came to Jesus with an anguished heart and bitterness of soul. She left with a humble heart and a broken spirit. Humility and brokenness He does not despise; in fact, it is the kind of heart He loves. It is also the kind of heart He responds to. Our LORD Jesus tells His grieving daughter the wonderful news she had so longed to hear: "Your brother will rise again." Death for the child of God—the one who has made the LORD Jesus their Savior is not the end. Death is the beginning. We will rise from the grave to everlasting life again. Isn't that great news?

MARTHA AND US: I am very comforted and at peace in that while my sister was alive, she made Jesus Christ, her LORD and Savior. Her spirit is with the LORD, and I will see her again. This is wonderful news!

GOD SPEAKS: "If you, then, though you are evil, know how to give good gifts to your children, how much more will your Father in heaven give good gifts to those who ask him!" (Matthew 7:11 NIV) The question to ask is, "Am I not the God of Supreme Love?" Since I am, then you can completely trust in My Love. You can know beyond any doubt that what I allow or hold back from you is for your best, because I only give the best. There will be times when you do not understand what I am doing. In those times, just rely on My loving, caring heart.

WANDA'S PRAYER: Lord, we are going to do just that—rely on Your big old loving heart!

September 19

THANKS FOR ANSWERING MY PRAYER LORD, BUT THAT'S OK

"MARTHA ANSWERED, 'I KNOW HE WILL RISE AGAIN IN THE RESURRECTION AT THE LAST DAY.'"
(JOHN 11:24 NIV)

When I read Martha's response to Jesus telling her that her brother will rise again, I had to chuckle. I do not laugh because there is anything "ha-ha" funny about it, but because her statement is so similar to what I would say if I were in her shoes. Martha's response to Jesus telling her she would see her brother again reminds me of a commercial I loved watching several years ago. It was about a woman who went into the bank to get a loan. Before the loan officer could say one word, the frustrated woman quickly interrupted him. She quickly and convincingly talked herself out of getting the loan. After thoroughly convincing herself she does not qualify, she gets up and "mousey" walks out of the bank, leaving the loan officer speechless. Martha does the same thing. In the previous verse, she pleads with Jesus to ask God to intervene in her brother's death, "But I know that even now God will give You whatever You ask." Now here in the next breath she says, "Naw, I won't see my brother again until resurrection day." To Martha's credit, her interpretation of this statement was correct. In John 6:39, Jesus says He will resurrect the dead on the last day. So, her seeming contradiction of statements is possibly because of her remembering this statement, as well as the grief and shock of her brother's quick death. Though she may have wanted a quick resurrection, she would rely on His previous words of last day resurrection. (John 6:39) To His words, "Your brother will rise," she brushed off the immediate answer she desperately wanted, and she responds, "I know LORD, it's going to work out in the end." (Writer's paraphrase) She does not make the faith stretch—meaning she does not reach out to grasp the Master's words at face value, nor does she seek further clarification of what He means. She just assumes His meaning and responds in kind. Jesus is about to do a wonderful work. He wants to reveal this work to her, but she cannot see the supernatural, because she was only focused on the natural.

MARTHA AND US: I am so much like Martha; I do not make the faith stretch to just believe what my LORD Jesus is saying. Therefore, I like Martha, miss the true and immediate blessing my LORD has in store for me.

GOD SPEAKS: "Jesus heard that they had thrown him out, and when he found him, he said, 'Do you believe in the Son of Man?'" (John 9:35 NIV) I ask you, "Do you believe that I, Jesus Christ, exist? Am I your LORD?" If your answer is "yes," then put "feet" to your faith. Take up my Word, the Bible, and follow me.

WANDA'S PRAYER: "… 'Lord, I believe…'" (John 9:38 NIV) Now teach us to worship You in how we live. We want to worship You, as Your Word says.

September 20

MIND EXPANSION (PART 1)

"JESUS SAID TO HER, 'I AM THE RESURRECTION AND THE LIFE'"... (JOHN 11:25 NIV)

Here, so magnificently displayed before our eyes, is the patience and gentleness of our LORD and Heavenly Dad. He scolds His daughter's unbelief. He tenderly peels back the layers of her understanding with His words. The first thing she needs to understand is that HE IS RESURRECTION AND HE IS LIFE. What does this mean to her and to us? The words, "I AM," denote our LORD Jesus as the Self-Existing One; who is everything we need Him to be. She needed a "rising" or "standing up" of her brother from the dead. Jesus was telling her and us, He was the ONE! Only He alone brings life back from the dead, and Martha's brother needed life. Jesus looks His distraught daughter in the face, and with Godly compassions says to her, "I AM LIFE." So, putting the two together, He says to the one He loves, "My daughter, I AM the 'Riser' from the dead, and I AM the 'life,' your dead brother and your dead soul need. I AM the complete package all rolled into one." (Writer's paraphrase) This earth-shattering statement of our LORD is a difficult statement to grasp—then and now. It says that everything I need for life and eternity is in JESUS! This is a mind expander, is it not?

MARTHA AND US: Just chewing on this thought alone is enough to blow my mind—He is simply everything, and everything means everything! He is the source and substance; sustainer and maintainer of my life. He gives my old body of sin (which must die), His pure spotless life when I give it to Him.

GOD SPEAKS: "In the beginning was the Word, and the Word was with God, and the Word was God. Through him all things were made; without him nothing was made that has been made. In him was life, and that life was the light of all mankind (me)." (John 1:1,3-4 NIV) I, your LORD, made everything. I AM the source of life and the true light. I AM everything you need now, and I AM everything you will ever need. You can bring all of you and lay yourself at My feet and rest.

WANDA'S PRAYER: Whew! Thank You Father. We can take the shackles off and drop the heavy load at Your feet—it is Yours!

September 21

MIND EXPANSION (PART 2)

"... THE ONE WHO BELIEVES IN ME WILL LIVE, EVEN THOUGH THEY DIE;"
(JOHN 11:25 NIV)

I imagine when Jesus announced to Martha that He was the "Stander Upper" from the dead (The Resurrection), the Life, and the source of life, her eyes must have rolled around in her head, or her mouth may have flown open. At the very least, she must have had that "Da" look on her face. The reason I say this is that He continues to make His meaning clearer to her, and to us. He says to her, "If anyone who believes that I AM GOD (believing in Me to be whatever you need), you will LIVE. No matter what dead state a person finds himself in—physically, spiritually, or emotionally, they will live BECAUSE Jesus says, I AM LIFE! This is great news in every way. It was great for Martha, because she did not have to wait until all the dead would be resurrected or brought back to life. Sista' girl would see her brother—now! It is great news for us because we do not have to wait for a future event to experience true life in Jesus. We can have "every spiritual blessing in Christ" now! (Ephesians 1:3). Peace, joy, true love, and contentment are ours now—in abundance, no matter our surroundings. He is the LIFE that lives within our hearts. This is the life our LORD wants us to live. To Martha, He says I am going to bring your brother back, disease free, now. To us, He says I can resurrect your spirit, sin free, because I have washed your sins away with My precious blood. It is great to know that death is no hindrance to our LORD. He can work with death to bring new life, and He can work despite death, to accomplish His divine purposes.

MARTHA AND US: I also struggle to understand the greatness of my LORD. Many times, He has to explain, remind, and rehearse things over and over again with me in my mind. I am just so glad He does. Thanks Dad, for Your wondrous gifts to me; and even more, for Your long suffering and patience in dealing with me.

GOD SPEAKS: "This day I call the heavens and the earth as witnesses against you that I have set before you life and death, blessings and curses. Now choose life, so that you and your children may live and that you may love the LORD your God, listen to his voice, and hold fast to him. For the LORD is your life, and he will give you many years in the land…" (Deuteronomy 30:19-20 NIV) My promises to you are eternal life in Me. I will give you every spiritual gift in Christ, as you hold fast to My words. Read My Word daily; meditate on them throughout the day. They will keep you on the path I have set for you. Then one day soon, I will take you to be with Me forever.

WANDA'S PRAYER: LORD, keep us close to You always.

September 22

MIND EXPANSION (PART 3)

"AND WHOEVER LIVES AND BELIEVES IN ME SHALL NEVER DIE ..."
(JOHN 11:26 NKJV)

This is wonderful how our LORD uses His discourse with Martha to bring the gospel to the world. The invitation of eternal life is given to all. Jesus excludes no one when He says, "Whoever lives and believes in Me shall never die." (John 11:26) But what do these simple words mean? They mean exactly what the verse says it means, which is: the sum of my total existence—my ever-beating heart, every effortless breath I take, every slight movement of my joints, and everything else that makes up who I am (me), is in Christ Jesus, my LORD. When I throw the full weight of everything I am onto Him (which is my belief in Him), I have access to this "LIFE." In doing this, I shall never die. My body may sleep in the earth's dust (1 Thessalonians 4:16-17 and John 11:11-13); but I am never separated from my LORD. Death or separation from Him is never an option, for those who live in and for Him—those whose complete substance is held meshed together in Him! This is the gospel in a nutshell. He says to Martha (and to us), "Without Me, you are dead and lifeless; but for you who live and believe in Me, I AM forever life." Putting the entire statement of Jesus together, it reads like this to me: "Martha, your brother is dead and gone, but do not worry, my daughter. I AM (the whatever you need Me to be), the ONE who can bring your brother back to life. I AM here, I AM now, and I AM life! Life started from Me—I gave life its existence. Martha, all I need you to do is to put all of who you are onto Me. Then simply walk like it, rest in it, and believe in My words. If you do this, not only will I raise your brother back to life, but I will give eternity to your grieving, dead spirit life as well. Then one day I will give eternity to all of you who have believed in Me." (Writer's paraphrase)

MARTHA AND US: The implication here is so very clear. Life and eternity are ours for the believing. We must accept His words as fact and allow Him to always live in us. It is Him in us forever, which gives us forever life, because He is forever.

GOD SPEAKS: "Most assuredly, I say to you, he who believes in Me has everlasting life. I am the bread of life. This is the bread which comes down from heaven, that one may eat of it and not die." (John 6:47-48,50 NKJV) Believe that I AM, who I say I AM. Consume this thought completely. Take this thought and eat of it daily, hourly—when and wherever you need it. I in you, living and abiding, equals living forever.

WANDA'S PRAYER: Father, may this be our focus forever. Totally consume us, as we place all that we are in Your hands.

September 23

THE BALL IS IN YOUR COURT—SISTER

"… DO YOU BELIEVE THIS?" 'YES, LORD,' SHE REPLIED, 'I BELIEVE THAT YOU ARE THE MESSIAH, THE SON OF GOD, WHO IS TO COME INTO THE WORLD.'"
(JOHN 11:26-27 NIV)

For so long, I read this text in error. I mistakenly thought Martha had missed the mark and did not understand what Jesus was saying. She did not. What she (nor I) could not understand was the full magnitude of what all Jesus our Savior meant by His statements. We will all spend an eternity searching out the depth to the meaning of His words regarding having eternal life in Him. Having heard Jesus' words about who He was and what His mission was, the ball was now in Martha's court. She could accept His words at face value and live her life as His child, or she could reject His statements as utter nonsense. This is the same choice each of us has today. This is the same choice each person on the planet has ever had—to choose life (the Eternal God as seen in the face of Jesus), or to choose eternal separation and hell. The choice is clear, and Martha made the right choice. She says, "I believe that You are the Messiah, the Son of God, who is to come into the world." She is saying, I believe (I know) that You are God in the flesh. Martha makes a choice we too must make. Someone once said that Christ is LORD of ALL, or LORD of none. The question we must ask ourselves is which is He to me? I demonstrate my answer not just in what I say, but more so in how I live.

MARTHA AND US: Over twenty-five years ago, I gave my heart to Jesus. Since then, there have been many times I sinned, and not represented my Father and LORD, as I should have. Twenty-five years later, I still only slightly understand the concept of believing in Him and living, as I say I believe. Living in Christ, or rather, allowing Him to fully live in and through me, is freeing and peaceful. The battles become His. He gets the victory, and He gets the glory. The problem I have is remaining in His Word, spending time in prayer—daily suiting up in His armor. My defeats come when I do not do these things.

GOD SPEAKS: "For we are God's handiwork, created in Christ Jesus to do good works, which God prepared in advance for us to do." (Ephesians 2:10 NIV) "for it is God who works in you to will and to act in order to fulfill his good purpose." (Philippians 2:13 NIV) Sit down and get out of the way; just let ME do what I do best—everything good.

WANDA'S PRAYER: Ok LORD, we are sitting, and we are still—do Your thing, which is everything good.

September 24

THE GIGANTIC LIE: GOD DOESN'T HURT WHEN YOU HURT

"JESUS WEPT." (JOHN 11:35 NIV)

The shortest verse in the Bible speaks much about our LORD. Though He was 100% God, He was also 100% human. This math does not work on anyone else but Jesus. As a human, He was moved with compassion and feelings, just as I am. As the All-Knowing LORD of Creation, He knew and felt the hurts and pains so much more. The word for our LORD'S weeping is "Dak-roo'-o." In the Greek it means to weep silently. Our Dad and LORD suffer in silence at times for His children. He does not make a fanfare or a spectacle of Himself. He does not make a show or a joke of our circumstances, but He hurts, nevertheless. But why does He who holds time and eternity in His hands hurt? Because He alone knows by experience, the deep agony sin has brought upon this planet. He who created us, to be forever with Him, knows the searing of death's powerful sting. He loves us so much that He gave our parents the power to choose. They chose self, and with this choice came sin and death. The choice of self has caused pain and heartache since the death of Abel by Cain (Genesis 4). These silent tears did not go unnoticed by Martha and the crowd, who see the tears well up in the eyes of her LORD. They know too, that He hurts for her and for Himself. He feels her pain and grief, and as a man He feels His own. Remember, Lazarus was a friend He truly loved. (John 11:5) Yes, He is about to fix the problem. His tears show us very clearly there is a problem to be fixed. The immediate problem is the death of Lazarus, and He is the solution. The long-term problem is sin, and He is also the solution to it as well.

MARTHA AND US: This verse is so comforting to me. I see He cried with me over my hurts and pain. He cried because of the pain He had to allow me to go through. Yes, my pain grew me up, but what a painful growth it was. He felt everything I felt. I know if there were another way to spare me, He would have done so. How do I know? I just have to look at His nail-scarred hands and the piercing of His side.

GOD SPEAKS: "Those who sow with tears will reap with songs of joy. Those who go out weeping, carrying seed to sow, will return with songs of joy, carrying sheaves with them." (Psalm 126:5-6 NIV) Allow Me to make the pile of rocks and dried earth of pain, into a harvest of joy for My glory. This field will not only bless you, but will bless those around you as well. During the cutting away and tough pruning, I will be with you. I need you to stay with Me.

WANDA'S PRAYER: We are Yours Oh LORD! You can cut, pull, and prune whatever You need to. Remind us, when we are crying out in pain, that You are crying too.

September 25

JUST TAKE A STEP MARTHA

"JESUS, ONCE MORE DEEPLY MOVED, CAME TO THE TOMB. IT WAS A CAVE WITH A STONE LAID ACROSS THE ENTRANCE. 'TAKE AWAY THE STONE,' HE SAID…"
(JOHN 11:38-39 NIV)

The background of this verse is that Jesus is now at the grave of His beloved friend Lazarus, brother of Martha and Mary. He is very upset, disturbed, or angry. Pick one or all of these words, and you would be correct in describing how our LORD felt at this moment. The word used for "deeply moved" is "Embrimaomai," which means to snort with anger—to have indignation, to blame. Jesus was very upset about the things which caused Martha pain. Though He knows this scene in Martha's life must play out this way, He is not at all happy or joyful at Martha's sorrow. In this, our LORD shows true meekness. This is Universal power held in check. Jesus, the Omnipotent One, is able to do what is absolutely best for everyone, despite His own hurt and pain. The salvation of our little earth rests on the shoulders of One who, despite His own feelings and emotions, will do what is the absolute best and not error in sin, as did our fore parents. With His angry feelings about the devil, sin, and pain, our LORD moves forward in His Father's will. He sees the massive stone covering the cave where the body of Lazarus lay and tells the bystanders to take away the stone. What did this stone represent and why would Jesus ask "them" to move the stone? Wasn't He God? Couldn't He have spoken the stone away or just tapped it and caused it to crumble? He could have done all of these things and more. The stone covered the tomb of the dead brother, the source of all her hurt and grief. Her moving the stone was her exposing all of this intense hurt and pain to the only one who could take it away. He told Martha her brother would rise again. He tells her He (alone) is resurrection, and He is life. (John 11:23-25) He alone could repair the damage. All Jesus needs from her is total trust in Him, as seen by her obedience to His words. She proclaims her faith in verse twenty-seven of this chapter. Now was the time for her to put her feet to her faith. "You believe Martha, now take away the stone. I need you to do what I say, despite how you feel." (Writer's paraphrase)

MARTHA AND US: My faith in my LORD, Jesus, has greatly increased! Life with my LORD is like climbing a mountain. Each step up the mountain only strengthens my leg muscles for the next step. I am asked to believe His word. The fruit of that belief is obedience.

GOD SPEAKS: "… Obey me, and I will be your God and you will be my people. Walk in obedience to all I command you, that it may go well with you." (Jeremiah 7:23 NIV) I know you believe in me; now by faith, go forward in Me, your LORD, and do the things I have told you to do. Stay in Me and I will wipe out all of your enemies. It does not matter the number; I can destroy them all.

WANDA'S PRAYER: You alone, MY LORD and MY GOD, are strength and power! Help us focus only on You; and to do what You tell us to do.

September 26

LORD, I OBJECT

"... BUT, LORD," SAID MARTHA, THE SISTER OF THE DEAD MAN, 'BY THIS TIME THERE IS A BAD ODOR, FOR HE HAS BEEN THERE FOUR DAYS.'" (JOHN 11:39 NIV)

As you see in the above scripture, the NIV translation uses the words "bad odor." In the King James version of the Bible, it uses the word stench ("… by this time he stinketh…"). Lazarus' body had been in that cave for four hot, smelly days. Decomposition on the corpus of Martha's brother had taken place; filled with maggots, ants, and other creatures that feast on dead organisms. To unleash Lazarus from the grave would amount to an all-out assault on the olfactory nerves. Making it plain, the smell of a dead corpus was torture on the nose. Considering all of this, Martha, from a human standpoint, rightfully and forcefully objected. This would be a fine, well deserving, and notable objection, if it were humans asking her to make this sacrifice. However, it was not a human—it was the God man, Jesus, whom she earlier called her LORD. (John 11:27) Our God cannot just be our LORD in some things, He must be our LORD OVER EVERYTHING. But like Martha, we have brief lapses in this "LORD over all things" area of life. It is ok for me to call You LORD in church, at work, or around other Christians, but not around sinners. I do not know if I want You to LORD over the "darling sins of my life." I will lord over them, LORD. Martha had a good reason to put up a fight; to voice an objection, and so do we—we think. Again, if our Heavenly Father and Jesus, is not LORD IN ALL, IT IS BECAUSE HE IS NOT LORD OF ALL — OR, OVER ANY AREAS OF OUR LIVES. The answer to Martha's stress was in remembering our LORD'S words and believing in them. He said, "YOUR BROTHER WILL RISE AGAIN," and "I AM THE RESURRECTION AND THE LIFE." (John 11:23-25) After remembering Jesus' words, Martha holds on tight to her confession. "I BELIEVE THAT YOU ARE THE MESSIAH, THE SON OF GOD." (John 11:27) We too must remember His Word, confess our faith in Him, walk in that, and just do what He tells us to. After that, go take a nap—rest girl; Daddy's got things under control.

MARTHA AND US: There are many issues I struggle with in allowing my LORD complete LORDSHIP over me. Areas like my finances and submission. I give Him a little piece of the pie, and then I consider the rest to be mine. LORD help!

GOD SPEAKS: "… Does the LORD delight in burnt offerings and sacrifices as much as in obeying the LORD? To obey is better than sacrifice, and to heed is better than the fat of rams. For rebellion is like the sin of divination, and arrogance like the evil of idolatry…" (1 Samuel 15:22-23 NIV) When you deliberately go against My Word, you practice witchcraft or devil worship, and your pride stinks in My nostril, like a four-day-old corpus. Then you have the nerve to call Me LORD—I DON'T THINK SO! You say you love Me, right? Then show Me, by doing as I say.

WANDA'S PRAYER: Father, LORD Jesus, forgive us for our horrible, rotten sins. Give us Your pure heart to do Your perfect will.

September 27

OK MS. MARTHA, LET ME TELL YOU ONE MO' GIN!

"THEN JESUS SAID, 'DID I NOT TELL YOU THAT IF YOU BELIEVE, YOU WILL SEE THE GLORY OF GOD?'" (JOHN 11:40 NIV)

As a kid, I grew up in the "deep-south." As Southerners, we sometimes used many words to say a few things. Things such as "I's a be a gonna fixin' that there thang ret na." Instead of saying, "I'll fix it now." Other times, we used too few words to describe things such as the title of today's devotional. What Jesus was saying based on today's verse was, "Martha, let Me just explain to you once more." (One Mo' Gin) No matter how we say it, the message is clear: Jesus was rehearsing His lesson to Martha again. Either Martha did not get the message the first time, or the message that Jesus was trying to teach did not stick to her brain cells. The end result was that our LORD had to repeat Himself. It sort of sounds like the "Martha, Martha" story of Luke 10:38-40. Jesus reminds Martha that He told her, if she would only believe, she would see the "GLORY OF GOD." Martha needed to stand on her LORD Jesus' words alone. In doing so, she would see God's power and majesty on display. Is that awesome or what? As Christians, we all want to see God's glory expressed in our lives. To see God's grand show, all I need to do is to believe in the Word of the One who holds the universe in His hands. My faith is seen through my obedience. One might say, "I have been obedient, and I have not seen God manifested or shown in my life." Oh really? Ponder for a moment. Think about how you were before God saved you and look at where you are now. Now what were you saying about not seeing the Glory of our Loving LORD in your life?

MARTHA AND US: This display of God's glory is not limited to Martha's behalf. My obedience to my Lord Jesus Christ affords me this privilege as well. Like Martha, when Jesus reminds me of the benefits of obedience, how could I ever think of saying no? The cost of disobedience carries such a high price. As a writer once put it, "He paid a cost that He did not owe, so that I no longer owe a cost that I could not pay." Because He paid it all, my debt to Him is obedience.

GOD SPEAKS: "I will glory in the LORD; let the afflicted hear and rejoice. Glorify the LORD with me; let us exalt his name together." (Psalm 34:2-3 NIV) To exalt Me—to lift Me up, you must bow low. For your soul to make her boast in Me, you must be full of Me. In order for Me to fill you, you must first be empty.

WANDA'S PRAYER: LORD, we can never ask You enough to continually empty us of self, and fill us always with You.

September 28

THE POWER OF SURRENDER

"SO THEY TOOK AWAY THE STONE. THEN JESUS LOOKED UP AND SAID, 'FATHER, I THANK YOU THAT YOU HAVE HEARD ME. I KNEW THAT YOU ALWAYS HEAR ME, BUT I SAID THIS FOR THE BENEFIT OF THE PEOPLE STANDING HERE, THAT THEY MAY BELIEVE THAT YOU SENT ME.' WHEN HE HAD SAID THIS, JESUS CALLED IN A LOUD VOICE, 'LAZARUS, COME OUT!'" (JOHN 11:41-43 NIV)

There is a simple, but profound truth this verse points out. When the stone was removed, all in attendance saw the Glory of God that day! When Martha allows the stone to be removed, then Jesus does the rest. By allowing the stone to be taken away, she also allows the pains and/or angers she may have had to be exposed by the Master's touch. Our LORD Jesus, who first called our world into being, is about to call His son and friend back from the dead. Notice how He first looks to heaven. He doesn't look at the tomb housing the dead man; but He looks to heaven and addresses His (and our) Dad. (Matthew 6:9) He is conversing with Dad; there is no pleading. In fact, based on what He is saying, it would appear we are getting the tail end of the conversation. He is just filling us "Johnny come lately's," in on what He and the Father had previously talked about. Listen to what Jesus says: "Dad, I want to thank You for having heard Me." Notice the resurrection is already a done deal. Then Jesus continues, "You always hear Me when I talk to You." (This tells us God hears us too.) "But Dad, this audible conversation is for the folk listening, so they can believe and trust in You." At this, the Son of God — Jesus Christ calls in a loud voice, "Lazarus come forth," and Lazarus comes out. He comes out of the grave upright and walking. All it took on Martha's part was faith in Jesus, as seen in her obedience in rolling away the stone.

MARTHA AND US: As I look back at the stones of my past, with all of its unresolved hurts and seemingly unanswered prayers, I can see now my LORD heard me. Not only has He heard, but He has answered. He answered "yes" to some, "no" to others, as well as there have been some "waits." But this I know now—He always hears me. His answers are from a loving heart of perfection. He will always do things for His glory and my good. On that, I can rest.

GOD SPEAKS: "Who among the gods is like you, LORD? Who is like you—majestic in holiness, awesome in glory, working wonders? In your unfailing love you will lead the people you have redeemed. In your strength you will guide them to your holy dwelling." (Exodus 15:11,13 NIV) The answer is, there is none like ME! I ALONE, AM GOD—AND NO ONE ELSE. Now, little girl of mine, you can rest your little head on that.

WANDA'S PRAYER: LORD, we completely rest in that because we completely rest in You.

September 29

WE'RE IN THIS THING TOGETHER

"WHEN HE HAD SAID THIS, JESUS CALLED IN A LOUD VOICE, 'LAZARUS, COME OUT!' THE DEAD MAN CAME OUT, HIS HANDS AND FEET WRAPPED WITH STRIPS OF LINEN, AND A CLOTH AROUND HIS FACE. JESUS SAID TO THEM, 'TAKE OFF THE GRAVE CLOTHES AND LET HIM GO.'" (JOHN 11:43-44 NIV)

The beginning of this verse points back to the two previous verses. In those verses, (John 11: 41-42) Jesus reminds the crowd at Martha's home that the God of Heaven is His Father, and that He is His one and only Son. He goes on to tell them this miracle will validate that fact. After His dialogue, Jesus turns His attention to the deceased Lazarus. Looking at the open tomb, Jesus cries with a loud voice, "Lazarus, come out!" The dead man came out without hesitation or pause. I imagine Martha, after recovering from fainting, must have been filled with joy. Her long night of agony and grief was finally over with just a few words from our LORD Jesus. This was an effortless gesture by our LORD, but there was still work to do. Though Jesus raised the dead Lazarus back to life with only a few words, He did not remove from him the look and smell of death. The verse says, "The dead man came out, his hands and feet wrapped with strips of linen, and a cloth around his face." Jesus looks to Martha and the crowd and tells them to take off the grave (dead) clothes that tightly bound Lazarus. This tells us two things: First, the act of receiving a new life in Christ Jesus is instantaneous to those who believe in Him. Second, living like a new man is an ongoing process that will require the assistance of others. To show us the need for fellowship, Jesus leaves the job to his "church" family and friends. In the work of removing the "dead man's wear," our LORD gives the needed help to Lazarus, and increases the group's faith in Jesus. As Martha and the others remove the smelly clothes from Lazarus, they were given a deeper appreciation of the glory of God.

MARTHA AND US: A while back, I slipped and fell at work. I was fine at first; then later in the day, I needed a wheelchair to get around. As I think back on the events of the evening, I realized how much the act of helping benefited the "helpers," as well as it benefited me.

GOD SPEAKS: "Is it not to share your food with the hungry and to provide the poor wanderer with shelter—when you see the naked, to clothe them, and not to turn away from your own flesh and blood? Then your light will break forth like the dawn, and your healing will quickly appear; then your righteousness will go before you, and the glory of the LORD will be your rear guard." (Isaiah 58:7-8 NIV) Your blessings and answered prayer will often come when you become My hands extended out to others.

WANDA'S PRAYER: Father, take control of our lives. We want to become Your hands and heart to those around us in need.

September 30

IN PERFECT ORDER

"HERE A DINNER WAS GIVEN IN JESUS' HONOR. MARTHA SERVED, WHILE LAZARUS WAS AMONG THOSE RECLINING AT THE TABLE WITH HIM." (JOHN 12:2 NIV)

We see the context of this verse in the first verse of this chapter. In that verse, we see the Passover was near, and Jesus has now returned once again to Bethany—the house of Martha and her family. Jesus had previously come to her house for dinner. (Luke 10:38-40) For deeper insight into this verse, let us compare the two dinners that Jesus attends at Martha's home. As we examine the two dinners, we will see real spiritual growth in Martha. At the first dinner, she opens up her home to Him, and shortly after, becomes swallowed up by her "preparations" for Him. "They" (and not Him), become her priority. At this point, her focus has turned away from Jesus. We see her getting "bogged down" with the preparations until they become an angry distraction for which she lashes out at Jesus. At the first dinner, Christ was only a guest in the home, and the preparations were her primary focus. At this final dinner, however, things are very different. First, as previously noted, Jesus comes to the home. At this dinner, He is given the seat of honor. He is the reason for the dinner. The focus is on HIM! Even though Martha was "working for Jesus" at the first dinner, she was not serving Him. At the first dinner, her service was given over to the preparations. At this second dinner, the above verse tells us she "served" Him (waited on, attended to, and performed menial tasks). We can see it was not about Martha anymore; it was all about Jesus. Because it was all about Jesus and not her, she could submit and serve freely with joy. She had now received a peace beyond comprehension, from her service to Him. Her sister is still not helping, but Martha does not complain. Her focus and goal is to serve and please Him alone. Martha, girl, you are preaching a sermon to me now!

MARTHA AND US: Like Martha, I find that when my focus is fixed on Him, and I am carrying out His will for my life, this is when I find my greatest joy and peace. Like Martha, when He is my focus, He does not just occupy the building where I am, but He fills my heart as well.

GOD SPEAKS: "The light of the body is the eye: if therefore thine eye be single, thy whole body shall be full of light." (Matthew 6:22 KJV) That word for single means clear; some text render the word "good." The point is that as the focus of your heart and life is on Me, I will transform you from the inside out. Remember, "I Am the light of the world..." (John 8:12)

WANDA'S PRAYER: LORD, we thank and praise You for being the Light of our lives. Help us stay focused on You always!

Notes

Notes

October

INTRODUCTION

MARY

Mary is the sister of Martha and Lazarus. Her life, as presented in scripture, is one of complete love for the LORD Jesus. She shows us what it looks like when we are passionately in love with Jesus. We make Him the priority and make everything else a distant second. This woman does not allow anything—nothing and no one — to come between her and her LORD. Every time we read of her in God's Word, Mary is either at or near the feet of Jesus, basking in His presence; taking in our LORD'S every word.

What's the outcome of such a life consumed by her LORD? Peace and calm commitment, no matter the circumstances of life. Mary's life teaches us important lessons. First, that our love for our LORD and His love for us, does not shield us from suffering and sadness in this world of sin. Second, when we experience the deep pain of life's tragedies, we automatically know where or who we can take them to. Finally, Mary's life shows us that the God of all peace and comfort will carry us to the other side.

Notes

October 1

MARY, IT'S A PRIORITY THANG

"SHE HAD A SISTER CALLED MARY, WHO SAT AT THE LORD'S FEET..."
(LUKE 10:39 NIV)

Looking at this verse, I see I started in the middle of a conversation; so let me backtrack. I am starting at verse thirty-eight of this chapter. In that verse, we see Jesus has just entered the home of Mary and Martha. When Jesus comes into this home, we see two quick, but different decisions (or approaches), are made to our LORD. Martha decides to approach her LORD by doing for Him. Mary, however, decides to sit at His feet and allow Him to do for her. Here is the clear-cut question we must all ask ourselves in our encounters with our LORD: Are we a "Martha" or a "Mary?" Is our LORD starving and in desperate need of a meal, or are we the hungry ones? Our answer to this question will decide our approach to our LORD. Another interesting fact about this partial verse is that Mary sits, not stands, at the feet of Jesus. Her "sitting" at His feet puts her in a position of submission. This is a form of worshiping Jesus. Mary made a deliberate decision that the first thing she would do when she met Jesus was to sit at His feet. This time at His feet was special for her, and she would let no one take it away.

MARY AND US: Mary is bold in her "sit in" or "sit down" time with Jesus. It screams conviction to my soul about the precious, missed times and opportunities I could have with my LORD; especially during those early, fresh hours of my day. Many times, I become a Martha. I get my priorities mixed up. I often think Jesus needs me to do for Him, more than I need His doing for me. LORD, speak to my heart.

GOD SPEAKS: "The poor will eat and be satisfied; Those who seek the Lord will praise Him—May your hearts live forever!" (Psalm 22:26 NIV) First, sit at My table and eat the meal I have prepared for you. This meal will satisfy you throughout the day. My meal consists of studying My word and prayer.

WANDA'S PRAYER: LORD, we know this so well. Yet, we need Your constant reminders. Thank You for Your gentle tug upon our hearts.

October 2

THIS IS THE PLACE FOR ME

"SHE HAD A SISTER CALLED MARY, WHO SAT AT THE LORD'S FEET LISTENING TO WHAT HE SAID." (LUKE 10:39 NIV)

No, reader, you are not on page one again; nor are you about to read a repeat—just an expanded version. To review, we see the LORD has entered the home. Next, we see Mary choosing to spend intimate time at Jesus' feet, which is an act of worship. As she sits at His feet, giving Him worship, she also receives from Him. She is listening to what He says. His words to Mary's ears are waters of life to her very thirsty soul and, boy, is she lapping it all up. She must have thought to herself as she sat at His feet, "How often will I get these precious Words of life, from the Source of Life." Mary is sitting at Jesus' feet receiving nourishment from Him for her life—her necessary sustenance. This is an opportunity of a lifetime that Mary would not pass up. But what about you and me? Are we given the same opportunity as Mary? Yes! Our LORD invites us daily, even many times during the day, to spend intimate moments with Him. He is just waiting for us to put everything else aside, grab His word, and, with prayer and worship, sit at His feet. We may not see His physical form as Mary did. But He is waiting and wanting to show us His heart. He wants to feed us with the bread of Heaven. All He asks is that we come to the table. How often would you go without physical food? Do we go days, weeks, or months at a time without eating? NO! So why do we go through these starvation diets from the Source of Life? Our LORD is ready and willing to fill us with Himself; all He wants of us is our time and attention. The blessing is ours for the sitting.

MARY AND US: Mary's "sit down" with her LORD shows me I need at least a daily "sit down" time with my LORD. From her life, I can see I too must start my day with a good meal. That meal is Him and His Word—the Bible.

GOD SPEAKS: "And Jesus said to them, 'I am the bread of life. He who comes to Me shall never hunger, and he who believes in Me shall never thirst.'" (John 6:35 NKJV) Sit down for a while with Me; and let me fix you a little "something to eat."

WANDA'S PRAYER: Father, as we sit at Your feet, we give You praise. We lift up Your Name and give You all honor. You alone are worthy of receiving praise. It is You alone, who flung the stars in space. You alone call for time and can make it stand still. We thank You for the love and mercy You have continually shown to us. Fill us with Your Spirit; empty us of self and forgive us of all our sins and unrighteous ways. As we study Your Word, teach us Your perfect ways, so we can give You glory in how we live our lives.

October 3

DON'T BE HATIN'

"… TELL HER TO HELP ME!" (LUKE 10:40 NIV)

Today's young people use the term "hatin" when they are describing someone who is jealous of them, or describing a person they perceive is trying to "spoil their fun." Such is the case in this verse. The phrase used in our study verse is the last part of Luke 10:40. In the previous verse, we see Mary planted firmly at Jesus' feet. Based on her sister Martha's comments to Jesus, it does not appear Mary was moving in any way to help her with all the work needed to be done around the house. "But Martha was distracted by all the preparations that had to be made. She came to Him (Jesus) and asked, 'LORD, don't You care that my sister has left me to do the work by myself? Tell her to help me!" (Luke 10:40 NIV) This verse clearly points out one thing—where or what is our focus? Mary's focus was on Jesus and Him alone. Her sister's focus was first on the distractions of her tasks, and then second on her sister. Mary's focus remained a single one—fixed on Jesus. Her sister's focus was on everything but Jesus. Notice that Mary's focus seemed to Martha to be an idle waste of good time. She was condemned for wasting time and not doing the "good, necessary thing." But Mary shows us that there is nothing more necessary than spending our first and precious hours with our LORD.

MARY AND US: In the past, when I read this verse, I saw Mary as lazy and not wanting to do her share of the work around the house. But now I see a new perspective on this story. LORD, what's Your answer?

GOD SPEAKS: "Do not work for food that spoils, but for food that endures to eternal life, which the Son of Man will give you. For on him God the Father has placed his seal of approval." (John 6:27 NIV) Everything, and everyone else on this planet of yours, is temporary. It will all burn one day. I alone AM the Eternal GOD! You are to seek Me first, last, and in all points in between.

WANDA'S PRAYER: LORD Jesus, help us do just that. We want to seek You and Your ways, always.

October 4

JESUS TO THE RESCUE

"MARTHA, MARTHA," THE LORD ANSWERED, 'YOU ARE WORRIED AND UPSET ABOUT MANY THINGS, BUT FEW THINGS ARE NEEDED—OR INDEED ONLY ONE...'" (LUKE 10:41-42 NIV)

There are several delectable delights we can nibble on from our Scripture reading today. Our first tasty delight is, as our focus remains on our LORD Jesus, He will fight the battles of our lives for us. Notice how Mary does not have to say a word. Her LORD spoke up in her defense. The second chewable is that as Mary kept herself firmly planted at the feet of her (our) LORD, the "many worries" which "upset" Martha did not trouble her. No, Sista' Mary was not bothered by any of the things which were driving her sister Martha to drink. She just sat calmly and remained at the feet of her LORD. Mary's sister had "many things" on her mind and in her heart, which caused her to be worried and upset. The third and tastiest of all the nuggets is there was only "one thing needed." Mary had discovered this "one needed thing"—passion of life and feasting on "Him." At Jesus' feet, Mary sat and inhaled His every word. This was the only thing Mary needed or desired. The first meal of her day was time with her LORD Jesus. With Him in her system, she was ready to face her day. She knew her LORD Jesus was the Master Chef, and dinner was on Him. So, she parked herself at His feet and thoroughly enjoyed the meal.

MARY AND US: On days when I do not set aside time in the morning with my LORD, by mid-day, I am starving. At times, I am acting like a raving maniac, with no restraint. Mary teaches me the importance of making and keeping first things first. Jesus is to be the first, middle, and last thing to focus on. I can see from her life that if Jesus is my priority, He will handle everything else.

GOD SPEAKS: "Jesus said to them, 'Very truly I tell you, unless you eat the flesh of the Son of Man and drink his blood, you have no life in you.'" (John 6:53 NIV) Daily come into My presence; sit at my table—let Me feed you with My WORD, prayer, and worship.

WANDA'S PRAYER: Lord, we want to consume every morsel of Your Word to us; We want to bask in Your Presence all throughout the day. So, continually feed us until we are full of You!

I'VE GOT TO HAVE IT

"BUT FEW THINGS ARE NEEDED—OR INDEED ONLY ONE. MARY HAS CHOSEN WHAT IS BETTER, AND IT WILL NOT BE TAKEN AWAY FROM HER." (LUKE 10:42 NIV)

Have you ever craved something or someone? You know… you have that, "gotta have it, or you'll just lie down and die" feeling? To quench that "thirst" or satisfy this need, you would risk all—and perhaps you did. Well, this is how Mary felt about her LORD. How do I know? Look at what she did and what she went through to meet her need. Jesus enters the home with His disciples and probably others. In those days, the "womanly" thing to do would have been to serve the men. Certainly, you would want to serve the LORD, right? There was a lot to do—cooking and washing the dirty feet of the guest. But Mary does none of this. No, while her sister is running around like a "chicken with no head," Sista' girl just plopped herself at the feet of Jesus and became an immovable statue. Even when her sister goes to Jesus to make her help, Mary still does not move. Mary had an emptiness of soul—a hunger in her heart. She was determined to get satisfaction today at the feet of her Master and LORD. Like a strong pair of grip pliers, Ms. Mary has locked herself in at the feet of Jesus. She is so enraptured by His words of life to her thirsty soul that she is not letting go. All in the room that day could roll their eyes and say what they pleased, but Mary knew this was where she belonged. Jesus confirmed this to her, as well as to all who were in the house that day, and to us on this day. The verse tells us, "Only one thing is needed." He says to us—there is only ONE thing needed and "I AM IT!" He tells us "I AM the Source of Life; I AM all you need." He also says you must choose Me. I will not force Myself on you; the choice is yours. Next, He says when you choose Me, "It will not be taken from you." You can have as much of Me as you desire.

MARY AND US: Through Mary's story, I see how I have not always chosen the LORD first. Many days, I did not choose Him at all. Then halfway through the day, I wondered why I felt so empty and dry. On the other hand, on those days when I put Him first and meditated on His words throughout the day, I noticed I felt so full and satisfied. As I reflect on those days, I am reminded He was all I truly needed.

GOD SPEAKS: "The LORD is my light and my salvation—whom shall I fear? The LORD is the stronghold of my life—of whom shall I be afraid? One thing I ask from the LORD, this only do I seek: that I may dwell in the house of the LORD all the days of my life, to gaze on the beauty of the LORD and to seek him in his temple." (Psalm 27:1,4 NIV) I AM to be your every need and desire you have now, or will ever have.

WANDA'S PRAYER: Father GOD, fill us with You. Keep us at Your feet always.

October 6

LORD, NOW WHAT?

"NOW A MAN NAME LAZARUS WAS SICK. HE WAS FROM BETHANY, THE VILLAGE OF MARY AND HER SISTER MARTHA." (JOHN 11:1 NIV)

In this verse, we see Ms. Mary, the child of God, has a big problem. Her brother Lazarus is sick. In fact, as we continue the story, we shall see he is very sick. This part of the story answers the question of the sincere Christian experiencing illness or even death. The answer is yes; we as children of GOD can and will experience illness and death. Our love for the LORD and His love for us does not shield us from tragedies. The reason we mortals suffer sickness and death is because we live in a world damaged by the evils of sin. Sin brings his twin sister—suffering, and brother death with him. That is the bad news. I could sit and wallow in my pain, or I could give it away. Mary and her sister did the latter. They took the brother's illness to Jesus. "So the sisters sent for Jesus, 'LORD, the one you love is sick.'" (John 11:3) They knew there was nothing they could do about Lazarus, but to take it to the LORD Jesus. Notice the request or prayer. They recognize Jesus as LORD— meaning He is the one in control and not the sisters. Next, they inform Jesus of the problem or need— "the one YOU love is sick." Tucked in those few words is a calm assurance. "The one YOU love." The sisters are very aware of the LORD'S love for Lazarus and for them. In this love, they rest and wait for His answer. This should speak libraries to us about what we do with the problems we face in life.

MARY AND US: Unlike Mary, when I face heartache, pain, sickness, and/or death, unfortunately, my first words are not to the LORD, but to my own resources—a friend, the doctor, or the medicine cabinet for a pain pill. Then, when those things do not work, or work fast enough, then I take my very stressed-out-self to Jesus. Looking at Mary, I see that if I had gone to Jesus first, I would have left with His quiet assurance that He is LORD over me, as well as LORD over all my problems.

GOD SPEAKS: "Cast your cares on the LORD and he will sustain you; he will never let the righteous be shaken." (Psalm 55:22 NIV) With My big hands, I formed this Universe, and still hold it in place. Surely they are big enough to take care of your minor problems. Give them to Me, your LORD, and rest, My child.

WANDA'S PRAYER: Thank You, Father God, for taking care of our every pain. We know You will not let us fall, because You are carrying us through all the hurt and pain.

October 7

MY CHILD, I HEARD YOU—DO YOU HEAR ME?

"WHEN HE HEARD THIS, JESUS SAID, 'THIS SICKNESS WILL NOT END IN DEATH. NO, IT IS FOR GOD'S GLORY SO THAT GOD'S SON MAY BE GLORIFIED THROUGH IT.'" (JOHN 11:4 NIV)

I love this verse—it is like soft silk to my hurting soul. Reader, do you hear His words? Jesus received the request of the sisters (He heard their prayer), and He gave an immediate answer. "When He heard this, Jesus said..." This shows the child of God that He hears our every call, and He responds to our needs. So what did He say? "... This sickness will not end in death. No, it is for GOD'S glory so that GOD'S SON may be glorified through it." Well, what does that mean? It means, "I got this ... and I will work it out. I need you to let Me (Jesus, your LORD) do what I do." Death is separation from GOD. Jesus is saying to the sisters, and to all of us, that our tragic illnesses, heartaches, or pains will not separate us from Him—not at all! We will be with our LORD Jesus in this life, or face to face with Him in Heaven. In fact, as you leave your issue with Him, GOD'S Kingdom and the Kingdom of His SON will be glorified. In other words, every aspect of your life, when given to Him, will give Him glory and praise. This is a promise. When I place my complete self in His arms, I cannot lose. The sisters received the LORD Jesus' message. How do I know? Because of what Jesus said in verse forty of this same chapter, let's take a quick look: Then Jesus said, "Did I not tell you that if you believe, you will see the glory of God?" (John 11:40 NIV) Jesus made this comment when He asked the crowd to remove the stone, and Martha objected. He could ask her to believe because He had sent word earlier that Lazarus' problem would give Him glory! Now, what did Mary do with the LORD'S response? She just waited.

MARY AND US: Thank You Jesus! As I look at Mary's life, I see what I should do when I have hard, trying times. I need to give You my "whatever's." As I place my "it's" in Your loving hands, I can rest, knowing the end results will be for Your glory. Since You are a very good GOD, what is for Your glory is also for my good. I can then rest and not fret over the problem.

GOD SPEAKS: "Who shall separate us from the love of Christ? Shall trouble or hardship or persecution or famine or nakedness or danger or sword? As it is written: 'For your sake we face death all day long; we are considered as sheep to be slaughtered.' No, in all these things we are more than conquerors through him who loved us. For I am convinced that neither death nor life, neither angels nor demons, neither the present nor the future, nor any powers, neither height nor depth, nor anything else in all creation, will be able to separate us from the love of God that is in Christ Jesus our Lord." (Romans 8:35-39 NIV) I knew and loved you before you existed; and I will love you forever. Nothing will interfere with that love—it will only grow stronger.

WANDA'S PRAYER: LORD, we thank You for the warm-fuzzy assurance of Your tender love for us. We never want to climb out of those big old hands.

October 8

I GOT YOUR WORD, BUT MY PROBLEM AIN'T FIXED

"NOW JESUS LOVED MARTHA AND HER SISTER (MARY) AND LAZARUS. SO WHEN HE HEARD THAT LAZARUS WAS SICK, HE STAYED WHERE HE WAS TWO MORE DAYS," (JOHN 11:5-6 NIV)

True love always does what is best. Jesus is true love and will do what is best for all. He would do what is completely perfect in this or any other situation of life. The question is, "did Mary understand and learn this lesson?" Earlier in the chapter of Mary, we discussed how she sat at the feet of Jesus and received His every word. Class time is now over, and the real-life test was here to see what she had learned at the Master's feet. Mary and her sister had made their prayer request. Jesus told them He was going to handle the problem. (See John 11:4-5) Now all that was left to do was for the sisters to wait and believe that Jesus would do what He does best—everything! But Jesus did not just leave Mary in limbo; He left her with an important piece of Himself. He says in this verse, "(He) LOVED Martha, her sister (Mary) and Lazarus…" What is Jesus saying here? When the sisters sent word to Jesus that their brother was ill, they said, "The one You love (Your good friend, the one You are fond of) is sick. But our text says, "Jesus loved Martha and her sister and Lazarus"—all three are mentioned. (I love this family with the passion of God.) Their word for love is friendship; whereas His love is Love from the heart and soul of God. Yet with all of this "love," our LORD waits. Why? He told them already. "I AM waiting and Mary, you need to trust what you cannot see. I want you to believe this is for the Glory of God and His Son. So just wait on me—ok?" (Writer's paraphrase) Mary did just that—she waited in calm quietness. She could rest in His words because she had heard His heart earlier.

MARY AND US: As I look at this very painful episode in Mary's life, I see that true love must sometimes wait; and while waiting, we must believe the LORD is in complete control.

GOD SPEAKS: "In the morning, LORD, you hear my voice; in the morning I lay my requests before you and wait expectantly." (Psalm 5:3 NIV) "Wait for the LORD; be strong and take heart and wait for the LORD." (Psalm 27:14 NIV) Waiting on Me (your LORD) requires trusting, serving, and resting in Me, as you wait for My glory. Can you do this for Me?

WANDA'S PRAYER: LORD, we can do all things, as You give us Your strength. Empower us to do what You tell us to do.

October 9

I'VE GOT THE HOOK UP

"AFTER HE HAD SAID THIS, HE WENT ON TO TELL THEM, 'OUR FRIEND LAZARUS HAS FALLEN ASLEEP; BUT I AM GOING THERE TO WAKE HIM UP.' ... SO THEN HE TOLD THEM PLAINLY, 'LAZARUS IS DEAD, AND FOR YOUR SAKE I AM GLAD I WAS NOT THERE, SO THAT YOU MAY BELIEVE. BUT LET US GO TO HIM.'"
(JOHN 11:11,14-15 NIV)

When someone says they have the "hook up," it means they have insider or advanced information on a particular subject. Our LORD Jesus could truly say this as we look at this Scripture verse. In a day when there were no cell phones, emails, landlines, telegraphs or even the Pony Express, and though He was miles away from Lazarus, Jesus emphatically knew Lazarus had died. As He does to His disciples, Jesus speaks to let us know He is God in human flesh, and that He knows all things. As we look at this verse, we can see His Deity flashing through His humanity, as He states this fact with perfect accuracy, though He was not physically present to witness the event. His "hook up" does not stop there. Not only does Jesus tell the disciples Lazarus is dead, He goes on to say, "... But I AM going to wake him up ..." Say what? Only the All-Powerful Creator Himself could make such a bold statement about waking up the dead. In these words, He makes it known He has power over death. Mary was in for a wonderful surprise. Jesus was about to wake up her dead brother and bring him back to life. This recorded conversation tells us something of our Lord and Savior Jesus' heart towards Mary. It tells us He carried Mary's pain over the loss of her brother, with Him in His heart. It also tells us that, even though she could not see His plans, Jesus was working things out for the perfect good of all. As God, our LORD Jesus, considers the good of all, not just the good of one. What a loving LORD we serve! Thus, His dealing with Lazarus would be a benefit to us all. Mary must wait and believe that the heart of her LORD truly has her heart on His mind. This part of the story should speak to us in the same way it does to Mary. As she is unaware of the events which are about to happen, so are we concerning our life events. Jesus wants everyone reading this story to know He is God, and He has the All-Powerful hook-up!

MARY AND US: I am very comforted when I read this part of the story. From this passage of Scripture, I can see a few things: Jesus has me on His mind; He is very "hooked up" to my hurts and pain; I can trust Him; and there will be times of waiting on Him. I can and will wait patiently; assuredly knowing He is working all things out well.

GOD SPEAKS: "Yours, LORD, is the greatness and the power and the glory and the majesty and the splendor, for everything in heaven and earth is yours. Yours, LORD, is the kingdom; you are exalted as head over all. Wealth and honor come from you; you are the ruler of all things. In your hands are strength and power to exalt and give strength to all." (1 Chronicles 29:11-12 NIV) As long as you hold on to this belief about Me, your LORD, you will never go wrong.

WANDA'S PRAYER: LORD, we give You thanks and we praise Your name!

October 10

WILL THE REAL MARY... SIT DOWN?

"WHEN MARTHA HEARD THAT JESUS WAS COMING, SHE WENT OUT TO MEET HIM, BUT MARY STAYED AT HOME." (JOHN 11:20 NIV)

It is often said a time of crisis will reveal the "real you." We can definitely see the "real you's" of Mary and Martha coming out in this part of the story. The real Martha was going to confront Jesus for His perceived inaction regarding her deceased brother, Lazarus. In contrast, Mary's way of dealing with her tragedy was to stay at home, waiting on her LORD. Why didn't she go with the menacing Martha, to confront Jesus and find out the "where, why, and how come's" regarding His delay? Possibly she was still in a state of shock over her brother's untimely death and had no words for Jesus at this time. Perhaps she was too angry to speak. Or maybe all those moments at the feet of Jesus, taking in His words, now gave her an unshakable peace which was guarding her heart. Though she was now experiencing a time of extreme agony over the loss of her brother, she still would not abandon what she knew about her LORD; nor for what she could not understand about her circumstance. She would allow His beautiful, soothing word of life to grip her hurting heart like a vice grip. All those times at the feet of Jesus had taught her she could completely trust His heart. This absolute trust in the Master's (Jesus) heart would keep her sitting at home in peace instead of running "willy-nilly" all over the place in search of answers to the unanswered "whys" of life. Mary chose to sit, rest, and reflect on the goodness of her LORD despite any present pain she was suffering. She could rely on the LORD fully and trust His heart and leading.

MARY AND US: Wow! To have this kind of unwavering faith is something I desperately desire to have. Spending a lot of time with Jesus is what makes it happen. I can spend time in His Word (the Bible); I can also spend time in prayer, praise, and worship to Him. Or I can do all of these things. I just need to fall at His feet and stay there, in thought, word and deed.

GOD SPEAKS: "I remember the days of long ago; I meditate on all your works and consider what your hands have done. I spread out my hands to you; I thirst for you like a parched land." (Psalm 143:5-6 NIV) Mary could sit and wait for Me (Jesus) in the time of her greatest storm, because she had sat at My feet when the sun was shining. Can you do the same?

WANDA'S PRAYER: LORD, only You know the answer to that. We ask You to prepare our failing hearts now, in our time of calm. Keep us always at Your feet. We realize if we stay at Your feet now, we will not move later—no matter what comes.

October 11

TIME TO BLOW THIS POPSICLE STAND

"AFTER SHE HAD SAID THIS, SHE WENT BACK AND CALLED HER SISTER MARY ASIDE. 'THE TEACHER IS HERE,' SHE SAID, 'AND IS ASKING FOR YOU.' WHEN MARY HEARD THIS, SHE GOT UP QUICKLY AND WENT TO HIM.'" (JOHN 11:28-29 NIV)

Looking at Mary's actions in the above verse, I am reminded of an old Kenny Rogers song, "The Gambler." In the song's chorus, it says, "You better know when to hold 'em … know when to fold 'em … know when to walk away, and know when to run …" Mary gives us several practical applications to our Christian walk, during times of suffering. First, she shows us when to "hold them" by joyfully and graciously receiving comfort from friends and family in times of pain and sorrow. Second, she continues to "hold them" by waiting patiently on her LORD, when she did not know what to do. Mary held a steady course of doing nothing until she received a clear word from the LORD. Third, she knew when to "fold them," when she got word from her sister that the Teacher, Jesus, called her. And fourthly, she knew, "when to run." When Jesus called, she quickly responded. Despite her heartache over her brother's loss, or any possible disappointment she may have had over her LORD not acting the way she thought He should have, when Jesus called, Mary ran to Him. What would make her do such a thing? Two things I think: One, Jesus had her heart. Mary had developed a bond with her LORD, which was stronger than the current hurt. Two, she knew the comfort and healing she so desperately needed was at the feet of Jesus. Mary points out to us that "timing is everything," as my friend Debra used to say to me. The time for her to go to Him was when He called, and the time was now!

MARY AND US: As I look at this story, I see there are some things which cannot be hurried; and other things which cannot wait. I also see how to get wisdom to know the difference, and that is only as I remain at the feet of Jesus, like my sister Mary did.

GOD SPEAKS: "Never be lacking in zeal, but keep your spiritual fervor, serving the Lord. Be joyful in hope, patient in affliction, faithful in prayer. (Romans 12:11-12 NIV) The key is to remain connected to Me, your LORD. Mary could remain calm because she held tightly to My words, and she stayed "spiritually" connected to Me. The word for you, my daughter, is to "abide in Me and let Me abide in you."

WANDA'S PRAYER: Lord, give us a heart to always want to be near You. Hold us ever so close to You.

October 12

THEY'RE WATCHING ME

"WHEN THE JEWS WHO HAD BEEN WITH MARY IN THE HOUSE, COMFORTING HER, NOTICED HOW QUICKLY SHE GOT UP AND WENT OUT, THEY FOLLOWED HER, SUPPOSING SHE WAS GOING TO THE TOMB TO MOURN THERE." (JOHN 11:31 NIV)

At this point, Mary's life has been lived in a fish tank. Her every move is being watched by all in the community. They had come to comfort the sisters in their time of sorrow, and it now seems they were watching her like a laboratory rat. They watched her remain in the home for several days after her brother's tragic death. Now suddenly, she just sprung up and, in their minds, was going to the gravesite of Lazarus. They thought she was continuing her mourning process. What they did not know is she was more interested in seeing her living LORD, than she was in mourning her dead brother. Notice Mary did not forbid them from following her because she had nothing to hide. Mary knew she was going to see her LORD, and she welcomed the company. What a wonderful thing for a life to say: "I have mourned over my loss; I have waited for my LORD. Now He bids me to come to Him and I am making a 'beeline' to Him. You may come if you want." Mary would lead others to Jesus, even in her time of grief.

MARY AND US: I must admit, I have not mourned my losses as gracefully as Mary. Nor have I displayed a willing spirit to bring those to the LORD, while going through times of sorrow. Mary teaches me to remember that I am to be a testament of His goodness, no matter the circumstances of life.

GOD SPEAKS: "Follow my example, as I follow the example of Christ." (1 Corinthians 11:1 NIV) I purchased your life from the clutches of hell; you now belong to Me. Everything you do will reflect Me—for the good, or for the bad. Remember, "… to live is Christ (Me), and to die (you dying to flesh) is gain." (Philippians 1:21 NIV)

WANDA'S PRAYER: LORD, help us lead others to You, even in our time of grief. We are sorry, Father; obviously, we forgot who owned whom. Continue to remind us of Your order of things.

October 13

THIS IS A GOOD TIME FOR WORSHIP

"WHEN MARY REACHED THE PLACE WHERE JESUS WAS AND SAW HIM, SHE FELL AT HIS FEET AND SAID, 'LORD, IF YOU HAD BEEN HERE, MY BROTHER WOULD NOT HAVE DIED.'" (JOHN 11:32 NIV)

Mary's posture towards seeing the LORD Jesus after her brother's death totally differs from that of her sister. When her sister Martha heard Jesus had come back to town (John 11:20-27), she went to confront Him. She had questions and wanted immediate answers. To the contrary, Mary just wanted to be at the feet of her loving LORD. The verse says she reaches Him, falls at His feet, and worships Him. This was her place of solace and comfort. It is at those beautiful feet of her LORD; she pours out her heart's cry. Heartache did not demand answers, only comfort. Her statement to Jesus is a confession of fact, rather than one of accusation: "LORD, if You had been here, my brother would not have died." It is as if she is saying, "LORD, if only You were here, You would have never allowed my brother to die." (Writer's paraphrase) I say this is what she must have felt, because she makes this statement while clinging to the LORD'S feet. Mary makes this lone statement and, according to the next verse, says nothing more; she just weeps at the feet of Jesus. Mary does not have to say anymore. She may not have all the answers, but she has all she needs—His perfect comfort. She has accepted her LORD's divine plan for her brother, though she does not understand. To coin a very popular phrase, "Though she can't trace the hands of her LORD Jesus, she has chosen to trust His heart." So she sobs bitterly at the feet of her Master, giving Him all the hurt and pain of her brother's death. Mary shows us what we must do with the misfortunes of our lives. We must bring them to the feet of Jesus, and in worship, as well as with tears, we must leave them there.

MARY AND US: Mary is showing us that while it is ok to receive consolation from friends and family, what we really need is consolation from our LORD. I used to think I needed answers to all my questions—No! All I need, like Mary, is to know my Jesus is near. I can trust in knowing that the same One who holds the world in place, is also holding me.

GOD SPEAKS: "Come, let us bow down in worship, let us kneel before the LORD our Maker; for he is our God and we are the people of his pasture, the flock under his care …" (Psalm 95:6-7 NIV) I have big feet and wide arms; I can handle anything you give Me.

WANDA'S PRAYER: Thank You, LORD, for being everything we will ever need. Thank You for constantly working with us, as You create Your masterpiece out of our lives.

October 14

A DOUBLE TAKE AT THE VERSE

"WHEN MARY REACHED THE PLACE WHERE JESUS WAS AND SAW HIM, SHE FELL AT HIS FEET AND SAID, 'LORD, IF YOU HAD BEEN HERE, MY BROTHER WOULD NOT HAVE DIED.'" (JOHN 11:32 NIV)

As I re-read this verse of Scripture, the LORD poured a few life lessons into my heart, four of which I will share. First, Mary teaches us that no matter the problem or circumstance, we need to always make our way to the feet of Jesus. Notice the verse says, "When Mary reached the place where Jesus was…" Let's keep in mind that in this flawed world, problems and pain are a way of life—they are attached to our skin. So, in the midst of our problems and pain, we need to always go to Jesus, as Mary did. The place where you meet with Him may be your prayer closet or bathroom, whatever—just get to Jesus. Second, as she entered His presence, she fell at His feet. The verse says, "… and saw Him, she fell at His feet …" This was Mary's recognition of her place and His. She placed Him as LORD, and she placed herself as a servant. In falling at His feet, it was as if she was saying, "LORD, despite what I am going through, You are still in control, and this is the only place I need to be. So, Jesus, I come and bow to Your perfect will and authority over my life. I know in the end, what You allow for me is for my good and for Your glory." Third, while at the feet of Jesus, Mary poured out her complete heart to Him; she held nothing back. I once heard on television how some people pay as much as $300 to $500 for an hour of counseling, which is a lot of money to give someone just to listen to your problems. Our LORD offers His perfect counseling for free! Jesus is called, "WONDERFUL COUNSELOR…" (Isaiah 9:6). Our LORD Jesus is the perfect Counselor. Mary knew this, so she poured out her heart to Him. Fourth, after making every effort to reach Him, falling at His feet, and emptying ourselves on Him, then we finally wait to receive His comfort. Note how Mary said nothing more; she just remained at His feet. The rest of Isaiah 9:6 says, "…Mighty GOD, Everlasting Father, Prince of Peace." Our LORD Jesus is so awesome! As we leave all of our baggage with Him, we rest in knowing He will work everything out for our perfect good, according to His perfect plan for our lives. While we wait, He gives us His total peace, because He is the "Prince of Peace." Our LORD rules and reigns over Peace. We can trust Him because He is our forever (Everlasting) Father, and He loves us.

MARY AND US: If only we would keep these things in mind every day of our lives. As we go through life's ups and downs, may the storms that come our way not shake us.

GOD SPEAKS: "Therefore everyone who hears these words of mine and puts them into practice is like a wise man who built his house on the rock." (Matthew 7:24 NIV) The rains will come and beat against your life. Your only protection is to cement yourself around Me. I will keep your house from crashing.

WANDA'S PRAYER: As the songwriter says, "I need Thee every hour." Actually, Lord, we need You every moment.

October 15

I FEEL THE PAIN OF SIN—AND IT ANGERS ME

"WHEN JESUS SAW HER WEEPING, AND THE JEWS WHO HAD COME ALONG WITH HER ALSO WEEPING, HE WAS DEEPLY MOVED IN SPIRIT AND TROUBLED."
(JOHN 11:33 NIV)

Many times, as we are going through life's difficulties, we often wonder if God knows what we are going through. We may look up into the sky and shake our puny fists at our LORD and say, "Are You there?" or say, "Hello God, are You aware of my living hell?" This passage gives us a rare peak into the mind and heart of the LORD. The verse starts out by telling us the LORD Jesus saw. That word means to be fully aware, perceive, or considered. Our LORD "saw" and was fully aware of Mary and her companions weeping (crying loudly). But Jesus did not just "perceive or consider" her pain, nor did He just feel sorry for Mary. He felt the weight of her burden; her hurts were His hurts. As we see by His reaction, Jesus, our LORD, was deeply affected by what was going on in the lives of Mary and her friends. His response to her immense suffering was that "He was deeply moved in the Spirit and troubled." The Greek meaning for the words "deeply moved" means to be angry or indignant. To understand our LORD Jesus' feeling at this point, I will tell a story. Picture your six-year-old son. It is his first day of school. He is wearing his new uniform, has a nice new backpack, a delicious lunch, and you have given him some snack money. When he comes home from school, he is battered, torn, bleeding and scared. Even though you know you are going to do something about this, you also know that your injured, tearing son first needs your feeling of compassion for him. At that moment, you have the deepest compassion, yet you are also angry. Your anger is not at your son, but at the enemy who did this evil to your son. Well, this describes our LORD Jesus' feelings at the moment. His anger and indignation are at the devil for causing this hurt and pain upon His daughter. As Jesus climbed down into Mary's heart, the deeper He felt and saw into her pain. As He looked at what the enemy had done, He became very angry at him.

MARY AND US: In looking at Mary's life, I am assured the LORD Jesus sees my hurts and pain. He is here with me. LORD, You show me You are not in any way happy when I am hurting, but very angry at the enemy for causing me this pain.

GOD SPEAKS: "Surely he took up our pain and bore our suffering, yet we considered him punished by God, stricken by him, and afflicted. But he was pierced for our transgressions, he was crushed for our iniquities; the punishment that brought us peace was on him, and by his wounds we are healed." (Isaiah 53:4-5 NIV) I did not feel bad for you—I took away the total burden. All you feel are the fumes because I consumed the flames for the sins of this world. I paid the cost so that one day, you would never hurt again.

WANDA'S PRAYER: Thank You Jesus for paying the debt. Thank You for being the way out!

October 16

TAKE ME TO YOUR PLACE OF SORROW

"WHERE HAVE YOU LAID HIM?" HE ASKED. 'COME AND SEE, LORD,' THEY REPLIED." (JOHN 11:34 NIV)

The world in which we live often gives us an evil perception of our Loving LORD. It portrays Him as distant, cold, and uncaring to us as humans. This verse is like lens paper, cleansing the specks of our heart, which allows us to see clearer into the heart of God. This text reveals to us how our LORD wants us to take Him into the deepest places of our sorrows. Jesus asked Mary to take Him to the grave of Lazarus. Lazarus is the brother she and her sister Martha, so wanted Him to heal. Now he has been dead and buried for four days. After all this time, He now comes. The question our LORD posed to Mary is designed that she might allow Him access, not just to the literal burial place of her dead brother, but also into the "graveyard" of her heart. It represented her buried painful emotions. It is as if Jesus is saying, "Mary, reveal to me the place of your pain and death." Our LORD, Jesus, wanted total intimacy with Mary. He wanted her to open up this most devastating part of her life to Him. This is an invitation the LORD gives to us all. Our LORD would not come uninvited; He awaits her answer. She could have said, "LORD, I just can't go to that place—it's too painful." But she is so transparent to her LORD that she eagerly takes Him. I can almost see her grabbing Jesus' hand as she says, "Come and see, LORD."

MARY AND US: Mary teaches me four obvious lessons. (1) I have dead, buried areas in my life Jesus wants access to. (2) He is eagerly waiting; wanting me to take Him to those places. (3) He is a perfect gentleman and will not force me to take Him to those places. (4) Allowing Him access to those dead places is the start of a new life. It is, therefore, to my benefit, to take Him to those grave sites.

GOD SPEAKS: "O LORD, you have examined my heart and know everything about me. I could ask the darkness to hide me and the light around me to become night—but even in darkness I cannot hide from you…" (Psalm 139:1,11-12 NLT) I know your heart; I just need you to allow Me into it, so I can fill it with My perfect love.

WANDA'S PRAYER: LORD, come! We have the shovel—let us go dig up every grave.

October 17

WHY ARE YOU CRYING MY LORD?

"JESUS WEPT." (JOHN 11:35 NIV)

This two-word verse has much to say. It is the shortest verse in the Bible. The context of the verse is that Jesus has reached the burial site of Lazarus, Mary's dead brother. Upon arriving, He weeps. What would bring the Creator of the Universe to tears? Was it the stress of the moment? Was it seeing the intense wailing of family and friends? Was this His breaking point? Or was it the culmination of all these things? As Jesus stared at the tomb of Lazarus, did it finally hit Him that His friend was "really" dead? NO! From His own lips, He says, "This illness will not end in death, but it would give God glory." (John 11:4) So Jesus, why the tears? The eternal God in flesh knew that only moments from now, He would call His friend back from death to life. Usually, we cry over things that deeply move us. Shedding tears are a way of conveying intense feelings or powerful emotions. Our LORD knows the pain Mary is feeling. He feels her intense pain, as if it were His own. His heart is shattered over this—so He cries. Jesus had asked Mary to take Him to the burial place. Having now reached this place, God's compassion, mixed with human empathy, pours forth from the heart of Jesus. The result is God's great compassion towards her. It is seen through the humanness of Jesus' tears as He stands at the entombed Lazarus. Is He not, "a Man of sorrows acquainted and well aware of, or with, our grief?" God in flesh stands beside His hurting weeping daughters, and shares their pain.

MARY AND US: The message to me is loud and clear. Jesus is here with me in the midst of all my hurt and pain. He cries when I cry because He feels my agony as if it were His own. During those times in my life, when I am going through great difficulty and hurt, I want to know, does anyone hurt for me? Does anyone feel what I feel? In looking at this passage, the answer is a resounding YES! That Someone is Jesus, the Creator of the Universe. From this passage, I also glean that not only does He feel what I feel deeply, as if it were His own, but He intentionally comes very near to me and surrounds me with His unfailing love.

GOD SPEAKS: "Away from me, all you who do evil, for the LORD has heard my weeping. The LORD has heard my cry for mercy; the LORD accepts my prayer." (Psalm 6:8-9 NIV) As you read this entire Psalm, you will see how the writer was in a deep anguish of soul; but he held on to Me. As he held on to Me, I held on to Him. I will never let you go. I am in the middle of all your pain. Allow Me to comfort you through it all. Hold on to Me, as I am holding on to you.

WANDA'S PRAYER: "My shield is God Most High, who saves the upright in heart." (Psalms 7:10 NIV) Thank You, LORD, for not only being with us in all the difficulties and pains of life, but for carrying us through them all. You, alone, have been our shield and protector. Thank You for being our Savior through everything.

October 18

LOOK AND SEE—MY GOD DOES CARE

"JESUS WEPT. THEN THE JEWS SAID, 'SEE HOW HE LOVED HIM!'" (JOHN 11:35-36 NIV)

The Greek word for weeping in this verse is "dakruō." It means to be teary-eyed or silent crying. It is a quiet crying instead of a loud wailing. Jesus does not make a loud, obnoxious show, but quietly takes into Himself, Mary, and Martha's anguish. He is there with them in the midst of their loss, walking with them in this hardest of trials. This scene blows away all the theories of a distant, uncaring LORD. We have a God who is in the midst of our hurt and pain. Look, see Him sharing, yes, carrying Mary's pain. Her feelings and her hurts become His, as He bears them in His own body. So intense is His burden of bearing all that, though He weeps in silence, His cries are heard by all who were present that day. As they observe the Master's (Jesus) affections over the death of Lazarus, they are awestruck by His deep love for this man and his family, and it moved them. The crowd could see the "love" Jesus had for Lazarus and his sisters. The Greek word for love in this verse means to have a deep fondness or passion for. Thus, we could say the heart of God was so thick with emotion for Lazarus and his sisters that it was seen and felt by all in attendance that day.

MARY AND US: I get several things from this part of the story. One, our loving LORD is always involved in the lives of His children. This involvement may be quiet and sometimes very inconspicuous, but nonetheless, His involvement is ever present. Two, those around us can see the love of our LORD at times, even in our deepest of trials. Finally, I cannot escape His steadfast love for me. One time at work, I remember it seemed as though I was going through one terrible experience after another. While I was "trying" not to show my emotions over my continued "trials," all could see my days were not going well at all. Finally, a co-worker said, "Wanda, girl, I see you are going through one thing after another. I also see that God is going to bring you through them all." Yes, my LORD was in the midst of my hurt and carrying my pain, just as He had carried Mary's.

GOD SPEAKS: "Praise be to the God and Father of our Lord Jesus Christ, the Father of compassion and the God of all comfort, who comforts us in all our troubles, so that we can comfort those in any trouble with the comfort we ourselves receive from God." (2 Corinthians 1:3-4 NIV) Remember your perfect and complete Comfort is in GOD, in Him alone! I, your LORD, will bring you through every circumstance of life. Yes, I will carry you in My arms of love.

WANDA'S PRAYER: Father God, thank You for never taking Your eyes off of us. We know You always have our best interest at heart, even when it does not feel like it.

October 19

THE CRITIC—THERE'S ONE IN EVERY CROWD

"BUT SOME OF THEM SAID, 'COULD NOT HE WHO OPENED THE EYES OF THE BLIND MAN HAVE KEPT THIS MAN FROM DYING?'" (JOHN 11:37 NIV)

There is a saying which holds true in almost every setting of this sort. The saying is, "When looking at a partially filled glass, some will see the glass as half-filled, while others will see the same glass as half-empty." Critics will always see the emptiness of the glass. The saying goes much deeper, because in this saying are several questions, such as "Does the LORD Jesus have the power to fix this difficult problem?" "If He can fix the problem and does not, reason says, 'He does not really care about human hurts.' If He did, He would fix the problem the way 'our limited thinking,' says He should." These questions cast a negative eye on our LORD. Truth be told, we are still asking those same questions today, and reasoning the same erroneous way. Like the crowd of Mary's day, when difficulties of life come which we cannot handle, we turn to our LORD. Then when we do not get the answer we expected or hoped for, we, too, question His power and/or His love for us, just as the ancient wayward crowd did. On the other hand, Mary has the perfect word to us as we face the seemingly unanswered prayers. Listen carefully… can you speak in the midst of the grumbling critics? Did you hear her response? Listen quietly now and you will hear the answer. Mary says a very loud nothing! She does not join the crowd in their comments. She takes the advice of a good mother … "Say nothing at all!" Despite whatever she may have felt or thought—the "How comes…?" and the "Why didn't…?" things which may have plagued her mind, she kept them all to herself. Instead of joining the rebuking crowd, she took the advice of the late Pastor Chuck Smith, "not letting go of what she knew, to grab hold of what she did not know." She knew her LORD loved her and her brother. She knew she could hold on to His words, "that this sickness… would be for God's glory." Though her brother's death and burial were now beyond her comprehension, she would still cling tightly to the God she loved and wait patiently for Him.

MARY AND US: I must admit, during trying times in my life, my responses have been those of the critics. I remember at work one day; they floated me to a floor I had not been to in a while. Instead of thanking my LORD for work during a time of high unemployment, I complained, and complained, and complained; over and over again, about everything and everyone. Thinking back on that day brings me to shame.

GOD SPEAKS: "Rejoice in the Lord always. I will say it again: Rejoice! Let your gentleness be evident to all. The Lord is near. Do not be anxious about anything, but in every situation, by prayer and petition, with thanksgiving, present your requests to God. And the peace of God, which transcends all understanding, will guard your hearts and your minds in Christ Jesus." (Philippians 4:4-7 NIV) Not following My words, grieves My Spirit, and causes Me to hurt. Your witness of Me is shattered, and you miss the precious peace I am trying to give you.

WANDA'S PRAYER: Father God, We are so very sorry for the hurt our evil behavior causes You. Forgive us of all our sins, and the hurt we have caused. Consistently remind us that praying to You always, and leaving our cares at Your feet, is always for our good, as well as for Your glory.

October 20

YOUR FEELINGS MOVE ME

"JESUS, ONCE MORE DEEPLY MOVED, CAME TO THE TOMB. IT WAS A CAVE WITH A STONE LAID ACROSS THE ENTRANCE." (JOHN 11:38 NIV)

Jesus, God in flesh, comes face to face with the death of one of His closest friends. As He stands at this cave with a stone covering the entrance, He is horrifically moved at this scene. We are not specifically told about what in this scene moves Him, but as we look at the verse, we can glean from some things that may have touched the Master's heart. Death is the great separator from life. Lazarus' death separated him from a joyful life with his sisters, Mary, and Martha. This great divider, death, put Lazarus on one side of the cave and the sisters, the crowd, and Jesus on the other side of the cave. Death is the great jailer that held Mary's brother captive. The stone over the entrance to the cave meant Lazarus was powerless to break free from the thing that held him bound. Humanly speaking, death is forever the great divide. As He stands at the cave that held His dear friend, Jesus is painfully aware of these facts. This verse is another reminder of the terrible consequences of sin, which gives birth to death. The phrase "deeply moved" in this verse means our LORD was "touched or angered," by what He saw as He came to the tomb. Mary, looking on at her Master's visible hurt, was comforted to know that what was hurting her was also hurting the heart of God.

MARY AND US: When I look at verses like this, I know also that what breaks my heart also breaks the heart of my Savior. I, too, can be assured my wounds are His wounds, and that He has truly captured all my tears in His jar.

GOD SPEAKS: "Surely he took up our pain and bore our suffering…" (Isaiah 53:4 NIV) I am very aware of your most intimate hurts and pains. Your hurts are My hurts, and your pains are my pains. Not only are your hurts and pains Mine, but I take them into My own body.

WANDA'S PRAYER: Father God, we give You everything we are going through, from the large income tax bill to our crashing computers. We will continue to praise You, LORD, as You fix our "itty bitty" problems. Thanks!

October 21

TAKE A RETAKE, NOW WHAT DO YOU SEE?

"JESUS, ONCE MORE DEEPLY MOVED, CAME TO THE TOMB. IT WAS A CAVE WITH A STONE LAID ACROSS THE ENTRANCE. 'TAKE AWAY THE STONE,' HE SAID..."
(JOHN 11:38-39 NIV)

These two verses, as well as other companion ones, put to bed this nonsense of the All-powerful "weakling," that "soft headed" Christians worship as God. You may ask, "How so?" To answer this question, I will start at the end of this verse. Jesus looks at the stone covering this cave where His friend has been held captive in death's grip for four days. Then, turning to the crowd, He commands them, "Take away the stone." To our LORD, this one-ton slab of stone is only a pebble. This puny rock is a minor obstruction, and a small object in the Master's way. To Mary and the crowd, it was a major ordeal. So what is our LORD saying to Mary and to us, through this strange object lesson? He is saying that Lazarus' condition of death (separation, the end of life, the finished product), as "grave" as it is, is only a temporary one and not a permanent state. The Master of Life stands toe to toe with death. He looks death in the eye and tells him, "I AM removing your victory! I AM taking away your control, and I AM enlisting the help of weak human beings in this process." This entire show, Lazarus' sickness, and death were all for God's glory alone. Jesus declares that life does not end until He says so. Previously, He said, Lazarus is "sleeping" (a temporarily restful state) but I (alone) have come to wake him up. (John 11:11) Our LORD offers to Mary, and the crowd, the chance to take part in this miracle with Him. Our Lord is saying, "Join Me Mary, obey my command, and witness My glory." As she stood at that tomb, she had only two options—to believe His words, or not.

MARY AND US: Mary's options are my options every day of my life. If I say I believe Him, then I must put feet to my faith, and do what He commands of me as well. This speaks clearly to me. I must ask myself, "Wanda, do you really trust your LORD with every single area of your life? Have you given Him every 'outfit,' with matching shoes, in the closet?" In short, have you given Him your all? Is this act of surrender demonstrated in how you live your life before Him and the world?

GOD SPEAKS: "Where, O death, is your victory? Where, O death, is your sting?". (1 Corinthians 15:55 NIV) The answer to that question is wherever and whenever I (your LORD) allow death to have victory and to have a bite. I (God) create, and I destroy. I AM GOD AND BESIDES ME, THERE IS NO OTHER GOD. Believe this and live accordingly.

WANDA'S PRAYER: LORD, you are our God. Fill us with Your Spirit. Go through not only our clothes closet, but our entire house called ___ (say your name). You have our permission to straighten up, fix up, and tear down any and everything that is not like You.

October 22

MARY, I'VE GOT YOUR HEART—NOW TRUST MY WORD

"DID I NOT TELL YOU", REPLIED JESUS, 'THAT IF YOU BELIEVED, YOU WOULD SEE THE WONDER OF WHAT GOD CAN DO?'" (JOHN 11:40 PHILLIP'S TRANSLATION)

As Mary struggled in her mind, with a divided heart between obeying her LORD'S command to remove the stone, and her sister's strong opposition, Jesus spoke sweet words of comfort to her heart. "Mary, listen to Me. Did I not tell you that if you believed (My words), you would see the wonder of what God can do?" (Writer's paraphrase) Jesus is saying, "Mary, take your focus off of everything and everyone else, and listen to Me! Give Me your complete heart and put your total trust in Me." (Writer's paraphrase) Mary is like most of us. We want to see God's glory as shown by His awesome power. Jesus says, "Ok Mary, I will show it to you; but to see this show, you must step out in faith by walking out My words. Girl, just do what I tell ya' to do." (Writer's paraphrase) His words often times will defy the world's logic. Jesus asks us to believe, act, and think outside of this world's "box." How can He ask such a thing? The answer is because Jesus, the box maker, lives outside the "box" of this world—it is His box! He built it and He can do whatever He pleases with it. So, He looks at Mary and the crowd and says do not trust your eyes or your heart, but trust completely in me; let Me show you My glorious power.

MARY AND US: These words must have brought great comfort to Mary and the crowd, because in the next verse we see obedience to His command. Like Mary, Jesus' words are a great source of peace and comfort to me as well. I, too, can rest in complete obedience to His Word. The same Word that called this planet into being is more than capable of taking care of my every need.

GOD SPEAKS: "Offer the sacrifices of the righteous and trust in the LORD." (Psalm 4:5 NIV) Do you want to give Me (Jesus, your LORD) a gift? Well, this is the perfect gift for Me. Give Me your absolute trust and obedience to My Word. Let Me live in and completely through you. Be My heart, My arms, and My legs. Sacrifice—give up your will and rights, to do this thing for Me.

WANDA'S PRAYER: LORD, consume us completely. My God, we want our will to be totally lost in Yours.

October 23

CATCH AN EAR FULL MARY

"SO THEY TOOK AWAY THE STONE. THEN JESUS LOOKED UP AND SAID, 'FATHER, I THANK YOU THAT YOU HAVE HEARD ME. I KNEW THAT YOU ALWAYS HEAR ME, BUT I SAID THIS FOR THE BENEFIT OF THE PEOPLE STANDING HERE, THAT THEY MAY BELIEVE THAT YOU SENT ME.'"
(JOHN 11:41-42 NIV)

Here is another demonstration of our LORD'S love and care for His children. In the previous verse, Jesus, our loving LORD, has given His sweet words of comfort to Mary and the crowd. As evidenced by their obedience to the LORD's command to remove the stone, the crowd moves on in faith. As they do so, He gives them a greater revelation of Himself. He allows them the privilege of listening in on a private prayer between He and His Dad, the Father. This eavesdropping by the ancient crowd does several things. It shows us Jesus is not alone in the universe; He has a Dad, God the Father. It also shows us He (Jesus) is doing what His Dad told Him to do. This provides us with His own example of "doing as I do" (John 5:19). Next, it shows us that a wonderful event is about to take place. The resurrection of Lazarus was not a spur-of the moment thing; it had already been pre-approved by God the Father. Finally, it offers Mary and the crowd more opportunities to increase their faith. This is God-logic. You know who I AM, do what I say, and you will see more and more of Me, and what I can do.

MARY AND US: This verse shows me several things. I can see my LORD is just waiting with bated breath, to show me more of Himself and His great power. When I disobey His words, I lose so much. But when I obey, He gives me a greater display of His love and power. I cannot see the complete picture until the portrait is finished.

GOD SPEAKS: "When he had gone indoors, the blind men came to him, and he asked them, 'Do you believe that I am able to do this?' 'Yes, Lord,' they replied. Then he touched their eyes and said, 'According to your faith let it be done to you;' and their sight was restored…" (Matthew 9:28-30 NIV) Notice that the relationship between faith and works are like a double-sided coin. Faith in God is seen by obeying His words.

WANDA'S PRAYER: Father God, as You take control of our hearts and lives, may this faith be seen through our total obedience to You.

October 24

LOVE RESTORES LIFE

"WHEN HE HAD SAID THIS, JESUS CALLED IN A LOUD VOICE, 'LAZARUS, COME OUT!' THE DEAD MAN CAME OUT, HIS HANDS AND FEET WRAPPED WITH STRIPS OF LINEN, AND A CLOTH AROUND HIS FACE. JESUS SAID TO THEM, 'TAKE OFF THE GRAVE CLOTHES AND LET HIM GO.'" (JOHN 11:43-44 NIV)

The title of today's thought reminds me of a song I like to listen to by Helen Baylor, a Christian gospel artist. The chorus of that song is "Love Brought Me Back." In this song, she tells how our LORD repaired the mess of her life, and restored her for His glory. These words so aptly speak the contents of the above verses. True LOVE in flesh was at the cave of Lazarus that day. Jesus released him from the prison of death and returned him to life. Imagine Mary's reaction. I think her heart must have either skipped a couple of beats, or raced with lightning speed at seeing her dead brother return to life. An immense joy surely must have flooded her soul. Never in her wildest dreams could she have imagined her LORD giving her such a truly wonderful gift. Our LORD rewarded His daughter's love and trust in Him, with the gift of life—her once dead brother. But the work for Mary and the crowd was not over—oh no! The brother was alive and now he must look the part. Jesus says to the crowd, "Take off those dead man's clothes, he ain't dead—he's alive! Take off those old rags and let him go." (Writer's paraphrase) This shows us the work of the LORD is always ongoing. Our LORD is ever moving forward and wants us to move forward as well. We work as we wait for prayers to be answered, and we work when prayers are answered. We move from "faith to faith," ever-going forward in the Name of Jesus and in the cause of our LORD.

MARY AND US: This answered prayer shows me the LORD Jesus is still in the miracle-working business. This is also a preview for me of the excitement and joy I will feel when I am reunited with my dead loved ones. I think about my mother who died over twenty-five years ago. I will hear those words, "Come forth," and we will be reunited—never to part again.

GOD SPEAKS: "The LORD has done great things for us, and we are filled with joy. Those who sow with tears will reap with songs of joy." (Psalm 126:3,5 NIV) I am doing great and wonderful things on your behalf. Some things you will see now, but most, and so much more when we meet face-to-face. Give Me (Jesus) your tears and I will give you My joy.

WANDA'S PRAYER: LORD, thank You for giving us constant assurances of Your wonderful love for us.

October 25

WHAT'S IN YOUR DOGGY BAG?

"THEREFORE MANY OF THE JEWS WHO HAD COME TO VISIT MARY, AND HAD SEEN WHAT JESUS DID, BELIEVED IN HIM. BUT SOME OF THEM WENT TO THE PHARISEES AND TOLD THEM WHAT JESUS HAD DONE." (JOHN 11:45-46 NIV)

Recently, I went to one of my favorite restaurants where I enjoyed a delicious meal. It was so filling and so much that I just could not eat it all. I did not want to let it go to waste, so I asked for a "doggy bag" so I could take the "leftovers" home and savor the delectable morsels at a later time, when my stomach could accommodate them. This is the case in the verse of study today. The crowd of Jews had come to Mary's home to comfort her at the death of her brother Lazarus. Jesus had come there also. After crying at His feet with worship (John 11:32-37), she submitted herself, and the body of her deceased brother, totally over to the Divine plans of the LORD Jesus. He, the Master Chef, had so beautifully prepared for the crowd a delectable feast of His glory. He called Lazarus, who had been dead for four days, back to life. At this point, there was no doubt to all in attendance that God's power and magnificence was clearly seen in the person of Jesus. Such a display of power, along with the words He spoke, left many of them "spiritually stuffed." They had gorged on God's large, "Spiritual Platter." They were so filled from the giant "helpings" of God's love and grace shown that day, they needed spiritual "doggy bags" to take home the leftovers. But not all chose to eat from the "Café Ala Heaven." For those who did, they found this "spiritual cuisine" they took home, a tantalizing plate of faith in Jesus as LORD, seasoned with the sweet spices of peace and joy. The other group refused Jesus as LORD, thus choosing to fast from the Heavenly feast. This group left Mary's home starved for the source of life, which they willfully rejected. With empty spirits and starving souls filled with doubt and despair, they left the presence of the "true filling station." Having turned down the real meal, they now sought out the cheap, non-filling imitation of the Jewish leadership, the Pharisees.

MARY AND US: Mary's story tells me that when I give Jesus all the ingredients of my sorted life, and leave them to His perfect pleasure and awesome plans, in the end He will prepare for me a delight beyond my wildest dreams! Mary's "fixins" were herself, her home, and her dead brother. When Chef Jesus was done, He served to her, a resurrected brother and a crowd who would put their faith in Him.

GOD SPEAKS: "This is what the LORD says: 'In the time of my favor I will answer you, and in the day of salvation I will help you;… to say to the captives, 'Come out,' and to those in darkness, 'Be free!' "They will feed beside the roads and find pasture on every barren hill.'" (Isaiah 49:8-9 NIV) Give Me your life and let Me fill your starving, destitute soul with Me. I AM your soul's satisfaction.

WANDA'S PRAYER: LORD, feed our ravaged souls with Yourself, so that we "neither hunger nor thirst."

October 26

BEING IN HIS PRESENCE MOVES ME

"SIX DAYS BEFORE THE PASSOVER, JESUS CAME TO BETHANY, WHERE LAZARUS LIVED, WHOM JESUS HAD RAISED FROM THE DEAD. HERE A DINNER WAS GIVEN IN JESUS' HONOR…THEN MARY TOOK …" (JOHN 12:1-3 NIV)

Before we look at Mary's extraordinary act towards Jesus of taking, pouring, and washing, let us give some history as to what moved her to "take" what she "took." It was six days before the Passover. This holiday, "holy day," was the time when the Jews celebrated their deliverance from Egyptian slavery. At the start of this, the holiest of the Jewish holy days, an unblemished lamb was killed, and its blood sprinkled over the doorpost (the entryway) of the house, per God's command. (Exodus 12) The blood on the doorpost of that home was the lifesaving covering to its occupants. For on that very night, the death angel passed through the land of Egypt, killing its firstborn offspring, both human and animal. The angel spared the house where the lamb's blood covered the doorpost. As Jesus' earthly ministry was coming to a rapid close, He continued to rehearse to His followers that He was the "Lamb of God." Mary had spent many a day sitting and listening to His words. She must have sensed that at this Passover, He would present Himself as the "True Lamb," for which the Passover lambs represented. Convinced the LORD Jesus was about to take His precious blood as a covering for her sins, thus, shielding her from the penalty of death (death is the wages sin brings), and with eternal gratitude for raising her brother Lazarus from death, she intensely moved into action. So, "she took…" Mary was so filled with a deep love and awe for her LORD, she could not, and would not, let this wonderful occasion slip quietly by, without showing her extreme love in a very tangible way.

MARY AND US: In looking at Mary's heart for the LORD, I am forced to examine my own. There are not enough words or time to discuss the awesome thanks I have for my LORD; for dying for my sins and making me His child. Not only did He die for my sins, but He arose from the dead, giving me new life—now and for eternity. (Romans 6:4)

GOD SPEAKS: "The next day John saw Jesus coming toward him and said, 'Look, the Lamb of God, who takes away the sin of the world!'" (John 1:29 NIV) Look constantly at your precious Lamb, who takes away every last one of your sins. Never take your eyes off of Me. Each wound I was inflicted with says over and over, "I have loved you with an everlasting love."

WANDA'S PRAYER: Father God, as we constantly look at You, we see in the scars and bruises You suffered for us, new beauties. Thank You, LORD.

October 27

THE EMPTY JAR

"THEN MARY TOOK ABOUT A PINT OF PURE NARD, AN EXPENSIVE PERFUME; SHE POURED IT ON JESUS' FEET AND WIPED HIS FEET WITH HER HAIR..." (JOHN 12:3 NIV)

This verse raises many questions: What is this perfume called "Nard"? Why was it so expensive, and what was the significance of Mary's public act of pouring the entire bottle (about a pint) on Jesus' feet, and then washing His precious feet with her hair? First, let us start with the pure Nard or Spikenard perfume. This very costly fragrance was known for its soothing, calming qualities, as well as its rich aroma. According to Judas (Mark 14:5), it cost as much as one year's wages. The reason for its high cost was that the ingredients were grown in the Himalayan Mountains of India. So where could Mary have gotten the money to buy this very pricey perfume? Was she a descendant of royalty? Was she a high price "madam"? I do not think she was either; but the Bible is silent about where and how she got the perfume. Some have suggested this may have been her dowry given to her by her father. According to the teachings by Roeh Gibor, with excerpts from Joseph Good, based largely on Roland deVaux's Ancient Israel, "The minimal bride price (paid for humiliating a virgin) is 50 shekels of silver." According to the 1st National Reserve and Money from the Bible, "30 shekels equal one-half year's wages." So Mary, perhaps, took her entire life's savings, and purchased the expensive Nard, just for her LORD. Mary chose to perform her act of service, and show her extreme love for her LORD, at a dinner honoring Jesus. This greatest of honors she bestowed on our LORD would echo through the annals of time. Normally, she would have been relegated to kitchen work, the feeding and serving of the men. But Mary would have none of this; choosing not only to defy social norms, but risk public humiliation for herself and her family. It would have been scandal enough to pour perfume on the feet of Jesus, but Mary went a mile further when she got on hands and knees, and wiped His dusty feet with her hair. She did this at a time when Jewish women kept their heads covered in a public setting. Mary was breaking every societal "no-no," for her LORD. Mary did not care what others in the room thought of her; she only thought of how she could show the Lover of her Soul, how much she loved and appreciated Him. She made a deliberate effort to get and give her very best to Jesus.

MARY AND US: Mary's act of self-abandonment puts me to complete shame. Putting her story in perspective to my life left me with some deep soul searching. So I asked myself, "Self, would you mortgage your house, buy a bottle of 'Imperial Majesty' perfume at $215,000/bottle, and empty the entire bottle on the feet of Jesus in a public setting?" To be honest, I do not think I am there yet. I want to be, but I am not. Yet, I say and sing, "I surrender all"—but do I, really?

GOD SPEAKS: "Whoever finds their life will lose it, and whoever loses their life for my sake will find it." (Matthew 10:39 NIV) You have a true, fulfilling life outside of Me (God). Lose all that is you, and I will give you more than you've ever dreamt of.

WANDA'S PRAYER: We say to You, LORD, "I SURRENDER ALL!" We lay it all at Your feet.

October 28

WHAT'S THAT I SMELL?

"... AND THE HOUSE WAS FILLED WITH THE FRAGRANCE OF THE PERFUME."
(JOHN 12:3 NIV)

Cross references of this passage say the dinner took place at Simon the Pharisee's house. (Mark 14) The place must have been quite large in order to hold the town's "big wigs" along with Jesus (the guest of honor) and His disciples. Look again at the expensive foot washing Mary gave to Jesus. The verse says, "The house was filled with the fragrance of the perfume." According to "Organic Facts.com," the expensive Nard had an "earthy and somewhat wet soil like smell, resembling that of moss. It was used as a sedative and calming agent." When Mary broke open the alabaster box, generously pouring out its contents on the feet of Deity, her action spoke volumes. That one bottle of perfume quietly and effortlessly penetrated into every inch of the house. There was no escaping the creeping scent. The smell was on their clothing. It was in their nostrils. With every breath taken, they inhaled and exhaled the extravagance Mary so freely and unashamedly lavished on her LORD. No one in that house could escape the smell. The perfume affected everyone in the house. Without saying a "mumbling" word, Mary spoke. She testified to the "dignified" onlookers, with dropping mouths of her unrestrained—fanatical love of her LORD. Why was she so enamored with Jesus to the point of letting all the world know? Luke 7:36-50 appears to be a parallel story to this one in John 12. In Luke's account of the story, we are told this woman was a sinner. Jesus loved this woman completely; He forgave her of "many sins," and she was eternally grateful. In Luke 7, she not only washed His feet with her hair, but she continually kissed those precious feet as well. Everyone left the dinner that day with one question in mind as they carried the perfume odor with them: "What value do you place on Jesus?"

MARY AND US: As I look at this story, I am left with the same question: "What value do I place on Jesus?" In reflecting on the extravagant love, I see the LORD of the Universe has lavished His love on me by dying for my "many sins," and cleansing me from them as well. While I was never a prostitute, my lying, cursing, mean-spiritedness, gossiping and sometime foul mouth, are just as offensive to the spotless Son of God, Jesus. To show my love for what He has done, I would have to empty Fort Knox of all its gold, with that expensive perfume, and bathe my LORD a million times over.

GOD SPEAKS: "Therefore, I tell you, her many sins have been forgiven—as her great love has shown. But whoever has been forgiven little loves little." (Luke 7:47 NIV) As you continually empty yourself, and your sins, at the feet of your LORD, you will gain a greater appreciation for the cost of My (GOD'S) love. I want you, like Mary, to be totally unashamed of your love for Me. You can show your love for Me through a Holy, pure life lived for Me (your LORD).

WANDA'S PRAYER: LORD, may I never forget and always remember the extreme cost of love you paid to make me YOURS.

October 29

THE HIT DOG ALWAYS HOLLERS

"BUT ONE OF HIS DISCIPLES, JUDAS ISCARIOT, WHO WAS LATER TO BETRAY HIM, OBJECTED, 'WHY WASN'T THIS PERFUME SOLD AND THE MONEY GIVEN TO THE POOR? IT WAS WORTH A YEAR'S WAGES.'" (JOHN 12:4-5 NIV)

When I was a kid, I heard this saying. The meaning, unlike many of the sayings I have heard, was self-explanatory. "If you throw a rock into a pack of dogs, the one hit would be the one yelling out or hollering." Judas Iscariot is the first to complain about the "waste," and saying where he thinks the money could have gone. John points out in the next verse that it was not because he cared about the poor, but because he was the greedy treasurer who stole from the pot. (John 12:6) In his searing rebuke of Mary's heart pouring testimony, Judas revealed his own calloused heart. He called giving this gift to the LORD of Creation, the Lamb of God who took away all of our sins, a "waste." Then, in a fit of hypocrisy, in the next breath, he speaks of "helping the poor." This shows who the "real" sinner was, and it was not Mary. Mary must have known she would be misunderstood; much less appreciated, for the selfless deed done to her LORD. It did not matter to her at all. She was lost in complete love for her LORD, and nothing else mattered—not sneers or jeers, open rebuke, or quiet scorn. She was, as Gospel singing artist Helen Baylor would say, "Sold out to Jesus."

MARY AND US: My prayer and goal in life is to be that sold out to my LORD. I never want to embarrass Jesus through my words or actions. I want to get to the point in life where I do not mind humiliating myself for Him. LORD, what does that look like?

GOD SPEAKS: "Preach the word; be prepared in season and out of season; correct, rebuke and encourage—with great patience and careful instruction." (2 Timothy 4:2 NIV) "Preach" (tell someone) about Me (your LORD). Everyone on this planet needs to know I have provided a way of escape from their sins. Everyone needs to know that I am preparing a paradise for them, where they can be with (Me) God forever. Tell them how you spent time with Me and My word (the Bible). You are to live, breathe, and move in the love of your LORD. This proclamation of God is to be seen in every aspect of your life. As you do this for Me (God), you not only wash My feet, but you 'become' My feet, to the lost, hurting, and dying.

WANDA'S PRAYER: Father God, fill us with Your precious Spirit. Live out Your Holy life through us. Forgive us of all our many sins. Help us die to self and live for You.

October 30

THE LORD TO THE RESCUE—AGAIN

"LEAVE HER ALONE," JESUS REPLIED. 'IT WAS INTENDED THAT SHE SHOULD SAVE THIS PERFUME FOR THE DAY OF MY BURIAL. YOU WILL ALWAYS HAVE THE POOR AMONG YOU, BUT YOU WILL NOT ALWAYS HAVE ME.' (JOHN 12:7-8 NIV)

Jesus is always my knight and shining armor. We see in this verse, as Judas is hammering away at Mary, trying to give her a good "beat down," our LORD steps in and gives the cowardly, soon to be traitor, a knockout punch! Our LORD says to Judas, "Shut up—just be quiet; you do not know what's going on! But for your little 'pea brain' information, she knows I am going to die soon. So, she is giving Me my flowers (my perfume) while I can still smell it. The poor ain't going nowhere; they will always be here for you to take care of. However, I will not always be here." (Writer's paraphrase) If I were there, I would have said, "You go Jesus!" As we close our look at Mary, we see she was in a constant state of worshiping her LORD. At every opportunity, she was at the feet of Jesus. Because of her deliberate act of remaining close to Him in praise and worship, He will reveal Himself to her. She, like Moses, saw the LORD's ways, and not just His actions. Our LORD also wonderfully protected and defended His precious Mary. In this second round of criticism, Jesus was right there for His damsel in distress. He would allow no one to wound His child.

MARY AND US: In Mary's story, we see many things. She teaches us how to worship the LORD, as King and Savior. As we worship and praise Him, He reveals more of Himself to us. Looking at how Jesus protects His own, tells me I do not have to fight my battles; I just need to keep very close to Him and do what pleases Him. He will take care of me. Finally, as we stay close to Him, He will use our lives as a testament to His glory.

GOD SPEAKS: "Truly I tell you, wherever this gospel is preached throughout the world, what she has done will also be told, in memory of her." (Matthew 26:13 NIV) The search of most humans is immortality. Mary has found it. Immortality is in Jesus Christ, and in Him alone. She is immortalized in Scripture, and she has a place in My (God's) Kingdom. Mary gave herself to Me, and I gave her everything she needed. Let Me do the same for you!

WANDA'S PRAYER: LORD, to be even half as dedicated to You as Mary was would truly be an accomplishment. Please give us a desire, a passion, and an ongoing flame about our LORD, which continually consumes us. Thank You LORD!

MARY'S EPITAPH

"FOR IN POURING THIS FRAGRANT OIL ON MY BODY, SHE DID IT FOR MY BURIAL. ASSUREDLY, I SAY TO YOU, WHEREVER THIS GOSPEL IS PREACHED IN THE WHOLE WORLD, WHAT THIS WOMAN HAS DONE WILL ALSO BE TOLD AS A MEMORIAL TO HER." (MATTHEW 26:12-13 NKJV)

An epitaph are words written or spoken in memory of a person who has died. In this verse, our LORD gives Mary this eternal epitaph while she is still alive and for all to hear. This verse tells us that the little we give to our Lord does not compare with what He gives back to us. Mary has just bathed Jesus in this very costly perfume. This fragrant oil was probably her life savings. She had given Him her all. In return for her selfless act, she received much criticism. But our Lord boldly came to her defense. After rescuing Mary, our Lord gives her this wonderful living memorial. He tells her and us that through the annals of time, this woman's generous act would be told. Our Lord gives Mary an astounding honor, *"I say to you, wherever this gospel is preached in the whole world, what this woman has done will also be told in memorial to her."* Do you see the absolute privilege Mary is given? Worldwide and throughout history, every time we open our Bibles and read the gospel story of Jesus, she is given a place right next to our LORD.

MARY AND US: I am sure Mary never thought the LORD would honor her selfless act, much less memorialize it in this way. I think the lesson is very clear. The lesson reminds us that nothing we do for our LORD is ever lost or forgotten.

GOD SPEAKS: "The memory of the righteous is blessed, But the name of the wicked will rot." (Proverbs 10:7 NKJV) By your actions, you choose the category you will be in.

WANDA'S PRAYER: Lord, we want to be in the righteous category. Live out Your righteous ways in our lives.

Notes

Notes

November

INTRODUCTION

THE SAMARITAN WOMAN

If you have been a Christian for any length of time in your life, you have no doubt heard the scripture verse, "For God so loved the world that He gave his only begotten Son, that whoever believes in Him should not perish but have eternal life" (John 3:16). The Samaritan woman we are about to study embodies that scripture. She not only teaches us that God loves the world, but she also teaches us God loves the individuals in the world. Her life demonstrates to us how God goes to great heights to reach that individual, and to shower His love on them.

The Samaritan woman also shows us how our Lord comes to us even when we're not searching for Him. This is a great demonstration of His love for us. To quote the verse, "… It's not that we loved God, but that He loved us..." (1 John 4:10) This Samaritan woman clearly shows us how God is able to meet and deal with the deep-seated needs of our heart. He comes to us just as we are and deals with us there, thus bringing us to the heights He wishes us to be. Come, journey with me as we visit this lonely, isolated woman in a foreign land as she shows us the beautiful and wonderful love of our Lord.

Notes

November 1

GOD'S GOT HER ON HIS MIND

"NOW HE HAD TO GO THROUGH SAMARIA." (JOHN 4:4 NIV)

There is a general belief that women are better at multi-tasking (doing several things at once) than men. Jesus, in this section of Scripture (starting from John 3:22-4:3), shows us He is the "Master Multi-Tasker." In these verses (John 3:22-4:3), our LORD Jesus' popularity is increasing, as we see John the Baptist's ministry on the decline. You would think the rising "Super Star" (Jesus) would be far too busy for the "little folk." After all, He has large crowds to attract, mega miracles to perform, and religious leaders to battle. Surely, He does not have time to veer off the "planned" book signing tours and movie deals, to visit with one lonely foreign woman in Samaria, or does He? This short verse of today's study suggests otherwise. In those six words of John 4:4, we see a strong since of determination and urgency by our LORD. This verse implies He is not only driven to make this journey, but this stop is a big part of His planned itinerary. So, what is the big deal about going to a foreign soil? This foreign soil was considered "outcast soil," by all self-respecting Jews. The people who lived there were bi-racial Jews, mixed with other races. They were considered the "untouchables," and their land was considered contaminated soil. By setting foot in Samaria, Jesus was making a very bold statement! In this single act, He was tearing down centuries of racial barriers, while saving a damsel in distress. Only God, in human flesh, could juggle this schedule so effortlessly, and Jesus does not skip a beat or break a sweat in the process. Wow! You have to love the LORD for this.

SAMARITAN WOMAN AND US: This verse shows me just how my LORD cares about the individual. My LORD has "Eagle Eyes." He sees my needs at a distance and comes to my rescue. I see in this verse how He continually has me on His mind, even when I am not aware of it. The verse also tells me Jesus is a vindicator of unjust causes. In the end, He will "right" all the "wrongs."

GOD SPEAKS: "The LORD reigns forever; he has established his throne for judgment. He rules the world in righteousness and judges the peoples with equity. The LORD is a refuge for the oppressed, a stronghold in times of trouble." (Psalm 9:7-9 NIV) I, your LORD, have complete and total control. This is your LORD'S world, and He controls it. Beyond My (God's) awesome power is My extreme love for you. I am concerned about every minute and part of your little life. Never forget this!

WANDA'S PRAYER: LORD, thank You for always reminding us of Your great and tender love for us. As we look at that precious love called Jesus, may we be changed into His likeness.

ALL IN THE FAMILY

"SO HE CAME TO A TOWN IN SAMARIA CALLED SYCHAR, NEAR THE PLOT OF GROUND JACOB HAD GIVEN TO HIS SON JOSEPH." (JOHN 4:5 NIV)

In this verse, we are given some insight on how our LORD thinks. Taking the above verse, and the previous one (John 4:4), we clearly see the God man, Jesus, on a mission. Notice Jesus does not wander aimlessly throughout the country of Samaria. No, He goes to a specific town— "Sychar." Then, He goes to a specific place in the town— "A plot of ground Jacob had given to his son Joseph." This verse tells me my Savior, the LORD Jesus, knew exactly where this woman was. It also tells me He had pre-arranged plans to meet with her. This scene reminds me of a secret admirer showing up to meet the one his heart yearns for. Jesus, while busying Himself with the salvation of the world, takes out from His divine time to meet with a woman who does not yet know that He exists. Now this is LOVE! There is more. The fact that Jacob's well is in that place shows kinship with these people. After all, Jacob (Israel) was the "founder" of the Jewish nation. To Jesus, who is born of Jewish descent, this is family! Jesus comes to bring the "family," the Samaritans, home to the family of God. This was an amazing feat considering the strong hatred the Jews had for the Samaritans. While Jesus had these lofty ideas of tearing down racial bigotry and making the two nations one in Christ, the Jews held no such notions. So thick was the prejudice and hatred of these people, the Jews would rather walk an extra thirty to fifty miles out of their way, through the scorching desert, to maintain this despicable racism. For example, at that time, the average Jew journeying from Jerusalem (South of Israel) to Nazareth (Northern Israel) would never take the straight shot through the heart of Samaria, which was about sixty miles. Instead, they would go twenty miles out of the way to Jericho, then up through Perea, which was about another forty miles or so, to Decapolis. Then, finally, from Decapolis taking another forty miles to Nazareth. You know, the road of hatred and prejudice was a hard, long road then and now. Thank You, LORD, for paving a new highway through this bigotry.

SAMARITAN WOMAN AND US: Lessons learned: (1) My LORD knows exactly where I am. (2) I am always on His mind. (3) He constantly makes and carries out His plans, with me in mind. (4) He does all of this because I am His kid. I am a part of the family, and Jesus takes care of "family."

GOD SPEAKS: "Declare his glory among the nations, his marvelous deeds among all peoples. For great is the LORD and most worthy of praise; he is to be feared above all gods." (Psalm 96:3-4 NIV) When you look at Me (your God), and see the great lengths I went through to ransom and bring this lost world back to the family of God, I want you to give Me glory and honor.

WANDA'S PRAYER: Father God, we will give You much honor and praise! You, alone, are so worthy. We thank You LORD, for saving and caring for us on this planet.

November 3

HONEY, I'M HERE

"JACOB'S WELL WAS THERE, AND JESUS, TIRED AS HE WAS FROM THE JOURNEY, SAT DOWN BY THE WELL. IT WAS ABOUT NOON." (JOHN 4:6 NIV)

Many people have said to me, "if only I could find God, I would give Him a piece of my mind; I would tell Him all of my troubles. I just do not know where He is, or how to get in touch with Him." This verse tells me Jesus, God in the flesh, has solved that problem for us. We see in this verse it is the LORD who does the "finding," and not us. Our LORD and Savior, sets aside His successful ministry to go meet a woman in an out-of-the-way place. Jesus has come to Jacob's Well in the land of the "untouchables," to meet His "intended." This exhausting journey was no small trip for Jesus. Jacob's Well lies on the low slope of Mount Gerizim. Translation, it was on the side of a mountain. (Fausset's Bible Dictionary) He makes this grueling ascent in searing desert heat, which, the text says, leaves Him "tired" or worn out. What would make the God man, Jesus, do such a thing? He heard the silent heart cry of his daughter in a foreign land. The Bible tells us, "The LORD is near to all who call." (Psalm 145:18) He knew she needed Him. So, He scaled mountainous terrain and desert heat to reach this woman. It was about high noon ("the sixth hour"), when He arrived at His destination. The humanity in Him was tired, and He needed rest; so He sits down to wait. Though His flesh was tired and worn out, the God in Him was ready to bring this wayward daughter into His Kingdom.

SAMARITAN WOMAN AND US: I can relate well to this woman whose name we are not given. There was a time in my life when I was "just out there" in the middle of my sins. Jesus came to me because I did not know enough to come to Him. He reached out to pull me back into the fold. Even now, it is His sustaining power that keeps me ever close to Him.

GOD SPEAKS: "For he says, 'In the time of my favor I heard you, and in the day of salvation I helped you.' I tell you, now is the time of God's favor, now is the day of salvation.'" (2 Corinthians 6:2 NIV) I am as close as the whisper of your heart. It would be nice sometime if you called out My Name—Jesus! I love you and will always extend to you, My grace; that unearned favored.

WANDA'S PRAYER: LORD Jesus, we say Your name loudly! Thank You for saving us from all of our many, many sins. Keep us ever close in Your arms.

November 4

WHAT A LINE

"WHEN A SAMARITAN WOMAN CAME TO DRAW WATER, JESUS SAID TO HER, 'WILL YOU GIVE ME A DRINK?'" (JOHN 4:7 NIV)

Believe me, I have lived long enough to have heard some "come on" lines in my day (The lines men will use to get a date with a woman), but this one is a "showstopper!" Most men, wanting to get your attention, will usually say something "funny," "witty," or "macho." Not the King of Kings and LORD of LORDS. He approaches this woman in total humility and with a bit of helplessness. He politely asks this woman, a foreigner of a country despised by the Jews, for water. Why is this so remarkable you may say? Isn't He a man, hot and tired, needing water to quench His thirst? Yes, but our LORD is ever focused on His purpose—to seek and save lost souls. He approaches this woman, which is not what she is used to, but what she needs. She is used to men who are harsh, users and abusers of her; but what she truly desires is someone who is soft, gentle, compassionate, and loving—this is what the Prince of Love gives her. I imagine what she may have been thinking as she approached the well. She may have been expecting some brash "come-on" or some smooth line. When she recognized He was a Jew, she probably expected to be completely ignored by the man at the well. But this is not what she gets from the LORD of Love. Notice our LORD is first gentle. Next, He gives her options, "Will you give Me a drink?" She was not forced to do this, and could have said "no." Her actions (and ours), must be voluntary and never forced. Remember, reader, this well (Jacob's Well) was situated on the side of Mount Gerizim. Since it was not a city well, but a well in the middle of "nowhere," there was no bucket to draw with. She was carrying her bucket with her. The LORD was asking her to share herself and what she had with Him. Notice how He asks her to do for Him first; then she could get her water and go. This speaks to us as Christians. Our first and best is to our LORD. When we do this, He then supplies all our needs with "left overs" to share.

SAMARITAN WOMAN AND US: This is a "bucket-and-a-half" of information for me. I will start backward from the text. I note that when I give my LORD the first, no matter what it has cost me to do so, I am filled to overflowing. My day is filled with inner peace and joy, no matter how hard the chores are. I love the fact that My LORD always comes to me with love and compassion. He is unlike anyone I have ever known. I thank Him for giving me a choice; He never forces Himself on me.

GOD SPEAKS: "The LORD will indeed give what is good, and our land will yield its harvest." (Psalm 85:12 NIV) Remember, I (your LORD) am perfectly good. I give you what I AM—PERFECT and GOOD. I want the landscape of your life to yield a harvest for Me.

WANDA'S PRAYER: Father, take total control. Plow and prune in our lives what You have to, so You will get a great and bountiful harvest for Your glory.

November 5

IT'S JUST ME AND YOU

"(HIS DISCIPLES HAD GONE INTO THE TOWN TO BUY FOOD.)" (JOHN 4:8 NIV)

Here is another of those "in the middle of a though" verses. This verse actually piggybacks off of the previous verse. In that verse, Jesus asks this woman of Samaria for a drink of water. Let me paint the picture for you. Jesus makes this grueling expedition into the heart of Samaria, a land repulsed by the Jews, with His disciples. He, hot and tired, sits down next to the well. It is about noontime in this mountainous desert. He, as God in flesh, knows the woman whom He has come to meet is approaching. So, He sends the disciples away so He can have some quiet time with this woman. So, what is Jesus doing here? Has the humanity in Him taken over? Is He a "jack-leg" preacher trying to "score" on this helpless woman in the middle of the desert, with no one around? NO! NO! AND DOUBLE NO! The disciples of Jesus are ardent Jews. Though they loved and revered their Master, they wear their prejudices and bigotries like "robes of righteousness." Jesus needs to open up the heart and soul of this woman; she needed delicate, spiritual surgery to repair her. He keeps her private issues private; there is no need for an audience. Besides, she was not apt to lay bare her deep feelings and emotions to this stranger in the presence of a crowd. So, Jesus sends them to the city, a long way away, to buy food. This intricate procedure is going to take some time. He can now perform the fragile healing necessary. This verse reveals to us the deep care and concern our Savior has for us. See in this picture how our LORD truly loves and cares for his daughters. He has totally prepared the perfect place of healing for this stranger in a strange land. What a wonderful LORD we serve.

SAMARITAN WOMAN AND US: This verse reminds me of those times when I have been at a distance from my LORD. He was forever paving the way for me to come back to Him. The LORD longs for me to get alone with Him. He knows the complete me so very well. He knows the injury I, and others, have caused me. The LORD wants to expose those evil and damaged areas of my life; areas for which He knows I have buried deeply. Only He can do the delicate operation needed for true healing. Like this woman, it is in the "alone time" where this takes place.

GOD SPEAKS: "For the Lord God, the Holy One of Israel, says: Only in returning to me and waiting for me will you be saved; in quietness and confidence is your strength; but you'll have none of this." (Isaiah 30:15 TLB) I am the only cure for all your ills. Come, let us spend the day together. From there, we can spend an eternity together.

WANDA'S PRAYER: Ok, LORD, we are just gonna' stop right now and spend time with You, in prayer and in Your word. Speak words of healing to our heart and soul. We desperately need to hear from You.

November 6

YOU TALKIN' TO ME!

"THE SAMARITAN WOMAN SAID TO HIM, 'YOU ARE A JEW AND I AM A SAMARITAN WOMAN. HOW CAN YOU ASK ME FOR A DRINK?'" (FOR JEWS DO NOT ASSOCIATE WITH SAMARITANS.)" (JOHN 4:9 NIV)

The Samaritan woman gives Jesus an astonishing reply to His request for water. This is what I hear her saying: "Excuse me, sir! Haven't You forgotten who You are, and who I am? I have not, so let me just refresh Your memory. You, Sir are a Jew; I am a Samaritan. You know, I am a member of the race the Jews have rejected and debased. To add injury to insult, I am a woman from this despoiled people group. I am sure in this extreme heat, these facts must have slipped Your mind, Sir. But I am more than happy to refresh your memory. Do not forget now—Your people do not associate with my people. So, I will be more than happy to stay in my place, and will allow You the dignity of staying in Yours, Ok?" Our LORD Jesus knew her heart and her intense pain. It was from this place of hurt and anger that her mouth spoke. He came to her to allow her to unload her "tractor trailer contents" of stored up emotions on Him. Jesus was about to do the "great exchange." He would allow her to completely empty herself of all those venomous, deadly feelings which had for so long controlled her life. It was these feelings (and her lifestyle), which brought her to this well, far from her home in the middle of the day, in scorching heat. It was these feelings which held her captive. This day, however, it would be these same feelings she would feel no more. In place of the old passions, there would be new ones. She could stop eating from the rotten tree of bitterness. The "Tree of Life, with Healing in His Wings," stands only feet away. He offers her the fruit of, "Love, Joy, Peace, Patience, Kindness, Goodness, Faithfulness, Gentleness and Self-Control." (Galatians 5:25) Of this fruit, you could eat as much as you wanted, and still have room for more.

SAMARITAN WOMAN AND US: Wow! In reading this, I take a quick stroll down memory lane. For 16 years, I too, ate from the tree of bitterness. Its nourishment supplied me with the fuel of anger and resentment, which, for years, drove my embittered life. I met my LORD at the "Well of Life." It was at that "Well," where He took away the bad gas; along with the pain and grief which came with it. Now I am free! I have the Perfect Fruit, from the Perfect Spirit of God. It is sumptuous and delicious. My only regret is that I did not go to the "Well" sooner.

GOD SPEAKS: "Come to me, all you who are weary and burdened, and I will give you rest. Take my yoke upon you and learn from me, for I am gentle and humble in heart, and you will find rest for your souls. For my yoke is easy and my burden is light." (Matthew 11:28-30 NIV) My daughter, for years, you were needlessly strapped to the wrong yoke. Now that I have set you free, you are truly free! Stay free by being forever yoked to Me. I, alone, have the only light burden. I do all the work through you.

WANDA'S PRAYER: Father God, thank You for the freedom You give in and through Your Son, Jesus. Keep us continually very close to You.

November 7

WOMAN CHILL! I'VE GOT WHAT YOU NEED

**JESUS ANSWERED HER, 'IF YOU KNEW THE GIFT OF GOD AND WHO IT IS THAT ASKS YOU FOR A DRINK, YOU WOULD HAVE ASKED HIM AND HE WOULD HAVE GIVEN YOU LIVING WATER.'"
(JOHN 4:10 NIV)**

In my lifetime, I have heard many sermons preached on this text and the "Living Water." Every time I hear one, I am stirred all over again. Jesus Christ, the Bread from Heaven, the Word of Life, the answer to the craving of her heart, sits only inches away from her, and she is clueless about this fact. He says to her, "I AM (meaning that He is the God who has no beginning or end) the answer to your heart's true longing. I AM the Perfect Gift from God. I want to give you this free Gift. If you only knew this, you would ask 'Me,' and I would give you Living Water." Jesus could have said, "Madam, I am not the one in need—you are! I see the dryness of your hollow soul. The mere fact that you make this trek up these dusty slopes, in the searing heat of the day, to avoid contact with others in your town, shows the thirstiness of your unfilled spirit." (In those days, women went in the day's cool, to draw water, not in searing heat as this woman did.) Jesus knew all about this woman. His words proved He had read her soul like an open book. Every page of her life had written on it, "unsatisfied, empty—longing for more." He also knew He alone was the "More" she so desperately needed. Living water is water that sustains life. She made this daily journey to get the physical water to maintain her natural functions, while the recesses of her thirsty soul longed for the "More." Our LORD knew she was a hollow shell and that her insides were as dry as the desert ground she stood on.

SAMARITAN WOMAN AND US: Like this woman, the circumstances and situations of my life so battered and bruised me. In the end, I was left very empty and dry. I, too, longed for a filling of "Living Water." This is just what my LORD gave me, and I am so thankful!

GOD SPEAKS: "As the deer pants for streams of water, so my soul pants for you, my God." (Psalm 42:1 NIV) Of all the things in this world you may think you want or need, there is only One true want and need you really have, and I AM it. Open yourself up fully to Me, and I will give you not only what you need, but what your heart desperately desires.

WANDA'S PRAYER: Father God, thank You for being our total satisfaction. "You alone are our heart's desire and we long to worship You!" (Hymn)

November 8

SHOW ME THE BUCKET

"SIR," THE WOMAN SAID, 'YOU HAVE NOTHING TO DRAW WITH AND THE WELL IS DEEP. WHERE CAN YOU GET THIS LIVING WATER?'" (JOHN 4:11 NIV)

At this point in the story, we see Jesus is breaking ground in this woman's dry-hardened soul. Her interest in this "Living Water" has peaked, but she wonders aloud to Jesus how will He get water from a well, without a bucket. On the surface, the question appears to be one of skepticism, but in fact, it is more of a question from the heart of a "seeker," in search of the "Wellspring of Life." She points out the depth of the well; which its estimated range is from 100 to 130 feet deep. But her two-fold question is actually much deeper. Question 1: "How will You (Jesus) overcome these 'seeming' insurmountable odds (a very deep well and no bucket) to get this water?" Question 2: "You (Jesus) seem to talk about a different type of water than what is in this well, so where is Your water?" The Samaritan woman's questions are the same ones we ask our LORD today. She (and we) say to Him, "My problems, my predicaments, are so… big and so overwhelming. When I look at You, Jesus, I see nothing on You that tells me You can fix my problem." The next question we ask is, "Where are You (the God of the Universe, Creator of all things), going to get this promised solution to deal with my problem?" Actually, there is a third question also implied. That question is, "Jesus, You say You have a better plan? I need You to show it to me because I just do not see it!" Notice our LORD does not shut her down or make her feel bad. He allows her to speak freely and lay herself and her questions bare to Him.

SAMARITAN WOMAN AND US: When I face my issues of life, I have had the same questions and complaints about the LORD Jesus this woman had. Like this woman, my LORD never makes me feel ashamed about my questions, doubts, and fears. He allows me to lay myself bare and unashamed to Him. Then I realized, He uses this process to draw me to Him, and to build my faith in Him.

GOD SPEAKS: "When they saw him, they worshiped him; but some doubted. Then Jesus came to them and said, 'All authority (power) in heaven and on earth has been given to me.'" (Matthew 28:17-18 NIV) I have all power and authority in Heaven and on earth. Shouldn't all this power be enough to deal with your little problems?

WANDA'S PRAYER: Father, there is nothing wrong with Your authority or Your power; we just need to get out of the way, and let You do what You do so well. LORD, give us the faith to take You at Your Word—after all, those words spoke an earth into place. Power like that does not need our help; only our faith in it.

November 9

THE CHALLENGE

"ARE YOU GREATER THAN OUR FATHER JACOB, WHO GAVE US THE WELL AND DRANK FROM IT HIMSELF, AS DID ALSO HIS SONS AND HIS LIVESTOCK?"
(JOHN 4:12 NIV)

In this section of the story, we see something about both the woman and our LORD. The woman of Samaria calls Jacob (His name meant "deceiver" before God changed it to Israel, which meant prince of God) her father. In this statement, she exercises kinship to the Jews and to Jesus. In what she says, she has made this man (Jacob)—the deceiver, larger than life, and certainly larger than Jesus. She says he gave them that well. She credits nothing to God, who gave Jacob the well! Next, she magnifies the well. "This well is so… grand," (she is saying), "that it provided for Jacob (this larger-than-life figure)—he even drank from it. Not only him, but his sons (he had twelve sons, plus wives and children), their flocks (all those animals) and their herds. This well is so 'mighty' that it provided all this needed water." She continues talking to Jesus…, "And You know what? It provides for my needs, too." (Writer's paraphrase) This shows me how this woman (and I) lift people over and above God. She and I make frail, faltering humans into 'gods' and attempt to lower GOD into the weakness of flesh. Jesus shows perfect meekness as He listens to this woman's discourse. Jesus has all the power, yet it is perfectly restrained. He does not have an ego problem. He is well aware of who He is, and His absolute abilities. Man cannot deny it, and He does not need this woman to affirm it either. He simply awaits His opportunity to demonstrate it to her.

SAMARITAN WOMAN AND US: I can excuse the Samaritan woman's failing, because she has not yet seen Jesus' power and might, expressed in her life; but I have no such excuse. He (Jesus) has shown me His strength in my life, time and time again; and yet, at times, I still doubt and look to my surroundings, instead of to my GOD.

GOD SPEAKS: "For the LORD your God is God of gods and Lord of lords, the great God, mighty and awesome, who shows no partiality and accepts no bribes. He defends the cause of the fatherless and the widow, and loves the foreigner…" (Deuteronomy 10:17-18 NIV) I know who I AM! When you learn to believe and trust in who I AM, then we can get some work done in your life.

WANDA'S PRAYER: LORD, thank You for continually coming to us, and revealing Yourself. Strengthen us in You, as we take our baby steps of faith.

November 10

WRONG WATER—WRONG WELL

"JESUS ANSWERED, 'EVERYONE WHO DRINKS THIS WATER WILL BE THIRSTY AGAIN.'" (JOHN 4:13 NIV)

Having listened to all of her complaints, doubts, and fears, our LORD now responds. Jesus does not pull any punches, but goes straight to the heart of the matter, which was the matter of her heart. In the previous verse, she makes her forefather, Jacob, a god, as she heralds his accomplishments regarding the well. Jesus sets her straight. He tells her she is thirsty—very thirsty! Jesus also reveals she has not been, nor will she ever, be satisfied with "this water" she has been drinking. He tells her "this water" has only created a thirst for the True Living Water, which is God, in the person of Jesus Christ. This woman's soul was hollow, empty, and void. She could find no satisfaction in any of the things she did or consumed. Our LORD goes on to say she could drink from this well until the end of time, and never find the satisfaction she so frantically craved. In short, He, the LORD of life and fulfillment of all joy, looked at this parched soul, standing at the well in the heat of the day, and said to her: "Woman, you are drinking the wrong water, because you are at the wrong well." He would go on to tell her she needed a new watering source. There is a saying that insanity is doing the same thing and expecting different results. This phrase applies to her and me (at times).

SAMARITAN WOMAN AND US: This applied to my life before I gave it to Jesus Christ. It also applies to my life when I place other things before or ahead of Him. Anything or anyone I put in place of Him, in front of Him, and try to find satisfaction from, will leave me like this woman—only wanting more. This proves all the more that You, LORD, created me and I am Yours. You put a hunger and thirst inside me, which can only be filled by You—and only You alone.

GOD SPEAKS: "My people have committed two sins: They have forsaken me, the spring of living water, and have dug their own cisterns, broken cisterns that cannot hold water." (Jeremiah 2:13 NIV) Anything and anyone you put in place of Me, is your own broken water hole. When you place anything in your life higher than Me, you sin, break My law, and our relationship. Those "idols," broken water jugs, can hold nothing. In the end, it will leave you thirsty and unfulfilled.

WANDA'S PRAYER: LORD, always keep us near You; We need You to consume us. We (I) choose to die to sinful flesh, and we want You to live through us.

November 11

RIGHT WELL—SATISFYING WATER

"BUT WHOEVER DRINKS THE WATER I GIVE THEM WILL NEVER THIRST. INDEED, THE WATER I GIVE THEM WILL BECOME IN THEM A SPRING OF WATER WELLING UP TO ETERNAL LIFE." (JOHN 4:14 NIV)

When I read this verse, the word "satisfaction" flashes in my mind like a giant green neon sign. In the previous verse and in this one, Jesus reveals to this unnamed woman of Samaria just a little bit of His deity. He does this by first showing her He has read her tender heart like an open book. Then He gives her the perfect solution to her heart's ills—Himself! He tells her, "Woman, if you will only drink from the water I give, you will never thirst!" He continues, "Take Me into your heart and life, and I will completely satisfy your soul." (Writer's paraphrase) Of course, our LORD is speaking metaphorically about her spiritual condition. The God of the universe, in the person of Jesus, had crossed through the scorching desert and scaled mountains to rescue this woman from herself. Now, as the Savior and this woman sit by this well, which offers her a temporary quench for her thirst, our LORD makes a remarkable statement. He tells her He is the permanent fix for her problem. Jesus knew this woman's soul had a "God-shaped" hole. He had come to plug up that hole with Himself. Her ailment was an unfulfilled heart. The LORD Jesus presents Himself as the solution to this desperate need. This claim of Jesus can only be made by the God man, which He is. To make it plain, He says, "Lady, you need Jesus and here I am. If you take Me into your heart, and allow Me to live there, you will not thirst anymore." (Writer's paraphrase) Only the True God and Savior of Creation can make such a statement. Though that would have been enough, our wonderful LORD does not stop there. He gives her an additional promise. "This 'water' (Me) does not just satisfy, but it grows and changes into a 'spring' of water." In other words, "My satisfaction is not just a 'one time fix,' nor is it just a little satisfaction; but 'I AM' all you need whenever you need it. What I have will never end—it becomes a 'forever satisfaction'." He tells this woman, "I AM the Right Well—I AM the Satisfying Water."

SAMARITAN WOMAN AND US: Jesus also reads my heart like an open book. And, like this woman, He is my perfect solution, as well. I am amazed the LORD of Love cares for me so and has proved it by giving me Himself. Thank You Jesus!

GOD SPEAKS: "Come, all you who are thirsty, come to the waters; and you who have no money, come, buy and eat! Come, buy wine and milk without money and without cost. Why spend money on what is not bread, and your labor on what does not satisfy?…" (Isaiah 55:1-2 NIV) I can and will satisfy you in every way. Give yourself completely and continually to Me. You will find I AM all you need.

WANDA'S PRAYER: LORD, fill us completely with You and Your love.

November 12

OK, I BITE—I'LL TAKE IT

"THE WOMAN SAID TO HIM, 'SIR, GIVE ME THIS WATER SO THAT I WON'T GET THIRSTY AND HAVE TO KEEP COMING HERE TO DRAW WATER.'" (JOHN 4:15 NIV)

This woman says a mouthful in these few words. To understand her words, let us take a peek into her world. This woman is coming to get water in the middle of a very hot sweltering day, to an out-of-the-way well on the side of Mount Gerizim. Most of the town's women got their water in the evening because of the intense heat. (Genesis 24:10-11 and 29:7) According to Fausset's Bible Dictionary, this well she came to draw water from, was not the local "city well," but it was an out-of-the-way well. She went to this well for several reasons. She was avoiding people—she wanted to be alone. This was evident by the time of day she chose to go to the well. Also, perhaps she went to "Jacob's Well" for the spiritual significance. It was considered "hallowed ground." (John 4:12) Putting it all together, this woman has a past; a very painful one. She goes to extreme measures to avoid dealing with her past and her present as well. As she heard the words of Jesus telling her He has the better, more satisfying water, her soul cries out for the filling of the water He offers. "Sir, give me this (Your) water so that I won't get thirsty and have to keep coming here to draw water." (John 4:15) This is my translation of what I hear this woman is saying: "Sir, my life is so 'jacked up.' I have been making this long, hot journey up the side of this mountain for years. I am so exhausted from hiding out and avoiding people. It is so hot when I come, but I have to do it to avoid the scorning crowd. In the end, I find myself empty and dry. I am never satisfied. It is a trip that never ends and every day I have to do it all over again. It is a merry-go-round, and I want to get off. You say You have something better? You say Your water is satisfying and that it will satisfy me forever? Give it to me, so I never have to come back here anymore."

SAMARITAN WOMAN AND US: I hear this woman's heart because for years, it was my heart. I, too, was stuck on this never-ending merry-go-round. Like her, I was hollow and empty; I kept repeating the same actions—evil, unsatisfying actions, and expecting different results—insanity! When I heard my LORD offering the great "Water Exchange," I took His perfect deal, and I have never been more satisfied and more filled.

GOD SPEAKS: "Satisfy us in the morning with your unfailing love, that we may sing for joy and be glad all our days." (Psalm 90:14 NIV) I, Your LORD, gave you this thirst for Me. I am more than happy to satisfy you.

WANDA'S PRAYER: Heavenly Father, thank You for always reminding us—You alone are our heart's desire.

November 13

BEFORE I POUR IN THE NEW, LET ME FLUSH OUT THE OLD

"HE TOLD HER, 'GO, CALL YOUR HUSBAND AND COME BACK.'" (JOHN 4:16 NIV)

Our LORD Jesus is the Master at all He does. As the story continues, we see Jesus does not want to just give her salvation, or even eternal life. He wants to give her the "fullness" of life, in "this" life, as well. Previously, we saw this woman pleading for the "water" Jesus offered her. You would think that since she is now panting for this "Living Water" our LORD offers, He would have quickly given it to her—but no. Instead, He tells her to get her husband—what is that all about? Was He going to fix both of them at the same time? No! Jesus was getting to the root cause of all her problems—bad relationships, especially with men. Before she could receive this fresh, "Living Water," He needed to rid her of old stagnant "dead water," which had collected in the drains of her heart and soul. This clogged cesspool of bad relationships was the source of her hurt and pain. For her complete healing, Jesus needed total access to every part of her life, including this painful part. He would need to dig deep to rid her of the decay and death she suffered because of these bad relationships which plagued her soul. He commanded her, "Woman—go get the man!" This was the putrid area of her life and the source of all of her woes. She wore the foul odors of her failed affairs like grave clothing. The stench of her "man" problems caused her to avoid people. Her "man" problems brought her out in burning heat and took her to this faraway place to get water. This one sorrowful issue of her life kept her from the true life the Savior had in store for her. Jesus so wanted to pour into her, His "Living Water." But first He needed to flush out that "Dead Water" of bad relationships that had for so long, clogged the "pipes" of her soul. Our LORD knows you cannot fill an already filled cup. In order to fill her with His water, she must first be emptied of her own.

SAMARITAN WOMAN AND US: What I see in this passage is how Jesus completely satisfies me to the fullest. He deals with and fixes the total "me." Jesus shows His skills as the "Wonderful Counselor"—the Master Psychiatrist, as He probes deep into her psyche to heal her deep-seated pain. I can see both my LORD'S might and His love. His might, in that there is no area of my heart, He cannot reach. His love, in that He stops at nothing to save me.

GOD SPEAKS: "I will sprinkle clean water on you, and you will be clean; I will cleanse you from all your impurities and from all your idols. I will give you a new heart and put a new spirit in you; I will remove from you your heart of stone and give you a heart of flesh." (Ezekiel 36:25-26 NIV) My clean for you is a complete cleansing—nothing less.

WANDA'S PRAYER: LORD, wash us thoroughly and we will be whiter than snow. (Psalm 51)

November 14

OUCH! YOU TOUCHED A NERVE

"I HAVE NO HUSBAND," SHE REPLIED. JESUS SAID TO HER, 'YOU ARE RIGHT WHEN YOU SAY YOU HAVE NO HUSBAND.'" (JOHN 4:17 NIV)

A skilled brain surgeon can take an instrument and touch a particular area of the brain. Immediately after touching this exact spot, the person can have total recall of certain long forgotten memories. That recall is so complete, it is as if the person was transported back in time, and is now reliving the actual event. This is what our LORD is doing for the woman. Jesus, Creator of the Universe, knows what is in the heart and mind of this woman. To set her free from the emotional chains which hold her captive, He must touch this area of her life she has for so long tried to bury in the desert sands. The Master Surgeon opens up the layers of her wounded soul and gently touches the tender spot in her heart. I can almost hear her saying to our LORD, "ouch!" I picture her either speaking in mumbling tones, or with her bowed head, looking away in shame, as she says to Jesus, "I don't have a husband." Aha! This was Ms. Samaritan woman's problem—she was husbandless. Jesus, knowing her plight, probes still deeper. He knows this candid confession is only the first, but a necessary step, to her path of full healing. He gently replies to her, "You're right when you say you have no husband." Jesus knows this agonizing confession was the tip of a very dirty iceberg. With the words, "I don't have a husband," the Samaritan woman cracks open the door of her heart to the Savior. Having exposed her injured soul to the loving Savior, she could now allow Him to do His perfect work in her. The act of removing the layers of many years' worth of built-up pretense, which covered her shame and guilt, is the beginning of her healing process.

SAMARITAN WOMAN AND US: The Samaritan Woman's story is my story. I think the reason she is nameless and faceless is so I could put my name and my face in this story. I, too, walked around with layers of pretense and guilt for my many sins. One day I met the Savior, and He exposed the diseased areas and took it all away. I cannot thank You enough, LORD, for saving me from myself.

GOD SPEAKS: "Nevertheless, I will bring health and healing to it; I will heal my people and will let them enjoy abundant peace and security. I will cleanse them from all the sin they have committed against me and will forgive all their sins of rebellion against me." (Jeremiah 33:6,8 NIV) I was more than happy to take your damaged heart, and give you My perfect heart. Keep that heart ever beating for Me.

WANDA'S PRAYER: Father God, continue to allow us to live in Your presence always. Keep us ever close, so very close to You.

November 15

I'LL CUT IT ALL OUT

"THE FACT IS, YOU HAVE HAD FIVE HUSBANDS, AND THE MAN YOU NOW HAVE IS NOT YOUR HUSBAND. WHAT YOU HAVE JUST SAID IS QUITE TRUE." (JOHN 4:18 NIV)

In 1997, it took Dr. Ben Carson, a famous neurosurgeon, over 28 hours to successfully separate Siamese or conjoined twins. One reason for this is because the procedure was not one "big surgery," but many small surgeries done at one time. Conjoined twins are two individuals physically attached as one. The attachment is usually at a major body part, like the head, back, or hip, and includes the sharing of internal organs as well. The Samaritan woman has a similar malady. Her case is an emotional conjoining of her heart and soul, with her many failed relationships. Metaphorically speaking, she was connected at the hip, and joined at the heart, to these serial tragedies. Born with a "God-shaped" emptiness in her soul, she sought to fill it with human companionship. In her desperate search for satisfaction, she went through five marriages. Now she was so bruised by her botched relationships that she had given up on marriage and had now settled for living with a man who was not her husband; and, quite possibly, he was married to someone else. FAILED RELATIONSHIPS were so entwined in her psyche that they became her conjoined companion. The embarrassment of how she looked to the townsfolk kept her imprisoned in loneliness and isolation. To avoid the scorn and ridicule, she would go out in deadening heat, miles from home, to get the water she needed for her family. Our LORD, the Master Physician, who instantly diagnosed the problem, immediately starts the spiritual "microsurgeries" needed to separate her from her failures. With the scalpel of His gentle words, He cuts deep into the malady of her contorted soul. He says to her, (starting at the end of the verse) "Woman, you have spoken truth (though your true intent was to perpetrate a lie)—you have no husband. Now, let Me tell you why this is so. It is because you have had five husbands. You have tried five unsuccessful times to fill the hole in your heart, which only the LORD God can plug. It did not work out, and now you have just settled for having any old man in your house." (Writer's paraphrase) With the words of God, spoken by the God man, Jesus cuts clear through her cancerous facade, to begin her process of true and lasting healing.

SAMARITAN WOMAN AND US: When I reflect on what Jesus did to save me, I have to say, "ditto." The Samaritan woman's story is my story.

GOD SPEAKS: "Jesus answered them, 'It is not the healthy who need a doctor, but the sick. I have not come to call the righteous, but sinners to repentance.'" (Luke 5:31-32 NIV) Only the sick know they need help. People who are well think they are fine.

WANDA'S PRAYER: Father, all we know is that You have been there for us; healing all of our hurts, forgiving all of our sins, and ever drawing us closer to Your side. Thank You, so very much, LORD.

November 16

I CAN'T CONNECT THE DOTS

"SIR," THE WOMAN SAID, 'I CAN SEE THAT YOU ARE A PROPHET.'" (JOHN 4:19 NIV)

Some years ago, a new art form came along, which consisted of painting with "dots." The dots on the canvas were assorted in color. At first glance, the portrait just looked like multi-colored dots on a page. But with correct focus, the hidden picture was apparent. Veiled in the wall of dots were magnificent works of art such as majestic landscapes like the Grand Canyon or Yosemite National Forest. When I first saw one of those "dot pictures," all I could see were the varied colored dots. But with careful and continued focus, my eyes became trained to see the intended picture amid the dots. When I read this verse, I get the feeling the Samaritan woman could not connect the dots as to the true nature of Jesus, though He was only inches from her face. Let us review what has taken place so far. Jesus has crossed deep racial barriers, bore desert heat in mid-day, and trekked up a mountainside to meet this lonely woman. He has spent a great deal of time revealing Himself to her. He also displayed His Deity by recounting back to this stranger, her own life story with detailed accuracy. After all this, she looks at Him and says, "I can see that You are a (just) prophet." In other words, "Guy, you're a good fortune teller." (Writer's paraphrase) The portrait hidden from her eyes was that this "Man," was God's greatest and most wonderful "Gift," offered freely to her (John 4:10). He is the One her thirsty, unsatisfied soul panted for. She had said she wanted this "Living Water" (John 4:15), but she was unwilling to do all it took to accept the gift. She needed to empty herself, of herself, and "drink Him in" (John 4:13-14). How would she drink Him in? By focusing on His life-saving words— 'God's gift' (which was to be asked for), and 'Living Water,' (which causes growth and change). Then, by putting those statements together, along with His complete revelation of her life. All of those "dots" connected would reveal that only God can do those things. Had she connected the dots, she would have understood that Jesus Christ was not just a prophet, but God in human flesh.

SAMARITAN WOMAN AND US: I can relate well to this woman. I say I want Jesus to save me and take away the hurt. But when He starts to dig deep in order to show me the cause of my pain, I (like her) want Him to stop. Like her, I cut Him short guarding the wound that only He can heal.

GOD SPEAKS: "The seed that fell on the footpath represents those who hear the message about the Kingdom and don't understand it. Then the evil one comes and snatches away the seed that was planted in their hearts." (Matthew 13:19 NLT) Though the ground of her heart (and yours), is as "rock-stone," I am the perfect Gardner. When I am finished, those hearts will yield bumper crops. All I (your LORD) ask of you is that you would continue to give Me your heart.

WANDA'S PRAYER: LORD, do not just take our hearts, but take every inch of us. Remove all the stones, weeds and anything that does not give You glory.

November 17

I CHASE RABBITS

"OUR ANCESTORS WORSHIPED ON THIS MOUNTAIN, BUT YOU JEWS CLAIM THAT THE PLACE WHERE WE MUST WORSHIP IS IN JERUSALEM." (JOHN 4:20 NIV)

Now let us talk about the rabbits. In conversations, the phrase "chasing rabbits" refers to the aimless wandering all over the place, by the speaker; leaving the listener unable to make sense of what is being said. For example, the speaker may start out talking about cars, but end up talking about blades of grass—all in the same conversation. Meanwhile, the listener is clueless about what is being said. This is what the Samaritan woman was doing at this point in the story. Jesus calls her on the carpet about her deception on the "husband" topic (John 4:18). It was too sensitive and painful of a discussion for her to handle; so she quickly changed the subject. Now we just see her "out there," talking about places of worship. This is a great illustration as to what happens to us when we look truth in the face, then turn away. We, like this woman, go on long, endless, pointless rabbit trails. Her first pointless mission takes us to the "Do-It-Yourself" religion. With this statement to our LORD, "Our fathers (ancestors) worshiped…" She implies she does not really need a Savior, because she is not so bad. After all, she worships God too; though it is not the way the Jews worship. The second endless trail she is going down is, "since I worship God in my own way, this is acceptable to Him." This is the way of Cain, who offered God his "right way," instead of what God required. It did not work for him (Genesis 5), and it is not working for her either. If this self-made religion had worked for her, she would not have been at this obscure well in blistering heat, "ducking the crowds." To quote a gospel hymn, "What Can Wash Away My Sins? Nothing but the Blood of Jesus!"

SAMARITAN WOMAN AND US: When my hurts and sins have been too painful to deal with, I have done what the Samaritan Woman did. The only problem is that I dig myself into a deeper hole, and the issues are still not dealt with. It is only when I realize Jesus has the only remedy for all my ills, do I get relief. He does not just have the fix for all my problems; He is trying so desperately to give me His perfect solution.

GOD SPEAKS: "I do not set aside the grace of God, for if righteousness could be gained through the law, Christ died for nothing!" (Galatians 2:21 NIV) You can loosely paraphrase this verse to say, "If worship done in your own way, on some mountain; or if giving Me your 'goodness' was enough, then Christ died for nothing.

WANDA'S PRAYER: LORD, since we know You did not die in vain, we know we need a Savior. We know our Savior is the LORD Jesus Christ. Thank You for dying for our many sins and cleansing us of all our unrighteousness.

November 18

YOU'RE IN THE WRONG PLACE

"WOMAN," JESUS REPLIED (DECLARED), "BELIEVE ME, A TIME IS COMING WHEN YOU WILL WORSHIP THE FATHER NEITHER ON THIS MOUNTAIN NOR IN JERUSALEM." (JOHN 4:21 NIV)

I like the use of the word "declared" in this sentence. It means to make a firm statement. Jesus makes two firm but gentle statements to this woman of Samaria in one sentence. The first statement He makes to her is in continuing to reveal His Omniscience (God All-Knowing). He does this by telling her to believe Him (to trust in His certain—unfailing word). He then, again, gives her a future event. Our LORD says, "A time is coming… ('What I say is going to happen')." He knows the time is coming because He has already seen it. Second, He shows His erring woman that worship of the God of Heaven is not limited to time or place. "My dear lady, you have completely missed the point of true worship. You are hung up on a 'place' where you think you can meet with God." (Jesus might say), "I will tell you this: there is coming a time when the worships centers will not be on this mountain or in Jerusalem." (Writer's paraphrase) Jesus was telling her that the view she holds about worship and about God was small and insignificant. She thinks, as many of us do, that the God of the Universe is contained in, and restrained, to a place or time. Jesus points out to her He (as God Eternal) is any and everywhere she needs Him to be. Jesus wants the Samaritan woman to know that this God, who sits in her presence, is more than capable of satisfying her unsatisfied heart.

SAMARITAN WOMAN AND US: When I read this section, I get an additional reassurance of God being able to take care of all my needs. I am glad He does not get angry for having to remind her of who He is. As He is patient with her, He is patient with me as well. Finally, I am comforted in knowing my worship of the LORD Jesus is not relegated to time or place; but it should be continual and ongoing.

GOD SPEAKS: "Each of the four living creatures had six wings and was covered with eyes all around, even under its wings. Day and night they never stop saying: 'Holy, holy, holy is the Lord God Almighty,' who was, and is, and is to come." (Revelation 4:8 NIV) Sinless, Heavenly creatures know what you need to know. They know I AM GOD—THE ETERNAL, SELF EXISTENT, ALMIGHTY GOD. They know I am worship and praise.

WANDA'S PRAYER: LORD GOD, You are so worthy of our praise and worship. May we not only learn what worship is, but that we continually live in it. Show us how to worship You day and night.

November 19

THE DIVIDING LINE

"YOU SAMARITANS WORSHIP WHAT YOU DO NOT KNOW; WE WORSHIP WHAT (WHO) WE DO KNOW, FOR SALVATION IS FROM THE JEWS." (JOHN 4:22 NIV)

The Continental Divide is a set of mountain ranges in Australia. If rainfall lands on one mountain, it flows east, and if it falls on the opposite side, the water flows west. There is no middle ground. Jesus draws the dividing line in the sand with the woman of Samaria. He leaves no room for ambiguity (doubt/uncertainty). What the LORD Jesus gently, but firmly, tells her carves a line between her worship and His worship. The Samaritan woman had said to Him, her people worship the same God as the Jews; with the only difference being the 'place' of worship. The Samaritans worshipped on Mount Gerizim, and the Jews worshipped in Jerusalem. In her mind, this was a minor difference. In Jesus' mind, this was the Great Divide, which separated "known" worship from "unknown" worship. He says a definite 'no' to her false thinking of this point. He tells her in the above text that her worship is not known by herself, much less to the God of Heaven. To the LORD Jesus, this woman's worship is not an alternate style of the same worship; nor is it partial worship of God. He calls it a kind of, "you don't know what you are doing" worship. He does not stop there, but He says the Jews know (to be intimately familiar with) what the correct idea of worship is. In fact, He says that salvation (the way out of sin and death to life eternal) is from an only source—the Jews. He, the Savior (the one who will pay the penalty for sin), comes to earth in the body of a Jewish Carpenter. This was a startling statement in His day, and in ours. It blows away the theory that all roads lead to Heaven. Jesus says they do not.

SAMARITAN WOMAN AND US: Like the Samaritan woman, I started my Christian walk with a lot of missed information. I spent most of my life thinking I must 'work for' and not 'work out' my salvation. It was only when I spent intimate time with Jesus in His Word that I realized just how in error I was.

GOD SPEAKS: "Jesus said to him, 'I am the way, the truth, and the life. No one comes to the Father except through Me.'" (John 14:6 NKJV) I, your LORD, hold the only way to truth and life. Stay in communication with Me, and you will not go off track.

WANDA'S PRAYER: LORD, keep us connected with You continually; We never want to get off track.

November 20

LET'S BE CRYSTAL CLEAR

"BUT AN HOUR IS COMING, AND IS NOW HERE, WHEN THE TRUE WORSHIPERS WILL WORSHIP THE FATHER IN SPIRIT AND IN TRUTH. YES, THE FATHER WANTS SUCH PEOPLE TO WORSHIP HIM." (JOHN 4:23 CSB)

Jesus continues to give this woman a beautiful study in truth, and in Him (the Word of Life). In the last verse, He told her that her worship was unacceptable to God. In this verse, our LORD now defines and explains what God wants from those who say they are His children. The Samaritan woman discussed earlier of going to this place or that, to meet with God. These actions can become rigid, outward shows of piety which our LORD rejects. He wants worship (honor/adoration) of Him to come from the inner being of a person—from our spirit. Our spirit is the essence of who we really are—it is our nature. We cannot fake this part of us. We have all heard the terms, "mean spirited" or "gentle natured" person. These words describe the true character of a person. Our LORD does not want this inner person to worship Him with pretense or "put on." Jesus tells her that true worshippers are unveiled and unmasked as they lift up the LORD of glory. So rare is this type of worship that Jesus says the Father is "seeking such people to worship Him." The picture painted to her is the Father is searching to find this type of "true worshiper." In other words, Jesus is saying, "Lady of Samaria, if you really want to bring joy to the Father's heart, and put a smile on His face, give Him worship that comes from the deep recesses of your heart. Lift Him up in praise, in all that you do, and in all of who you are. It means nothing to Him for you to give Him areas, parts, and patches of your life. He wants and deserves it all." (Writer's paraphrase)

SAMARITAN WOMAN AND US: Like this lady, sometimes I want to give God worship my way. I want to give Him some, even most, but not all of my life. I realize, however, when I do this, I have given Him nothing at all.

GOD SPEAKS: "And you shall love the LORD your God with all your heart, with all your soul, with all your mind, and with all your strength…" (Mark 12:30 NKJV) As you well know, incomplete worship of Me (your God) is no worship at all. Either I AM LORD of all, or I AM LORD of none. I do not do "halves."

WANDA'S PRAYER: Father, in order for us to worship You the way You deserve, place Your Spirit in us. Give us a new nature. We want one that longs to follow You all the days of our lives.

November 21

I'LL TELL YOU WHY

"GOD IS SPIRIT, AND THOSE WHO WORSHIP HIM MUST WORSHIP IN SPIRIT AND TRUTH." (JOHN 4:24 NKJV)

To understand the meaning of this text, we need only to look at the lowly sparrow. He flies so effortlessly through the air. For centuries, we humans have looked with envy and wonder at his abilities to sail "on the wings of the wind." Finally, during the latter part of the 19th century, air travel was realized. Now, I can write this note at 35,000 feet above the earth, flying at over five hundred miles per hour. There are major differences between myself and my sparrow friend. I can fly higher than he, but I need help to reach this height. I reach my 35,000 feet height in a pressurized machine called an airplane, while the sparrow needs no such equipment. Artificial means must carry me through the air. This is what I believe our LORD is saying in this verse. The Godhead's essential nature is Spirit, though from time to time He has occupied a body, as in this case as He talks with the Samaritan woman. Since God is Spirit, true worship of Him must be worship in the realm in which He exists. No fleshly or intellectual worship can ever reach the level of the Spirit. We flawed humans can never reach the level of worship He requires on our own, no more than we could fly through the air without some sort of artificial device. The Jews understood they worshipped "the High and lofty One, who inhabits eternity." He is high and we are low, therefore, we must ascend to reach Him. The men of old had a dim concept of God's loftiness; whether they worshipped the God of Heaven or their own self-made deity. This is why they built altars of worship on high hills called "high places." Jesus offers this woman that new and perfect way to reach Him. She does not have to come to Him (because on her best day she could not). He comes to get her (and us), and takes us to Him in worship and praise, by way of His Holy Spirit. Jesus leaves her with one last jewel. He tells her God is also the total embodiment of truth. This means she (and we) need to look no further for absolute truth or the meaning of life.

SAMARITAN WOMAN AND US: As I read this verse, I am struck with just how much my LORD wants to share with me. All He wants me to do is to spend time with Him; listening and meditating on His words. If that were not enough, He wants to take me up into His presence.

GOD SPEAKS: "And don't get drunk with wine, which leads to reckless living, but be filled by the Spirit:" (Ephesians 5:18 CSB) How this statement applies to you is that your "pick-me-up," is not to be in the things of this world (i.e., alcohol, sex, or any other carnal pleasure). Your pleasure is to be in the LORD and in Him alone. This verse indirectly makes a bold statement. It says the Spirit is all the filling you will ever need.

WANDA'S PRAYER: LORD, since Your Spirit is the only filling we need, keep us always at Your service station. We want to be filled with You, continually!

November 22

I'M PEEKING THROUGH THE KEYHOLE

"THE WOMAN SAID TO HIM, 'I KNOW THAT THE MESSIAH IS COMING' (WHO IS CALLED CHRIST). WHEN HE COMES, HE WILL EXPLAIN EVERYTHING TO US.'"
(JOHN 4:25 CSB)

If you have ever looked through a keyhole, you know that at least two things are true. One is that you only get a glimpse of what is going on in the room behind the keyhole. Second, there is so much more you want to see, but cannot see through the little bitty hole in the door. This was the Samaritan woman's case. As Jesus opened the "Word of Life" (Himself) to this woman, she was seeing through the keyhole. But she had gotten a small portion of what was in the room behind the "Door" of the keyhole. From what little she could see, she spoke, "I know that the Messiah is coming" (who is called Christ). "When He comes, He will explain everything to us." (John 4:25) This (Man) speaking to her, brought back to her mind what she had been told about God. She recalls He is the "Promised God in flesh" (Messiah) who would come. She also knew He was to be the "Anointed of Heaven." In her next statement, she unknowingly reveals what had been foretold hundreds of years earlier. "When He comes, He will explain everything to us," she says. Isaiah says that He (the Messiah) would be "A light to the Gentiles." (Isaiah 49:6) Thus, our LORD is fulfilling Scripture to her very ears. What she had not yet realized, because she was only peering through keyhole understanding, was that He who spoke to her was that very Messiah, the Christ. The real beauty of this story is that He had scaled mountains and braved desert heat to bring her the Living Water of Himself. Now He takes His precious time to "explain everything" to her.

SAMARITAN WOMAN AND US: When I look and listen to my LORD through His "word" either spoken or written, I, too, see that I am only getting a dim picture of His total story of love for me. Like this woman, I see how very patient and loving He is with me, as He peels off the scar tissue that blocks my mind from understanding His word. He is such a very loving LORD.

GOD SPEAKS: "Love never fails. But where there are prophecies, they will cease; where there are tongues, they will be stilled; where there is knowledge, it will pass away. For we know in part and we prophesy in part, but when completeness comes, what is in part disappears." (1 Corinthians 13:8-10 NIV) I, the LORD, AM Perfect LOVE. Because I AM perfect love, I will never fail you. You may not always understand My ways, but you can always trust My loving heart.

WANDA'S PRAYER: LORD, thank You for a heart that continually loves us.

November 23

SHE HIT THE MOTHER LODE

"THEN JESUS DECLARED, 'I, THE ONE SPEAKING TO YOU—I AM HE.'" (JOHN 4:26 NIV)

The woman of Samaria had spent a great deal of time with Jesus that day. In this part of the story, we see she was about to receive a great revelation from Him. She had struck spiritual gold—she hit the mother lode! The information she had just received in this verse, kings, and prophets, would have died for. We see there is a direct correlation between time spent with God and revelation given from God concerning Himself. The more she stayed and talked with the LORD, and listened to His words, the more He fully revealed Himself to her; until finally, He gave her the grandest of all prizes. He tells her she has just had a private audience with the Creator of the Universe! Here He tells her, He, the Self-Existent God, was sitting at the well with her. He was that Messiah to whom she was just referring. He says to her, "I AM the one you, your people, and the entire world have been waiting for. The fulfillment of all your hopes and dreams sits before you now." (Writer's paraphrase) This woman shows us that our LORD Jesus cares for us as individuals. Jesus gave this great revelation in a one-to-one conversation. I also see in this story how Jesus comes to her; He did not wait until she came to Him. What a loving LORD we serve!

SAMARITAN WOMAN AND US: I am so glad my LORD comes to me with His love. I am also glad to know He longs to tell me more and more about Himself; and all it costs me is time with Him.

GOD SPEAKS: "For this is what the Sovereign LORD says: I myself will search for my sheep and look after them." (Ezekiel 34:11 NIV) I will always love, go after, and get what is Mine (your LORD's). You are Mine and I take very good care of what is Mine.

WANDA'S PRAYER: Thank You, LORD, for never leaving or forgetting about us. It is comforting to know we are never out of Your sight.

November 24

LISTEN, DID YOU HEAR THE PIN DROP?

"JUST THEN HIS DISCIPLES RETURNED AND WERE SURPRISED TO FIND HIM TALKING WITH A WOMAN. BUT NO ONE ASKED, 'WHAT DO YOU WANT?' OR 'WHY ARE YOU TALKING WITH HER?'"
(JOHN 4:27 NIV)

After our LORD gave His jaw-dropping declaration to this lowly woman at the well, it left her speechless. I am sure you could hear a pin drop on the desert floor that day. She was not the only one with a loss for words. The text says the disciples had returned and were surprised also. But, I imagine, with eyes-bucked and tongues wagging, they too were speechless as well. As my mother would say, "there wasn't a mumbling word." You might ask, "Why all that 'silence'?" We are not told for sure, but it is not too hard to figure out. The woman was in shock. Think for a moment if you had spent hours on end, talking with the Queen of England, or the President, or First Lady of the United States, in disguise. As you talked with this person, you found them to be so easy-going and such a beautiful person, only to find out you were conversing with an impressive VIP (Very Important Person). Now, multiply this event times a hundred billion and you have what is going on here. My heart would have stopped too! In the disciple's case, it was the racism "cat," which held their tongues. They simply could not believe "their" LORD would talk to a person of this despised race—and to make matters worse, this was a woman. This was the lowest of the low. Jesus had certainly blown their minds. He shows the disciples, the woman of Samaria, and us, that God is not a local, confining God. He is indeed the GOD of the Universe. As God of all, He does whatever He pleases; and who is going to tell God what to do?

SAMARITAN WOMAN AND US: The LORD Jesus shows us He rules over all. I can trust in the God who controls all. I love the fact that our LORD knows exactly what He is doing, and He does what is best for all, with no doubt or hesitation.

GOD SPEAKS: "How great you are, Sovereign LORD! There is no one like you, and there is no God but you, as we have heard with our own ears." (2 Samuel 7:22 NIV) I (your LORD) rule and reign over time, space, and everything in between. Allow Me to have the total reign of your little heart.

WANDA'S PRAYER: Father God and LORD Jesus, take total control of our hearts. Come, sit down—rule and reign as You should. I can see how much You truly love us. We want to give to You what You desire most—an undivided heart, which reflects in all we do.

November 25

I GOTTA' NEW RUN NOW!

"THEN, LEAVING HER WATER JAR, THE WOMAN WENT BACK TO THE TOWN AND SAID TO THE PEOPLE, ..." (JOHN 4:28 NIV)

This is what Jesus can do to a life that He has full rule and reign over. This is what a Christ-changed life looks like. You might say, "What you say, Wanda Faye?" Come on—go back with me to the beginning of the story of Jesus and this woman. Have you forgotten why she is on this distant hill side in searing heat hiding from the crowd? Let me just refresh your memory a little. She is ashamed and embarrassed at her lifestyle. But now, after just one afternoon on the King's couch (Jacob's well), instead of the psychoanalysis couch, she is running to the crowd she ran away from for years! In one afternoon, Jesus has done what years of therapy on a human couch could never do. He has changed her heart and we can see it through her actions. As the song says, "Just a little talk with Jesus (and Him alone) makes it right." The Samaritan woman can attest to this fact. She now embraces with joy, what only hours before she would have avoided. After being in the presence of the All-Seeing, All-Knowing LORD, she has no shame. She now boldly faces what was once her deepest hurt (her interpersonal relationships), by running towards them instead of running away from them. I tell you when the LORD Jesus changes a life—He really changes a life. AMEN!

SAMARITAN WOMAN AND US: One issue I had before I allowed Jesus to change my heart was depression. It displayed itself as anger. You could say I was an "angry, Black woman" (I could have written the script for Mr. Perry's movie). I spent time with my LORD in His Word (the Bible) and in prayer. As I continued to allow the LORD Jesus to strip me of all the hurt, pain, and guilt, I came away like the Samaritan woman—totally free and unashamed.

GOD SPEAKS: "So if the Son sets you free, you will be free indeed." (John 8:36 NIV) I have set you free—now be free and stay free.

WANDA'S PRAYER: LORD, we would like to paraphrase for a moment, and say this: "Since the LORD has set us free, we are truly free indeed!" Thank You for setting every inch of us free. Thank You for reminding us we do not have to get the rope and tie ourselves back down. Thank You for loving us so very much.

November 26

JUST KNOWING JESUS

"COME, SEE A MAN WHO TOLD ME EVERYTHING I EVER DID. COULD THIS BE THE MESSIAH?"
(JOHN 4:29 NIV)

The pastor's wife at the church wrote and sang this beautiful song I loved hearing. It was entitled, "Just Knowing Jesus." A couple of the verses were: "If you have always had a lot of friends, you would not know how it hurts to be lonely. I have seen hard times and been through many hard days; I have a testimony. I have somethin' to shout about—just knowing Jesus, just knowing God, paid off in my life." Verses like these must have bellowed through this woman's soul, as she ran back to town compelling everyone she met to "come and see" the Man Jesus who had completely changed her life. She was definitely singing, "Everybody Ought To Know Who Jesus Is." Her message to everyone she met was short and deliciously sweet, "Just come back with me and see this man. I just met Him myself. My life was a complete mess. I was torn up from the floor up, and beat down from the head down, with depression and heartache. He knew it all and loved me despite what He knew. Like a skilled surgeon, He opened up and exposed every nasty, discussing flaw I had. He did not just take away all the hurt and pain, He replaced it with His peace, joy, and wonderful love. He helped me and He can help you too. Let me take you to Him; see for yourself if the Man is indeed the Christ (God in flesh) or not?" (Writer's paraphrase) In a nutshell, this is the message of the Gospel—the good news that Jesus saves.

SAMARITAN WOMAN AND US: The song I could sing right now is called "Changed," sung by Tramaine Hawkins. The words are: "A change has come over me … He changed my life and now I am free …" I too, want to go and tell everybody I meet about how the LORD saved me from myself. He set me free from anger, depression, and sexual lust. Do I not still have "pop-ups" that enter my heart and mind from time to time? Yes! But in there now is freedom. He reigns and controls my emotions as I completely submit my life to Him. He becomes that firewall of protection to take away the sins and remove the thoughts.

GOD SPEAKS: "Turn to me and be saved, all you ends of the earth; for I am God, and there is no other." (Isaiah 45:22 NIV) I AM (your LORD) GOD; you do not have to look anywhere else. I AM all you will ever need. Make your complete dependence on Me (GOD).

WANDA'S PRAYER: Heavenly Father, You alone are God; there is no comparison to You or Your greatness.

November 27

I'M COMING, WAIT ON ME

"EVERYONE IN TOWN WENT OUT TO SEE JESUS." (JOHN 4:30 CEV)

This is a beautiful scene to behold. "Everyone in the town went out to see Jesus." (John 4:30) In this verse, as a result of the power of God displayed in this one woman's simple, heart-felt testimony, we see the town's people coming to see Jesus in masses. The Samaritan woman's words were genuine and very believable. She may have been known to them as the "woman that couldn't keep a man," or possibly, "the woman who took other women's husbands," or maybe no one knew of her at all because she avoided them. Whatever her story was the day before she met Jesus, today she has a new story. Today is a different day. This is the day Heaven came down (in the person of Jesus Christ) and filled her soul. Her prior reputation was not a good one, but now she had a new life in Christ. The old was gone, He (Jesus) had made all things new, and Sista' girl was shouting about it. She is now the "lady evangelist" running joyfully to the crowd she once avoided, pleading with them as she cries out with a loud voice, "Come and see a man who told me everything I ever did. Is this not the Christ?" She is no longer running away from them, but charging towards them at lightning speed. They could see she no longer cared about what they knew or thought of her. All that mattered to her is that they (the town's folk) would come to know this God-man—Jesus. She wanted everyone to experience the love and freedom from sin she now knew. So, she ran through the streets of Samaria compelling them to come, and come they did. Seeing her genuine sincerity, they came by the masses. Convinced of the miraculous change in her life, the town gladly came out to see Jesus. If He could fix her problems, they thought, surely He could fix theirs.

SAMARITAN WOMAN AND US: This woman screams to my heart and soul, twenty-five hundred years later. What she is telling me is to "keep is simple stupid." A simple testimony of God's displayed love in my life is all that is needed. This testimony will also be followed up by a changed life. When people see this changed life, they will want to come and meet this Jesus, who changed my life.

GOD SPEAKS: "That which was from the beginning, which we have heard, which we have seen with our eyes, which we have looked at and our hands have touched—this we proclaim concerning the Word of life." (John 1:1 NIV) You have a personal relationship with Me (the God of the Universe). If you love Me the way you say you do, let everyone know it in what you say, and in how you live.

WANDA'S PRAYER: Father God, give us a Holy boldness to live out our lives totally for you, and to tell everyone we meet about You.

November 28

A MESSAGE FROM THE MASTER'S HEART

"YOU MAY SAY THAT THERE ARE STILL FOUR MONTHS UNTIL HARVEST TIME. BUT I TELL YOU TO LOOK, AND YOU WILL SEE THAT THE FIELDS ARE RIPE AND READY TO HARVEST." (JOHN 4:35 CEV)

Jesus spoke the words of this verse to His disciples, as the entire town of Samaria was making their way to this obscure well outside of Sychar, on the slopes of Mount Gerizim. (John 4:30) His disciples, having just returned from the town on an errand to buy food, were concerned only with momentary physical needs of hunger and thirst. (John 4:31) Jesus' focus was on the larger, grandeur picture. His greatest concern was the spiritual hunger of the approaching throng. As the crowds were making their way to Him, He bellows to His disciples, "This is the food that satisfies Me. Hungering, thirsting souls, seeking the pure food of righteousness, only found in God, in the person of Jesus. Look at them, pouring out of their homes, as they seek the satisfaction that only the Son of God can give. This is the food I hunger for! This is My feast and its ready to eat." (Writer's paraphrase) This is our LORD'S tender heart and was the reason He made this necessary stop to these "heathen people." He saw the hunger and dryness of this community. In this lesson, we see what our LORD Jesus sees. He sees the inner core of man's heart—his inner desire, hidden from the rest of the world. He also sees that by reaching one genuine, committed person for Him, it would reap an entire town of saved souls. Our LORD Jesus changed the woman of Samaria's heart and spirit, and she quickly went out to compel others to come and receive that same wonderful touch she herself had received.

SAMARITAN WOMAN AND US: In this story, I see the heart of my LORD, Jesus. He does not want me to hoard up this beautiful gift of salvation for myself. As Gospel singing artist Yolanda Adams sings, "I've gotta tell it—I've gotta tell it!" Jesus came to this decaying world trapped in the dungeon of sin to provide its only key to freedom—Himself. The woman of Samaria found this out and told everyone in her town. In looking at her life, I see this is my only true function in life as well. I have been set free and sent back to show others the Way to true freedom.

GOD SPEAKS: "It is for freedom that Christ has set us free. Stand firm, then, and do not let yourselves be burdened again by a yoke of slavery." (Galatians 5:1 NIV) The freedom I have given you in Christ, you are to now let everyone know about it.

WANDA'S PRAYER: LORD, at times our problem is that we are so filled with self that we squeeze You out. We want to die of self and selfishness now! Father God, take over our lives—rule and reign over us completely.

November 29

A BUMPER CROP

"MANY OF THE SAMARITANS FROM THAT TOWN BELIEVED IN HIM BECAUSE OF THE WOMAN'S TESTIMONY, 'HE TOLD ME EVERYTHING I EVER DID.'" (JOHN 4:39 NIV)

Until now, I believed giving my testimony or "witnessing for the LORD," was so complicated and hard—no! It is simply telling others what Jesus has done for you. This is exactly what the woman of Samaria did. The verse tells us this woman's testimony was simple and to the point, "He told me everything I ever did." So, what is she saying? She is saying, "He knew me inside and out. He loved me despite what He knew about me, and He saved me from myself. For years, failed relationships held me captive. This caused me much agony and grief. I spent years hiding and avoiding people. I was so sad and lonely until Jesus met me at this distant well. In only a few hours, He dug deep into the inner parts of my heart and thirsty soul. He cleansed out all the garbage and then He washed me clean with His pure 'living water.' This 'living water' filled me with His joy and His peace. He saved me from me! Now, I've got to tell everyone of the wonderful love and joy I have. Come, go with me, and meet Him for yourself. See if He cannot fix you—just like He fixed me." (Wanda's paraphrase) The response to her genuine testimony was the conversion of "many Samaritans who believed in Him because of the woman's testimony…" The message is very clear.

SAMARITAN WOMAN AND US: The verse speaks for itself, and it screams truth in my ears. Sad to say, sometimes I did not want to give my testimony. I did not want to share the LORD Jesus' goodness to me with anyone else. I was embarrassed or afraid. This was not only a great loss to those needing to hear and receive the loving LORD—it was a great loss to me. Looking back, I can see I was selfish, very selfish. I made it all about me when it never should have been.

GOD SPEAKS: "And I, when I am lifted up from the earth, (I) will draw all people to myself." (John 12:32 NIV) Where in that verse are you alone mentioned? Nowhere! I (your LORD and God) the one with all power, alone, is to be "lifted up from the earth." I AM not subject to the contamination and failing of the earth because I AM so much higher. When I AM put in My rightful place (above and beyond this planet of woe), I will draw men (everyone) up and above, to where I am. I am all about the Kingdom of God. God is Savior, and God in Jesus is King. Wanda, lift up your LORD God—He will draw, and He will save.

WANDA'S PRAYER: Father God, please forgive us for our disobedience when we did not lift You up, as we should have. We were only exalting ourselves. Teach us to lift You, oh LORD, in everything we say and do.

November 30

WE NEED MORE WATER

"SO WHEN THE SAMARITANS CAME TO HIM, THEY URGED HIM TO STAY WITH THEM, AND HE STAYED TWO DAYS. AND BECAUSE OF HIS WORDS MANY MORE BECAME BELIEVERS." (JOHN 4:40-41 NIV)

The Samaritan woman's testimony was the spark that set the entire country of Samaria ablaze with the words of Jesus. Her compelling words caused the town to come out to hear Him. This brings up an excellent point to consider about witnessing (giving our testimony) for Jesus. Notice the Samaritan woman did not have to preach a sermon or sing a song. All that was needed was to simply say what Jesus had done for her. After hearing her words, they came to hear and see Jesus for themselves. After they came, He did the rest. The people were so taken with the Savior's (Jesus') life-giving words. His words to their ears and hearts were the refreshing water of life the woman had experienced earlier herself. As the people drank this spiritual water of life, it had a strange effect on them. His words were fully satisfying to them and yet, it left a desperate craving to hear more of His life-sustaining morsels. They simply could not get enough of Him or His words. To the dry, parched souls of Samaria, Jesus' words were cool springs of living water. They desired to hear more, so they urged Him to stay. Our Savior was all too happy to continue filling those empty vessels with His pure water of life. The end results were His words, saving more souls. The woman of Samaria is a picture of what happens when we do our small part. Jesus is more than capable of doing the rest. Her part may have seemed so insignificant. What if she had said, "I'm too afraid to share what Jesus has done for me, they might laugh to scorn." Keeping her mouth shut could have condemned these people to hell. Instead, we read this fairy tale ending of how the Prince of Glory (Jesus) saves the entire town through the witness of an outcast woman. Truly (as someone said), "little becomes much, in the Master's hands." From this little seed of a tiny testimony, we see the harvest of an entire town.

SAMARITAN WOMAN AND US: This woman's testimony cuts me like a knife. I stand accused. I am guilty of selfish grace. This is grace I have freely and lavishly received, yet kept it all to myself. I forgot that if it were not for someone coming and sharing the love of God with me, I, too, would still be lost. LORD, give me the love that You have for the lost soul. Break my heart, the way Your heart breaks, for Your lost creation. Then fill me with Your Spirit so that I cannot help but cry out to everyone I see of Your wonderful love.

GOD SPEAKS: "Surely God is my salvation; I will trust and not be afraid. The LORD, the LORD himself, is my strength and my defense; he has become my salvation." With joy you will draw water from the wells of salvation." (Isaiah 12:2-3 NIV) Do not be afraid. Just know that I want to save all who will allow Me, from the hell I saved you from. Draw from the "Wells of My salvation!" Drink from it yourself and also give it to others to quench their thirst.

WANDA'S PRAYER: My LORD God, always quench our thirst from the "Well of Your Salvation." Clear any obstruction which prevents the flow of Your Living water, from reaching into every part of our mind, heart, body, and soul. Fill us to overflowing with You! May we then, and always be a fountain through which Your Living Water will flow over and into the lives of others. May they be drawn and come close to You, through Your life-giving words. LORD, we want to freely give as You have so graciously given to us.

A TESTAMENT OF HER TESTIMONY

THEY SAID TO THE WOMAN, 'WE NO LONGER BELIEVE JUST BECAUSE OF WHAT YOU SAID; NOW WE HAVE HEARD FOR OURSELVES, AND WE KNOW THAT THIS MAN REALLY IS THE SAVIOR OF THE WORLD.'" (JOHN 4:42 NIV)

As we end our brief visit with the Woman of Samaria, we see it end as it began. You might ask, "Where is that?" It ends with the wonderful words of Jesus—the Word of Life—Jesus the Christ. The words of our LORD Jesus possess' creative power. (Genesis 1-2; John 1:1-4) First, we see how His words brought life to her dying soul. She was no longer hiding and avoiding the crowd. She is no longer ashamed of what she was. Now she passionately tells the town of how Jesus' words, those healing words, set her free. The people, having known her history, believed in His healing words spoken to her. Their belief in those words brought them out to meet Him. Now, having met Him for themselves, their faith has greatly increased. Having heard His words, they knew Him to be the Savior of the world. The statement is astounding, considering the people saying this have such limited knowledge, as compared to the known (the Old Testament). They only had the first five books of the Bible alone. They had also mixed God's words with pagan idol worship. But, when presented with the Word of Life (Jesus), it left no doubt in their minds, this Man is the "Savior of the World." In other words, this Jesus is the long-awaited Messiah. This was a revelation the learned Jews have yet to accept. The Samaritan woman (also known as the woman at the well) speaks two things very clearly to me. She tells me by example that when Jesus comes in, the change is as different as night and day. Finally, she says to me when the LORD OF LOVE has entered my soul, I want to share that love with everyone I meet, which is exactly what she did.

SAMARITAN WOMAN AND US: Thanks to this woman and others like her in the precious Word of God, I am reminded of how God loves the world so much that He Himself came to save us. Thank You, LORD, for Your wonderful Gift—Jesus the Christ!

GOD SPEAKS: "For God so loved the world that he gave his one and only Son, that whoever believes in him shall not perish but have eternal life." (John 3:16 NIV) God's love is universal, and it is eternal. The love I have will do everything to save you from destruction and eternal death. All you have to do is just believe in My words. Let Me live in your heart. Like the Samaritan woman, I can change you from the inside out.

WANDA'S PRAYER: LORD, thank You so much for Your free and beautiful gift! LORD Jesus, come and forever dwell in our hearts.

Notes

Notes

December

INTRODUCTION

MARY, THE MOTHER OF JESUS

When we think of honors bestowed upon humans, we can think of no greater honor than what was given to Mary, the mother of our Lord Jesus. God hand-picked, and chose the young Mary from all the women that have lived or who will ever live on planet earth. She would be given the privilege of bringing the God of Heaven to our world in human form. This was indeed a high privilege the King of the Universe would give her. Imagine being chosen for such a great honor.

This young woman is remarkable and teaches us many things. Her life teaches us that even at a young age we can decide to be totally committed to the LORD. As we walk through her life as given to us on the pages of scripture, we will see what genuine commitment looks like. The job our LORD gives her would not be an easy one—oh no! But this young woman would remain steadfast and unmovable as she carries out the task given to her. In carrying out her task as being the human mother of the Christ child, she performs her duty with little to no complaints. What a wonderful lesson this is for us all.

Journey with me through the life of Mary, mother of Jesus and let us gleam from God's beautiful words of life.

Notes

December 1

A PROMISE KEPT

"IN THE SIXTH MONTH OF ELIZABETH'S PREGNANCY, GOD SENT THE ANGEL GABRIEL TO NAZARETH, A TOWN IN GALILEE, TO A VIRGIN PLEDGED TO BE MARRIED TO A MAN NAMED JOSEPH, A DESCENDANT OF DAVID. THE VIRGIN'S NAME WAS MARY." (LUKE 1:26-27 NIV)

Notice how this verse starts in the middle of a conversation. It is planned this way, to show how our LORD is always working things out on our behalf. His loving plans of care for us are never an afterthought, but are continual and ever ongoing. If we go back a few verses, we can see what is going on. The good Doctor Luke tells us how the God man, Christ Jesus, is the ultimate promise-keeper. Following the fall of Adam and Eve (Genesis 3) in the paradise of Eden, our LORD promised to fix the mess they made. This verse reveals to us how our LORD is going to carry out His plans, to save this grievously infected world from the terminal ailment of sin. Six months prior to this event, our LORD opened the aged Elizabeth's closed womb to receive the forerunner of the Messiah (Christ in flesh). John the Baptist (the babe in Elizabeth's womb and forerunner to Jesus), would prepare the world to meet their Maker. Now, six months later, God the Son, whom we know as Jesus Christ, is Himself about to wrap His Divinity in a babe's flesh. Our Heavenly Dad chooses this most venerable and costly way of paying for our disobedience, by using the very thing that caused the sin in the first place—fragile human flesh. He will come as a man, to save man. The time has now come. So, God sends the mighty angel Gabriel to go to Nazareth (an ancient ghetto), to speak to a poor girl name Mary, who the text says is a virgin. This is very important because the sin "gene" was transmitted through Adam's seed. (Read Romans 5:12) Had Joseph impregnated Mary, the child would have been contaminated with sin and therefore, incapable of saving Himself, much less saving us. The fact that God chose to use a woman to cure us of sin is a beautiful thing to me. He, as Eternal Creator, could have used any other source at His disposal to save us from sin. But in using fallen woman, He allows women a small part in correcting the fault started in the Garden of Eden. After all, it was Eve, the first woman, who influenced her husband to eat from the tree of sin, thus causing the downfall of humanity in the first place. (Genesis 3:6 and 1 Timothy 2:13)

MOTHER MARY AND US: As I look at how our LORD enlisted Mary in His service for salvation, I see the Father has a part for me to play as well. He often sends people to speak to me, to give me a swift kick, in order to get me moving—into His service.

GOD SPEAKS: "For God did not send his Son into the world to condemn the world, but to save the world through him." (John 3:17 NIV) The purposes of God toward the sinful world is a purpose of salvation.

WANDA'S PRAYER: LORD, continue to use us as a living vessel in Your service; for the purpose of helping to bring the good news of salvation to others.

December 2

THE ULTIMATE PRIVILEGE

"THE ANGEL WENT TO HER AND SAID, 'GREETINGS, YOU WHO ARE HIGHLY FAVORED! THE LORD IS WITH YOU.'" (LUKE 1:28 NIV)

What would we think of as being a great privilege or honor in this life? The first thing that comes to my mind would be to be invited as a guest at the White House; to dine with the President and his wife. Or, perhaps, to meet the King/Queen of England. Our LORD, the Creator of a billion worlds, would honor a peasant girl with the privilege of caring God in flesh, inside her womb. This extremely high honor is the "mother of all honors." So special was this endowment, that Heaven would dispatch a special messenger—Gabriel, the angel who makes face-to-face visits with God Almighty, to make the important announcement. He tells this young girl (around the age of fourteen) how, out of all the women on planet earth, the God of Heaven hand-picked her for this special task. Imagine how she is feeling. She is going about the daily tasks of life, abruptly interrupted by an angel, a foreign being, suddenly appearing to her. This angelic creature from another world seeks to calm Mary's impending heart failure with the words, "Hail or Greetings." According to the Strong's Concordance, this word means to be "cheerful or happy; to celebrate or rejoice with me." The angel is saying to Mary, "Hello young daughter of Eve; come celebrate this very joyful occasion with me. Out of all the billions of women on planet earth, you have been selected for this special assignment. This is a time for extreme joy! The God of Heaven is with you." (Writer's paraphrase) This is a time of wonderful hope and joy. In fact, this was the hope and high honor every daughter of Abraham had longed for. Since the promise had been given to Eve in the Garden of Eden (Genesis 3:15), every Hebrew girl waited, wondered, and hoped for this astounding privilege. Now, the King of Eternity would bestow this ultimate honor on a lowly poor girl from Nazareth.

MOTHER MARY AND US: This was indeed an extreme privilege and great honor our LORD endowed Mary with, and the importance of her task cannot be diminished. She will encase the God man in human form, from single-cell inception to birth. This Child would grow up to save all of humanity from the grips of sin and give back to us again, the keys of paradise. The only minor comparison to me is now that our LORD has completed His mission, He allows me the privilege of housing His Holy Spirit, to live out that completed life as a saved Christian.

GOD SPEAKS: "To them God has chosen to make known among the Gentiles the glorious riches of this mystery, which is Christ in you, the hope of glory." (Colossians 1:27 NIV) As Mary was given an honor, so are you and every child born of God. That is the privilege of God in Spirit, living and having control over their lives. This privilege does not last for just nine months, but forever. Let the Spirit of God control your life. God in Spirit will birth in you new and wonderful things you cannot possibly imagine.

WANDA'S PRAYER: LORD, Your Spirit has been in me since I asked You to be my Savior at the age of nineteen. I still find that daily and sometimes hourly, I must ask and allow You to reign as my LORD.

December 3

I'M HAPPY—YOU'RE... TROUBLED

"MARY WAS GREATLY TROUBLED AT HIS WORDS AND WONDERED WHAT KIND OF GREETING THIS MIGHT BE. BUT THE ANGEL SAID TO HER, 'DO NOT BE AFRAID, MARY; YOU HAVE FOUND FAVOR WITH GOD.'" (LUKE 1:29-30 NIV)

In the previous verse, we see the angel Gabriel beaming with Heavenly news for Mary. But what was extreme joy to him troubled this child—soon to be mother of our LORD. To understand why, put yourself in the place of a young teenage girl in the ancient town of Nazareth. You live in abject poverty. You live in a home, probably one room, made of stone-mud brick. Your daily life consists of grinding wheat, barley, which you had to help harvest, into flour. After making the flour, you had to cook the bread over an open pit. Most likely, you also had to care for the smaller siblings while trying to cook and clean (the Jews are known for their strict cleanliness). Let us also not forget you are the one responsible for going to the town water well, to get the daily supply of water for household cleaning and ceremonial washings. Oh, did I mention the care of the household animals were also a part of the job description? Young Mary had her life planned, not just from dusk to dawn, but from birth to death. As we speak, she is already engaged to wed Joseph at her young age. Into this already, completely filled life, walks this extraterrestrial being, Gabriel, the angel sent from God with his very strange greeting of being "favored by God." As she thought of those words, "favored," she may have thought of the prophet Daniel who was also "favored" by our LORD. But he lived in the king's palace, and she was the child of peasants. Since she was not a child of privilege, she may have wondered if she had incurred the wrath of God for some unknown or secret sin. She could not imagine why the God of Heaven would give her His unearned and undeserved goodness. This entire scene must have seemed to Mary like a dream or an illusion of some sort. The angel Gabriel, seeing her stark with fear and concern, sought immediately to reassure her of God's goodness and love towards her with the words, "… Don't be afraid, Mary; you have found favor with God." You need not fear; but rejoice with me because you have been honored as no earthly woman has ever been.

MOTHER MARY AND US: This part of the story shows us how our LORD comes to us, just as we are. He wants to bless us. This is not based on our goodness; but it comes out of His greatness and deep love for us. God had a plan for Mary's life that only she could live out; it was tailor-made just for her. He also has a tailor-made plan for us. He wishes to favor us, as we live out our lives for His glory, just as He wanted Mary to.

GOD SPEAKS: "But the salvation of the righteous is from the LORD; He is their strength in the time of trouble." (Psalm 37:39 NKJV) There is only one thing wrong with having fear, and that is not knowing what to do with it. There is only one place to take your fears and get true relief. That place is to your LORD. I, your God, am your strength in times of fear and trouble.

WANDA'S PRAYER: Father God, we submit ourselves to you. We have many fears and troubles. So, before we start our day, we give them all to You. Father, take them and in return, give to us, Your awesome strength.

December 4

GUESS WHO'S COMING TO YOUR WOMB?

"AND BEHOLD, YOU WILL CONCEIVE IN YOUR WOMB AND BRING FORTH A SON, AND SHALL CALL HIS NAME JESUS." (LUKE 1:31 NKJV)

What I like about this verse is that it is written in "Southern ease." Born in the southern part of the United States, I relate well to what the writer is saying. Gabriel, the angel sent from God, continues to talk with Mary about this Child, as he gently and slowly unfolds her part in God's plan to save humanity from the clutches of sin. I hear him saying to her, "Look here, girl, your part in this grand scheme is this: you will become pregnant and have a Son—His name is Jesus." In Matthew, when Gabriel is speaking to Mary's espoused husband, Joseph (Matthew 1:21), he tells him Jesus' name means Savior of sins. Mary is told the part she is to play is 'host womb.' She is to give birth to God, wrapped in flesh. She will deliver the Savior, who will save earth from the sins of the world. As the songwriter says, "This Child that you deliver will soon deliver you" (and all of us). What could be more honoring than carrying deity in your womb for nine months? This God-honoring role is one she can readily play with His help. God does not ask us to do anything that He will not equip us to do. Women get pregnant and have babies, so Father God tells Mary she will become pregnant and have a baby. As Mary listens in amazement, the angel fills in some of the blanks, but the entire ordeal must be entered into by faith. Gabriel, the angel of God, assumes she will accept his words as God's words, and she does. Since childhood, Mary had been told about the prophesies concerning the Messiah, so she was well aware of them. Now, all she needed to do was to believe the time was now, and she would be the host womb—the place where the Savior would be conceived.

MOTHER MARY AND US: The plan sounds simple enough. The hard thing for Mary is accepting that she, "little ole' Mary," was the one the God of Creation, would choose to use to carry out His grand plan of salvation. It seems so beyond anything she could or would do. She was right—it was all beyond her. That is why He, and not her, was called Savior! When I look at Mary's life, I am assured that since He used her in His grand plans, He can and wants to use us as well. We, like Mary, must learn to trust His words.

GOD SPEAKS: "Trust in the LORD with all your heart and lean not on your own understanding; in all your ways submit to him, and he will make your paths straight." (Proverbs 3:5-6 NIV) To function for Me (your LORD), you must believe Me.

WANDA'S PRAYER: Father God, teach us to trust You. Show us more and more of You.

December 5

NOW, ABOUT THE BABY!

"HE WILL BE GREAT AND WILL BE CALLED THE SON OF THE MOST HIGH. THE LORD GOD WILL GIVE HIM THE THRONE OF HIS FATHER DAVID, AND HE WILL REIGN OVER JACOB'S DESCENDANTS FOREVER; HIS KINGDOM WILL NEVER END."
(LUKE 1:32-33 NIV)

As the angel Gabriel continues to speak to Mary, his message to her gets deeper and more intense. He tells her in no uncertain terms that the child in her womb is not an ordinary one. "This Child will be great (or the great One), and He will be called the Son of God." Mary was given a mouthful by Gabriel. Let us regurgitate what he is saying and pick apart each piece, shall we? In the Jewish mind, the title, "Son of God," meant this Child was God in flesh and co-equal with the God of the Universe. (John 5:17-22) This was also the same thing the angel told her husband Joseph in Matthew 1:23. "… And they shall call His name Immanuel, which is translated God with us." In other words, the angel Gabriel is saying, "Mary, girl you have got God in you—are you aware of this?" (Writer's paraphrase) Not only was this Child God in the flesh, but He would rule over the house of Jacob; and the throne of King David would be given to Him. This not only speaks of the type of King He would be, but the length of His reign—a Kingdom without end. This Child is an eternal King. Again, the verse emphasizes the fact that this baby is the Everlasting God! This tall honor would seem an impossible feat for this child, or any other little child, because it had been many centuries since Israel had been without a King to reign over them. Now, just "out of the blue," this kid would come to rule like the best King of Israel—David, and he would rule forever? Impossible. The statement Gabriel makes to Mary points back to the prophesies of the coming Messiah in the Old Testament. The angel is saying to her, "you, my dear, are indeed carrying Almighty God inside of you—believe it or not." (Writer's paraphrase)

MOTHER MARY AND US: Mary is given the extraordinary honor of bearing the Messiah to the world. Though her task was a one-of-a-kind order, I, too, have been given a wonderful task to perform for my LORD. As a Christian, I now have God in Spirit, ruling and reigning in my life. When I gave my heart to Jesus, I died to myself. (Galatians 2:20)

GOD SPEAKS: "I have been crucified with Christ; it is no longer I who live, but Christ lives in me; and the life which I now live in the flesh I live by faith in the Son of God, who loved me and gave Himself for me." (Galatians 2:20 NKJV) You no longer belong to you. I bought you when I paid the price for your sins. As you live your life, always remember this. Stay dead to sin and alive to Me, your LORD.

WANDA'S PRAYER: Father God, always remind us of the high and expensive price You paid for us on Calvary's tree (Your Cross).

December 6

QUESTIONS—QUESTIONS

THEN MARY SAID TO THE ANGEL, 'HOW CAN THIS BE, SINCE I DO NOT KNOW A MAN?'" (LUKE 1:34 NKJV)

This child bride and now, soon-to-be mother, asks a very curious question to the angel Gabriel. I picture Mary being ever so meek and respectful, but slowly raising her hand to speak, as if she were in school. "Excuse me, Mr. Angel, I know you said I am going to have a baby and I do not mean to question what you say, but I am a virgin and have never been with a man. (Luke 1:27) So could you please tell me how this pregnancy will take place?" (Writer's paraphrase) This was a "good honest" question, worthy of an answer, unlike the one asked by the priest Zacharias (Luke 1:18), for which he was struck dumb and unable to speak until John's birth. Mary's question had to do with the process. Dr. Luke, the author of this book, tells us Mary's account of events surrounding the birth of Jesus. In reading her account, we see she was given no explanation yet about the process of her conception. So, she asks the angel if he would not mind telling her what was going to take place. On the other hand, Zacharias has a wife, though she is past childbearing age. As a priest of God, he was well aware of the ancient matriarch Sarah's pregnancy and the delivery of Isaac at the ripe old age of ninety. His question was not one of process, or how it would happen, because it would happen the "natural way"—between a man and a woman. His question reflects his unbelief and therefore, he wanted a sign to look at, instead of just believing God's words spoken through the angel Gabriel. What this verse validates is the fact that Mary was truly a virgin and had never been intimate with a man. This shows this child is God's son, and not Joseph's. Only God's sinless Son, who is Himself God, can save us from our sins.

MOTHER MARY AND US: Mary shows me it is ok to ask questions and to take my concerns to the LORD. Even as in Zacharias' case, though he was struck dumb and could not speak until John's birth, our LORD did not take away what He promised—a son. Our LORD would have us come to Him for everything, even seemingly dumb questions.

GOD SPEAKS: "Casting all your care upon Him, for He cares for you." (1 Peter 5:7 NKJV) I, your LORD, want you to come to Me for every little thing that bothers you. What bothers you, bothers Me.

WANDA'S PRAYER: Father God, there is nothing impossible for You. Help us remember there is nothing too great or small that we cannot bring to You. Thank You for always listening, caring, answering, and just plain being there!

December 7

LITTLE GIRL, THE ANSWER IS SIMPLE

"AND THE ANGEL ANSWERED AND SAID UNTO HER, THE HOLY GHOST SHALL COME UPON THEE, AND THE POWER OF THE HIGHEST SHALL OVERSHADOW THEE: THEREFORE ALSO THAT HOLY THING WHICH SHALL BE BORN OF THEE SHALL BE CALLED THE SON OF GOD." (LUKE 1:35 KJV)

I picture the angel Gabriel beaming with a smile as bright as the noon sun and as wide as a crescent moon as he gives Mary the answer to her curious question. "Why it's simple, little Ms. Mary. This is how the pregnancy is going to take place. You see, the Holy Spirit will come on you. It is all God's doing, my child. His power is going to cover you completely. There is not going to be anything you have to do. In fact, the 'Holy thing' (the embryo), inside of you, that baby boy in the making, is called 'the Son of God.' And this, Ms. Mary, is how you are going to give birth to God's Son. The child in your womb will be 100% God and 100% human. I know it is a hard thing to swallow, but it is all true. Do you understand it all now?" If Mary is like me, the explanation would have gone right over her head. From the explanation in the above verse, we can see that our loving LORD, through Gabriel, is more than happy to answer her question. He goes into much detail about how she, a virgin, will become pregnant. We see her only part in this entire process is to be a willing vessel. We also see from this verse that God claims total responsibility for the inception and development of this Child. Mary is not given any credit, except that she is the host vessel. God claims paternity for this child! He is the Father, and the Child is His Son. This, in Hebrew vernacular, tells us the Child is God in flesh—the sinless One. Remember, it was God's Spirit covering (overshadowing) her and it was the "Power of the Highest" (God), causing the Creation of this in Mary's womb. The process had to be this way because only a sinless God man could pay the price for human sin. Sinful creatures like us are disqualified. Mary (and we) will just have to strengthen ourselves in Jesus.

MOTHER MARY AND US: In looking at this part of the story, I see our LORD is careful to assure my finite mind of His love and faithfulness to me. But like Mary, there is a muscle of faith I must exercise. This muscle, when strengthened, will hold me close to my LORD, during those times, when I lack understanding.

GOD SPEAKS: "The secret things belong to the LORD our God, but the things revealed belong to us and to our children forever, that we may follow all the words of this law." (Deuteronomy 29:29 NIV) I, your LORD, am more than happy to give you truths to strengthen your faith in Me. Hold on to Me and My word, and you will move "mountains."

WANDA'S PRAYER: Father God, help us to do what You say, and to trust in You completely; even when we do not understand.

December 8

HOLD ON TO THIS LITTLE NUGGET

"NOW INDEED, ELIZABETH YOUR RELATIVE HAS ALSO CONCEIVED A SON IN HER OLD AGE; AND THIS IS NOW THE SIXTH MONTH FOR HER WHO WAS CALLED BARREN. FOR WITH GOD NOTHING WILL BE IMPOSSIBLE." (LUKE 1:36-37 NKJV)

The first lady at our previous church uses this title-phrase often when she presents the words of God. She says, "Take this nugget and hold on to it." In these verses, God, through His angel, gives Mary a large nugget to hold on to. The gold nugget was "… nothing is impossible with God." The beautiful wrapping the nugget came in was a living, breathing example in the person of her relative Elizabeth. She was told by the angel the "barren" Elizabeth was now six months pregnant. This was obviously a big deal to young Mary. She knew her relative Elizabeth was a very old woman and well past her childbearing years. To be told this "grandmother" was now having a child was truly a lesson of her LORD'S mighty power. This magnificent gift our LORD gave to Elizabeth would be a warm fleece blanket to Mary on those cold days of persecution about her own pregnancy. Through this gift to Elizabeth, our LORD is also saying to Mary that if God cared enough to take away an old woman's reproach and give her unspeakable joy, then He would stop at nothing to take care of her and her needs. This was a tiny gesture on God's part, but it spoke volumes of His love and mighty power for His children. Our LORD was saying to Mary, "I displayed My mighty power for her (Elizabeth), and I will do the same for you." (Writer's paraphrase)

MOTHER MARY AND US: This story about God's provision for Mary and Elizabeth is a gold nugget for me to hold on to. As God shows His love and provision for these two daughters of His, I know He will also take care of me. I too am His daughter, and so are you. Like Mary and Elizabeth, we are well loved by Him. The verse also tells me I do not have to worry about my needs being too big for Him. They are not—NOTHING IS IMPOSSIBLE FOR HIM.

GOD SPEAKS: "This is the confidence we have in approaching God: that if we ask anything according to his will, he hears us. And if we know that he hears us—whatever we ask—we know that we have what we asked of him." (1 John 5:14-15 NIV) You can have complete confidence that I will do according to My (your God) perfect plan for your life. Your job is to seek My perfect will and trust in My loving hand and mighty power.

WANDA'S PRAYER: LORD, keep us very close to You always.

December 9

FATHER, I'M YOURS!

"I AM THE LORD'S SERVANT," MARY ANSWERED. 'MAY YOUR WORD TO ME BE FULFILLED.' THEN THE ANGEL LEFT HER." (LUKE 1:38 NIV)

There was a popular song I used to listen to during my childhood. Unfortunately, all I can remember is one line in the chorus, which I believe may also be the title of the song— "Baby I'm Yours." The theme of the song is very clear to me. The person singing the song is giving her lover a blank check over her life to do whatever the lover would choose to do with her. This is exactly what Mary, the mother of Jesus, is doing with the God of Heaven, as seen in the above verse. The difference is that Mary was giving the blank check of her life to the well-deserving, All-Knowing, King of Kings, and LORD of LORDS. It is to this flawless God, and Lover of her Soul, that she would put her complete and total trust in. The angel believed this child's innocent words and immediately left her. In looking at Mary's unwavering faith, we see the true character of this young woman as she demonstrates a maturity well beyond her years. She was totally sold out to her LORD. She knew this monumental task would not be an easy one. To start with, this innocent child would be branded with the title of "immoral woman" and seen as an adulterer by her beloved husband-to-be. And who would believe this incredible story? Her explanation of a miraculous pregnancy would sound like a crazy fantasy at best, and out and out lies at worse. But despite all she would face, from the start, she draws a line in the sand as she tells her LORD, "Father God, I'm Yours." She would make her bold statement without reservations or hesitation. This must have put a smile on our Heavenly Father's face.

MOTHER MARY AND US: I am, shall I say, considerably older than this young woman; yet I am just now learning what she seems to know instinctively already. Her childlike, steel-curtain faith is almost unrivaled in Scripture. Oh, that I would have half the faith and complete trust in my LORD, that young Mary has.

GOD SPEAKS: "Those who know your name trust in you, for you, LORD, have never forsaken those who seek you." (Psalm 9:10 NIV) Spend time with Me (your LORD). Learn My name—what My name means and what it stands for. In doing these things, you will learn to trust in Me. I will never leave you alone—ever!

WANDA'S PRAYER: LORD, give us eyes and a heart, fixed, and focused on You alone.

December 10

CAN I GET A WITNESS PLEASE?

"AT THAT TIME MARY GOT READY AND HURRIED TO A TOWN IN THE HILL COUNTRY OF JUDEA, WHERE SHE ENTERED ZECHARIAH'S HOME AND GREETED ELIZABETH." (LUKE 1:39-40 NIV)

To answer the question of "what time?" this verse is referring to, we need only look at the previous verses. In those verses (Luke 1:28-35), God commissions Mary to literally be the host womb, to the Christ Child or God in the flesh. From a simple human level, this seems an impossible task. I believe Mary sensed the heaviness of the load she was asked to bear. So she sought the strength and comfort from her elder sister of her soul, Elizabeth. After all, it was this aged relative to whom the angel referred in his discussions with Mary about her becoming the mother of our LORD. (Luke 1:36) So important was this confirmation to Mary (that she was indeed the chosen host vessel of God), that she would easily take a 50–60-mile journey, through the wild into hazardous brush, in her pregnant state, to see Elizabeth. What was going through this child's mind to bring her to a point of wanting to get away from it all, and maybe take a little "me time?" Backing up in the story for just a bit, we see Mary is now left alone to sort out and ponder over how all of "this" is going to work. Remember, she was already engaged to marry Joseph, and now she has just become the mother of our LORD, by unnatural, miraculous means. Explaining just her immaculate conception to anyone would take a lifetime. If you do not see the giant stress of it all, then try telling your fiancé, "yes, you are still a virgin, and yes, you're pregnant—by God." Then see how quickly you are carted off to the "nut house." I can see how Mary would need a visual in the life of Elizabeth (of God's power), to strengthen her faith just a bit. So "over the river, through the woods, and up the mountain" to Elizabeth's house she would go. Mary needed this private retreat. Our LORD, who was in toe, via her womb, provided it and would beautifully reward her there.

MOTHER MARY AND US: There have been times in my life when I, like Mary, have needed to do the same thing. I know the LORD has given me this task (not as extreme as Mary's by any means), but it seems crazy to explain it to anyone else. I need a kindred spirit to assure me I have not lost my mind.

GOD SPEAKS: "Be still and know that I am God; …" (Psalm 46:10 NKJV) Let Me rewrite that verse especially from My (your LORD'S) heart to yours. "Don't move, just stand still, very close to Me. Be absolutely certain and trust that I AM GOD." The rest of that verse says, "I will be exalted (lifted up) among the nations, I will be exalted in the earth." Mary was carrying God physically inside of her. She had all the power of the universe in her womb. You carry God in Spirit inside of you. This is all the power, comfort, and peace you will ever need. I AM forever with you—have no fear.

WANDA'S PRAYER: Thank You, LORD, for always calming our weary souls. We love You!

December 11

"DON'T LOOK FOR WHAT YOU ALREADY HAVE"

"WHEN ELIZABETH HEARD MARY'S GREETING, THE BABY LEAPED IN HER WOMB, AND ELIZABETH WAS FILLED WITH THE HOLY SPIRIT. IN A LOUD VOICE SHE EXCLAIMED: 'BLESSED ARE YOU AMONG WOMEN, AND BLESSED IS THE CHILD YOU WILL BEAR!'" (LUKE 1:41-42 NIV)

We see in the previous verse that Mary walks into Zechariah's home and makes a "beeline" to his wife, Elizabeth. It is as if she cannot wait another minute to see if what the angel says about the elderly Elizabeth's pregnancy is true. Immediately after she greets her, something beautiful happens. Baby John, in Mommy Elizabeth's womb, upon hearing Mary's voice, starts into an out-of-control "break dance" or doing the "two-step." He becomes a "womb acrobat" doing flips inside his mother's uterus. What is this all about? Remember, Baby John is filled with the Holy Spirit (God in Spirit) from birth. (Luke 1:15). Mary walks in the door of her relative carrying Baby Jesus, God the Son, in her womb. She greets Elizabeth. When the Spirit-filled Baby John hears Mary's voice, there is an instant connection. God the Spirit knows that God the Son, Jesus, is near. God the Spirit in Baby John begins Heavenly praise of God the Son, from inside the womb of his mother. Then, like an out-of-control flame, the Holy Spirit engulfs Mother Elizabeth and consumes her with the Spirit of God. God gets the glory as the praise party begins. Mary goes to Elizabeth in search of a blessing and instead, she becomes one! Elizabeth instantly bellows out a glorious blessing to Mary, "Girl, you are truly blessed among women." (Writer's paraphrase) The same Spirit that revealed to Baby John that Mary was carrying the Messiah (God in flesh), was now revealing this information to Elizabeth. She then turns verbal "flips" as she cries out how blessed (honored/favored) Mary is. What Mary may have considered for a moment to be a burden was truly an honor.

MOTHER MARY AND US: Many times, I have viewed the blessings or gifts from God as a burden and this has been to my utter shame. As a single mother raising two children, I found myself complaining to the LORD about my "lot in life." But now, 20 years later, what I would not give for just five minutes of my wasted time of whining. I love my children and now see how my LORD was honoring me with the privilege of being their mother.

GOD SPEAKS: "But we have this treasure in jars of clay to show that this all-surpassing power is from God and not from us." (2 Corinthians 4:7 NIV) You are just a jar of clay. Let the Spirit of God consume you and run wild in your life, as He did in Mary and Elizabeth's. Let Me (God) show you My glory.

WANDA'S PRAYER: As the songwriter says, "Have thine own way, LORD, have thine own way. You are the Potter; I am the clay. Mold me and make me after Your will, while I am waiting, yielded and still." Lord God, this is our prayer.

December 12

LET THE BLESSINGS FLOW

"AS SOON AS THE SOUND OF YOUR GREETING REACHED MY EARS, THE BABY IN MY WOMB LEAPED FOR JOY. BLESSED IS SHE WHO HAS BELIEVED THAT THE LORD WOULD FULFILL HIS PROMISES TO HER!" (LUKE 1:44-45 NIV)

These verses say something very basic. Elizabeth is saying to Mary that the very presence within her brought a great blessing to her. In other words, Mary, with Christ in her, gave Elizabeth joy and made her happy. "Girl, you walked into this room with me and the God in you (Jesus), stirred up the baby inside me, and then set my spirit on fire." (Writer's paraphrase) After receiving her blessing, Elizabeth then gives one of her own to Mary. "Blessed are you Mary, because you simply believed (trusted fully in and acted upon) the LORD'S word. You knew He would do what He (God) said He would do." This entire conversation represents the power of God on display. It was the power of the Holy Spirit who gave Elizabeth this revelation about Mary's conception. We know this because we read nowhere in the text of any human having given her this information. Also, Mary could not have been "showing" (had a visible sign of her pregnancy) when she saw Elizabeth. Remember, she took the next oxen driven wagon almost immediately after the angel told her she was going to be pregnant with Baby Jesus. Shortly after the angel left her, she left town for Elizabeth's house. (Luke 1:38-39) Nope! Our LORD put on this entire spectacle to encourage His daughter Mary and us. It is interesting to me that Mary may have gone to Elizabeth for a blessing, but instead, she became a blessing herself.

MOTHER MARY AND US: Walking in the faith of God's Word always produces a two-way blessing. Like Mary, when Jesus is inside of me, His Spirit in me will touch someone else's spirit and bless them. In return, I will also receive the blessing I need. This story tells me I need to believe God's words and act on them.

GOD SPEAKS: "Let us hold unswervingly to the hope we profess, for he who promised is faithful. And let us consider how we may spur one another on toward love and good deeds," (Hebrews 10:23-24 NIV) This is what Mary and Elizabeth are doing in the above verse. Because of their faithfulness, millions of people, down through the centuries, continue to be blessed by their actions. Will you also be this kind of blessing for Me (your LORD)?

WANDA'S PRAYER: Heavenly Father, we want nothing more in life than to be this kind of wonderful blessing for You. As we submit to Your complete will for our lives, live Your life through us to bless others.

December 13

IT WAS NEVER ABOUT ME

"AND MARY SAID: 'MY SOUL GLORIFIES THE LORD AND MY SPIRIT REJOICES IN GOD MY SAVIOR,'" (LUKE 1:46-47 NIV)

Mary breaks into magnificent praise to her LORD on the heels of Elizabeth's gracious words to her. She sings about Jesus as LORD. Notice, the verse does not say, "Liz, girl, you are so right. Just look at me. You know, I saw and spoke to the angel. And I received the special gift of God… And I am truly so much more loved and blessed by God than anyone else. And I… and I… and I…" No, the verse says she says, "My soul magnifies the LORD…" The word "soul" in this text is the essence or core of who she is. This statement refers to her inner self, the seat of her emotional being. Every fiber of her being wants to boast of the greatness of the LORD alone. Her praise song is not about her goodness, but God's alone, who is good. The word "magnify" means to make larger, bigger, or greater. Our LORD, already greater and larger than Mary's wildest imagination, is made even larger (magnified) by her becoming smaller (humble). Through her experience, our LORD has gone from big to enormous in her sight—more than she could have ever conceived! As "her spirit rejoices in the LORD," her "spirit" cries out to the Holy God—she wants to know Him! There is a "God-shaped hole" in her heart that only He can fill. His Word says we all have this longing for God in our hearts. Mary knows the Savior who is living in her womb is coming to our planet to save us from sins and death. She knows she only has a small part to play. She refers to the Baby in her womb (Jesus), as her Savior. In this, she is giving a hearty AMEN to the angel's words. After all, the name Jesus means Savior of sins.

MOTHER MARY AND US: Looking at Mary in these verses puts everyone and everything into perspective. She lets me know once again that God is the "Big Chief," and I am just a little "Indian." Since I know God alone is first, last, and all in between, this gives me such peace. Now, I can just relax in Him (God) and in His perfect plans for my life.

GOD SPEAKS: "But, Let the one who boasts boast in the Lord.' For it is not the one who commends himself who is approved, but the one whom the Lord commends." (2 Corinthians 10:17-18 NIV) My daughter, you do not boast in Me (your LORD) to give Me the "big head"—You boast in Me because I AM your power source. As you lift up the "high and holy One who lives forever," I will work on your behalf.

WANDA'S PRAYER: LORD, we will praise You in happy or sad times—always!

December 14

A CARING GOD FATHER

"HE CARES FOR ME, HIS HUMBLE SERVANT. FROM NOW ON, ALL PEOPLE WILL SAY GOD HAS BLESSED ME. GOD ALL-POWERFUL HAS DONE GREAT THINGS FOR ME, AND HIS NAME IS HOLY."
(LUKE 1:48-49 CEV)

I like the way this translation of Scripture reads. In this verse, Mary continues her song of praise to her God with a level head. She tells us she is God's possession (His humble servant), and she is well cared for by Him. "God cares for me…" This tells me God knows her individually, personally, and intimately. Although God is on a first name basis with her, she is not on a first name basis with Him. To her, He is still "All-Mighty God!" She is a servant—a "humble servant" to Him. Next, she tells us that God's blessings for her are something which can be seen by others; "all people will say God has blessed me." In fact, she goes on to say, "God hasn't just blessed me a little; this thing He has done for me is a 'great' thing." This is a wonderful statement. She sees the position she is given in this life as an awesome responsibility, not an enduring chore. Yes, she is pregnant with the King of Kings and LORD of Lords; but she is pregnant outside of marriage, which was scandalous in that day, and in this one. Mary can view her lot in life this way because her focus is not on her problems, but on her God. In looking at God, she sees Him as the One who can and will take care of her every need. As she keeps her focus on Him, she can rest in the fact that this "All-powerful One, whose name is Holy," has everything under perfect control.

MOTHER MARY AND US: Well, this lesson is a no brainer to me. As I look at this story, I see a woman whose eyes and heart are totally fixed and focused on her LORD. Mary reminds me that every part of my life is a privilege. The circumstances are opportunities to give Him glory. Finally, I see that continuing to gaze at Him gives peace; as I am constantly reminded He is taking care. He is the perfect caretaker.

GOD SPEAKS: "The LORD is good, a refuge in times of trouble. He cares for those who trust in him,…" (Nahum 1:7 NIV) Never forget your LORD is so very good. Continually rehearse in your mind His wonderful, unending love for you.

WANDA'S PRAYER: Father God, You are so very good to us, and Your mercies never end. You alone love us with an unending love. Thank You LORD! Now, live in us and enable us to walk worthy in all the privileges You have given us.

December 15

THE PRAISES KEEP COMING

"HIS MERCY EXTENDS TO THOSE WHO FEAR HIM, FROM GENERATION TO GENERATION." (LUKE 1:50 NIV)

Have you ever been around someone genuinely grateful? Such a person goes on and on about the person or object of their gratitude. It is as if the person expressing the heart-felt thanks cannot say enough good things about the object of their praise. Such is the case in this verse. As we read the text, we hear Mary joyfully continue to give God her grateful praise. In this verse, she discusses the LORD'S mercy. Mercy is a wonderful thing. While "grace" is getting what is undeserved, "mercy" is not getting what is well-deserved. As children of a fallen race plagued by sin and evil, we are well-deserving of death and hell. Instead, our God gives us ungrateful ones, much undeserved love, and offers us an eternal paradise with Him. Surely, as Mary is speaking, she is reflecting on the undeserved gift God is giving us by sending His one and only Son, who now resides in her womb. In reflection of this gift of undeserved "mercy," she speaks to all of us—those in her day and in ours. She tells us this undeserving act of mercy covers all people everywhere who "fear" Him. In this verse, the word "fear" means to place one in an exalted or lifted up position; to reverence or to worship. As she tells us, she shows us how it is done; praise is an act of worship from her grateful heart. She knows that we, as humans, owed a debt we could not pay. But the babe in her womb, the God Man, has come to us—to pay our debt that He did not owe.

MOTHER MARY AND US: Mary reminds me to have an "attitude of gratitude." God has blessed us with so many wonderful things. I have life. Despite some aches and pains, I have good health. I have a place to stay and food on my table. But most of all, I have God's wonderful gift in His Son, Jesus. He saved me from my sins and has given me eternal living, which starts now. So, I, like Mary, can go on and on about the goodness of my Savior and His love for me.

GOD SPEAKS: "I will be glad and rejoice in Your mercy, For You have considered my trouble; You have known my soul in adversities, And have not shut me up into the hand of the enemy; You have set my feet in a wide place." (Psalm 31:7-8 NKJV) I, your LORD, want you to have joy and to be glad. I have everything in your life under My perfect control. I need you to always trust Me! Be free to live at peace in Me, the Creator God.

WANDA'S PRAYER: LORD, our hearts overflow with joy and extreme happiness. Our hearts sing the lyrics to the song called "This Joy," by Yolanda Adams, which says, "I don't have to worry because He takes care of me. And I know where my strength comes from. I know where my joy comes from. It's in Jesus. I can lean on Him. I can depend on Him. Wonderful, Counselor, What is His Name? What is His Name? Jesus!"

December 16

THE LONG ARM OF OUR GOD

"HE HAS SHOWN STRENGTH WITH HIS ARM; HE HAS SCATTERED THE PROUD IN THE IMAGINATION OF THEIR HEARTS. HE HAS PUT DOWN THE MIGHTY FROM THEIR THRONES, AND EXALTED THE LOWLY." (LUKE 1:51-52 NKJV)

A poet once wrote, "Your arms are too short to box with God." What that means is our LORD'S reach is long and strong. Thus, in the fight between us and Him—He wins by a knockout. As I continue to read Mary's wonderful song of praise to her God, I liken this reading to eating a delectable box of caramel nuts, covered in chocolate. From her delicious box of praises, she pulls out one scrumptious morsel after another for us to sample. In this verse, she speaks of the strength of the wonderful arm of our LORD. She tells us we have a God and Savior who can take care of our every need. Is there someone or something "big and bad" standing in our way? That "thing or person" is no problem for the strong "arm" of our LORD. Our God has a powerful "arm" (figuratively) that can just move or scatter the proud at a whim. Proud, stubborn people tend to see themselves as immovable objects. This verse says—NOT! The proud and mighty of our world is no match for the God of Heaven. He reads their thoughts as an open book; the verse says, and with ease, He deals with them by scattering them to the wind. Mary goes on to say that effortlessly our God topples the "thrones" of the proud and puts the lowly ones in their place. Looking at this verse, we can rest in the fact that our God is the "righter of wrongs"—He settles everything in perfect order. Mary reminds us that this is still God's world, and He has ultimate control.

MOTHER MARY AND US: This is so comforting to me. It is like a warm blanket on a cold, rainy day. I can snuggle up close in these words. As a songwriter says, "I will rest in You, I will rest in You. Not just when this race is over, but in these earthly moments, too. I will rest in You (God)." (Shannon Wexelberg). I just need to stay under the "covers" of Your care.

GOD SPEAKS: "My soul shall make its boast in the LORD; The humble shall hear of it and be glad." (Psalm 34:2 NKJV) "In God we boast all day long, And praise Your name forever." (Psalm 44:8 NKJV) I, your God, give you two words of thought to delight in. In giving you these verses, I want you to rest and be at peace with Me. Let Me wrap you up in the warm covers of My love. Give me your every care and concern.

WANDA'S PRAYER: Father God, keep us snuggled up very close to the Cross. We want to always remain in Your wonderful presence.

December 17

THE GOODNESS OF GOD ON DISPLAY

"HE HAS FILLED THE HUNGRY WITH GOOD THINGS, AND THE RICH HE HAS SENT AWAY EMPTY. HE HAS HELPED HIS SERVANT ISRAEL, IN REMEMBRANCE OF HIS MERCY, AS HE SPOKE TO OUR FATHERS, TO ABRAHAM AND TO HIS SEED FOREVER." (LUKE 1:53-55 NKJV)

As Mary ends her praise to our LORD and King, she goes out with a bang! In reading the entire section of her praise song, I am struck by her knowledge of Scripture. She is very well versed in God's promises to her people—the Jews. In the first part of this text, she quotes almost verbatim, from the Psalms and the book of Samuel (Psalm 107:9 and 2 Samuel 2:5). This young woman is a serious student of God's Holy Word, and it shows in her speech. I can see one reason why our LORD chose her for this most precious of all missions. Here she tells us that our God "has filled the hungry with good things" while sending away the rich empty-handed. This is probably a reference to the Jews who, for hundreds of years, received no direct words from God between the "Old and New Testaments." At this point in time, they were starving for a Word from God. She goes on to remind us that our God is the Ultimate Promise Keeper, as she tells us that not only has He (God) helped His servant, Israel, He never forgot about them throughout all those years. Mary tells us our God has big plans, which He carries out in and at just the right time. The application to us is simple. As children of the fallen race, when we come to our LORD hungry and empty, He will fill us to overflowing. On the other hand, if we are "rich" or full of ourselves, we will go away empty and emaciated. Mary tells us our LORD is a God who never forgets. He will do what He says with perfect timing. She also tells us His great and precious promises for us are forever. Isn't that great news?

MOTHER MARY AND US: Just reading these verses of Mary has certainly filled me to overflowing. She has shown me I need to look no further than Jesus. He is truly all I need. LORD, keep me so very near to You always.

GOD SPEAKS: "For He satisfies the longing soul, And fills the hungry soul with goodness." (Psalm 107:9 NKJV) Let Me (the God of Creation) be your filling station. Do not go anywhere else for satisfaction. I am, and I have, all you will ever need.

WANDA'S PRAYER: LORD, thank You for constantly reminding us of Your love and goodness. Thank You for reminding us You will never leave or forsake us—ever! I love You LORD.

December 18

CAN'T STAY ON THE MOUNTAINTOP FOREVER

"MARY STAYED WITH ELIZABETH FOR ABOUT THREE MONTHS AND THEN RETURNED HOME."
(LUKE 1:56 NIV)

In this three-month respite at the home of Elizabeth, our LORD gave Mary what must have seemed to us like an extended stay at Disney World; with every conceivable accommodation paid for by Oprah Winfrey. In short, this was an indescribable joy. Elizabeth and Zachariah were in a group of the few. These two were the only ones so far who believed without a doubt that she carried the Messiah in her womb. For those first three months of her pregnancy, she was accepted and loved for being the one who accepted God's call on her life. It must have been a pleasure to be believed in and not thought of as "one of the foolish ones." Here in this home on the mountain, she was heralded, and not scandalized. But she could not stay on this mountaintop. The valley with its large, looming shadows of death awaited her. In the valley, she must face her beloved Joseph. He did not see the pregnancy as God granted, nor did he yet share her angelic vision of prophecy, about being the chosen one to carry the LORD'S Christ. But in this verse, we see how much our LORD truly loved His little daughter. He saw in advance the pain this young girl would experience in the not-too-distant future. He would be with her through it all. Before she faced the valley's bitter cold and biting hurts, He provided her with a summer mountain retreat—away from the world and its woes. When the world would close in on her, in an attempt to snuff out her last hope, she would remember and be reminded that her God spoke to her His wonderful words of love. Through His daughter Elizabeth, He says, "Mary, you are my obedient daughter, and I am well pleased in what you are doing for Me." Where did our LORD say these words, you might ask? He said it in these words, "Blessed is she who believed that what the LORD has said to her will be accomplished." (Luke 1:45)

MOTHER MARY AND US: Mary's life teaches me that God uses my mountaintop experiences to carry me through deep valleys. I like to be reminded of those times, because when I hit rock bottom, I remember my LORD GOD is still with me.

GOD SPEAKS: "Lord, you have been our dwelling place throughout all generations. Before the mountains were born or you brought forth the whole world, from everlasting to everlasting you are God." (Psalm 90:1-2 NIV) Never lose sight of your God—His might and awesome power. If you do this, then you will praise Me (your God) no matter where life takes you.

WANDA'S PRAYER: "I will sing of the LORD's great love forever; with my mouth I will make your faithfulness known through all generations." (Psalm 89:1 NIV)

December 19

MY DARK LONELY VALLEYS

"SO HER HUSBAND, JOSEPH, BEING A RIGHTEOUS MAN, AND NOT WANTING TO DISGRACE HER PUBLICLY, DECIDED TO DIVORCE HER SECRETLY."
(MATTHEW 1:19 CSB)

As told, there are two sides to every story and somewhere in the middle is the truth. This text is based on that case. Matthew gives Joseph's side of the story about the birth of our LORD. Starting with verse eighteen, Mary and Joseph were engaged to be married, when the unthinkable happens. Mary is pregnant by the Holy Spirit. It is said the information about Mary's pregnancy was "discovered" by Joseph. How this "discovery" came about, we are not told. In any case, he has a real dilemma on his hands. Though the couple is considered "married," the marriage has not been consummated by intimacy; Mary is still a virgin, yet very pregnant. These two things, in Joseph's mind, are impossible to reconcile. Joseph knows he is not the father of this child in Mary's womb. He believes she has been unfaithful and is crushed by this thought. He rejects the idea that her pregnancy is a miraculous event and wants to be rid of her. Despite the pain of betrayal he feels, he loves her deeply. Thus, he will preserve her life from a public stoning. He will instead divorce her quietly. While I am sure Mary could understand Joseph's reasoning, his decision to abandon her in her deepest hour of need must have been to her, a devastating blow. She would now have to raise this child alone in First Century Bethlehem; with the stigma of an immoral woman forever branded to her chest. We are not told of Mary's internal struggles. She gives those thoughts and feelings to her LORD alone. So, we do not see her groveling at Joseph's feet for marriage, instead she falls at the feet of the LORD. She holds on to the LORD's love and strength as she goes from the mountaintop of acceptance to the valley of rejection.

MOTHER MARY AND US: Here again we see why our LORD chose this young girl to bear the Christ child. I do not read about her complaining or whining about her lot in life. No, she accepts Joseph's, and God's decision for her. She bears up under this cross with "flying colors." I think if it were me—the readers would read of my many woes and tears. LORD, help me to do as Mary did and give You all my problems.

GOD SPEAKS: "Even though I walk through the darkest valley, I will fear no evil, for you are with me; your rod and your staff, they comfort me." (Psalm 23:4 NIV) My daughter, notice what the verse says. It says your God is with you in the valley. It also says you are going "through" the valley. The valley is not your home—it is only part of the journey. Finally, the verse says God is your comfort and protection—in and through this valley. Hold on to your God and never let go!

WANDA'S PRAYER: LORD, the words are a little different from the original lyrics, but I will sing You a song. "So, I thank You for my mountains, and I thank You for my valleys. I thank You for all You have brought me through. For in every situation, You have given me great consolation; You've used all my trials to make me strong."

December 20

MARY, I'LL TALK TO HIM

"BUT AFTER HE HAD CONSIDERED THIS, AN ANGEL OF THE LORD APPEARED TO HIM IN A DREAM AND SAID, 'JOSEPH SON OF DAVID, DO NOT BE AFRAID TO TAKE MARY HOME AS YOUR WIFE, BECAUSE WHAT IS CONCEIVED IN HER IS FROM THE HOLY SPIRIT. SHE WILL GIVE BIRTH TO A SON, AND YOU ARE TO GIVE HIM THE NAME JESUS, BECAUSE HE WILL SAVE HIS PEOPLE FROM THEIR SINS.'"
(MATTHEW 1:20-21 NIV)

Yesterday's lesson talked about Joseph not believing the Holy Spirit had immaculately impregnated Mary. Mary did not argue with Joseph; nor did she try to change his mind about his action to divorce her. She would quietly trust God, who chose her for this special mission, that He would do what was absolutely best for her in this situation. Mary trusted it was God's responsibility to speak to her husband. Our LORD does a wonderful thing. He comes to Joseph in a dream. While sleeping, our LORD had Joseph's complete attention as He spoke to him. First God acknowledges Joseph's fears by saying, "Don't be afraid…" Then God validates Mary's pregnancy as a divine act of His will, "What is conceived in her is from the Holy Spirit." Next, the Father God establishes Joseph's place as head of the home, "you are to give Him the name Jesus." Finally, God tells Joseph the supreme mission of the Child, "He will save His people from their sins." Mary's attitudes and actions regarding Joseph teach us as women great principles of Scripture: (1) God's man is seeking to hear God's voice; and not our (my) nagging. (2) When I am quiet and still, the man of God will hear and obey God's voice without my interference and possible negative influence.

MOTHER MARY AND US: These verses teach me I do not have to fight my battles. My LORD is so much better at fighting on my behalf, and He always wins! I can give Him every problem, big or small. As I surrender to His perfect will and plans, He carries out His plans for my life perfectly.

GOD SPEAKS: "Wives, in the same way submit yourselves to your own husbands so that, if any of them do not believe the word, they may be won over without words by the behavior of their wives, when they see the purity and reverence of your lives." (1 Peter 3:1-2 NIV) The principle is universal—whether you are married or single. Your best influence is a quiet, holy life. Let your blameless life speak, and not your nagging words.

WANDA'S PRAYER: Father, close our mouths and open our hearts. Live out Your life through us.

December 21

GOD'S MAN DOES WHAT GOD TELLS HIM

"WHEN JOSEPH WOKE UP, HE DID WHAT THE ANGEL OF THE LORD HAD COMMANDED HIM AND TOOK MARY HOME AS HIS WIFE. BUT HE DID NOT CONSUMMATE THEIR MARRIAGE UNTIL SHE GAVE BIRTH TO A SON. AND HE GAVE HIM THE NAME JESUS." (MATTHEW 1:24-25 NIV)

I once watched a movie about Mary, the mother of Jesus. In the movie, it took Joseph months to finally take Mary as his wife; poor Mary was near delivery before the marriage took place. As I read the accounts of Matthew and Luke, the timelines are blurred as to what took place, when. But one thing is clear from this passage—Our LORD had the final word! God said it and in Joseph's mind, this settled the matter! Father God spoke to his boy Joseph in a dream and said, "Marry the woman—now!" When he woke up from his dream, Joseph made a "beeline" to Mary's house to make the nuptials (the marriage) official. This shows our God knew what He was doing when He chose Joseph to be the husband of Mary. Joseph was a man who sought after God's heart. Mary was getting a man who would hear and instantly obey his LORD'S voice. Joseph was a man who was used to hearing God's voice and would not act until he was certain that what he heard was from his LORD. Joseph is also a man that shows complete trust in his God; as evident by the faith he shows in his complete obedience to God's word. Notice how completely the man acted on God's words. He knew the child was conceived by our LORD. He would not become intimate with Mary until after she gave birth. Thus, Mary would retain her virginity until after the birth of God's Son. There would be no question this Child was God's Son. What a man of integrity!

MOTHER MARY AND US: I like the fact that this verse gives instructions to us, whether we are single or married. For single women, this is the kind of man our LORD would have us marry. For married women, this is the kind of man our LORD would have us to pray our husband would become.

GOD SPEAKS: "… Speak, Lord, for your servant is listening…" (1 Samuel 3:9 NIV) Take a page out of Mary's book; spend more time with Me, your LORD, pondering My words and hearing My voice. Allow Me to speak in and through you. My words give perfect peace to take away your worries.

WANDA'S PRAYER: Help me, LORD, to start my day with You. Then remind me You are with me all throughout the day.

December 22

WE'LL HONEYMOON IN—BETHLEHEM?

"SO JOSEPH ALSO WENT UP FROM THE TOWN OF NAZARETH IN GALILEE TO JUDEA, TO BETHLEHEM THE TOWN OF DAVID, BECAUSE HE BELONGED TO THE HOUSE AND LINE OF DAVID. HE WENT THERE TO REGISTER WITH MARY, WHO WAS PLEDGED TO BE MARRIED TO HIM AND WAS EXPECTING A CHILD." (LUKE 2:4-5 NIV)

Before we start our discussion of this passage, I must clear up what may seem to be a contradiction between these verses and the previous ones. In this verse it says, "… Mary who was pledged to be married to him (Joseph)." The previous verse in Matthew 1:24 tells us, "He took Mary home as his wife." Mary was his wife, but the marriage was not yet consummated by intimacy, until after the birth of Jesus. (Matthew 1:25) Now, back to our story. As a kid from Alabama, I never thought I would see California (about 2,000 miles from my birthplace), except on TV. Yet, as I pen these words, I have lived here in California now for the past 20-plus years. I think this may have been Mary's idea as well. She was born and raised in Nazareth. Her hometown was a small village inside of a valley, of only five miles or so (according to Dr. Ferrell of Ferrell's blog). But in the ninth month of her pregnancy, she would make at least a 75-mile journey on a donkey, uphill but down south, to Bethlehem. I came to California by car from Oklahoma. It was a terrible experience. My ex-husband insisted we drive straight through with a minimal amount of stops. At the time, I had a six-week-old baby on breast milk. Looking at Mary, I can multiply my journey a thousand times, and never equal her agony. Yet, unlike me, she never complains. I do not hear her saying, "Now wait a minute God, just what are you doing?" Perhaps she did not know the prophecy of Micah, which foretold that the Christ (Jesus) would be born in Bethlehem. (Micah 5:2) She only knew she and Joseph were one; and she would go wherever our LORD lead him to go.

MOTHER MARY AND US: Mary's journey from Nazareth to Bethlehem must have been a very adventurous one, for sure. What fascinates me about the story is her meek and quiet spirit. Her life speaks to my heart about silently, patiently trusting in God, and following His leading. I want to be like her when I "grow up" in my old age.

GOD SPEAKS: "Follow God's example, (be imitators) therefore, as dearly loved children and walk in the way of love, just as Christ loved us and gave himself up for us as a fragrant offering and sacrifice to God." (Ephesians 5:1-2 NIV) Mary is a very good example but I, your LORD, am the perfect example. Imitate Me in all your ways.

WANDA'S PRAYER: LORD, as we study Your word, show us how to live as You ask.

December 23

UNWELCOME RECEPTION

"WHILE THEY WERE THERE, THE TIME CAME FOR THE BABY TO BE BORN, AND SHE GAVE BIRTH TO HER FIRSTBORN, A SON. SHE WRAPPED HIM IN CLOTHS AND PLACED HIM IN A MANGER, BECAUSE THERE WAS NO GUEST ROOM AVAILABLE FOR THEM." (LUKE 2:6-7 NIV)

This was the time all the world was waiting for, or should have been waiting for. Since the fall of Creation, our sin-sick world has been crying out, "Save me, I'm dying." The Savior is poised to enter our world and save us. Yet, we show our thanks by ignoring Him and His earthly parents in their deepest time of need. Picture the scene with me. Mary has just made this trying journey to Bethlehem, on a donkey's back, with no time to spare. She is now in active labor and perhaps her bag of water has broken. Hear the intense moaning and groaning she makes with each gripping contraction? The birth of the Christ child is eminent. Yet, in a town full of "passers-by and on lookers" viewing this very pregnant woman on the verge of delivery, it is astounding no one offers any assistance. How much would have been required? A mat on the floor and some warm water to clean the mom and baby was all that would have been needed—but they got nothing! It looks as if she will give birth on the streets of Bethlehem. See Joseph runny frantically going from door to door, pleading for someone—anyone to open their home and let them in. The answer to his desperate cries, the pathetic answer is, "We're full and haven't any room." Why is everyone so uncaring, so cold? It is Rome's April 15th, or tax day. All are in fear of mighty Rome and must do what she says. They are in their own world, consumed with their own problems. There is no time or interest for this girl about to have a baby. Finally, the couple makes their way to a cave as Mary shrieks in the agonizing pain of labor. As best he can, Joseph assists with the delivery. In this dirty cave, Mary gives birth to the King of Glory! After giving birth, and probably not fully clean herself, she wraps our LORD in strips of cloths, and places Him in a feeding trough, "Because there is no room in the inn."

MOTHER MARY AND US: WOW! I am in awe of this couple, this woman or young girl. I do not hear her complaining at all. She just does what she has to do. I wonder what I would have done if I were back in those days. But, I guess I do not really have to wonder. There are times now when my LORD asks me to stop and spend some time with Him, and I say "my Rome calls" with its eminent requests. Like the people of Mary's day, I too, become a "passer's by."

GOD SPEAKS: "If we are faithless, He remains faithful; He cannot deny Himself." (2 Timothy 2:13 NKJV) Aren't you very glad I am not like you? I am God, so My love never changes. It is not subject to change depending on how I feel. I knew you needed a Savior, so I came to pay the price.

WANDA'S PRAYER: LORD, thank You for loving and caring for us. Thank You for being that dependable, changeless God.

December 24

HEAVENLY CONFIRMATION

"BUT THE ANGEL SAID TO THEM, 'DO NOT BE AFRAID. I BRING YOU GOOD NEWS THAT WILL CAUSE GREAT JOY FOR ALL THE PEOPLE. TODAY IN THE TOWN OF DAVID A SAVIOR HAS BEEN BORN TO YOU; HE IS THE MESSIAH, THE LORD.'"
(LUKE 2:10-11 NIV)

Though the earth's inhabitants seemed to have forgotten their Savior and LORD, the Heavenly host had not. Shortly after the birth of Jesus on our planet, they burst into our world to proclaim this most wonderful of all news. The announcement is done with a bang! Here in our verses of Scripture, we see the angels of God showing up on the hills above Bethlehem. With a bright light illuminating the night, they startle the lowly shepherds, calling them to attention. (Luke 2:8-9) While the shepherds cower in fear at this spectacle, the angelic chorus breaks out in an uncontrollable praise to God. In their chorus, the angels announce the birth of the Christ Child. As the grand praise session closes, the shepherds rush down the mountain to see Jesus. In their haste to see this site the angels proclaimed, they leave the sheep unattended. On reaching the cave where Jesus lay, they witnessed God's fulfilled words and worshipped Him. They relayed the story of angelic sightings to the lonely couple (Mary and Joseph). Then they proceeded to spread the news to all who would listen. This was the confirmation Mary and Joseph needed. This tidbit from Heaven, by way of the shepherds, would spur the couple on in faith. I am sure moments of doubt plagued their minds. They must have thought, "Did we really hear from God?" And, of course, Satan was there to whisper all sorts of lies into their ears. But this night, in a filthy obscure cave perfumed with animal odor, indeed did lay the King of Creation in a feeding trough wrapped in strips of cloth. The angels of glory had confirmed it.

MOTHER MARY AND US: This speaks a quiet firmness to my heart. It says that at times, when I am in a "fog," waiting on God's will to come to pass in my life, I can hold on tight to His words. The story reminds me that my God cannot and will not lie. I only need to hold on and wait for the fulfillment of the promise.

GOD SPEAKS: "Your kingdom is an everlasting kingdom, and your dominion endures through all generations. The LORD is trustworthy in all he promises and faithful in all he does." (Psalm 145:13 NIV) Hold on to Me (your God) always! Trust My words and stay close to Me.

WANDA'S PRAYER: "Jesus, keep us (always) near your Cross, where there is a precious fountain. Free to all, the healing stream that flows from Calvary's fountain." (Fanny J. Crosby) LORD GOD, this is our prayer to You!

December 25

DO YOU WANT ANOTHER SIGN?

"SIMEON TOOK HIM (BABY JESUS) IN HIS ARMS AND PRAISED GOD, SAYING:…" (LUKE 2:28 NIV)
"COMING UP TO THEM AT THAT VERY MOMENT, SHE GAVE THANKS TO GOD AND SPOKE ABOUT THE CHILD TO ALL WHO WERE LOOKING FORWARD TO THE REDEMPTION OF JERUSALEM." (LUKE 2:38 NIV)

One thing I love about the LORD is that He leaves nothing to chance, and He makes many allowances for our frailties. Here is a perfect example. At the birth of the Christ Child, He sent angels to shepherds to trumpet this wonderful news. And now lest anyone forget, to broadcast the news further, our LORD incites His children to cry out the news of His Son's coming. Luke 2:21-38 are two such examples of this. In these verses are the stories of two of God's human messengers of salvation. The first, Simeon. Simeon is an elderly righteous man, who was promised he would live to see the Messiah's coming. (Luke 2:25-26) On seeing the Baby Jesus being dedicated to God on the eighth day as commanded (Leviticus 12:2-8), he takes the Child from the couple and offers loud songs of praise to God for keeping His promises. He tells the couple (and us) that this is God's salvation for us. This is our ticket out of this world of sin back into paradise. (Luke 2:29-32) As Simeon is speaking, another senior citizen takes the stage. Her name is Anna, a prophetess of God. She has also been waiting to see the promised Messiah. The Holy Spirit gives her this revelation also, as He had done with Simeon. (Luke 2:36-38) At this holy prompting, she goes about the temple preaching and thanking God loudly to all who would hear her. (Luke 2:38) In giving these dramatic presentations, our LORD increases Mary and Joseph's faith; assuring them this is truly His Son. Here are two independent confirmations of this fact. In this display, our God gives the busy, bustling, indifferent Jews another chance of hearing and seeing the Good News of Salvation.

MOTHER MARY AND US: I am so glad my LORD does not mind repeating the same thing over and over again to me. He loves to remind this "thick-sculled" woman of the wonderful love He has for me.

GOD SPEAKS: "Glory in his holy name; let the hearts of those who seek the LORD rejoice. Look to the LORD and his strength; seek his face always. Remember the wonders he has done, his miracles, and the judgments he pronounced," (1 Chronicles 16:10-12 NIV) I never want you to forget how much I love you, and how good I (your LORD), am to you. I will remind you a million times a day if I have to.

WANDA'S PRAYER: As long as we glorify your Holy Name Father God, and constantly seek Your face, we will forever be reminded of Your tender love and goodness for us. Thank You, LORD, for Your forever love.

December 26

I HAVE ANOTHER WITNESS

"AFTER JESUS WAS BORN IN BETHLEHEM IN JUDEA, DURING THE TIME OF KING HEROD, MAGI FROM THE EAST CAME TO JERUSALEM AND ASKED, 'WHERE IS THE ONE WHO HAS BEEN BORN KING OF THE JEWS? WE SAW HIS STAR WHEN IT ROSE AND HAVE COME TO WORSHIP HIM.'"
(MATTHEW 2:1-2 NIV)

A rule of law says the more credible your witnesses, the better your chances of winning your case. In "proving" His case in the courtroom of human opinion that Jesus is the Son of God, our LORD has given three sets of distinguished witnesses. The first were the angels witnessing to the shepherds who went on to witness to the people of Bethlehem. (Luke 2:8-18) Eight days later, our LORD gives us Simeon and Anna as witnesses at the Temple. (Luke 2:21-38) Now our LORD brings His third set of witnesses from the other side of the globe. These witnesses are astrologers, wise men called the Magi. They have traveled many miles over the past several years to bring us this good news. We see a grand spectacle on the streets of Jerusalem according to the text. The Magi and their entourage make their way to the palace of King Herod. They have only one question, "Where is the One who was born King of the Jews? We saw His star…" (Matthew 2:1-2) The men receive word from the Jewish Scribes that the Child they seek is born in Bethlehem. (Matthew 2:6) From there, the Star continues leading the Magi until they reach the very home of Jesus. This knock at Mary's door brought confirmation and amazement to her heart. On reaching the humble earthly home of our LORD, "… they fell down and worshipped Him." (Matthew 2:11) The witness did not stop at the worship of zealous, strange foreigners. It continues with the giving of precious gifts; gold, frankincense, and myrrh. These gifts witness to Mary, Joseph, and us, the 3-fold mission of our LORD Jesus. The gold testifies of His royalty as King of Kings and LORD of Lords. Frankincense speaks of His mission as Priest of the Most High God and the perfect mediator between us and Father God. Myrrh foretells us of death on the cross as payment for our sins.

MOTHER MARY AND US: To believe that Jesus Christ is the One and only Son of God, Mary, me, and the entire planet, have all the witness we will ever need. As the song says, "I need no other evidence, I need no other plea; it is enough that Jesus died and rose again for me." I so appreciate my LORD continuing to remind me over and over again who He is; and also for continuing to whisper His sweet love to me.

GOD SPEAKS: "keeping our eyes on Jesus, the source and perfecter of our faith, who for the joy that lay before Him endured a cross and despised the shame and has sat down at the right hand of God's throne." (Hebrews 12:2 HCSB) Just keep your eyes on Me, your LORD. Look at My face and you will see the joy I had (and still have), as I paid the price for your salvation on that cross. Do you see My wonderful love for you?

WANDA'S PRAYER: Thank You Jesus, for being all we will ever need.

December 27

HE'S ONLY ON LOAN TO YOU

"AND HE SAID TO THEM, 'WHY DID YOU SEEK ME? DID YOU NOT KNOW THAT I MUST BE ABOUT MY FATHER'S BUSINESS?'" (LUKE 2:49 NKJV)

I cannot tell you how many times I have borrowed things from others and kept them as my own. Later, when the thing I "borrowed" and kept was requested back, I then felt sheepishly foolish as I had to give back what was never mine to start with. In reading the circumstances surrounding this verse, I see the same issue with Mary. The family goes up to Jerusalem with 12-year-old Jesus, to the Passover—a required attendance. After the festival had completed, the family, along with others, headed home. It took them about a day to remember they had "lost Jesus." He was not really lost because He had remained in the Temple "blowing the minds" of the Jewish intellectuals, with His grasp of everything about God. A panicking Mary found Jesus in the temple after three days of diligent searching. As a mother of two, I completely understand her fears. Especially, as she must have recalled how Herod tried to kill Him when He was just a child. (Matthew 2:16-18) Upon finding Jesus in the temple, she starts to give our LORD a verbal spanking for their losing track of Him. (Luke 2:48) In her conversation, she tells Jesus He worried her and His father, Joseph. At these words, Jesus gently reminds her He was only on loan to her. He tells her He was doing His Father in Heaven's business. In this statement, our LORD reminds His earthly parents that He is the Son of God, who came to earth for a visit only. The next verse tells us Mary did not have a clue what Jesus had said to her. She had forgotten about the angelic message which told her the Child in her womb was the Son of God.

MOTHER MARY AND US: When I was a teenager and a Christian, I got into an attitude of thinking of Jesus as my "homie" or someone from my neighborhood. I remember calling Him that one day. The Spirit gently, but firmly reminded me that though our LORD is a "friend that sticks closer than a brother," He is still LORD! I have never forgotten this rebuke!

GOD SPEAKS: "But when the fullness of the time had come, God sent forth His Son, born of a woman, born under the law, to redeem those (us) who were under the law, that we might receive the adoption as sons (children)." (Galatians 4:4-5 NKJV) I AM your LORD, Savior, and Friend.

WANDA'S PRAYER: LORD, teach us how to always revere Your name. We want to give You due honor all the time. I thank You, LORD, for being our friend.

December 28

HAVE YOU MET MY BOY—HE'S GOD!

"HIS MOTHER SAID TO THE SERVANTS, 'WHATEVER HE SAYS TO YOU, DO IT.'"
(JOHN 2:5 NKJV)

I remember once meeting a couple of famous people. The next time I went back to work, I could not wait to let everyone (who also knew of those people), that I'd held a long conversation with them. I enjoyed having the "bragging rights." I think this was the case with Mary. Her pregnancy and subsequent birth of Jesus was questionable, at best, in the eyes of the world. She was thought of as an immoral woman by the people of her day. In this story, Jesus had just started His ministry; and the gathering of His disciples for Himself. (John 1:35-51) Here in Chapter 2, we see Jesus at a wedding, probably a family member, since His mother was also in attendance. At the wedding, a small tragedy took place—the family ran out of wine. In those days, weddings lasted several days. Since the Jews had a southern mentality of always being good, gracious hostesses, it was therefore very important to keep the guest supplied with food and drink at all times. Thus, the running out of wine posed a big problem. Mary saw a chance to "kill two birds with one stone." She could have the family save face, and she could introduce everyone to her Son—God Himself! So, she goes to Him and explains the no more wine dilemma. After a slight hesitation by Jesus, Mother Mary turns to the servant, telling them to follow her Son's instructions to the "tee." They do, and the result is vintage wine in abundance—complements of Jesus! This was our LORD'S first recorded miracle. The servants knew it was a miracle and soon everyone would know this miracle God man was Mary's Son. This was her proof. She was not a loose woman, as so many had long thought. She had given birth to the Son of God, and this miracle was the proof.

MOTHER MARY AND US: I like the fact Jesus, despite whatever misgivings He may have had, went on to perform the miracle for His mom; and at a wedding, of all places. This story tells me Jesus cares about those things in my life which are deeply personal, and sometimes self-serving.

GOD SPEAKS: "I will glory in the LORD; let the afflicted hear and rejoice. Glorify the LORD with me; let us exalt his name together. (Psalm 34:2-3 NIV) I do not mind your boasting about Me, your LORD. As you think of My goodness, you will know I am certainly worthy of all the boasting.

WANDA'S PRAYER: "I will extol the LORD at all times; his praise will always be on my lips." (Psalm 34:1 NIV) LORD Jesus, it is You who causes our hearts to beat about 4,200 times an hour; and cause us to take about 1,000 uninterrupted breaths within that same hour. We do not have to ask You to do these things. You do them just because You love us. Thank You!

December 29

THE PIERCING OF THE SOUL (PART 1)

"HE REPLIED TO HIM, 'WHO IS MY MOTHER, AND WHO ARE MY BROTHERS?'" (MATTHEW 12:48 NIV)

These were stinging words spoken by Mary's precious first-born Son, Jesus. The setting takes place as Jesus is battling the Jewish leadership as they dog His every step, seeking to condemn Him. He has just had a knockdown, drag out fight, over the way He keeps the Sabbath Day in Matthew 12. Because of this conversation, they call Him a devil or Beelzebub. At the end of this vicious fight, His mother and brothers show up wanting to talk to Jesus. Perhaps Mother Mary wants to shield or comfort Him. So, as they stood outside of the place where He was, they send word to Jesus that they need to speak with Him. Instead of running right to see them, or saying that He was on His way, He sends out these stinging words, "Who is my mother and who are my brothers?" He then goes on to say that His family members are those who obey God's will. (Mark 3:35) These words had to have been like a very sharp, piercing knife; slicing her soul in two. As she stood there with her soul in deep pain, she recalled how, thirty years prior, those words were prophesied to her. Eight days after Jesus' birth, Simeon, the old prophet, spoke to this piercing of her soul: "This child is destined to cause the falling and rising of many in Israel, and to be a sign that will be spoken against, so that the thoughts of many hearts will be revealed. And a sword will pierce your own soul too." (Luke 2:34-35 NIV) This was the dagger of which the old man spoke. Was Jesus being evil or mean-spirited to His earthly mother? NO! NO! NO! Our LORD responded as He did, for her sake, as well as ours. She had to know that "For God so loved the world (everyone in this messed up world) that He gave His one and only Son, (Jesus) so that whoever (you, me, all of us) believes in Him shall not perish but have a forever life with God in Heaven." (John 3:16) Our LORD could not play favorites, even with His own mom and brothers. We are all equally loved by God and in this statement, He proves it.

MOTHER MARY AND US: Even though I understand why Jesus had to do what He did, as I read this passage, I still ached for Mary as I read His words. I have heard spurning words from my children. Those words are also very painful to the heart and soul of mothers.

GOD SPEAKS: "But he was pierced for our transgressions, he was crushed for our iniquities; the punishment that brought us peace was on him, and by his wounds we are healed." (Isaiah 53:5 NIV) I, your LORD, understand the deep piercing and slicing of the soul. Mine was also cut open—for you. I would do it all over again, to save you.

WANDA'S PRAYER: LORD, thank You for loving and saving us!

December 30

THE PIERCING OF THE SOUL (PART 2)

"NEAR THE CROSS OF JESUS STOOD HIS MOTHER, ..." (JOHN 19:25 NIV)

There is a popular Christian song today called, "Mary, Did You Know?" The song poses several hypothetical questions to Mary about the life and mission of her Son—Jesus. I would like to parody on that song and ask several questions of my own. Mary, did you know your baby boy, though sinless and all loving, would be treated worse than a serial killer? Did you know your own church leaders would hand your precious baby over to the Roman authorities? Did you know your baby boy would be beaten beyond the point of recognition? Did you know your baby boy would be stripped of His clothing, and forced to be paraded through the streets of Jerusalem, carrying His own instrument (the cross) of death? Did you know they would mock Him by placing a piercing crown of thorns on His head? Mary, had you known all of these things, would you still have agreed to the assignment asked of you? As Mary stood at the foot of the cross where her beloved Son hung, her soul, mind, and body were not just pierced, it was seared to the max. Of all the areas of Mary's life that I revere, I have the most admiration for how she carries herself through this "mother" of tragedies. And yet, through all of what Mother Mary sees and hears, we hear not a single complaint from her. No, she like her Son, "opened not her mouth."

MOTHER MARY AND US: I, too, am a mother of a son. I have watched him go through the heartbreak of a divorce and single parenthood. I have held and wiped away the tears of childhood diseases and broken bones. My son's and my life, in no way compared to what Ms. Mary and her Son have gone through. The only thing I can say is the LORD of Glory was beside both of us, with His arms of comfort. He loved and carried us through it all.

GOD SPEAKS: "This is love: not that we loved God, but that he loved us and sent his Son as an atoning sacrifice for our sins." (1 John 4:10 NIV) Never forget He was My (your LORD'S) Son, before He was Mary's borrowed Child. Please remember and never forget that if it could have been done any other way than this way, it would have been. I allowed My Son to die, so your son could live forever.

WANDA'S PRAYER: LORD, words are not enough. All I can think of is the song, "Jesus paid it all. All to Him I owe. Sin had left a crimson stain. He washed it white as snow." Thank You, Father, for loving me and my son, so very much!

December 31

A SON'S PROVISION

"WHEN JESUS SAW HIS MOTHER THERE, AND THE DISCIPLE WHOM HE LOVED STANDING NEARBY, HE SAID TO HER, 'WOMAN, HERE IS YOUR SON,' AND TO THE DISCIPLE, 'HERE IS YOUR MOTHER.' FROM THAT TIME ON, THIS DISCIPLE TOOK HER INTO HIS HOME." (JOHN 19:26-27 NIV)

This is the Jesus I truly love and could spend eternity with. This is the God man who has everything under complete control. In this part of God's Word, some readers see a weak Jesus, with the tide turned against Him, hanging helplessly on the Cross; but nothing is further from the truth. Look closer at the scene and the truth will almost knock you to your feet. The Crucifixion scene as described in John 19 was predicted hundreds of centuries before (See Psalms 22 and Isaiah 53). Jesus, our LORD, would die on the Passover; and the LAMB OF GOD would be WITHOUT BLEMISH. This was not an accident or a terrible miscarriage of justice. The God of Heaven planned this and carried it out. His grand provision was to save our world from the destructive power of sin. While doing the work of salvation, He would take care of His earthly mom just before completing His last works. As He hung on the cross, one of His seven last statements was concerning the mother He loved so dear. He deeply felt her pain and sorrow. Before He died, Jesus made provisions for her care. Looking at John, His beloved disciple, He said to him, "Take her and care for her; love her as your very own mother." (Writer's paraphrase) To His mother, writhing in deep agony, He says, "Mommy, I gotta go away for a while. I am leaving you in the hands of my boy, John. He is gonna take real good care of you—ok?" (Writer's paraphrase) Jesus shows us He is a good Son of Father God and Mother Mary.

MOTHER MARY AND US: In looking at this part of the story, I see Jesus completing His mission to us all. As He takes care of the needs of the entire world, He stops for a moment to consider His own mother. I never have to worry if He has forgotten about me. If He shows tender compassion while in extreme agony, I know that even now, while in Heaven, He is making provisions for me.

GOD SPEAKS: "The earth is the Lord's, and everything in it, the world, and all who live in it." (Psalm 24:1 NIV) This is all Mine; it all belongs to your LORD. You never have to worry about Me not taking care of My stuff.

WANDA'S PRAYER: LORD, thank You for making us a part of Your stuff.

IT'S ALL RIGHT NOW

"THEY ALL JOINED TOGETHER CONSTANTLY IN PRAYER, ALONG WITH THE WOMEN AND MARY THE MOTHER OF JESUS, AND WITH HIS BROTHERS."
(ACTS 1:14 NIV)

This is the most beautiful scenes in all of Scripture. In Acts 1, Dr. Luke tells us Jesus has risen from the dead. He had visited His followers off and on for the past forty days. He commissioned them to go and tell the world of His love, and to bring to them the gift of salvation in Jesus Christ. But before they can do this, they would need the power of God. He, the Son of God, will no longer be with them. However, He will dispense the power source of the Holy Spirit to come upon and live in them. Mary is ecstatic at this point. Jesus has completed the work of saving the souls of men. The horror of the crucifixion and burial of her beloved Jesus is now just a distant, awful memory. The new phase of dispensing the finished work of Christ has now begun. This handful of faithful followers have been given the awesome responsibility of taking this "Good News" (The Gospel) to the entire planet. She and her other sons take their place in the upper room waiting for further orders not from Jesus her Son, but Jesus her LORD and Savior. Truly, as she fades from the pages of Scripture, all is right with her world.

MOTHER MARY AND US: Like Mary, this phase of my work is complete. I await my next assignment to help take His (Jesus') word to a lost and dying world. He has given me His Holy Spirit to live and abide in me. He (the Holy Spirit) is the power source to live a life of Holiness, and to tell others of the one who will save them from their sins.

GOD SPEAKS: "Jesus is 'the stone you builders rejected, which has become the cornerstone.' Salvation is found in no one else, for there is no other name under heaven given to mankind by which we must be saved." (Acts 4:11-12 NIV) Take this "Word" (Jesus) to your part of the planet. Tell this "Word" to everyone you meet.

WANDA'S PRAYER: LORD, give us Your Spirit and energize us to take the Good News of the Gospel to the world.

Notes

Notes

About the Author

 Wanda F. Hicks began her born-again Christian journey 40+ years ago. This journey has propelled her into being an energetic speaker, author, and teacher of God's Word. Wanda is passionate about teaching through the Word of God, and has taught a variety of Bible classes for children and adults over the same time period. Her gift of teaching and writing has opened the doors for her to speak at various women's ministry venues, and through social media platforms.

Wanda is married to Willie Hicks, Pastor of Harvest Care Christian Fellowship, in Highland, California. As a very hands-on servant of God, and loving wife, she humbly and dutifully serves alongside her husband in many areas of the ministry. She demonstrates humble leadership as she oversees, teaches, and participates with Harvest Care's Children's ministry, as well as with the church's local community outreach events.

Wanda is the proud mother of two adult children, and a very involved grandmother. She has been a practicing nurse for over 30 years, and currently works in the Obstetrics-Postpartum department.

Be on the Lookout!

Sisters of the Soul: A Devotional Exploring Women In God's Word
Monthly Journal Editions

Other Notable Book Credits Authored by Wanda Hicks

Sisters of the Soul: Every Woman's Devotional
Published February 20, 2014 — ISBN No. 9781312036024

Sisters of the Soul: Every Woman's Devotional, Book 2 Sarah's Story
Published March 11, 2014 — ISBN No. 9781304931719

Connect With Wanda on Social Media

YouTube: Moments in God's Word
Facebook: Moments in God's Word

Author's Contact Information

Wanda F. Hicks, Harvest Care Christian Fellowship
2595 Date Street East — Highland, CA 92346
Email Address: wandahicks2008@yahoo.com
(909) 862-3572

www.ingramcontent.com/pod-product-compliance
Lightning Source LLC
Chambersburg PA
CBHW081352070526
44583CB00020B/2528